Restorative Justice Through the Lens of Jesus

A Journey from Retribution to Restoration

DR. MAXWELL SHIMBA

Published in Manhattan, New York by Shimba Publishing, LLC.

Shimba Publishing LLC

Table of Contents

Preface v
Chapter 1 1
UNDERSTANDING RESTORATIVE JUSTICE 1
Chapter 02 25
THE TEACHINGS OF JESUS ON JUSTICE 25
Chapter 03 60
PARABLES AND RESTORATIVE JUSTICE 60
Chapter 04 86
FORGIVENESS AND RECONCILIATION 86
Chapter 05 112
RESTORATIVE JUSTICE IN BIBLICAL CONTEXT AND IN THE CHURCH 112
Chapter 06 149
HISTORICAL PERSPECTIVE OF JUSTICE 149
Chapter 07 181
MODERN RESTORATIVE JUSTICE 181
Chapter 08 209
JESUS AS A MODEL FOR RESTORATIVE JUSTICE 209
Chapter 09 252
RESTORATIVE JUSTICE IN CHRISTIAN COMMUNITIES 252
Chapter 10 293
CHALLENGES AND CRITIQUES 293
Chapter 11 327
OVERCOMING THE OBSTACLES 327
Chapter 12 371
RESTORATIVE JUSTICE AND HEALING 371
Chapter 13 403
RESTORATIVE JUSTICE AND CRIMINAL JUSTICE 403

Chapter 14 428
RESTORATIVE JUSTICE IN THE GLOBAL CONTEXT 428
Chapter 15 457
RESTORATIVE JUSTICE IN EDUCATION 457
Chapter 16 483
RESTORATIVE JUSTICE IN FAMILY RELATIONSHIPS 483
Chapter 17 510
CASE STUDIES IN RESTORATIVE JUSTICE 510
Chapter 18 534
RESTORATIVE JUSTICE AND THEOLOGY 534
Chapter 19 555
FUTURE DIRECTIONS AND CHALLENGES 555
Chapter 20 580
EMBRACING RESTORATIVE JUSTICE THROUGH THE LENS OF JESUS 580

Preface

In the long and complex history of human civilization, few concepts have proven as foundational—or as fiercely contested—as justice. From the ancient codes etched in stone to the modern statutes debated in legislatures, humanity has perpetually grappled with a singular, haunting question: How do we rightly respond to wrongdoing? The answers to this question have shaped our laws, defined our societies, and determined the fate of countless individuals. We have navigated a wide spectrum of approaches, oscillating between the stark severity of punitive retribution and the aspirational vision of transformative, healing-centered paradigms. On one end lies the cold calculus of pain for pain, a system designed to exact a price. On the other lies a more difficult, more hopeful path—one that seeks not merely to punish, but to repair, to heal, and to restore.

It is within this dynamic and often contentious spectrum that the figure of Jesus of Nazareth casts a unique and compelling light. For two millennia, the teachings of Jesus have served as a moral compass for billions, influencing not only personal piety but also profound philosophical and ethical debates about the nature of a just society. To examine justice through the lens of His life and words is to encounter a radical reorientation of the entire concept. It is to move from a framework dominated by abstract rules and punitive outcomes to a lived experience centered on concrete relationships, communal healing, and personal transformation. This book, *Restorative Justice Through the Lens of Jesus*, is an invitation to embark on that very examination. It is an exploration of the profound and harmonious intersection between the transformative philosophy known as restorative justice and the timeless, revolutionary teachings of the Gospels.

This work is not a detached academic exercise, though it is built upon a foundation of rigorous inquiry. It is, rather, a journey—a narrative exploration that weaves together the wisdom of theology, the insights of psychology, the frameworks of law, and the deep questions of philosophy. Our purpose is to demonstrate that restorative justice is not merely a modern sociological invention, but a paradigm deeply rooted in the very fabric of the biblical narrative, finding its most perfect expression in the person and work of Jesus Christ. This is what we will come to understand as the **Jesus Paradigm**: a comprehensive model for justice that is at once ancient and urgently contemporary, profoundly spiritual and practically applicable.

The Theological Foundation: A God of Justice and Mercy

Theologically, this book posits that the God revealed in Scripture is not content with a justice that merely settles accounts. The Hebrew concept of *mishpat* (justice) is inextricably linked with *shalom*—a vision of comprehensive peace, wholeness, and right relationship among all people and with God. As the prophet Micah famously declared, "He has shown you, O man, what is good; and what does the LORD require of you but to do justly, to love mercy, and to walk humbly with your God?" (Micah 6:8). Here, justice and mercy are not opposing forces but divine companions. The entire biblical narrative, from the laws given to Israel to the warnings of the prophets, consistently calls God's people to a justice that prioritizes the vulnerable, defends the oppressed, and seeks the restoration of the community. When the Apostle Paul, in his epistle to the Romans, speaks of a righteousness from God revealed through faith in Jesus Christ, he is unveiling the ultimate expression of this restorative heart—a divine initiative to reconcile a broken world to Himself, not counting our trespasses against us. This is the **Gospel of Restorative Justice**: the good news that the Creator of the universe is in the business of making all things new, of restoring what was lost, and of healing what was broken.

The Philosophical Inquiry: Rethinking the Nature of Wrongdoing

Philosophically, the Jesus Paradigm challenges the foundational assumptions of purely retributive models. For centuries, Western philosophy, from Immanuel Kant's emphasis on "just deserts" to the utilitarian calculations of social benefit, has shaped legal systems that define crime as an offense against the state and justice as the infliction of proportionate pain. Restorative justice, viewed through the lens of Jesus, offers a profound counter-narrative. It asks a different set of questions: not merely "What law was broken, and what punishment is deserved?" but "Who was harmed, what are their needs, and whose obligations are these?" This shift moves the focus from an abstract violation of a statute to the concrete reality of injured human beings and fractured relationships. It resonates with the ancient wisdom of the prophets and the ethical teachings of Jesus, who consistently prioritized the person over the rule, mercy over sacrifice, and the transformative potential of love over the sterile demands of the law.

The Psychological Dimension: Healing the Wounds of Harm

The psychological dimension of this paradigm is equally critical. Crime and conflict leave deep, invisible scars—not only on direct victims but on offenders and the wider community as well. Victims often suffer from trauma, a profound sense of powerlessness, and a gnawing need for answers that a punitive system rarely provides. Offenders, too, are often trapped in cycles of shame, denial, and dehumanization that make genuine accountability and change nearly impossible. Restorative justice, through its structured processes of dialogue and encounter, creates a psychologically safe space for these wounds to be acknowledged and addressed. It offers victims a voice and a pathway to empowerment, allowing them to express their pain and participate in shaping the resolution. It confronts offenders with the human impact of their actions, fostering genuine empathy—a critical precursor to true repentance and behavioral change. This process, where an offender is moved to see the person behind the crime, is a powerful psychological intervention that breaks down the walls of abstraction that allow harm to be repeated. The ultimate goal is not just the cessation of harmful behavior, but the restoration of the offender's own psychological and spiritual health, reintegrating them as a contributing member of the community.

The Legal Context: A Framework for Justice, Not an Alternative to It

This exploration is grounded in a realistic understanding of law and legal systems. We will examine how restorative justice is not a replacement for all forms of legal oversight but a complementary and, in many cases, a more effective framework for achieving the true aims of justice. From the victim-offender mediation programs successfully implemented in Europe to the family group conferencing models in New Zealand and the community courts emerging in the United States, we will see how these principles are being codified and practiced within existing legal structures. We will explore how the law can be used not just to punish, but to facilitate accountability, mandate restitution, and support the reintegration of offenders. The book will draw on case studies and legal scholarship to demonstrate that a restorative approach can lead to higher rates of victim satisfaction, lower rates of recidivism, and a more profound sense of public safety—outcomes that purely punitive systems often fail to achieve. The legal framework, when infused with restorative principles, can become an instrument of healing rather than merely an engine of punishment.

The Practical Application: Living the Paradigm

Ultimately, the Jesus Paradigm is a call to action. It is a summons for individuals, churches, and communities to become agents of reconciliation in a fractured world. This book will serve as a guide for that calling, providing practical frameworks for application in diverse contexts:

- **In the Church:** We will explore how Christian communities can embody restorative justice internally, addressing conflicts with grace and truth, and externally, becoming beacons of hope and healing for those impacted by crime in their neighborhoods.
- **In Criminal Justice:** We will examine the role of restorative justice as a catalyst for meaningful reform, offering pathways to address the root causes of crime, reduce mass incarceration, and break the destructive cycles of recidivism.
- **In Education:** We will see how restorative practices can transform schools, replacing punitive zero-tolerance policies with a culture of dialogue, empathy, and accountability that prevents bullying and fosters a positive learning environment.

- **In Families and Relationships:** We will discover how these principles can mend broken trust, heal deep-seated conflicts, and build stronger, more resilient family units.

As you journey through these pages, you will encounter not only the teachings of Jesus on justice but also the voices of philosophers, theologians, psychologists, legal scholars, and—most importantly—the real-life stories of victims, offenders, and communities who have walked the path of restoration. You will grapple with the challenges and critiques of this approach, and you will be equipped with the knowledge and inspiration to overcome those obstacles. This book is an invitation to see the world differently, to imagine a justice that is not satisfied with an "eye for an eye" but dares to hope for a world made whole. It is an invitation to embrace the Jesus Paradigm, to live out the Gospel of Restorative Justice, and to become, in your own sphere of influence, an instrument of reconciliation and restoration. The journey begins now.

INTRODUCTION

In the long and arduous quest for justice, humanity has traversed a complex and often contradictory landscape. From the ancient codes of Hammurabi, with their stark pronouncements of "an eye for an eye," to the towering philosophical constructs of the Enlightenment, and down to the intricate legal statutes of our modern age, we have ceaselessly sought a framework to address harm, wrongdoing, and conflict within the intricate tapestry of society. This quest has yielded a spectrum of approaches, each reflecting the values, fears, and aspirations of its time. At one pole stands retributive justice, a system calibrated to measure out punishment proportional to the offense, to settle the moral ledger through the infliction of deserved consequences. At the other lies the nascent but increasingly vital paradigm of restorative justice—a vision that dares to ask not only what law was broken, but who was hurt, what they need, and whose obligation it is to make things right.

At the very heart of this contemporary exploration, however, lies an ancient and profound intersection. It is the place where the radical teachings of a first-century Jewish carpenter meet the most pressing questions of twenty-first-century criminology and social ethics. It is the convergence of the philosophy of restorative justice with the life and ministry of Jesus of Nazareth. This book, *Restorative Justice Through the Lens of Jesus*, is an invitation to stand at that crossroads and to see, perhaps for the first time, the full panorama of a justice that is at once divinely inspired and profoundly practical. We will embark on a transformative journey, unraveling the threads that weave these two realms together, inviting you to ponder the depths of what justice can truly mean when viewed through the lens of compassion, reconciliation, and redemption.

Restorative justice, as a paradigm, is far more than a mere procedural alternative within the criminal justice system. It emerges not simply as a departure from punitive measures but as a radical reimagining of justice itself. It is a vision grounded in the recognition that crime and conflict are first and foremost injuries to people and relationships, not merely violations of abstract legal codes. This foundational insight echoes through the corridors of history, finding resonance in the legal traditions of ancient Israel, where restitution and restoration were woven into the very fabric of the Law given at Sinai. When an ox was stolen, the Law did not merely prescribe punishment; it demanded repayment—five oxen for one (Exodus 22:1). This was not retribution for its own sake; it was a mechanism designed to restore the victim, to hold the offender accountable in a tangible way, and to repair the social fabric torn by the offense. This ancient legal principle, rooted in the character of a God who declares Himself "merciful and gracious, longsuffering, and abounding in goodness and truth" (Exodus 34:6), provides the deep biblical foundation upon which the entire structure of restorative justice is built.

Theologically, this book is grounded in the conviction that the Scriptures present a unified and coherent vision of justice that culminates in the person of Jesus Christ. The Hebrew prophets thundered against a justice that was merely ceremonial, a piety that ignored the plight of the orphan, the widow, and the poor. "Let justice roll down like waters," Amos proclaimed, "and righteousness like an ever-flowing stream" (Amos 5:24). This was a call for a justice that was active, life-giving, and restorative in its very nature. It was a justice that sought to lift up the fallen, to defend the defenseless, and to restore the marginalized to their rightful place within the covenant community. In the teachings of Jesus, this prophetic vision finds its fullest and most perfect expression. When He stands in the synagogue of Nazareth and declares His mission to "preach good tidings to the poor... to proclaim liberty to the captives, and recovering of sight to the blind, to set at liberty them that are bruised" (Luke 4:18), He is announcing the inauguration of God's great restorative project. The **Jesus Paradigm** is not a system of rules but a movement of redemption, a divine initiative to heal the broken, reconcile the estranged, and restore the dignity of every human being created in the image of God.

Philosophically, this paradigm issues a profound challenge to the assumptions that have undergirded Western legal thought for centuries. The influential philosophy of Immanuel Kant, with its emphasis on retribution as a moral imperative—the idea that the criminal must be punished because they "deserve" it, and for no other reason—has cast a long shadow over our conceptions of justice. This view, often summarized as "just deserts," holds that the primary purpose of punishment is to restore an abstract moral balance by inflicting pain on the offender. Restorative justice, viewed through the lens of Jesus, offers a fundamentally different philosophical anthropology. It sees the offender not as an abstraction, a mere "law-breaker" whose debt to society must be paid in suffering, but as a human being, created with inherent dignity and worth, who has caused harm and who is also capable of change, redemption, and restoration. It recognizes, with the Apostle Paul, the universal human condition: "For all have sinned and fall short of the glory of God" (Romans 3:23). This shared condition of brokenness calls not for a hierarchy of condemnation but for a community of mutual accountability and grace. The philosophical foundation of the Jesus Paradigm is not the cold calculus of desert but the warm embrace of love—a love that seeks not the satisfaction of vengeance but the transformation of the human heart.

The psychological dimensions of this approach are equally compelling and empirically supported. Decades of research in victimology have revealed the profound and lasting trauma inflicted by crime—a trauma that the impersonal processes of the traditional criminal justice system often exacerbate rather than alleviate. Victims frequently report feeling re-victimized by a system that treats them as mere witnesses, sidelines their emotional needs, and leaves them with unanswered questions about the crime and the offender. Restorative justice processes, such as victim-offender mediation, directly address these psychological wounds. They provide a safe and structured environment where victims can give voice to their pain, ask the questions that haunt them, and confront the person who caused them harm. For many, this encounter is profoundly cathartic, restoring a sense of power and agency that the crime stripped away. For offenders, the psychological journey is equally transformative. Confronted not with an abstract charge but with the living, breathing reality of the person they have harmed, the defenses of denial and rationalization begin to crumble. They are invited to experience genuine empathy—to see and feel the impact of their actions. This experience of "godly sorrow" (2 Corinthians 7:10), as Paul describes it, is the psychological wellspring of true repentance, a sorrow that leads not to despair but to a fundamental reorientation of life.

Within the legal context, restorative justice is not a utopian fantasy but a practical and increasingly influential framework. Around the world, from the family group conferencing models pioneered in New Zealand to the restorative justice protocols embedded in the juvenile justice systems of numerous European nations, and in the growing number of community courts and diversion programs across the United States, the principles of this paradigm are being tested, refined, and proven effective. The United States Department of Justice has itself recognized the potential of restorative justice, funding programs and supporting research that demonstrates its capacity to reduce recidivism, increase victim satisfaction, and do so at a fraction of the cost of traditional incarceration. This is not a call to dismantle the legal system but to infuse it with a deeper, more complete understanding of its own purpose. It is an invitation for lawmakers, judges, and legal professionals to consider how the law can become an instrument not only of punishment but of healing, not only of isolation but of reintegration.

As we navigate through the chapters that follow, we will traverse this rich and varied terrain. We will delve into the theological underpinnings of justice in the Gospels, exploring how the parables of Jesus—the Good Samaritan, the Prodigal Son, the Unforgiving Servant—serve as timeless narratives that speak directly to the core of restorative principles. We will examine the historical development of justice, from the ancient codes of the Near East to the modern prison system, tracing the emergence of the restorative alternative. We will explore the practical applications of this paradigm in diverse contexts: within the criminal justice system, where it offers a path to break the cycles of recidivism; within our schools, where it can transform disciplinary practices and create cultures of respect; within our families, where it can mend broken relationships and build stronger bonds; and within our churches, where it calls us to be the embodiment of Christ's reconciling love in a fractured world.

This book is not a mere academic exercise, though it is built upon a foundation of rigorous scholarship. It is, at its core, a call to action—an invitation to a transformative journey. It invites you, the reader, to reflect deeply on your own understanding of justice, to question the punitive instincts that may have become ingrained by a retributive culture, and to open your heart to the radical possibility of a healing-centered justice. It asks you not only to contemplate these principles but to consider how you might embody them in your own life, in your own relationships, and within your own community. How might a conversation with a family member be different if approached with a restorative mindset? How might a conflict at work be resolved if the goal were not to win, but to understand and repair?

As we explore the pages that lie ahead, we will encounter poignant case studies that bring these principles to life—stories of victims who found a voice, of offenders who embraced accountability and transformation, and of communities that discovered the power of reconciliation. We will grapple honestly with the challenges and critiques that restorative justice faces, from institutional resistance to the complexities of ensuring equity and addressing systemic injustice. And we will be equipped with the knowledge and inspiration to become agents of this healing justice in our own spheres of influence.

May this journey through the intersection of restorative justice and the teachings of Jesus inspire within you a renewed vision for justice—one that is compassionate, empathetic, and unshakably grounded in the transformative power of forgiveness. It is our hope that this exploration will contribute to a broader and more urgent conversation, inviting individuals, communities, and entire societies to consider the potential of a justice that does not merely condemn the past but actively redeems the future. This is the promise of the Jesus Paradigm. This is the hope of the Gospel of Restorative Justice. And this is the invitation now extended to you.

CHAPTER 1

UNDERSTANDING RESTORATIVE JUSTICE

What is justice? This question has haunted humanity since the dawn of conscious society. It has filled libraries with philosophical treatises, sparked revolutions, toppled governments, and shaped the moral contours of civilizations. Yet for all our collective pondering, justice remains one of the most elusive and contested concepts in human experience. We sense its absence with visceral clarity—when we are wronged, when we witness oppression, when the vulnerable are crushed by the powerful—but we struggle to define its presence with equal certainty. What does justice look like when it is fully realized? What does it feel like to experience it? And most importantly, how do we, as individuals and communities, actually practice it?

These are not merely academic questions. They are the most practical and urgent inquiries of our time, touching every dimension of human relationship—from the quiet conflicts that simmer within families to the public harms that fracture entire societies. The answers we give to these questions determine whether our responses to wrongdoing will heal or wound, whether they will restore or destroy, whether they will break cycles of harm or perpetuate them across generations.

This chapter invites you into a foundational exploration of restorative justice—not as an abstract theory to be memorized, but as a living paradigm to be understood, embodied, and ultimately practiced. We will examine its core principles, trace its ancient roots, and discover its profound resonance with the biblical vision of a world made whole. For at the heart of this exploration lies a conviction that will unfold throughout this entire book: that restorative justice, understood through the lens of Jesus, is not merely one approach among many, but the very heartbeat of God's redemptive purposes for humanity.

The Nature of Justice: Beyond Retribution to Restoration

Restorative justice is, at its most essential level, a profound and transformative approach to addressing harm and conflict in society. Unlike traditional punitive models that focus almost exclusively on determining guilt and administering punishment, restorative justice asks a different set of questions—questions that cut to the heart of what it means to be human in relationship with others.

Consider the contrast. In a conventional criminal justice proceeding, the central inquiries are these: What law was broken? Who broke it? What punishment do they deserve? The entire apparatus of the court is designed to answer these three questions with precision and procedural fairness. The state, representing the abstract entity of "the people," prosecutes the offender. The victim, ironically, is reduced to the role of witness—a source of evidence rather than a participant in justice. The community is relegated to the gallery, passive observers of a drama in which they have no active role. And the offender? The offender becomes the object of punishment, their humanity obscured by the label of "criminal," their needs and potential for change rendered irrelevant to the legal calculus.

Restorative justice fundamentally reorients this entire framework. It begins with a radically different set of questions: Who has been harmed? What are their needs? Whose obligations have arisen from this harm? How can we, as a community, address the underlying causes and repair the damage done? These questions shift the focus from abstract lawbreaking to concrete human injury, from punishment to accountability, from isolation to reintegration.

At its core, restorative justice seeks to restore relationships, promote healing, and reintegrate individuals who have caused harm back into their communities. It recognizes that when wrongdoing occurs, the fabric of human connection is torn. The victim is wounded, often in ways that extend far beyond material loss—their sense of safety shattered, their trust in others damaged, their dignity violated. The offender is alienated, not only from the victim but from the community and often from their own better self. The community itself is diminished, its bonds of mutual trust weakened, its collective well-being compromised.

Traditional punitive justice, with its focus on punishment and isolation, too often exacerbates these wounds. It isolates offenders behind walls, severing the very relationships that might support their transformation. It sidelines victims, denying them voice and agency in the resolution of their own suffering. It treats the community as irrelevant, missing the opportunity to mobilize collective resources for healing. In contrast, restorative justice offers a more holistic and empathetic perspective—one that sees in every harm an opportunity for repair, in every wrongdoer a potential for change, and in every community a capacity for collective healing.

The Victim at the Center: Honoring the Wounded

One of the most distinctive and essential features of restorative justice is its unwavering commitment to placing victims at the center of the justice process. This victim-centered approach is not merely a matter of procedural preference; it is a fundamental recognition of the dignity and worth of every human being created in the image of God.

When harm occurs, the victim is not an abstraction. They are a person—a living, breathing human being with feelings, memories, fears, and hopes. They have been directly affected by the harm caused, and their suffering demands recognition. Too often, in conventional legal proceedings, victims feel re-victimized by a system that treats them as means to an end. Their pain becomes evidence, their testimony becomes a tool for prosecution, and their ongoing needs—for answers, for acknowledgment, for a sense of closure—are systematically ignored.

Restorative justice seeks to change this entirely. It provides victims with a platform to express their feelings, to ask the questions that haunt them, and to have a meaningful say in how the offender can make amends. This is not about vengeance or extracting maximal concessions. It is about restoring to victims what the crime stripped from them: their voice, their agency, their sense of being seen and heard as persons of inherent worth.

The psychological dimensions of this victim-centered approach are profound and well-documented. Decades of research in victimology have revealed that the trauma of crime extends far beyond the immediate incident. Victims often experience a constellation of psychological wounds: hypervigilance and anxiety, depression and hopelessness, a persistent sense of violation and powerlessness. They are haunted by questions they cannot ask: Why me? What were you thinking? Do you have any idea what you took from me? Do you feel any remorse? These unanswered questions become a form of ongoing torment, a loop of rumination that prevents healing.

Restorative justice processes, particularly victim-offender mediation, create a structured and safe environment in which these questions can finally be asked and answered. When victims have the opportunity to confront the person who harmed them—to speak their truth, to express their pain, to receive answers—the psychological benefits can be transformative. Studies consistently show that victims who participate in restorative processes report significantly higher levels of satisfaction than those whose cases proceed through conventional channels. They are more likely to feel that justice has been done, that their needs have been addressed, and that they can begin the process of moving forward.

But the benefits extend beyond subjective satisfaction. Research has demonstrated that restorative processes can reduce symptoms of post-traumatic stress, decrease feelings of anger and desire for revenge, and restore a sense of safety and control. When victims see that the offender genuinely understands the harm caused and is taking concrete steps to make amends, the psychological grip of victimization begins to loosen. The victim is no longer defined solely by what was done to them; they become an active agent in their own healing.

This victim-centered approach is not merely a modern psychological insight. It is deeply rooted in the biblical vision of justice. Throughout the Scriptures, God repeatedly demonstrates a particular concern for those who have been harmed, marginalized, and oppressed. The Law of Moses is replete with provisions designed to protect the vulnerable and ensure that victims are not forgotten in the administration of justice. The prophets thunder against a justice system that ignores the cries of the wounded. And Jesus Himself, in His encounters with the broken and marginalized, consistently prioritizes their healing and restoration. When He meets the woman caught in adultery, He does not minimize her sin, but neither does He allow the legal machinery to crush her. He restores her dignity, speaks words of grace, and sends her forward into a new life. This is restorative justice incarnate.

The Offender's Journey: Accountability as Transformation

Restorative justice, however, is not solely concerned with victims. It also involves holding offenders accountable for their actions—but accountability is understood in a fundamentally different way than in punitive systems. The question is not simply, "What punishment do you deserve?" but rather, "What can you do to make things right?"

This distinction is crucial and often misunderstood. Critics of restorative justice sometimes assume that it is "soft on crime," that it lets offenders off the hook, that it prioritizes the needs of wrongdoers over the rights of victims. Nothing could be further from the truth. Restorative justice demands a deeper, more demanding form of accountability than conventional punishment ever could.

Consider what happens in a typical criminal proceeding. The offender is represented by counsel, whose job is to minimize consequences. The offender is advised to say as little as possible, to admit nothing beyond what the evidence forces, to portray themselves in the most favorable light. The entire process incentivizes denial, deflection, and minimization. The offender never has to look the victim in the eye, never has to hear the full extent of the pain they caused, never has to grapple with the human consequences of their actions. They serve their time—passively, often bitterly—and emerge from incarceration no more accountable than when they entered, and often far more damaged and alienated.

Restorative justice reverses this entire dynamic. Offenders are encouraged—indeed, required—to take genuine responsibility for their actions. They are confronted, not with an abstract charge, but with the living reality of the person they have harmed. They hear, in the victim's own words, the impact of their behavior. They are asked to explain themselves, to answer questions, to grapple with the consequences of their choices. And then they are given the opportunity—the profound privilege—of making amends.

This accountability process is not punitive in nature but restorative. Its goal is not to inflict pain but to repair harm. Offenders are invited to understand the harm they have caused, to feel genuine remorse, and to actively participate in making things right. This participation can take many forms: a sincere apology that acknowledges the specific harm done, restitution that compensates for material losses, community service that gives back to those affected, or other actions tailored to the particular circumstances of the case.

The psychological journey involved in this process is transformative. When offenders are shielded from the human consequences of their actions, they remain trapped in cycles of denial and self-justification. They can tell themselves that the victim deserved it, that they had no choice, that everyone does it, that the system is unfair. These rationalizations protect them from the painful truth of what they have done—but they also prevent any genuine change.

Restorative justice dismantles these defenses. When a victim looks an offender in the eye and describes, with tears, the ongoing impact of the crime, the walls of denial begin to crumble. The offender can no longer hide behind abstractions. They are confronted with a person—a person who is hurting because of choices they made. This confrontation evokes what the Apostle Paul called "godly sorrow"—a grief over wrongdoing that leads not to despair but to genuine repentance and transformation (2 Corinthians 7:10). This is sorrow that produces change, that motivates amends, that reorients a life.

Research consistently demonstrates the effectiveness of this approach. Offenders who participate in restorative justice programs have significantly lower recidivism rates than those processed through conventional channels. They are less likely to reoffend because they have undergone an internal transformation, not merely endured external punishment. They have faced the harm they caused, made amends where possible, and been welcomed back into community. They have experienced accountability not as something done to them but as something they actively participated in—a journey of taking responsibility and making things right.

The Community's Calling: Collective Responsibility for Healing

Restorative justice extends its reach far beyond the immediate parties involved in a conflict. It emphasizes the broader community's essential role in facilitating healing and reconciliation. This is not merely a practical consideration but a theological and philosophical commitment to the reality that we are all interconnected, that no harm occurs in isolation, and that collective healing requires collective participation.

In traditional justice systems, the community is largely absent. The state acts on behalf of "the people," but this representation is abstract and impersonal. Community members have no meaningful role in the process, no opportunity to contribute to resolution, no responsibility for supporting either victims or offenders. The result is a justice system that happens *to* communities rather than *with* them—a system that disempowers the very people most affected by crime and conflict.

Restorative justice restores the community to its rightful place. Communities play an active role in supporting both victims and offenders in their journey toward resolution. This support can take many forms: providing resources and assistance to victims, offering mentorship and accountability to offenders, creating structures of welcome for those returning from incarceration, and addressing the underlying social conditions that contribute to crime.

This community involvement creates a profound sense of shared responsibility and collective healing. When a crime occurs, it is not just an offense against an individual; it is a tear in the social fabric. The community itself is diminished, its trust eroded, its sense of safety compromised. For true healing to occur, the community must be actively involved in repairing that tear. This involvement communicates to victims that they are not alone, that their suffering matters to others, that the community stands with them. It communicates to offenders that they are still members of the community, that their restoration is a shared priority, that there is a place for them to return. And it communicates to all that justice is not something done by experts and officials but something the community collectively owns and pursues.

The biblical foundations of this community-centered approach run deep. Israel was constituted as a covenant community, bound together by shared relationship with God and mutual responsibility for one another. When harm occurred, it was not merely a private matter but a breach in the community's covenant relationship. The entire community was implicated, and the entire community was involved in restoration. The prophetic vision of shalom—of peace, wholeness, and right relationship—was always a communal vision, a picture of all creation dwelling together in harmony under God's reign.

In the New Testament, the church is described as the body of Christ—a living organism in which each member is connected to every other, and the health of the whole depends on the health of each part. When one member suffers, all suffer together. When one member is restored, all rejoice together. This is the theological reality that restorative justice seeks to embody: that we are created for relationship, that our lives are intertwined, and that our healing is inseparable from the healing of others.

The Practices of Restorative Justice: Structures for Encounter

Restorative justice is not merely a set of abstract principles; it is a practical discipline embodied in specific practices and processes. These practices provide structured opportunities for encounter, dialogue, and resolution—creating the conditions in which healing can occur.

The most widely used method within restorative practices is Victim Offender Mediation. This process brings together the victim and offender in a safe, structured setting, facilitated by a trained mediator. The victim has the opportunity to describe the impact of the crime, to ask questions, and to express their feelings. The offender has the opportunity to hear this impact directly, to explain their actions, and to take responsibility. Together, they work toward an agreement about what the offender will do to make amends.

Victim Offender Mediation differs fundamentally from traditional mediation. In conventional mediation, the parties are presumed to have equal standing, each with legitimate interests to negotiate. In restorative mediation, there is a clear recognition that harm has been done, that one party has caused injury to another. The process is not about finding a middle ground between competing claims but about addressing the harm, holding the offender accountable, and working toward restoration. This recognition of harm is essential to the integrity of the process.

Family Group Conferences extend this model to include the broader networks of support surrounding both victim and offender. Originally developed in New Zealand, drawing on Maori indigenous practices, these conferences bring together victims, offenders, and their respective families and supporters. Together, they discuss the harm that has occurred, the needs that have arisen, and the steps necessary for repair and reintegration. The presence of family and supporters creates a powerful context for accountability and healing—offenders must face not only their victims but also their own loved ones, who witness the consequences of their actions. And both victims and offenders receive the ongoing support of their communities as they move forward.

Circle processes represent another form of restorative practice, drawing on indigenous traditions from North America and elsewhere. Participants sit in a circle, symbolizing equality and mutual respect. A talking piece is passed from person to person, ensuring that each voice is heard without interruption. Circles can be used for a wide variety of purposes: addressing conflicts within communities, supporting victims and offenders, making decisions about sanctions and reparation, and celebrating successful reintegration. The circle creates a space of safety and respect in which even the most difficult conversations can occur.

What is remarkable about these practices is their ancient resonance. Long before the modern restorative justice movement, the Apostle Paul employed essentially these same techniques in addressing a conflict that threatened the early church. The Epistle to Philemon provides a stunning biblical example of restorative justice in action.

Onesimus, a slave belonging to Philemon, had run away—an offense that under Roman law could carry the death penalty. In his flight, Onesimus encountered Paul and became a Christian. Paul found himself in a delicate position. He had come to love Onesimus as a son in the faith, but he knew that justice required accountability. He could not simply ignore the harm Onesimus had caused to Philemon. Nor could he unilaterally command Philemon's forgiveness. What he did instead was to orchestrate a restorative encounter.

Paul sent Onesimus back to Philemon—but not alone. He sent with him this letter, a masterpiece of restorative advocacy. In it, Paul acknowledges the harm: Onesimus had been "unprofitable" to Philemon. He affirms the relationship: Onesimus is now Paul's "son" and "my very heart." He takes responsibility for making amends: "If he has wronged you or owes anything, put that on my account." And he appeals to Philemon to receive Onesimus back "no longer as a slave but more than a slave—a beloved brother."

Paul could have commanded. He could have asserted his apostolic authority. Instead, he created the conditions for encounter, accountability, and voluntary restoration. He brought together the victim (Philemon), the offender (Onesimus), and the community (the church that would hear this letter read aloud). He facilitated a process in which all parties could participate freely, in which accountability was embraced rather than imposed, in which restoration was possible. This is restorative justice, embodied in Scripture, centuries before the term was coined.

The Biblical Vision: Justice as Shalom

The biblical conception of justice is rooted in and stems from the vision of shalom. This Hebrew word, often translated simply as "peace," carries a richness of meaning that far exceeds the absence of conflict. Shalom denotes wholeness, completeness, well-being, flourishing—the state of being fully and rightly related to God, to others, to oneself, and to creation. It is the condition of life as God intended it to be, the harmony of all things in right relationship.

The prophet Isaiah paints a breathtaking picture of this shalom:

Justice will dwell in the desert and righteousness live in the fertile field. The fruit of righteousness will be peace; the effect of righteousness will be quietness and confidence forever. My people will live in peaceful dwelling places, in secure homes, in undisturbed places of rest. (Isaiah 32:16-18)

Here justice and peace are intertwined, inseparable. Justice is not merely the absence of wrongdoing but the positive presence of right relationship. It yields peace, quietness, confidence, security, rest—the fruits of a flourishing community.

The prophet Hosea envisions an even more expansive shalom, extending beyond human relationships to encompass all creation:

In that day I will make a covenant for them with the beasts of the field and the birds of the air and the creatures that move along the ground. Bow and sword and battle I will abolish from the land, so that all may lie down in safety. I will betroth you to me forever; I will betroth you in righteousness and justice, in love and compassion. (Hosea 2:18-19)

Here justice embraces all creation—humanity, animals, the land itself. It abolishes the instruments of violence and establishes safety for all. It is grounded in love and compassion, betrothing God's people to Him in covenant faithfulness.

This is the biblical vision of justice: not merely giving each person their due, but actively cultivating the conditions in which all can flourish. It is forward-looking, seeking to restore what has been broken and to build a future of wholeness. It is relational, concerned with the quality of connections between people and with God. It is communal, encompassing the well-being of the entire society and even all creation.

Compare this with the commonly accepted notion that justice means each person gets what they deserve. In this view, honest work merits appropriate reward; wrongful behavior deserves proportionate punishment. Justice is backward-looking, settling accounts from past wrongs. It is individualistic, concerned with what each person merits based on their actions. It is abstract, administered by impartial judges applying universal rules.

As important as these concerns are—and they are not unimportant—the biblical vision expands far beyond them. It calls us to a justice that is not merely fair but restorative, not merely proportional but transformative, not merely individual but communal. It calls us to a justice that seeks shalom.

When wrongdoing occurs between people, shalom suffers. Relationships are fractured, trust is broken, well-being is diminished. It is unjust to leave unresolved both the wrongdoing and the resulting harm. Practicing justice, in the biblical sense, means actively rebuilding and increasing shalom for all affected—victims, offenders, and the community alike. It means not stopping at punishment but pressing on toward restoration.

The Law and the Prophets: Restorative Threads in the Old Testament

The restorative vision of justice is woven throughout the Old Testament, often in surprising places. Even within the legal codes that seem most punitive, restorative principles are embedded.

Consider the case of a master who strikes out the eye of a servant. Under the principle of *lex talionis*—"eye for eye, tooth for tooth"—we might expect the master to lose his own eye. But Exodus 21:26-27 prescribes something quite different: "If a man hits a manservant or maidservant in the eye and destroys it, he must let the servant go free to compensate for the eye." The servant receives not vengeance but freedom—a restoration of liberty that far exceeds any punitive measure. The principle of proportional retaliation is here transformed into a principle of restorative compensation.

This pattern recurs throughout the Mosaic Law. Theft is not punished by imprisonment but by restitution—often multiple times the value of what was stolen. The goal is not to inflict pain but to repair harm, to restore the victim, to hold the offender accountable in a way that produces tangible repair. The Law creates a system in which wrongdoers must face the consequences of their actions and actively participate in making things right.

The prophets amplify this restorative vision. Micah famously distills God's requirements into three essentials: "to act justly and to love mercy and to walk humbly with your God" (Micah 6:8). Justice and mercy are not opposing forces but complementary dimensions of faithful living. To act justly is to seek right relationship; to love mercy is to extend compassion even in the administration of justice. Both flow from humble walk with God.

Isaiah calls God's people to a justice that goes beyond ritual observance:

Is not this the kind of fasting I have chosen: to loose the chains of injustice and untie the cords of the yoke, to set the oppressed free and break every yoke? Is it not to share your food with the hungry and to provide the poor wanderer with shelter—when you see the naked, to clothe him, and not to turn away from your own flesh and blood? (Isaiah 58:6-7)

Here justice is active, practical, restorative. It means freeing the oppressed, feeding the hungry, sheltering the homeless, clothing the naked. It means repairing relationships and meeting needs. It is not a matter of correct ritual but of transformed relationship.

These prophetic calls are not optional additions to the Law; they are expositions of its deepest intent. The Law was given to shape a community of shalom, a people whose relationships reflected God's character. The prophets recall Israel to this purpose when they have forgotten it in favor of empty ritual and self-serving religion.

Jesus and the Fulfillment of Restorative Justice

In the teaching of Jesus, the restorative vision of the Old Testament finds its fullest expression. Jesus does not abolish the Law but fulfills it—bringing to completion its deepest intentions, embodying in His own life and ministry the justice that the prophets proclaimed.

Consider Jesus' teaching on the law of retaliation. The principle of "eye for eye" had been given, as we have seen, to limit vengeance, to ensure that punishment did not exceed the offense. But Jesus pushes His followers beyond even this limited retribution:

You have heard that it was said, 'Eye for eye, and tooth for tooth.' But I tell you, do not resist an evil person. If anyone slaps you on the right cheek, turn to them the other cheek also. (Matthew 5:38-39)

This teaching is not a counsel of passivity in the face of injustice. It is a call to transcend the cycle of retaliation altogether, to respond to harm not with counter-harm but with creative, transformative action. Turning the other cheek is not weakness; it is a powerful refusal to be drawn into the logic of violence. It breaks the cycle and opens the possibility of genuine reconciliation.

Jesus consistently embodies this restorative approach in His encounters with wrongdoers. When the woman caught in adultery is brought before Him, the legal machinery is already in motion. The law is clear: such women should be stoned. But Jesus refuses to play the role of judge in this punitive drama. He challenges those without sin to cast the first stone—and one by one, they depart. Then He turns to the woman. He does not condemn her, but neither does he minimize her sin. "Go now and leave your life of sin," He says (John 8:11). He offers her both grace and challenge, both acceptance and a call to transformation. He restores her dignity and sends her forward into a new life. This is restorative justice incarnate.

The parables of Jesus consistently illustrate restorative principles. The Good Samaritan (Luke 10:25-37) portrays a justice that transcends ethnic boundaries and religious categories, that sees need and responds with compassion, that restores the wounded stranger to wholeness. The Prodigal Son (Luke 15:11-32) depicts a father who, when his wayward son returns, does not demand punishment but runs to embrace him, restores him to the family, and celebrates his return. The Unforgiving Servant (Matthew 18:21-35) warns of the consequences of receiving mercy but refusing to extend it to others—a stark reminder that restorative justice received must become restorative justice practiced.

Jesus does not merely teach about restorative justice; He embodies it. His entire ministry is a work of restoration—healing the sick, freeing the oppressed, forgiving sinners, reconciling the estranged, restoring the marginalized to community. And His death and resurrection are the ultimate restorative act: the innocent one takes responsibility for the guilty, bears the consequences of their wrongdoing, and opens the way for their restoration to God. This is the gospel of restorative justice: that in Christ, God was reconciling the world to Himself, not counting our trespasses against us, and entrusting to us the ministry of reconciliation (2 Corinthians 5:18-19).

The Contemporary Crisis: Why Restorative Justice Matters Now

The need for restorative justice has never been more urgent. Around the world, criminal justice systems are in crisis—overburdened, expensive, ineffective, and often unjust. The United States, with less than five percent of the world's population, incarcerates nearly twenty-five percent of the world's prisoners. This mass incarceration has not made communities safer; recidivism rates remain stubbornly high, with about two-thirds of released prisoners rearrested within three years.

The human cost of this system is incalculable. Young people, in particular, bear the brunt of its failures. Those incarcerated as juveniles often spend significant portions of their lives in the system, cycling in and out of prison, their futures truncated, their potential unrealized. About one-third of all people incarcerated when young return to prison within a few years of release. Those who manage to stay out face diminished lifetime earnings and persistent stigma. While incarcerated, they must cope with solitary confinement, increased risk of suicide, inadequate mental health care, and ever-present physical and sexual abuse. Rather than learning to interact with others appropriately, they spend years with minimal human contact, their social development arrested, their capacity for relationship damaged.

The legal process itself compounds these harms. The focus on the actions of the criminal often overshadows the needs of the victim. The adversarial system incentivizes denial and minimizes accountability. The media sensationalizes crime while ignoring the human beings affected by it. The entire apparatus seems designed to process cases rather than to heal wounds, to assign blame rather than to restore relationships.

Restorative justice offers a different path—a path that addresses the underlying causes of crime, that holds offenders accountable in meaningful ways, that supports victims in their healing, and that engages communities in the work of restoration. It is not a panacea, not a simple solution to complex problems. But it is a proven approach, supported by decades of research, that can reduce recidivism, increase victim satisfaction, and strengthen communities at a fraction of the cost of conventional incarceration.

A Global Vision: Restorative Justice Across Cultures

Restorative justice is not a Western invention imposed on other cultures. Its principles resonate with indigenous traditions around the world, reflecting a deep human wisdom about how to address harm and restore relationships.

In Africa, restorative justice has deep roots. Among the Kinga community in southern Tanzania, conflicts between family members or clans were traditionally addressed through restorative mechanisms. When disputes arose, the community gathered around a communal fire in a setting called *Lugono*. A complainant would recount the incident; the defendant would respond. Through questioning and dialogue, the community helped unravel the complexities of the problem and uncover the truth. The goal was not to determine who could make the most convincing case but to understand what had really happened and why.

Reconciliation was sealed through symbolic acts: sharing locally brewed alcohol (*ukupelanila ulupelo*), consuming roasted meat together (*okukatelanila inyama*), and blowing medicinal substances into each other's faces (*ukupulilanila untuguva*). These rituals embodied the restoration of relationship, the healing of the breach. Offenders had to voluntarily confess or acknowledge responsibility and display genuine remorse. Only then could the path to reconciliation unfold.

Similar practices existed throughout Africa. In Nigeria, reconciliation following dispute mediation might involve both parties eating from the same bowl, drinking palm wine from the same cup, and breaking kola nuts together. These shared activities symbolized the restoration of unity, the rebuilding of trust, the healing of the community.

These indigenous practices were not naive or simplistic. They recognized that the social cohesion of the community depended on truth, on understanding root causes, on genuine reconciliation. They empowered ordinary people to participate freely in addressing disputes, without interference from distant state authorities. They prioritized the restoration of relationships over the imposition of punishment.

The colonial imposition of Western legal systems disrupted these indigenous practices, often with devastating effects. Post-independence African nations largely retained the legal systems of their colonizers, systems that have proven ill-suited to resolving the conflicts that afflict these nations. The result has been a loss not only of effective justice mechanisms but of cultural practices that embodied communal values and sustained social cohesion.

The global restorative justice movement represents, in part, a recovery of this indigenous wisdom—a recognition that Western punitive models are not the only or the best way to achieve justice. Around the world, communities are reclaiming their traditional practices and integrating them with contemporary insights. The result is a rich diversity of restorative approaches, each adapted to its cultural context, each embodying the universal principles of healing, accountability, and restoration.

The Way Forward: A Call to Embrace the Jesus Paradigm

As we conclude this foundational exploration, we stand at a crossroads. The path of punitive justice, despite its dominance, has proven itself inadequate—costly, ineffective, and often unjust. It fails victims, who are sidelined and silenced. It fails offenders, who are damaged rather than transformed. It fails communities, who are excluded from the work of healing. It fails to address root causes, to repair harm, to restore relationships.

The path of restorative justice, illuminated by the teachings of Jesus and embodied in the Jesus Paradigm, offers a different way—a way of healing rather than hurting, of accountability rather than denial, of restoration rather than isolation. It is a way rooted in the deepest truths of Scripture, confirmed by the best insights of psychology and criminology, and validated by the lived experience of communities around the world.

This way is not easy. It demands more of us than punitive justice ever could. It calls victims to the difficult work of engaging with those who have harmed them. It calls offenders to genuine accountability and transformation. It calls communities to active participation in the work of healing. It calls all of us to see in every harm an opportunity for repair, in every wrongdoer a potential for change, in every community a capacity for collective restoration.

But this way is also hopeful. It believes that healing is possible, that relationships can be restored, that even the deepest wounds can be transformed. It trusts that the God who reconciled the world to Himself in Christ has entrusted to us the ministry of reconciliation—a ministry that we are called to embody in our relationships, our communities, and our institutions.

As we move forward through the chapters of this book, we will explore in greater depth the teachings of Jesus on justice, the application of restorative principles in diverse contexts, and the challenges and promises of embracing restorative justice through the lens of Jesus. We will encounter real-world case studies that illustrate both the possibilities and the difficulties of this approach. We will grapple with the critiques and concerns that restorative justice raises. And we will be equipped to become practitioners of this healing justice in our own spheres of influence.

The journey is long, but the destination is glorious: a world in which justice is not merely done but seen to be done, in which harm is repaired rather than compounded, in which relationships are restored rather than destroyed, in which communities are strengthened rather than divided. This is the vision of shalom. This is the promise of the gospel. This is the call of restorative justice through the lens of Jesus.

CHAPTER 02

THE TEACHINGS OF JESUS ON JUSTICE

The teachings of Jesus on justice are not merely scattered sayings or incidental remarks within the Gospel narratives. They constitute the very heart of His proclamation, the central thrust of His ministry, and the foundational ethic of the kingdom of God that He came to establish. To understand Jesus is to understand His vision of justice; to follow Jesus is to embody that vision in the world. This chapter invites you into a deep and sustained exploration of what Jesus taught about justice not as abstract doctrine but as living reality, not as distant ideal but as present imperative.

The Gospels present Jesus as a teacher unlike any other. The crowds were astonished at His teaching, for He taught them as one having authority, not as the scribes (Matthew 7:29). That authority derived not from credentials or position but from the intrinsic truth of His message and the perfect congruence between His words and His life. When Jesus spoke of justice, He was not merely interpreting texts or applying principles; He was revealing the very heart of God and embodying the justice that God requires.

As we immerse ourselves in His teachings, we will discover that Jesus consistently redirects our understanding of justice away from abstract rules and toward concrete relationships, away from mere compliance and toward transformed hearts, away from retribution and toward restoration. His vision of justice is nothing less than the blueprint for a new social order—a order in which love is the fundamental law, compassion is the default response, and reconciliation is the ultimate goal.

The Sermon on the Mount: The Constitution of the Kingdom

The Sermon on the Mount, recorded in Matthew chapters five through seven, stands as the most comprehensive and revolutionary statement of Jesus' ethical teaching. It is not merely a collection of beautiful sayings but a coherent vision of life in the kingdom of God—a vision that fundamentally reorients human relationships and reconceives the very nature of justice.

The sermon begins with the Beatitudes, a series of blessings that turn the world's values upside down. "Blessed are the poor in spirit, for theirs is the kingdom of heaven. Blessed are those who mourn, for they shall be comforted. Blessed are the meek, for they shall inherit the earth. Blessed are those who hunger and thirst for righteousness, for they shall be filled" (Matthew 5:3-6). Here Jesus declares blessed those whom the world considers unfortunate, weak, and disadvantaged. He locates the kingdom not with the powerful, the wealthy, and the satisfied but with the humble, the grieving, and the hungry.

This reversal is foundational for understanding Jesus' vision of justice. In the conventional order, justice is about giving people what they deserve—rewarding the deserving and punishing the undeserving. But Jesus announces blessings upon those who, by conventional standards, have received nothing but misfortune. He is not denying the reality of their suffering but declaring that God's justice transcends the present order, that divine blessing is not contingent on worldly success, and that those who hunger for righteousness will ultimately be satisfied.

The Beatitudes culminate in a double blessing: "Blessed are the merciful, for they shall obtain mercy. Blessed are the pure in heart, for they shall see God. Blessed are the peacemakers, for they shall be called sons of God" (Matthew 5:7-9). Here we encounter qualities essential to restorative justice—mercy, purity of heart, peacemaking. These are not passive virtues but active dispositions that shape how we relate to others, especially those who have wronged us.

To be merciful is to extend compassion to those who do not deserve it—precisely the posture that restorative justice requires. Victims who participate in restorative processes must draw upon deep reserves of mercy to engage with those who have harmed them. Offenders who seek restoration must receive mercy from victims and communities. The promise attached to this beatitude—that the merciful shall obtain mercy—reflects the reciprocal nature of restorative justice: as we extend mercy to others, we position ourselves to receive it when we need it.

To be pure in heart is to be single-minded in one's devotion to God and to goodness—free from the divided loyalties and hidden agendas that corrupt human relationships. In restorative justice, purity of heart manifests as genuine commitment to healing rather than hidden desires for vengeance or self-justification. It means entering the process not to manipulate outcomes but to seek genuine restoration.

To be a peacemaker is to actively work for reconciliation—not merely to avoid conflict but to actively repair broken relationships. Peacemakers are not passive; they are agents of restoration who invest themselves in the difficult work of bringing divided parties together. Jesus calls such people "sons of God," for in their peacemaking they reflect the character of the God who reconciles the world to Himself.

Later in the Sermon, Jesus addresses the heart of the justice system: "You have heard that it was said, 'An eye for an eye and a tooth for a tooth.' But I tell you not to resist an evil person. But whoever slaps you on your right cheek, turn the other to him also" (Matthew 5:38-39). This teaching has been widely misunderstood as a call to passive acquiescence in the face of injustice. Nothing could be further from the truth.

The law of retaliation—*lex talionis*—had been given to limit vengeance, to ensure that punishment did not exceed the offense. In a world where personal vendettas could escalate into blood feuds that destroyed families and communities, this principle represented a significant advance in justice. It said, in effect: you may take only one eye for an eye, not the offender's life; you may extract only one tooth for a tooth, not all their teeth.

But Jesus calls His followers beyond even this limited retribution. Turning the other cheek is not weakness; it is a powerful refusal to be drawn into the cycle of retaliation. In the cultural context of first-century Palestine, a slap on the right cheek would typically be delivered with the back of the hand—a gesture of insult and degradation, an assertion of dominance. By turning the other cheek, the victim says, in effect: strike me again if you will, but as an equal, not as a subordinate. You cannot degrade me without my consent.

This teaching opens a third way beyond passive submission and violent retaliation. It is the way of creative nonviolence, of assertive dignity, of refusing to let the offender define the terms of the encounter. It is the way that Jesus Himself would walk to the cross—not submitting to evil but overcoming it through sacrificial love. And it is the way of restorative justice, which refuses either to ignore harm or to respond to it with counter-harm, seeking instead a path of accountability and healing.

The Sermon on the Mount also gives us the Golden Rule: "Therefore, whatever you want men to do to you, do also to them, for this is the Law and the Prophets" (Matthew 7:12). This simple yet profound principle encapsulates the essence of restorative justice. It calls us to imagine ourselves in the other's position, to consider what we would want if we were the one who had been harmed, and to act accordingly.

If we were victims of crime, what would we want? We would want to be heard, to have our pain acknowledged, to receive answers to our questions, to see the offender take responsibility, to receive restitution for our losses, to find closure and healing. The Golden Rule therefore requires that we extend these same opportunities to victims when we are in positions of power. If we were offenders, what would we want? We would want the opportunity to explain ourselves, to make amends, to be restored to community, to have a future beyond our past failures. The Golden Rule therefore requires that we extend these same possibilities to offenders when we are the ones who have been harmed.

This principle, Jesus says, sums up the Law and the Prophets. It is not a new commandment but the distillation of all that God had been teaching Israel throughout their history. It is the hermeneutical key to understanding what justice requires in every situation. And it is the foundation upon which restorative justice builds its practices.

The Parable of the Good Samaritan: Justice as Compassion in Action

The parable of the Good Samaritan, found in Luke 10:25-37, is perhaps the most powerful illustration in all of Scripture of what restorative justice looks like in practice. It is Jesus' answer to the question, "What must I do to inherit eternal life?"—a question about ultimate justice, about being rightly related to God. And His answer takes the form of a story about a man who was victimized and the unexpected neighbor who restored him.

The context is crucial. A lawyer—an expert in the Law of Moses—stands up to test Jesus. "Teacher," he asks, "what shall I do to inherit eternal life?" Jesus turns the question back to him: "What is written in the law? What is your reading of it?" The lawyer answers correctly: "You shall love the Lord your God with all your heart, with all your soul, with all your strength, and with all your mind, and your neighbor as yourself." Jesus affirms his answer: "You have answered rightly; do this and you will live."

But the lawyer, wanting to justify himself, asks a follow-up question: "And who is my neighbor?" This question reveals the lawyer's underlying assumption. He assumes that "neighbor" is a limited category, that some people count as neighbors and others do not, that he can fulfill the commandment by loving those within his circle while remaining indifferent to those outside it. His question seeks to define the boundaries of obligation, to determine the minimum requirements of love.

Jesus responds with a story that demolishes all boundaries and redefines neighbor beyond any human limitation.

A man was traveling from Jerusalem to Jericho—a notoriously dangerous route, winding through rocky terrain that provided cover for robbers. He fell into the hands of bandits, who stripped him, beat him, and left him half dead by the side of the road. The victim is anonymous—no name, no ethnic identification, no religious affiliation. He could be anyone. His humanity alone is his identity.

First, a priest comes down the road. He sees the wounded man—and passes by on the other side. The priest is a religious professional, trained in the Law, charged with teaching others what God requires. Yet when confronted with a concrete opportunity to love his neighbor, he averts his eyes and continues on his way. Perhaps he feared ritual impurity if the man were dead. Perhaps he feared the robbers might still be lurking. Perhaps he simply didn't want to be bothered. Whatever his reasons, his inaction condemns him.

Next, a Levite comes to the place and sees the man. Levites were temple assistants, also religious functionaries, also charged with serving God and God's people. He too sees the wounded man—and passes by on the other side. The repetition is damning. Two representatives of Israel's religious establishment, both entrusted with the Law that commands love of neighbor, both fail to act when love is most needed.

Then comes a Samaritan. For Jesus' Jewish audience, this detail was shocking. Samaritans were despised as half-breeds and heretics, enemies of the Jewish people, beyond the pale of neighbor-love as conventionally defined. If anyone could be excluded from the category of neighbor, surely it was a Samaritan.

But when the Samaritan sees the wounded man, he does not pass by. He is moved with compassion—a visceral, emotional response to suffering that overrides every cultural and religious barrier. And his compassion issues in action: he goes to the man, bandages his wounds, pouring on oil and wine. He lifts him onto his own animal, brings him to an inn, and takes care of him. The next day, he gives the innkeeper two denarii—two days' wages—with instructions to care for the man further, promising to cover any additional expenses on his return.

Jesus then turns the lawyer's question upside down. He does not ask, "Who is my neighbor?"—a question that seeks to limit obligation. Instead, He asks, "Which of these three do you think was neighbor to him who fell among the thieves?" The question shifts from defining the object of love to embodying the practice of love. Neighbor is not a category to be defined but a relationship to be enacted. The one who shows mercy is the true neighbor, regardless of ethnic or religious identity.

The lawyer answers correctly: "He who showed mercy on him." And Jesus issues the command: "Go and do likewise."

This parable is a masterclass in restorative justice. Consider its elements:

First, it centers on a victim. The wounded man is anonymous but vividly present—stripped, beaten, half dead. His suffering is real, his need is urgent, his humanity is undeniable. The parable refuses to let us forget the victim's experience.

Second, it exposes the failure of institutional religion to provide justice. The priest and Levite, representatives of the established order, do nothing. Their religion has become routine, their compassion atrophied, their obedience to Law reduced to avoidance of impurity. They are not evil but they are useless—and their uselessness is itself a form of injustice.

Third, it reveals that true justice transcends boundaries. The Samaritan, the one least expected to act righteously, is the one who embodies righteousness. Justice is not confined to those who share our religion, our ethnicity, or our social position. It is a human obligation, arising from our common humanity.

Fourth, it demonstrates that justice requires action. The Samaritan does not merely feel compassion; he acts on it. He goes to the man, bandages his wounds, transports him to safety, provides for his ongoing care. Justice is not a sentiment but a practice, not an attitude but a set of actions that repair harm and restore wholeness.

Fifth, it shows that justice is costly. The Samaritan expends time, energy, and resources. He risks his own safety on a dangerous road. He spends his own money for a stranger's care. He commits to ongoing involvement, promising to return and cover any additional costs. Restorative justice is not cheap; it demands investment from those who practice it.

Sixth, it illustrates that justice creates community. The Samaritan does not merely provide immediate aid and move on. He creates a network of care involving the innkeeper, and he commits to ongoing relationship. The wounded man, once anonymous and alone, is now embedded in a community of support.

Finally, the parable calls us to imitation: "Go and do likewise." Restorative justice is not something we admire from a distance but something we practice in our own lives. Every encounter with suffering, every opportunity to respond to harm, is an invitation to be neighbor—to show mercy, to bind wounds, to restore the broken.

This is the justice that Jesus teaches. It is not about determining who deserves what but about responding to need with compassion, transcending boundaries with love, and restoring the broken with costly care. It is justice as love in action—the very heart of the restorative paradigm.

The Beatitudes: The Character of the Just

The Beatitudes, with which the Sermon on the Mount begins, provide a portrait of the character that undergirds authentic justice. They describe not what we do but who we are—the inner dispositions that shape our outer actions. And these dispositions are precisely those that restorative justice requires.

"Blessed are the poor in spirit" (Matthew 5:3). To be poor in spirit is to recognize our own spiritual poverty, our dependence on God, our need for grace. This recognition is essential for restorative justice because it undermines the self-righteousness that fuels condemnation. When we know our own need for mercy, we are more likely to extend mercy to others. When we have received grace, we are more equipped to offer grace. The poor in spirit do not stand in judgment over others from a position of imagined moral superiority; they stand alongside others, fellow recipients of divine compassion.

"Blessed are those who mourn" (Matthew 5:4). Mourning is the appropriate response to suffering—our own and others'. Restorative justice begins with mourning: mourning the harm that has been done, the relationships that have been broken, the lives that have been damaged. It refuses to rush past pain to resolution, insisting that grief must be acknowledged before healing can begin. Those who mourn are open to the full reality of suffering, and that openness is prerequisite to genuine restoration.

"Blessed are the meek" (Matthew 5:5). Meekness is not weakness but strength under control—the power to refrain from dominating others, to listen rather than assert, to serve rather than control. In restorative justice, meekness enables victims to engage with offenders without seeking to dominate them, and offenders to accept accountability without defensive posturing. It creates the space for genuine dialogue, for mutual recognition, for the kind of encounter that heals.

"Blessed are those who hunger and thirst for righteousness" (Matthew 5:6). This hunger and thirst is not a passive wish but an active longing, as urgent as the body's need for food and water. It is the deep desire for things to be made right, for justice to prevail, for relationships to be restored. Restorative justice is fueled by this hunger—not for vengeance but for genuine righteousness, for the shalom that comes when harm is repaired and community is healed. And the promise attached to this beatitude—that the hungry shall be filled—assures us that this longing is not in vain. God's justice will ultimately prevail.

"Blessed are the merciful" (Matthew 5:7). Mercy is the disposition to show compassion to those who have wronged us, to extend forgiveness rather than demand payment, to seek restoration rather than retribution. This is perhaps the most counter-cultural of all the beatitudes, for the world teaches us to demand what we deserve, to insist on our rights, to make others pay for their offenses. But Jesus declares blessed those who transcend this calculus, who give not what is deserved but what is needed. Restorative justice is mercy institutionalized—creating structures and processes through which mercy can be extended and received.

"Blessed are the pure in heart" (Matthew 5:8). Purity of heart is singleness of purpose, undivided devotion to God and goodness. In restorative justice, purity of heart means entering the process with genuine desire for healing, not hidden agendas of manipulation or revenge. It means transparency, honesty, and integrity in all our dealings. The pure in heart have nothing to hide and nothing to prove; they can engage with others openly and authentically, creating the conditions for genuine encounter.

"Blessed are the peacemakers" (Matthew 5:9). Peacemakers are not merely peace-lovers but peace-activists—those who actively work to reconcile divided parties, to heal broken relationships, to build bridges across chasms of conflict. This is the central work of restorative justice: bringing together victims and offenders, facilitating dialogue, negotiating agreements, supporting restoration. Peacemakers are called "sons of God" because in their work they reflect the character of the God who reconciles the world to Himself.

These beatitudes are not merely admirable qualities; they are the essential character traits for those who would practice restorative justice. They form a coherent portrait of the just person—humble enough to recognize their own need for mercy, grieving over harm rather than rushing past it, strong enough to refrain from domination, hungry for genuine righteousness, merciful toward wrongdoers, pure in intention, and active in peacemaking. This is the character that Jesus blesses, and this is the character that restorative justice requires.

The Golden Rule: The Measure of Justice

The Golden Rule stands as one of the most universally recognized ethical principles in human history. Its positive formulation—"whatever you want men to do to you, do also to them"—distinguishes it from merely negative formulations like the silver rule ("do not do to others what you would not want done to you"). Jesus calls His followers to proactive goodness, to actively do for others what we would want done for us.

This principle provides a simple yet profound test for every action and every system. Before we respond to harm, we must ask: If I were the victim, how would I want to be treated? What would I need? What would help me heal? And if I were the offender, what would I need to take responsibility and change? What would enable me to make amends and be restored?

Applying this test to our current justice systems reveals their inadequacy. If we were victims, would we want to be sidelined, silenced, and ignored—treated as mere witnesses in a process that belongs to the state? Would we want our questions to go unanswered, our pain to go unacknowledged, our needs to go unmet? Would we want the offender simply locked away, with no opportunity for us to confront them, to hear their remorse, to receive restitution? The answer is clearly no. Yet this is precisely what conventional justice systems offer.

If we were offenders, would we want to be defined solely by our worst act, reduced to the label of "criminal," stripped of our humanity and our hope for change? Would we want to be isolated from community, denied opportunities for growth and transformation, released back into society more damaged than when we entered? The answer again is no. Yet this is the reality of mass incarceration.

The Golden Rule therefore stands as an indictment of punitive justice and a mandate for restorative alternatives. It calls us to create systems that treat victims as we would want to be treated—with respect, with voice, with opportunities for healing. It calls us to treat offenders as we would want to be treated—with accountability that leads to transformation, with opportunities to make amends, with pathways back to community. It calls us to do for others what we would want done for us.

This principle also illuminates the relationship between justice and love. The Golden Rule is a practical expression of love—not sentiment but action, not feeling but doing. It translates the abstract command to love your neighbor into a concrete test for every decision. And it reveals that love and justice are not opposing forces but complementary dimensions of right relationship. Love without justice becomes sentimentality, ignoring the reality of harm and the need for accountability. Justice without love becomes cruelty, inflicting punishment without regard for healing or restoration. The Golden Rule unites love and justice, calling us to act toward others with the same care and concern we would want shown to us.

The Judgment of the Nations: Justice as Care for the Marginalized

In Matthew 25:31-46, Jesus presents a powerful vision of final judgment that reveals the essential connection between justice and care for the marginalized. The Son of Man comes in glory, surrounded by angels, seated on His throne. Before Him are gathered all the nations, and He separates them as a shepherd separates sheep from goats. To those on His right, He says:

"Come, you blessed of My Father, inherit the kingdom prepared for you from the foundation of the world: for I was hungry and you gave Me food; I was thirsty and you gave Me drink; I was a stranger and you took Me in; I was naked and you clothed Me; I was sick and you visited Me; I was in prison and you came to Me."

The righteous are bewildered. When, they ask, did we see You hungry and feed You, or thirsty and give You drink? When did we see You a stranger and take You in, or naked and clothe You? When did we see You sick or in prison and come to You? The King answers: "Assuredly, I say to you, inasmuch as you did it to one of the least of these My brethren, you did it to Me."

To those on His left, He speaks words of judgment. "Depart from Me, you cursed, into the everlasting fire prepared for the devil and his angels: for I was hungry and you gave Me no food; I was thirsty and you gave Me no drink; I was a stranger and you did not take Me in; naked and you did not clothe Me; sick and in prison and you did not visit Me." They too are bewildered, protesting that they never saw Him in need. And He answers: "Assuredly, I say to you, inasmuch as you did not do it to one of the least of these, you did not do it to Me."

This passage is revolutionary in several respects. First, it identifies Jesus Himself with the marginalized and suffering. The hungry, the thirsty, the stranger, the naked, the sick, the imprisoned—these are not merely objects of charity but representatives of Christ. To care for them is to care for Jesus; to neglect them is to neglect Him. This identification elevates care for the vulnerable from optional piety to essential worship.

Second, it makes care for the marginalized the criterion of final judgment. The nations are not judged on the basis of correct doctrine, proper worship, or moral purity—though these matter. They are judged on the basis of whether they fed the hungry, clothed the naked, welcomed the stranger, visited the imprisoned. The test of righteousness is practical compassion for those in need.

Third, it reveals that the righteous were unaware of their righteousness. They did not feed the hungry in order to earn reward; they fed them because they were hungry. Their compassion was spontaneous, uncalculated, genuine. They did not keep score of their good deeds or expect recognition. Their righteousness was not self-conscious but instinctive—the natural outflow of transformed hearts.

Fourth, it condemns not only active wrongdoing but passive neglect. The cursed are not accused of committing atrocities but of failing to act—of not feeding the hungry, not clothing the naked, not visiting the imprisoned. Their sin is omission, not commission. They are condemned for what they did not do.

This passage has profound implications for restorative justice. The imprisoned are explicitly named among "the least of these" with whom Jesus identifies. To visit prisoners is to visit Christ Himself. This is not merely a recommendation but a requirement—a test of righteousness, a criterion of judgment. Those who claim to follow Jesus cannot ignore those behind bars.

But the passage extends beyond prison visitation to encompass all who are marginalized and suffering. The hungry, the thirsty, the stranger, the naked, the sick—these are the ones with whom Jesus identifies, and these are the ones whose needs justice must address. Restorative justice, in its concern for victims and offenders and communities, seeks to care for all these groups. Victims are often traumatized, sick in spirit, in need of healing. Offenders are often among the hungry, the naked, the stranger—marginalized long before they committed crimes. Communities affected by crime need restoration and support.

The passage also challenges the tendency to separate spiritual concerns from material needs. Jesus does not say, "I was hungry and you preached to Me," or "I was naked and you shared the gospel with Me." He says, "I was hungry and you gave Me food; I was thirsty and you gave Me drink; I was a stranger and you took Me in." Spiritual care without material provision is hollow. Proclamation without action is empty. Justice requires meeting concrete needs—food for the hungry, clothing for the naked, welcome for the stranger, presence for the imprisoned.

Finally, the passage affirms that how we treat the most vulnerable among us reveals our true relationship with God. We cannot claim to love God whom we have not seen if we do not love our neighbor whom we have seen (1 John 4:20). Our treatment of "the least of these" is the measure of our love for God. Restorative justice, in its commitment to the marginalized and wounded, is therefore not merely a social program but a spiritual practice—a way of loving God by loving those with whom He identifies.

Forgiveness and Reconciliation: The Heart of Restorative Justice

Jesus' teachings on forgiveness are among His most challenging and most essential. They cut against every natural human inclination, demanding of His followers a radical generosity of spirit that seems beyond human capacity. Yet they are central to His vision of justice and indispensable for restorative practice.

In the Sermon on the Mount, Jesus links divine forgiveness to human forgiveness with startling directness: "For if you forgive men their trespasses, your heavenly Father will also forgive you. But if you do not forgive men their trespasses, neither will your Father forgive your trespasses" (Matthew 6:14-15). This is not a mechanical formula but a recognition that our reception of grace is inseparable from our extension of grace. Those who have truly experienced God's forgiveness cannot refuse to forgive others. Those who withhold forgiveness from others reveal that they have not truly received it themselves.

This teaching raises profound psychological and theological questions. How can forgiveness be commanded? Is it not a feeling, an emotion, something that cannot be produced at will? Yet Jesus speaks as though forgiveness is a choice, an act of will, a decision we can make regardless of our feelings. The psychological research supports this distinction: forgiveness is not the same as forgetting, not the same as ceasing to feel hurt, not the same as reconciliation. Forgiveness is the decision to release the offender from the debt of guilt, to relinquish the right to revenge, to open the door to possible reconciliation. Feelings may follow, but forgiveness itself is an act of will—a choice that can be made even when emotions lag behind.

Later, when Peter asks how many times he must forgive his brother—suggesting seven times, which seemed generous—Jesus responds: "I do not say to you, up to seven times, but up to seventy times seven" (Matthew 18:21-22). The number is not literal but symbolic, indicating limitless forgiveness. There is no point at which we are released from the obligation to forgive, no number of offenses beyond which we may finally withhold grace.

This teaching is immediately followed by the parable of the unforgiving servant (Matthew 18:23-35), which illustrates the catastrophic consequences of refusing to extend the forgiveness we have received. A servant owes his king an astronomical debt—ten thousand talents, millions of dollars in modern currency, a sum impossible to repay. When the servant pleads for mercy, the king forgives the entire debt. But that same servant, immediately upon leaving the king's presence, encounters a fellow servant who owes him a paltry sum—a hundred denarii, a few thousand dollars, a debt that could reasonably be repaid. He seizes the man by the throat, demands payment, and when the man pleads for patience, has him thrown into prison.

When the king hears of this, he is furious. "You wicked servant! I forgave you all that debt because you begged me. Should you not also have had compassion on your fellow servant, just as I had pity on you?" He delivers the unforgiving servant to the torturers until he should pay all that was due. And Jesus concludes: "So My heavenly Father also will do to you if each of you, from his heart, does not forgive his brother his trespasses."

This parable cuts to the heart of restorative justice. It reveals that forgiveness is not optional for those who have received it. The staggering disproportion between the debts—the first incalculable, the second trivial—underscores the absurdity of refusing forgiveness. If God has forgiven us the infinite debt of our sin against Him, how can we refuse to forgive the finite debts others owe us?

But the parable also illuminates the nature of forgiveness in restorative justice. The king does not ignore the debt or pretend it never existed. He acknowledges it fully—ten thousand talents is a real debt, a serious obligation. But he chooses to release the debtor from that obligation, to absorb the loss himself, to forego what was rightfully his. Forgiveness is not denial but release—not pretending harm didn't happen but choosing not to hold it against the offender.

This is precisely what restorative justice seeks to facilitate: not the minimization of harm but the release from its grip. Victims are not asked to pretend they weren't hurt; they are invited to acknowledge the full extent of their injury and then to choose a path that leads to healing rather than perpetual resentment. Offenders are not let off the hook but held accountable in ways that enable them to make amends and be restored. Forgiveness is the goal, but it is a forgiveness that fully acknowledges the reality of harm.

The psychological benefits of forgiveness are well-documented. Research shows that people who forgive experience lower levels of depression, anxiety, and anger; they have better cardiovascular health, stronger immune function, and greater overall well-being. Forgiveness breaks the cycle of rumination that keeps victims trapped in the past, allowing them to move forward with their lives. It does not benefit the offender alone; it liberates the victim from continuing bondage to the offense.

But forgiveness is not reconciliation. Reconciliation requires the willing participation of both parties; it involves the rebuilding of trust and the restoration of relationship. Forgiveness can be offered unilaterally; the victim can forgive even if the offender remains unrepentant. Restorative justice seeks to create the conditions for both forgiveness and reconciliation—offering victims the opportunity to forgive and offenders the opportunity to receive that forgiveness and work toward restored relationship.

The Rich Young Ruler: Justice and Economic Equity

The encounter between Jesus and the rich young ruler, recorded in Mark 10:17-27, reveals another dimension of Jesus' teaching on justice: the call to economic equity and the sharing of resources with those in need.

A man runs up to Jesus and kneels before Him, asking, "Good Teacher, what shall I do that I may inherit eternal life?" Jesus responds by pointing him to the commandments: "You know the commandments: 'Do not commit adultery,' 'Do not murder,' 'Do not steal,' 'Do not bear false witness,' 'Do not defraud,' 'Honor your father and your mother.'" The man replies that he has observed all these from his youth.

Then Mark records a detail of stunning significance: "Then Jesus, looking at him, loved him." This is not the cold appraisal of a moral teacher but the warm gaze of divine love. Jesus sees this man, recognizes his sincerity, and loves him. And because He loves him, He tells him the truth he most needs to hear: "One thing you lack: Go your way, sell whatever you have and give to the poor, and you will have treasure in heaven; and come, take up the cross, and follow Me."

The man's face falls, and he goes away sorrowful, for he had great possessions. Jesus then turns to His disciples and delivers a shocking pronouncement: "How hard it is for those who have riches to enter the kingdom of God!" The disciples are astonished, and Jesus repeats Himself: "Children, how hard it is for those who trust in riches to enter the kingdom of God! It is easier for a camel to go through the eye of a needle than for a rich man to enter the kingdom of God."

This encounter reveals that authentic discipleship requires more than moral conformity; it requires the radical reordering of our relationship to possessions. The man had kept the commandments—or so he thought. But Jesus exposes the hidden idolatry in his heart: his wealth had become his god. When confronted with the choice between his possessions and following Jesus, he chose his possessions. His righteousness was incomplete because his heart was divided.

The command to sell everything and give to the poor is not a universal requirement for all followers of Jesus. Many of Jesus' disciples, including women who supported His ministry from their means, retained their property. But for this man, at this moment, the command was necessary because his wealth stood between him and wholehearted discipleship. Jesus loved him enough to tell him the truth about what he truly valued.

This encounter has profound implications for restorative justice. It reveals that justice cannot be separated from economic reality. The accumulation of wealth while others lack necessities is incompatible with the kingdom of God. Those who have been blessed with resources are called to share them with those in need. This is not optional charity but essential righteousness.

In the context of restorative justice, this teaching calls us to consider the economic dimensions of harm and restoration. Victims often suffer material losses that require restitution. Offenders often come from backgrounds of poverty and deprivation that contributed to their criminal behavior. Communities affected by crime need resources for healing and prevention. Restorative justice must address these economic realities, seeking not only emotional healing but material restoration.

The encounter also challenges the comfortable assumption that we can follow Jesus while ignoring the needs of the poor. The rich young ruler was morally upright, religiously devout, and sincerely seeking eternal life. Yet he walked away from Jesus because he could not let go of his possessions. His story stands as a warning to all who would separate spiritual devotion from economic justice.

The Teachings in Mark's Gospel: A Case Study in Restorative Praxis

The Gospel of Mark provides a particularly vivid portrait of Jesus' restorative justice in action. From His first public acts to His final teachings, Mark presents Jesus as one who consistently prioritizes healing, inclusion, and restoration over rigid adherence to religious rules and social conventions.

Mark records Jesus' initial public miracles—both unfolding on the Sabbath. First, He casts out an unclean spirit in the synagogue at Capernaum (Mark 1:21-28). The people are amazed at His authority, for He teaches and acts with power unlike the scribes. Then He heals Simon's mother-in-law, who lies sick with fever (Mark 1:29-31). He takes her by the hand and lifts her up; immediately the fever leaves her, and she begins to serve them.

These healings on the Sabbath are significant. The Sabbath was sacred, a day of rest ordained by God Himself. Religious tradition had surrounded it with numerous restrictions, defining in minute detail what constituted work and what was permissible. By healing on the Sabbath, Jesus was not breaking God's law but challenging human additions that had obscured its purpose. The Sabbath was made for man, He would later declare, not man for the Sabbath (Mark 2:27). Human need takes precedence over ritual observance.

In these inaugural public demonstrations, Jesus exemplifies a profound love and compassion that transcends societal norms. His actions extend to individuals irrespective of their social standing. He heals a man possessed by an unclean spirit—one of the most marginalized and feared members of society. He heals a woman, challenging gender norms that limited women's public roles. He touches the sick, disregarding purity concerns. He violates Sabbath conventions, prioritizing human need over religious tradition.

This commitment to reaching out to the disenfranchised and marginalized becomes a foundational theme woven throughout Mark's Gospel. Jesus consistently crosses boundaries that separated people from community and from God. He touches lepers, dines with tax collectors and sinners, converses with Samaritan women, welcomes children. His justice is not abstract but embodied—a relentless movement toward those whom society has pushed away.

Importantly, these acts of compassion are not isolated incidents but integral components of a broader narrative. After healing many, Jesus withdraws to a solitary place to pray. When Simon and others find Him and tell Him that everyone is looking for Him, Jesus responds: "Let us go into the next towns, that I may preach there also, because for this purpose I have come" (Mark 1:38). The miracles are signs, pointers to a deeper reality. Their significance lies not in themselves but in the kingdom they announce and the King they reveal. Jesus' purpose is to proclaim the good news of God's reign—a reign in which justice, healing, and restoration are the norm.

The Paralytic: Forgiveness Precedes Healing

Another poignant lesson on forgiveness emerges in the healing of the paralytic (Mark 2:1-12), underscoring the inseparable connection between forgiveness and restoration. Jesus returns to Capernaum, and news spreads that He is home. So many gather that there is no room left, not even outside the door. As Jesus preaches the word to them, four men arrive carrying a paralytic. Unable to get near Jesus because of the crowd, they go up on the roof, dig through it, and lower the man down on his mat.

The faith of these four men is remarkable. They overcome every obstacle—the crowd, the roof, the difficulty of lowering a paralyzed man to bring their friend to Jesus. Their determination reveals the depth of their love and the strength of their faith. They believe that if they can just get this man to Jesus, something will happen.

Jesus sees their faith—and says to the paralytic: "Son, your sins are forgiven you." This declaration is unexpected. The man came for healing, not forgiveness. But Jesus sees deeper. He knows that this man's deepest need is not physical but spiritual, not temporal but eternal. Before addressing the paralysis of his body, Jesus addresses the condition of his soul.

Some of the scribes sitting there begin reasoning in their hearts: "Why does this Man speak blasphemies like this? Who can forgive sins but God alone?" They are correct in their theology—only God can forgive sins. But they fail to recognize who stands before them. Jesus perceives their thoughts and responds: "Why do you reason about these things in your hearts? Which is easier, to say to the paralytic, 'Your sins are forgiven you,' or to say, 'Arise, take up your bed and walk'? But that you may know that the Son of Man has power on earth to forgive sins"—He says to the paralytic—"I say to you, arise, take up your bed, and go to your house."

Immediately the man rises, takes up his mat, and walks out in full view of everyone. The crowd is amazed and glorifies God, saying, "We never saw anything like this!"

This episode reveals a profound truth: forgiveness must precede healing. The man's physical restoration flows from and demonstrates his spiritual restoration. Jesus addresses the root cause before dealing with the symptom. He forgives the sins that separate the man from God, and then He heals the body that separates the man from full participation in community.

For restorative justice, this sequence is instructive. True restoration requires addressing the fundamental breach in relationships—the wrong that has been done, the harm that has been caused. Before material restitution, before community reintegration, there must be acknowledgment of wrongdoing and the possibility of forgiveness. The offender must hear words of forgiveness, or at least the possibility of forgiveness, before healing can proceed. The victim must be able to release the offender from the debt of guilt, or at least to hold that debt in a new way, before restoration can occur.

The episode also demonstrates the connection between forgiveness and community. The paralytic is brought to Jesus by his friends; their faith plays a role in his healing. After his restoration, he returns to his community, able now to participate fully in its life. Forgiveness is not a private transaction between the individual and God but a communal event with social consequences. The restored man is restored to relationship—with God, with himself, and with his community.

The Parables of Growth: Patience in the Work of Restoration

In Mark chapter four, Jesus imparts four parables intended to inspire His disciples and anyone with receptive ears: the parables of the sower, the lamp, the growing seed, and the mustard seed. These parables address a question that must have been pressing for His followers and remains pressing for us: How can a small, seemingly insignificant movement transform the world? How can the work of restoration succeed against the entrenched powers of injustice and oppression?

The parable of the sower (Mark 4.3-9) describes a farmer scattering seed. Some seed falls by the wayside, where birds devour it. Some falls on rocky ground, where it springs up quickly but withers for lack of root. Some falls among thorns, which choke it so that it yields no grain. But some falls on good ground, yielding fruit that multiplies thirty, sixty, or a hundred times over.

Jesus explains that the seed is the word—the message of the kingdom. The soils represent different responses to that message. The path represents those who hear but allow Satan to snatch the word away. The rocky ground represents those who receive the word with joy but have no root; when tribulation arises, they fall away. The thorny ground represents those who hear but allow the cares of the world, the deceitfulness of riches, and the desires for other things to choke the word. The good ground represents those who hear, receive, and bear fruit.

This parable speaks directly to the work of restorative justice. The message of healing and reconciliation, like the seed, must find receptive hearts to take root and bear fruit. Some will reject it outright. Others will embrace it enthusiastically but fall away when difficulties arise—and difficulties will arise, for restorative work is demanding. Others will be distracted by competing concerns—the demands of daily life, the pursuit of wealth, the attractions of other interests. But some will receive the message deeply, allowing it to transform them and bear fruit in their lives and communities.

The call of the parable is to be good soil—to cultivate hearts that are receptive to the message of restoration, to remove the rocks and thorns that impede growth, to nurture the seed until it bears fruit. It is also a call to patience and persistence, recognizing that not all will receive the message and that fruitfulness takes time.

The parable of the lamp (Mark 4:21-25) follows: "Is a lamp brought to be put under a basket or under a bed? Is it not to be set on a lampstand?" The obvious answer is no. A lamp's purpose is to give light, and it must be placed where it can fulfill that purpose. So too with the message of the kingdom: it is not to be hidden but displayed, not kept secret but proclaimed openly.

This parable is a call to action—a reminder that teaching love and compassion is insufficient; one must act upon these lessons. The message of restorative justice must not remain hidden in books and seminars; it must be lived out in communities, demonstrated in practices, embodied in relationships. It must shine like a lamp in the darkness, illuminating a different way of responding to harm and conflict.

The parable of the growing seed (Mark 4:26-29) describes a farmer who scatters seed on the ground and then goes about his daily life. Night and day, whether he sleeps or rises, the seed sprouts and grows, he knows not how. The earth produces of itself—first the blade, then the head, then the full grain. When the grain ripens, the farmer puts in the sickle, for the harvest has come.

This parable addresses the question of how the kingdom grows. The farmer plays his part—scattering the seed, being present, harvesting when the time comes. But the growth itself is mysterious, beyond his comprehension or control. The earth produces of itself; the seed has its own intrinsic power.

So too with restorative justice. We play our part—planting seeds of healing, facilitating encounters, supporting restoration. But the growth is not entirely in our hands. Transformation occurs through dynamics we do not fully understand. Healing happens in ways we cannot predict. The process has its own mysterious power. Our task is to be faithful in planting and present for the harvest, trusting God for the growth.

The parable of the mustard seed (Mark 4:30-32) completes the series. The kingdom of God is like a mustard seed, which is the smallest of all seeds on earth. Yet when it is sown, it grows up and becomes the greatest of all shrubs, putting out large branches so that the birds of the air can nest in its shade.

This parable addresses the apparent disproportion between the kingdom's humble beginnings and its glorious future. Jesus' movement began with a handful of Galilean peasants—insignificant by any worldly measure. Yet it would grow to encompass the world. The mustard seed, tiny but containing within itself the potential for great growth, symbolizes this dynamic.

For restorative justice, this parable offers hope. The movement may seem small against the massive institutions of punitive justice. The number of practitioners may be few, the resources limited, the successes modest. But the seed contains within itself the potential for great growth. Under suitable conditions—nurtured by faithful practitioners, supported by receptive communities, blessed by God—it can grow into something far larger than its beginnings would suggest. The birds of the air—all those who need shelter and rest—can find refuge in its branches.

These parables together address the challenge of transformative change. The work seems impossible, the obstacles insurmountable, the progress slow. But Jesus assures His disciples—and us—that growth will come. The seed will bear fruit in good soil. The lamp will give light if placed on a stand. The seed will grow, mysteriously but surely. The tiny mustard seed will become a great shrub. The call is to faithfulness, patience, and trust—to sow the seed, to let our light shine, to be present for the harvest, and to trust God for the growth.

The Fig Tree: Judgment on Fruitless Institutions

Following His entry into Jerusalem, Jesus enacts a strange and striking parable. Seeing a fig tree in leaf, He approaches it looking for fruit. Finding none—for it was not the season for figs—He curses it: "Let no one eat fruit from you ever again" (Mark 11:14). The next day, Peter notices the tree withered from the roots and points it out to Jesus. Jesus responds with a teaching on faith and prayer, then adds: "And whenever you stand praying, if you have anything against anyone, forgive him, that your Father in heaven may also forgive you your trespasses" (Mark 11:25).

Between the cursing of the fig tree and the disciples' discovery of its withered state, Mark places another event: Jesus' cleansing of the temple (Mark 11:15-18). He enters the temple courts and drives out those who were buying and selling there, overturning the tables of the money changers and the seats of those selling doves. He declares: "Is it not written, 'My house shall be called a house of prayer for all nations'? But you have made it a 'den of thieves.'"

The placement of these events is significant. The fig tree, cursed for its fruitlessness, frames the cleansing of the temple, suggesting that the temple itself is the object of Jesus' judgment. The tree looked promising—full of leaves—but bore no fruit. The temple looked impressive—magnificent architecture, bustling activity—but bore no fruit of righteousness. It had become a den of thieves rather than a house of prayer for all nations.

In the Old Testament, the fig tree often symbolizes Israel. The prophets used the image of fruitless vines and barren fig trees to depict God's judgment on His unfruitful people. Jesus' action continues this prophetic tradition. The temple, the center of Israel's religious life, had failed in its purpose. It was meant to be a place where all nations could encounter God, but it had been corrupted by commerce and exclusion. It was meant to produce the fruits of justice and mercy, but it produced only the leaves of religious observance.

The curse on the fig tree therefore serves as a warning to every institution that claims to serve God but fails to bear fruit. The justice system, the church, the government—all are subject to this judgment. If they exist only for themselves, if they serve the powerful at the expense of the powerless, if they produce leaves of activity without fruits of righteousness, they will wither.

But the placement of the forgiveness teaching immediately after the withered fig tree is also significant. Jesus connects judgment on fruitlessness with the call to forgive. The temple's failure was, in part, a failure of forgiveness. It had become a place of exclusion rather than inclusion, of condemnation rather than mercy. The forgiveness that Jesus teaches—forgiveness that flows from faith in God—is the antidote to fruitlessness. Forgiving communities bear fruit; unforgiving communities wither.

For restorative justice, this passage underscores the importance of institutional integrity. Systems that claim to pursue justice must actually produce justice. Courts that claim to serve victims must actually serve them. Prisons that claim to rehabilitate must actually rehabilitate. If they fail to bear fruit—if they produce only leaves of activity without fruits of restoration—they stand under judgment.

The passage also calls us to examine our own lives and institutions for fruitfulness. Are we producing the fruits of justice, mercy, and forgiveness? Or are we like the fig tree, full of leaves but empty of fruit? The time for bearing fruit is now; the season for figs has come.

The Teachings of Jesus and Restorative Justice

As we survey Jesus' teachings on justice, a coherent vision emerges—a vision that aligns remarkably with the principles and practices of restorative justice.

Jesus consistently prioritizes victims. In the Good Samaritan, the wounded man is the center of attention; all action revolves around meeting his needs. In the healing narratives, Jesus responds to suffering with compassion, restoring individuals to wholeness and community. In the judgment of the nations, care for the hungry, thirsty, stranger, naked, sick, and imprisoned is the criterion of righteousness. Victims are not sidelined but centered.

Jesus holds offenders accountable while offering them restoration. The woman caught in adultery is not condemned, but neither is her sin minimized; she is called to leave her life of sin. The rich young ruler is confronted with the idolatry of his wealth and invited to follow Jesus. Zacchaeus, the tax collector, is welcomed by Jesus and responds by promising restitution fourfold. Accountability and restoration are not opposed but intertwined.

Jesus involves community in the work of justice. The paralyzed man is brought to Jesus by his friends; their faith participates in his healing. The disciples are sent out to proclaim the kingdom and heal the sick; they are agents of God's restorative justice. The church is called to be a community of forgiveness and reconciliation, embodying in its life the justice it proclaims.

Jesus teaches forgiveness as essential to justice. The unforgiving servant is condemned not for his original debt but for his refusal to forgive. The Lord's Prayer links divine forgiveness to human forgiveness. The call to forgive seventy times seven demands limitless mercy. Forgiveness is not optional for those who would follow Jesus.

Jesus insists that justice requires action, not mere sentiment. The Good Samaritan does not merely feel compassion; he acts on it. The sheep in the judgment scene do not merely sympathize with the needy; they feed, clothe, and visit them. The lamp must be placed on a stand, not hidden under a basket. Justice is love in action.

Jesus teaches that justice is costly. The Samaritan expends time, resources, and ongoing commitment. The disciples must take up their crosses. The rich young ruler must sell all he has. Restorative justice demands investment—emotional, material, relational—from all who participate.

Jesus promises that justice will ultimately prevail. The hungry will be filled, the mourners comforted, the meek inherit the earth. The mustard seed will become a great shrub. The seed sown in good soil will yield a bountiful harvest. The work of restoration, though small and slow, participates in God's ultimate victory over all that harms and destroys.

This is the Jesus Paradigm: a vision of justice rooted in love, expressed in compassion, seeking forgiveness, and working toward restoration. It is a vision that challenges every punitive system, every retributive instinct, every assumption that justice means giving people what they deserve. And it is a vision that invites us to become agents of healing in a wounded world—to embody in our lives and communities the restorative justice that Jesus taught and lived.

CHAPTER 03

PARABLES AND RESTORATIVE JUSTICE

The parables of Jesus are among the most beloved and enduring teachings in all of human history. These simple stories, drawn from everyday life in first-century Palestine, have transcended their original context to speak universal truths about God, humanity, and the nature of authentic relationship. Yet for all their familiarity, the parables remain radically challenging, subverting our assumptions and inviting us into a transformed way of seeing the world. They are, in the fullest sense, narratives of restoration—stories that illuminate the heart of God and reveal the path to genuine reconciliation.

When we read the parables through the lens of restorative justice, we discover that they are not merely illustrations of moral principles but profound explorations of how harm is addressed, relationships are restored, and community is rebuilt. Each parable, in its own way, embodies the core values of restorative justice: acknowledgment of wrong, accountability for harm, compassion for the wounded, forgiveness for the repentant, and celebration of restoration. They provide a narrative foundation for the Jesus Paradigm, showing us what restorative justice looks like when lived out in the complexities of human relationships.

This chapter invites you into a deep exploration of five parables that are particularly rich in restorative meaning. We will examine each story carefully, drawing out its theological insights, psychological wisdom, and practical implications for how we respond to harm and pursue healing. We will see how these ancient narratives anticipate and illuminate the principles of restorative justice, and we will discover in them a vision for reconciliation that is as relevant today as when Jesus first spoke them.

The Prodigal Son: The Anatomy of Restoration

The parable of the prodigal son, found in Luke 15:11-32, is often called the greatest short story ever told. Its narrative sweep, psychological depth, and emotional power have captivated readers for two millennia. But beneath its literary brilliance lies a profound exploration of restorative justice—a vision of how wrongs can be righted, relationships healed, and the estranged restored to community.

The story begins with a rupture. A younger son demands his share of the inheritance from his father—a request that, in the cultural context of ancient Israel, was tantamount to wishing his father dead. Inheritance was normally received only after the father's death; to ask for it while he lived was to declare that one wished him gone. The father, remarkably, accedes to this request, dividing his property between his two sons. The younger son then gathers all he has, travels to a distant country, and squanders his inheritance in reckless living.

This opening scene establishes the nature of the harm. The son has not merely made a poor financial decision; he has broken relationship with his father, rejected his place in the family, and dishonored his name. His sin is not against property alone but against personhood—against the bond that should unite father and son. The legal framework of inheritance provides the occasion, but the injury is relational at its core.

The consequences follow swiftly. A severe famine strikes the distant country, and the son finds himself in desperate need. He hires himself out to a citizen of that country, who sends him into the fields to feed pigs—a task that, for a Jewish audience, represents the depths of degradation. Pigs were unclean animals; to tend them was to become unclean oneself. The son is so hungry that he longs to fill his stomach with the pods the pigs are eating, but no one gives him anything.

This descent into degradation serves a crucial psychological function. The son must hit bottom before he can begin the journey home. His suffering strips away the illusions of independence and self-sufficiency that led him to leave. He comes to himself—a phrase that suggests a recovery of sanity, a return to right mind. In his desperation, he remembers what he has lost: "How many of my father's hired servants have bread enough and to spare, and I perish with hunger!"

This moment of remembrance is the beginning of repentance. The son acknowledges his condition honestly: he is perishing. He recognizes the contrast between his state and the abundance in his father's house. And he formulates a plan: "I will arise and go to my father, and will say to him, 'Father, I have sinned against heaven and before you, and I am no longer worthy to be called your son. Make me like one of your hired servants.'"

Note carefully the content of this confession. The son acknowledges that his sin has two dimensions: against heaven and against his father. He recognizes that his wrongdoing has both vertical and horizontal consequences—it offends God and harms human relationship. He accepts that he has forfeited the status of son; he no longer deserves that place. And he proposes a form of restitution: let him be as a hired servant, working to repay what he has squandered, earning his place through labor.

This confession embodies the psychological dynamics of genuine repentance. The son does not minimize his wrongdoing or make excuses. He does not blame his father for being too permissive or the distant country for being too tempting. He takes full responsibility for his choices and their consequences. He accepts that he deserves nothing and proposes to earn whatever he receives. This is the godly sorrow of which Paul writes—sorrow that leads to repentance without regret (2 Corinthians 7:10).

But the story takes an unexpected turn. While the son is still far off, his father sees him and is moved with compassion. The father runs—an act of undignified haste for an elderly patriarch—and falls on his son's neck, kissing him. The son begins his prepared speech: "Father, I have sinned against heaven and in your sight, and am no longer worthy to be called your son." But before he can complete his proposal to become a hired servant, the father interrupts. He calls to his servants: "Bring out the best robe and put it on him, and put a ring on his hand and sandals on his feet. And bring the fatted calf here and kill it, and let us eat and be merry; for this my son was dead and is alive again; he was lost and is found."

This response is the heart of restorative justice. The father does not wait for the son to complete his penance; he does not require a period of probation or a demonstration of reformed character. He sees the son's return—his willingness to come home, his confession of sin—and he runs to meet him with extravagant grace. He restores the son immediately and fully to his place in the family. The robe signifies honor, the ring authority, the sandals free status (servants went barefoot). The fatted calf signifies celebration, joy, community. The son who was dead is alive; the one who was lost is found.

This restoration is not cheap grace. The son has suffered real consequences—the loss of his inheritance, the degradation of the pigsty, the hunger and humiliation. He has acknowledged his wrongdoing and accepted responsibility. But the father does not require him to earn his way back. Restoration is a gift, not a wage. It is received, not achieved. The celebration is not a reward for good behavior but a response to restored relationship.

The parable then introduces a third character: the elder son. He has been working in the field, and when he comes near the house, he hears music and dancing. Learning from a servant that his brother has returned and his father has killed the fatted calf, he becomes angry and refuses to go in. The father comes out and pleads with him, but the elder son protests: "Lo, these many years I have been serving you; I never transgressed your commandment at any time; and yet you never gave me a young goat that I might make merry with my friends. But as soon as this son of yours came, who has devoured your livelihood with harlots, you killed the fatted calf for him."

The elder son's complaint reveals a different conception of justice. He sees relationship in terms of merit and reward. He has served faithfully and never transgressed; therefore, he deserves recognition and celebration. His brother has transgressed grievously; therefore, he deserves exclusion and punishment. When the father treats the younger son with grace, the elder son perceives an injustice. His own faithful service seems devalued; his brother's misdeeds seem rewarded.

The father's response corrects this distorted view: "Son, you are always with me, and all that I have is yours. It was right that we should make merry and be glad, for your brother was dead and is alive again, and was lost and is found." The father does not deny the elder son's faithfulness or diminish his place. He affirms the ongoing relationship and the shared inheritance. But he insists that restoration is cause for celebration, not resentment. The return of the lost is not a threat to the faithful but an occasion for communal joy.

This parable illuminates restorative justice in multiple dimensions.

First, it shows that genuine restoration requires acknowledgment of wrongdoing. The son must come to himself, remember his father's house, and confess his sin. Without this acknowledgment, there can be no authentic restoration. The father does not impose forgiveness on an unrepentant son; he responds to the son's return and confession. Restorative justice requires offenders to take responsibility for their actions.

Second, it demonstrates that restoration can be immediate and complete. The father does not put the son on probation or require a period of proving himself. He restores him fully to sonship the moment he returns. This does not mean that all consequences are erased—the inheritance is gone, the memories remain—but the relationship is restored. Restorative justice seeks full restoration, not partial or conditional acceptance.

Third, it reveals that restoration is costly to the restorer. The father absorbs the loss of the inheritance, the dishonor of the son's request, the pain of the separation. He runs to meet the son, embracing him before knowing whether he has truly changed. He hosts a celebration that expends resources. Restoration is not cheap; it demands sacrifice from those who extend it.

Fourth, it exposes the resentments that can hinder restoration. The elder son's anger threatens to poison the celebration, to exclude himself from the joy, to replicate the very separation he condemns in his brother. Restorative justice must address not only the relationship between offender and victim but also the attitudes of the wider community. Those who have remained faithful must be helped to share in the joy of restoration rather than resenting the grace extended to others.

Fifth, it locates restoration within community. The celebration involves the whole household—servants, family, friends. The lost son is restored not merely to his father but to the community. The fatted calf is shared; the music and dancing are communal. Restorative justice is not a private transaction but a public event, involving and affecting the entire community.

The psychological wisdom of this parable is profound. It recognizes that shame can be a barrier to restoration—the son expects to be rejected, to be made a servant. It shows that grace can overcome shame—the father's embrace communicates acceptance despite unworthiness. It acknowledges that resentment can block joy—the elder son's anger prevents him from participating in the celebration. And it affirms that restoration is cause for communal rejoicing—the dead is alive, the lost is found.

Theologically, the parable reveals the heart of God. The father represents the divine—running to meet the returning sinner, extending grace before words of confession are complete, restoring fully and freely, celebrating the return of the lost. This is the God whom Jesus came to reveal—a God of extravagant mercy, eager to forgive, quick to restore. The gospel of restorative justice is rooted in this divine character.

The Unforgiving Servant: The Necessity of Extending Mercy

If the parable of the prodigal son illustrates the joy of receiving restoration, the parable of the unforgiving servant, found in Matthew 18:21-35, warns of the consequences of refusing to extend it. The two parables are complementary: the first shows what it means to be restored; the second shows what it means to be a restorer.

The parable is prompted by Peter's question about forgiveness. "Lord, how often shall my brother sin against me, and I forgive him? Up to seven times?" Peter's suggestion of seven times seems generous, exceeding the common rabbinic teaching that one should forgive three times. But Jesus responds: "I do not say to you, up to seven times, but up to seventy times seven." The number is not literal but symbolic, indicating limitless forgiveness. There is no point at which we may cease to forgive.

Then Jesus tells a story to illustrate this teaching. The kingdom of heaven is like a certain king who wants to settle accounts with his servants. One servant is brought to him who owes ten thousand talents—an astronomical sum. A talent was worth about twenty years' wages for a laborer; ten thousand talents would be tens of millions of dollars in modern currency, a debt impossible to repay. The servant cannot pay, so the king commands that he, his wife, his children, and all that he has be sold to make payment.

The servant falls down before the king, pleading: "Master, have patience with me, and I will pay you all." The king, moved with compassion, does more than grant patience. He releases the servant and forgives the entire debt. The staggering magnitude of the debt underscores the magnitude of the mercy. The servant has received grace beyond all calculation.

But that same servant, going out from the king's presence, finds a fellow servant who owes him a hundred denarii—a paltry sum, a few thousand dollars, a debt that could reasonably be repaid. He seizes the man by the throat, demanding payment. The fellow servant falls down and pleads with him, using the exact words the first servant had used to the king: "Have patience with me, and I will pay you all." But the first servant refuses. Instead of showing mercy, he has the man thrown into prison until he should pay the debt.

When other servants see what has happened, they are grieved and report it to the king. The king summons the unforgiving servant and confronts him: "You wicked servant! I forgave you all that debt because you begged me. Should you not also have had compassion on your fellow servant, just as I had pity on you?" In anger, the king delivers him to the torturers until he should pay all that was due to him. And Jesus concludes: "So My heavenly Father also will do to you if each of you, from his heart, does not forgive his brother his trespasses."

This parable cuts to the heart of restorative justice. It reveals that the forgiveness we have received creates an obligation to forgive others. The staggering disproportion between the debts—the first incalculable, the second trivial—underscores the absurdity of refusing to extend the mercy we have received. If God has forgiven us the infinite debt of our sin against Him, how can we refuse to forgive the finite debts others owe us?

The parable also illuminates several key principles of restorative justice.

First, it shows that forgiveness is not optional for those who have received it. The king does not suggest that the servant might consider forgiving his fellow servant; he expects it as the natural and necessary response to the mercy he has received. Forgiveness is not a supererogatory act of extraordinary virtue but the basic obligation of those who have been forgiven. Restorative justice is not an optional add-on for Christians but an essential expression of the faith.

Second, it demonstrates that forgiveness must be from the heart. Jesus specifies that forgiveness must be "from your heart"—not merely external compliance but internal transformation. The unforgiving servant went through the motions of pleading for mercy but did not internalize the mercy he received. His heart remained unchanged, and so he could not extend to others what had been extended to him. Restorative justice requires genuine heart change, not merely behavioral conformity.

Third, it reveals the consequences of unforgiveness. The servant who refuses to forgive is delivered to the torturers—a vivid image of the inner torment that unforgiveness produces. Bitterness, resentment, and anger do not harm only those against whom they are directed; they torture the one who holds them. Research in psychology confirms this: unforgiveness is associated with higher levels of depression, anxiety, and stress; with poorer physical health; with damaged relationships. The torturers are real, and they work from within.

Fourth, it connects divine forgiveness to human forgiveness. Jesus teaches that our forgiveness of others is the condition of our receiving forgiveness from God. This is not because God's forgiveness is earned by our forgiving but because an unforgiving heart cannot receive what it refuses to give. The same passage that warns of the consequences of unforgiveness also promises that the merciful will obtain mercy (Matthew 5:7). Forgiveness and mercy are reciprocal; we can only truly receive what we are willing to extend.

Fifth, it exposes the hypocrisy of accepting grace while refusing to extend it. The servant was happy to receive mercy but unwilling to show it. He wanted the king to treat him graciously but refused to treat his fellow servant the same way. This inconsistency is at the heart of Jesus' condemnation. Restorative justice calls us to consistency—to treat others as we have been treated, to extend the grace we have received.

The legal dimensions of this parable are also significant. The king's initial judgment—selling the servant, his family, and his possessions—reflects the harsh realities of debt law in the ancient world. Debtors could be imprisoned or enslaved for nonpayment. The king, however, transcends the strict requirements of law to show mercy. He does not merely delay payment but forgives the debt entirely. Law gives way to grace.

But when the forgiven servant refuses to extend the same grace, the law reasserts itself. The king reinstates the debt and delivers the servant to the torturers. The legal consequences that had been suspended are now enforced. This dynamic illustrates the relationship between law and grace in restorative justice. Law provides the framework of accountability, establishing what is owed and what is just. Grace operates within that framework, offering forgiveness and restoration. But grace that is received and not extended can revert to law, leaving the unforgiving subject to the very judgment they escaped.

The psychological wisdom of this parable is profound. It recognizes that forgiveness is not merely a feeling but a decision—a choice to release the debtor from the obligation to pay. The servant could have chosen to forgive his fellow servant even if his feelings lagged behind. But he chose instead to demand payment, to seize by the throat, to imprison. His feelings followed his choices, hardening into the bitterness that ultimately destroyed him.

The parable also illuminates the social dimensions of forgiveness. The other servants see what happens and are grieved. They report the matter to the king. The community is affected by the unforgiving servant's actions; his refusal to forgive damages not only his relationship with his fellow servant but the fabric of trust within the community. Restorative justice must attend to these communal dimensions, recognizing that forgiveness and reconciliation are not merely private matters but public goods.

The Good Samaritan: Compassion as the Heart of Justice

The parable of the Good Samaritan, found in Luke 10:25-37, is so familiar that its radical edge can easily be blunted. We have heard it so often that we may miss its revolutionary message. But when we read it through the lens of restorative justice, we discover a profound challenge to conventional understandings of who deserves care and what justice requires.

The parable arises from a lawyer's question: "Teacher, what shall I do to inherit eternal life?" Jesus turns the question back to him: "What is written in the law? What is your reading of it?" The lawyer answers correctly: "You shall love the Lord your God with all your heart, with all your soul, with all your strength, and with all your mind, and your neighbor as yourself." Jesus affirms his answer: "You have answered rightly; do this and you will live."

But the lawyer, wanting to justify himself, asks a follow-up question: "And who is my neighbor?" This question reveals the lawyer's assumption. He assumes that "neighbor" is a limited category, that some people count as neighbors and others do not, that he can fulfill the commandment by loving those within his circle while remaining indifferent to those outside it. His question seeks to define the boundaries of obligation, to determine the minimum requirements of love.

Jesus responds with a story that demolishes all boundaries.

A man is traveling from Jerusalem to Jericho—a notoriously dangerous route, descending through rocky terrain that provides cover for robbers. He falls into the hands of bandits, who strip him, beat him, and leave him half dead by the roadside. The victim is anonymous—no name, no ethnic identifification, no religious affiliation. He is simply a human being in desperate need.

First, a priest comes down the road. He sees the wounded man—and passes by on the other side. The priest is a religious professional, trained in the law, charged with teaching others what God requires. Yet when confronted with a concrete opportunity to love his neighbor, he averts his eyes and continues on his way. Perhaps he feared ritual impurity if the man were dead. Perhaps he feared the robbers might still be lurking. Perhaps he simply didn't want to be bothered. Whatever his reasons, his inaction condemns him.

Next, a Levite comes to the place and sees the man. Levites were temple assistants, also religious functionaries, also charged with serving God and God's people. He too sees the wounded man—and passes by on the other side. The repetition is damning. Two representatives of Israel's religious establishment, both entrusted with the law that commands love of neighbor, both fail to act when love is most needed.

Then comes a Samaritan. For Jesus' Jewish audience, this detail was shocking. Samaritans were despised as half-breeds and heretics, enemies of the Jewish people, beyond the pale of neighbor-love as conventionally defined. If anyone could be excluded from the category of neighbor, surely it was a Samaritan. Yet when the Samaritan sees the wounded man, he does not pass by. He is moved with compassion—a visceral, emotional response to suffering that overrides every cultural and religious barrier.

And his compassion issues in action. He goes to the man, bandages his wounds, pouring on oil and wine. He lifts him onto his own animal, brings him to an inn, and takes care of him. The next day, he gives the innkeeper two denarii—two days' wages—with instructions to care for the man further, promising to cover any additional expenses on his return. The Samaritan does not merely provide emergency first aid; he ensures ongoing care. He does not merely offer sympathy; he invests his own resources. He does not merely do the minimum; he goes above and beyond.

Jesus then turns the lawyer's question upside down. He does not ask, "Who is my neighbor?"—a question that seeks to limit obligation. Instead, He asks: "Which of these three do you think was neighbor to him who fell among the thieves?" The question shifts from defining the object of love to embodying the practice of love. Neighbor is not a category to be defined but a relationship to be enacted. The one who shows mercy is the true neighbor, regardless of ethnic or religious identity.

The lawyer answers correctly: "He who showed mercy on him." And Jesus issues the command: "Go and do likewise."

This parable is a masterclass in restorative justice. Consider its elements:

First, it centers on a victim. The wounded man is anonymous but vividly present—stripped, beaten, half dead. His suffering is real, his need is urgent, his humanity is undeniable. The parable refuses to let us forget the victim's experience. Restorative justice begins with victims, with their pain and their needs.

Second, it exposes the failure of institutional religion to provide justice. The priest and Levite, representatives of the established order, do nothing. Their religion has become routine, their compassion atrophied, their obedience to law reduced to avoidance of impurity. They are not evil but they are useless—and their uselessness is itself a form of injustice. Restorative justice challenges institutions that claim to serve justice but fail to serve the wounded.

Third, it reveals that true justice transcends boundaries. The Samaritan, the one least expected to act righteously, is the one who embodies righteousness. Justice is not confined to those who share our religion, our ethnicity, or our social position. It is a human obligation, arising from our common humanity. Restorative justice must be accessible to all, regardless of identity, and must be practiced across all divisions.

Fourth, it demonstrates that justice requires action. The Samaritan does not merely feel compassion; he acts on it. He goes to the man, bandages his wounds, transports him to safety, provides for his ongoing care. Justice is not a sentiment but a practice, not an attitude but a set of actions that repair harm and restore wholeness. Restorative justice is verbs, not nouns—doing, not merely feeling.

Fifth, it shows that justice is costly. The Samaritan expends time, energy, and resources. He risks his own safety on a dangerous road. He spends his own money for a stranger's care. He commits to ongoing involvement, promising to return and cover any additional costs. Restorative justice demands investment from those who practice it.

Sixth, it illustrates that justice creates community. The Samaritan does not merely provide immediate aid and move on. He creates a network of care involving the innkeeper, and he commits to ongoing relationship. The wounded man, once anonymous and alone, is now embedded in a community of support. Restorative justice rebuilds the social fabric torn by harm.

Seventh, it calls us to imitation. "Go and do likewise." Restorative justice is not something we admire from a distance but something we practice in our own lives. Every encounter with suffering, every opportunity to respond to harm, is an invitation to be neighbor—to show mercy, to bind wounds, to restore the broken.

The psychological dimensions of this parable are profound. The Samaritan's compassion is not merely intellectual but emotional—he is moved. This visceral response to suffering is the psychological foundation of restorative action. Empathy—the capacity to feel with another—motivates care and sustains commitment through difficulty. The priest and Levite may have felt nothing, or may have suppressed their feelings in favor of other concerns. The Samaritan allows himself to be moved, and that movement issues in action.

The parable also addresses the psychological dynamics of victimization. The wounded man is stripped, beaten, left half dead. He has been dehumanized, reduced to an object of violence. The Samaritan's care restores his humanity—bandaging his wounds, lifting him onto his own animal, providing for his needs. He is treated as a person, not a problem. Restorative justice must attend to this psychological restoration, helping victims recover their sense of dignity and worth.

Theologically, the parable reveals that love of God and love of neighbor are inseparable. The lawyer's original question was about inheriting eternal life—about being rightly related to God. Jesus' answer connects that vertical relationship to horizontal relationship. We cannot love God whom we have not seen if we do not love our neighbor whom we have seen (1 John 4:20). Restorative justice is not merely a social program but a spiritual practice—a way of loving God by loving those who bear His image.

The Lost Sheep and the Lost Coin: The Value of Every Person

In Luke 15, Jesus tells two short parables that introduce and illuminate the longer parable of the prodigal son. Together, these parables form a triptych on the theme of seeking and restoring the lost. They reveal the heart of God as one that actively pursues those who have strayed and rejoices when they are found.

The parable of the lost sheep (Luke 15:3-7) begins with a question: "What man of you, having a hundred sheep, if he loses one of them, does not leave the ninety-nine in the wilderness, and go after the one which is lost until he finds it?" The implied answer is that any shepherd would do exactly that. A sheep is valuable; no shepherd would casually write off a lost animal. He would search diligently until he found it.

When he finds it, he lays it on his shoulders, rejoicing. And when he comes home, he calls together his friends and neighbors, saying, "Rejoice with me, for I have found my sheep which was lost!" Jesus then applies the parable: "I say to you that likewise there will be more joy in heaven over one sinner who repents than over ninety-nine just persons who need no repentance."

The parable of the lost coin (Luke 15:8-10) makes a similar point. "What woman, having ten silver coins, if she loses one coin, does not light a lamp, sweep the house, and search carefully until she finds it?" The coin is valuable—a day's wage, significant enough to warrant a thorough search. The woman searches diligently, sweeping and lighting, leaving no corner unchecked. When she finds it, she calls her friends and neighbors together, saying, "Rejoice with me, for I have found the piece which I lost!" Jesus applies this parable as well: "Likewise, I say to you, there is joy in the presence of the angels of God over one sinner who repents."

These two parables establish several foundational principles for restorative justice.

First, they affirm the intrinsic value of every person. The lost sheep matters. The lost coin matters. The shepherd does not say, "I still have ninety-nine; one loss is acceptable." The woman does not say, "I still have nine; one loss is affordable." They search diligently because what is lost has value. Restorative justice rests on this conviction: every person, victim and offender alike, possesses inherent dignity and worth as one created in the image of God. No one is disposable; no one is beyond restoration.

Second, they demonstrate that seeking the lost requires effort. The shepherd leaves the ninety-nine and goes into the wilderness. The woman lights a lamp, sweeps the house, searches carefully. Restoration is not passive; it requires active pursuit. Those who would practice restorative justice must be willing to invest time, energy, and resources in seeking the lost—whether lost victims who need healing or lost offenders who need restoration.

Third, they reveal that restoration is cause for rejoicing. The shepherd calls his friends and neighbors to celebrate. The woman shares her joy with others. The finding of the lost is not a private relief but a public celebration. Restorative justice should be marked by joy—joy at healing achieved, relationships restored, community strengthened. Too often, justice is associated with solemnity and severity; these parables remind us that restoration is also a party.

Fourth, they connect earthly restoration to heavenly rejoicing. Jesus explicitly states that there is joy in heaven over one sinner who repents. The angels of God share in the celebration. Our restorative work on earth participates in and reflects the joy of heaven. This theological dimension elevates restorative justice from mere social policy to participation in divine joy.

Fifth, they emphasize the individual within the community. The shepherd leaves the ninety-nine to find the one. The woman searches diligently for the single coin. The individual matters; no one is lost in the crowd. Yet the celebration is communal—friends and neighbors are called to share the joy. Restorative justice must hold together individual care and communal celebration, attending to each person while involving the whole community.

The psychological wisdom of these parables is profound. They recognize that feeling lost is a universal human experience—the sense of being disconnected, adrift, separated from community and purpose. They affirm that the response to being lost should not be abandonment but pursuit. They acknowledge that being found—being restored to relationship—is cause for deep joy. And they suggest that this joy is magnified when shared.

The parables also address the psychology of the seeker. The shepherd and the woman are not motivated by duty alone but by love—the love that values what is lost and will not rest until it is found. This love sustains them through the effort of seeking, through the uncertainty of the search, through the possibility of failure. Restorative justice requires this kind of love—persistent, hopeful, unwilling to give up.

The Workers in the Vineyard: The Generosity of Grace

The parable of the workers in the vineyard, found in Matthew 20:1-16, challenges our deepest assumptions about fairness and reward. It presents a vision of justice that transcends merit-based calculation, revealing the extravagant generosity of God and inviting us to share in that generosity.

A landowner goes out early in the morning to hire laborers for his vineyard. He agrees to pay them the usual daily wage—a denarius—and sends them into the vineyard. At the third hour (about nine in the morning), he goes out again and sees others standing idle in the marketplace. He hires them as well, promising to pay them whatever is right. At the sixth hour and the ninth hour, he does the same. Finally, at the eleventh hour (about five in the afternoon, with only one hour of work remaining), he goes out again, finds still others standing idle, and hires them.

When evening comes, the landowner instructs his foreman to call the laborers and give them their wages, beginning with the last and ending with the first. Those hired at the eleventh hour come first and receive a full denarius—a full day's wage for one hour's work. When those hired first see this, they expect to receive more. But they too receive a denarius each.

They begin to grumble against the landowner: "These last men have worked only one hour, and you made them equal to us who have borne the burden and the heat of the day." The landowner responds to one of them: "Friend, I am doing you no wrong. Did you not agree with me for a denarius? Take what is yours and go your way. I wish to give to this last man the same as to you. Is it not lawful for me to do what I wish with my own things? Or is your eye evil because I am good?"

Jesus concludes: "So the last will be first, and the first last. For many are called, but few chosen."

This parable challenges our notions of justice in several ways.

First, it reveals that God's generosity exceeds our calculations of merit. The workers who labored all day received exactly what they had agreed to receive—a fair wage for a fair day's work. They were not cheated. But the landowner chose to be generous to those who had worked less, giving them the same wage out of his own goodness. The complaint of the all-day workers is not that they were underpaid but that others were overpaid—at least by their reckoning. They measure justice by comparison, by what others receive, rather than by what they themselves have received.

Second, it exposes the envy that can poison our response to grace. The landowner asks, "Is your eye evil because I am good?" The evil eye was a Hebrew idiom for envy or jealousy. The all-day workers are not angry because they have been wronged but because others have been blessed. Their resentment reveals a heart that cannot rejoice in generosity extended to others. Restorative justice must guard against this envy, learning to celebrate the restoration of others rather than resenting the grace they receive.

Third, it affirms the landowner's freedom to be generous. "Is it not lawful for me to do what I wish with my own things?" The landowner has the right to dispose of his property as he chooses. He is not obligated to give everyone the same wage; he is free to be generous to some without being unjust to others. This freedom is an aspect of grace—God's sovereign right to show mercy to whom He will show mercy.

Fourth, it reverses human expectations about worth and reward. "The last will be first, and the first last." Those who come late to the vineyard receive the same reward as those who came early. Those who have labored long are not disadvantaged, but neither are they privileged. In the kingdom of God, worth is not measured by duration of service or intensity of labor but by the gracious acceptance of the landowner. Restorative justice must reflect this reversal, offering restoration to all regardless of when they come or how long they have strayed.

This parable has profound implications for restorative justice. It challenges the notion that justice is primarily about giving people what they deserve based on their merits. Instead, it points toward a justice that is infused with grace—a justice that goes beyond strict calculation to embrace generosity. This does not mean ignoring accountability or disregarding the seriousness of harm. The all-day workers received what they had earned; the landowner did not cheat them. But the landowner chose to be generous beyond strict desert, and that generosity is the heart of the parable.

For restorative justice, this means that while accountability is essential—offenders must take responsibility for their actions and make amends where possible—the ultimate goal is not the strict accounting of debts but the restoration of relationships. And restoration, like the landowner's generosity, goes beyond what strict justice would require. It involves forgiveness that releases debts, grace that welcomes the undeserving, and celebration that rejoices over the restored.

The parable also speaks to those who have labored long in the work of justice—the faithful servants, the consistent workers, the ones who have borne the burden and heat of the day. It warns them against resentment when others are restored more quickly or more easily than seems fair. It calls them to share in the landowner's generosity, to rejoice in the restoration of others, to see grace extended to the undeserving as cause for celebration rather than complaint.

Psychologically, the parable addresses the human tendency toward social comparison. We measure our worth not absolutely but relatively, comparing ourselves to others. When others receive more than we think they deserve, we feel diminished even if we have received what we were promised. This tendency can undermine restorative justice, leading victims to resent the restoration of offenders, or faithful community members to resent the welcome extended to the repentant. The parable calls us to transcend this comparative mindset, to find our satisfaction not in how we stack up against others but in the goodness of the one who gives.

Theologically, the parable reveals the nature of God's grace. God does not dispense grace according to our calculations of merit. He is free to be generous to whom He will be generous, and His generosity does not diminish His justice. Those who have labored long receive what they were promised; those who come late receive what they did not earn. Both are treated justly, but one is treated graciously as well. The gospel of restorative justice is that God's grace is available to all—to those who have labored long in faithfulness and to those who come at the eleventh hour.

The Parables as Restorative Narratives

When we read these parables together, a coherent vision of restorative justice emerges. The prodigal son shows us the joy of restoration and the danger of resentment. The unforgiving servant warns us of the consequences of refusing to extend mercy. The Good Samaritan calls us to compassionate action that transcends boundaries. The lost sheep and lost coin affirm the value of every person and the joy of finding the lost. The workers in the vineyard challenge our merit-based calculations and invite us into God's generous grace.

These parables are not merely illustrations of abstract principles; they are narratives that shape our imagination and form our character. They invite us into a story—the story of God's relentless pursuit of the lost, His extravagant mercy toward the undeserving, His joy over every one who is restored. And they call us to live within that story, to embody its values, to practice its ways.

For those who would practice restorative justice, these parables provide both foundation and guidance. They ground our work in the character of God, who is the ultimate restorer. They shape our attitudes, calling us to compassion rather than judgment, generosity rather than calculation, joy rather than resentment. They inform our practices, showing us what restoration looks like in concrete situations—the father running to meet the son, the Samaritan bandaging wounds, the shepherd searching for the lost sheep, the landowner paying the latecomers a full wage.

The parables also address the obstacles to restorative justice. They expose the self-righteousness that refuses to forgive, the envy that resents grace extended to others, the hardness of heart that passes by on the other side. They warn us of the consequences of these attitudes—the torturers of unforgiveness, the exclusion from the celebration, the judgment of the king. And they call us to repentance, to a change of heart that enables us to receive and extend mercy.

Finally, the parables point us to the ultimate source of restorative justice: the God who is Himself the great Restorer. The father in the prodigal son, the king in the unforgiving servant, the Samaritan in the parable, the shepherd seeking the lost, the woman searching for the coin, the landowner paying the workers—all these figures reflect aspects of the divine character. God is the one who runs to meet the returning sinner, who forgives astronomical debts, who shows compassion across every boundary, who searches diligently for the lost, who rejoices over every one who is found, who gives generously beyond all desert. Restorative justice is not our invention but our participation in God's own work of restoration.

As we continue our journey through this book, we will explore how these parable principles can be applied in various contexts—in criminal justice systems, in schools, in families, in churches. But always we will return to the parables, for they are the foundational narratives of restorative justice, the stories that shape our vision and sustain our hope. In them, we see the heart of God revealed, and in them, we find our calling made clear: to be agents of restoration in a broken world, to embody the compassion of the Samaritan, the forgiveness of the father, the generosity of the landowner, the diligent seeking of the shepherd and the woman. This is the Jesus Paradigm. This is the gospel of restorative justice.

CHAPTER 04

FORGIVENESS AND RECONCILIATION

Of all the teachings of Jesus, none are more central to the restorative justice paradigm—and none are more challenging to the human heart—than His instructions on forgiveness and reconciliation. These twin concepts lie at the very core of the gospel, embodying the divine initiative to restore broken relationship with humanity and calling us to extend that same restorative grace to one another. Without forgiveness, restorative justice collapses into mere conflict management; without reconciliation, it remains incomplete. Together, forgiveness and reconciliation form the beating heart of the Jesus Paradigm, the animating force that transforms harm into healing and estrangement into embrace.

Yet for all their centrality, forgiveness and reconciliation remain deeply misunderstood. They are often conflated with forgetting, with excusing, with pretending that harm never happened. They are dismissed as weakness, as capitulation, as letting offenders off the hook. They are demanded prematurely, extended incompletely, or withheld altogether in the name of justice. To understand forgiveness and reconciliation as Jesus taught them—and as restorative justice practices them—requires a radical reorientation of our thinking, a willingness to see these concepts in their full biblical, theological, psychological, and philosophical dimensions.

This chapter invites you into that reorientation. We will explore what forgiveness means in the teachings of Jesus, how it functions psychologically, what it requires legally, and how it relates to justice. We will examine the process of reconciliation, distinguishing it from forgiveness while recognizing their intimate connection. We will grapple with the hard questions: Can forgiveness be commanded? Is it always possible? What about cases where the offender remains unrepentant? How does reconciliation work in practice? And we will discover that forgiveness and reconciliation, far from being naive ideals, are the most practical and powerful forces for healing that the world has ever known.

The Foundation of Forgiveness in the Teachings of Jesus

Jesus' teachings on forgiveness are woven throughout the Gospels, appearing in His sermons, His parables, His prayers, and His actions. They are not peripheral to His message but central, not optional for His followers but essential. To understand forgiveness as Jesus taught it is to understand the very heart of the gospel.

The most familiar expression of Jesus' teaching on forgiveness comes in the prayer He gave His disciples, what we call the Lord's Prayer. In Matthew's version, the petition reads: "Forgive us our debts, as we forgive our debtors" (Matthew 6:12). The parallelism is striking and deliberate. Our forgiveness of others is linked to God's forgiveness of us—not as a cause but as a condition, not as earning but as evidencing. Those who have truly received forgiveness cannot help but extend it; those who withhold forgiveness reveal that they have never truly received it.

Luke's version uses different language: "Forgive us our sins, for we also forgive everyone who sins against us" (Luke 11:4). The shift from "debts" to "sins" makes explicit what was implicit: the forgiveness we need from God is forgiveness for our offenses against Him, and the forgiveness we must extend to others is forgiveness for their offenses against us. The vertical and horizontal dimensions of forgiveness are inseparable.

Immediately following the prayer, Jesus adds a commentary that underscores the seriousness of this connection: "For if you forgive men their trespasses, your heavenly Father will also forgive you. But if you do not forgive men their trespasses, neither will your Father forgive your trespasses" (Matthew 6:14-15). These words are stark, even alarming. They seem to make divine forgiveness conditional on human forgiveness. Yet they are not a legal formula but a spiritual principle: an unforgiving heart cannot receive forgiveness because it is closed to the very reality of grace. To refuse forgiveness to others is to place ourselves outside the flow of forgiving love.

This teaching is not unique to the Sermon on the Mount. Throughout the Gospels, Jesus consistently links divine and human forgiveness. When Peter asks how often he must forgive his brother—suggesting seven times, which seemed generous—Jesus responds: "I do not say to you, up to seven times, but up to seventy times seven" (Matthew 18:21-22). The number is not literal but symbolic, indicating limitless forgiveness. There is no point at which we may cease to forgive, no number of offenses beyond which grace may be withheld.

This teaching is immediately followed by the parable of the unforgiving servant, which we examined in the previous chapter. That parable drives home the point with unforgettable force: the servant who had been forgiven an astronomical debt—ten thousand talents, millions of dollars—refused to forgive a trivial debt—a hundred denarii, a few thousand dollars—and was handed over to the torturers until he should pay all that was due. The message is clear: forgiveness is not optional for those who have been forgiven. To refuse forgiveness to others is to invite judgment upon ourselves.

Jesus also taught forgiveness in the context of worship and prayer. In the Sermon on the Mount, He instructs: "Therefore if you bring your gift to the altar, and there remember that your brother has something against you, leave your gift there before the altar, and go your way. First be reconciled to your brother, and then come and offer your gift" (Matthew 5:23-24). Worship is unacceptable if offered by an unreconciled heart. The vertical relationship with God cannot be right if horizontal relationships are wrong. Reconciliation with others is prerequisite to acceptable worship.

On the cross, Jesus exemplified the forgiveness He taught. As the soldiers drive nails through His hands and feet, as the religious leaders mock Him, as the crowds pass by and hurl insults, Jesus prays: "Father, forgive them, for they do not know what they do" (Luke 23:34). This is forgiveness without condition, without waiting for repentance, without requiring acknowledgment. It is the purest expression of divine mercy—

forgiveness extended even to those who are actively engaged in crucifying the forgiver.

This prayer does not mean that repentance is unnecessary or that all will be automatically saved regardless of their response. It means that Jesus' heart toward sinners is forgiveness, that His disposition is mercy, that even in the moment of His deepest suffering He is pleading for those who inflict it. This is the model for all Christian forgiveness: a heart so saturated with grace that it continues to love even when wronged, continues to pray even when persecuted, continues to seek the good of those who seek its harm.

The Psychological Dimensions of Forgiveness

The teachings of Jesus on forgiveness are not merely theological assertions; they are deeply consonant with what psychology has discovered about the nature and benefits of forgiveness. Modern research has confirmed what Jesus taught two thousand years ago: that forgiveness is essential for human flourishing, that unforgiveness harms the one who holds it, and that forgiveness is possible even when feelings lag behind.

Psychologists define forgiveness as a conscious, deliberate decision to release feelings of resentment or vengeance toward a person or group who has harmed you, regardless of whether they actually deserve your forgiveness. It is not the same as forgetting, excusing, or reconciling. Forgetting denies the reality of harm; excusing minimizes its significance; reconciling requires the participation of the offender. Forgiveness is something the victim can do alone—a release of the offender from the debt of guilt, a relinquishment of the right to revenge.

Research has demonstrated impressive benefits of forgiveness. Studies show that people who forgive experience lower levels of depression, anxiety, and anger. They have better cardiovascular health, stronger immune function, and greater overall well-being. They report higher levels of life satisfaction and more positive relationships. Forgiveness breaks the cycle of rumination that keeps victims trapped in the past, allowing them to move forward with their lives.

These findings are not surprising to those familiar with Jesus' teachings. When He taught that the merciful obtain mercy, He was not only making a theological statement but describing a psychological reality. The merciful are blessed because mercy opens the heart to receive mercy, because forgiveness liberates the forgiver from the prison of resentment, because releasing others from debt releases us from the burden of collecting.

But forgiveness is not easy. It often requires a process—a journey through pain, anger, grief, and ultimately release. Psychologists have identified stages in this journey: acknowledging the hurt, experiencing the anger, considering the humanity of the offender, making a decision to forgive, and working through the process of emotional release. This process takes time and often requires support. It cannot be rushed or forced.

Jesus' teaching on forgiveness acknowledges this complexity. He does not demand that victims pretend they were not hurt or that they immediately feel warm feelings toward offenders. He calls them to release the debt, to relinquish the right to revenge, to open the door to possible reconciliation. The feelings may follow, or they may lag behind. But the decision to forgive is an act of will that can be made even when emotions are still raw.

The parable of the unforgiving servant illustrates the alternative. The servant who refused to forgive was delivered to the torturers—a vivid image of the inner torment that unforgiveness produces. Bitterness, resentment, and anger do not harm only those against whom they are directed; they torture the one who holds them. They consume mental energy, disrupt emotional peace, damage physical health, and poison relationships. The torturers are real, and they work from within.

Forgiveness, then, is not primarily for the benefit of the offender but for the liberation of the victim. When we forgive, we are not doing the offender a favor; we are freeing ourselves from bondage to the past. We are choosing not to let the one who harmed us continue to harm us by occupying our thoughts, dictating our emotions, and shaping our lives. Forgiveness is an act of self-liberation.

This does not mean that forgiveness is selfish or that the offender's response is irrelevant. Genuine forgiveness seeks the good of the offender as well—willing their restoration, hoping for their repentance, desiring their well-being. But even if the offender remains unrepentant, the victim can still forgive, can still release the debt, can still move forward. The forgiveness that Jesus taught and modeled does not depend on the offender's response.

The Philosophical Framework of Forgiveness

Philosophically, forgiveness raises profound questions about justice, desert, and the nature of moral obligation. If justice means giving each person what they deserve, then forgiveness seems unjust. The offender deserves condemnation, punishment, at least the continued resentment of the victim. To forgive is to withhold what is deserved, to treat the offender better than they deserve. How can this be right?

Various philosophical traditions have grappled with this question. Some, following Immanuel Kant, have argued that justice requires retribution—that the offender must be punished because they deserve it, and for no other reason. From this perspective, forgiveness appears as a violation of justice, a failure to give the offender what they have earned.

Other philosophers have challenged this view. They note that retributive justice, taken to its logical extreme, leads to endless cycles of vengeance and counter-vengeance. They observe that justice is not the only moral value; mercy, compassion, and love also have their place. They argue that forgiveness, far from violating justice, actually transcends it, moving beyond the calculus of desert to the更高 reality of grace.

Jesus' teaching on forgiveness aligns with this second perspective. He does not deny that offenders deserve punishment; the unforgiving servant's debt was real, and the king would have been justified in collecting it. But He insists that mercy is higher than justice, that grace can and should transcend desert. The king's forgiveness of the astronomical debt was not unjust; it was super-just, going beyond what justice required to what love made possible.

This does not mean that justice is irrelevant. The parable also shows that justice reasserts itself when mercy is rejected. The unforgiving servant, having refused to extend mercy, is subjected to the full rigor of the law. Justice without mercy becomes condemnation; mercy without justice becomes license. True forgiveness holds justice and mercy together, acknowledging the reality of wrong while choosing to release the wrongdoer from its consequences.

The philosophical foundations of forgiveness also intersect with questions about human freedom and moral responsibility. If we are not free agents, if our actions are determined by forces beyond our control, then forgiveness seems meaningless—there is no one to forgive, only causes and effects to be managed. But if we are genuinely free, genuinely responsible for our actions, then forgiveness becomes both necessary and possible. We can hold offenders accountable while also releasing them from the debt of guilt.

Jesus' teaching assumes human freedom and moral responsibility. He calls people to repent, to change their lives, to take responsibility for their actions. He holds offenders accountable while offering them forgiveness. This balance—accountability without condemnation, forgiveness without license—is the heart of restorative justice.

Reconciliation: The Goal of Forgiveness

If forgiveness is the release of the offender from the debt of guilt, reconciliation is the restoration of broken relationship. Forgiveness can occur unilaterally; the victim can forgive even if the offender remains unrepentant. But reconciliation requires the willing participation of both parties. It involves the rebuilding of trust, the restoration of communion, the reestablishment of relationship.

Jesus' teaching on reconciliation is as central as His teaching on forgiveness. In the Sermon on the Mount, He calls His followers to be peacemakers, promising that they will be called children of God (Matthew 5:9). Peacemakers are not merely those who avoid conflict but those who actively work to resolve it, to reconcile divided parties, to restore broken relationships. They are agents of reconciliation, reflecting the character of the God who reconciles the world to Himself.

The parable of the prodigal son provides the most powerful illustration of reconciliation in all of Scripture. The father does not merely forgive his wayward son; he restores him to full sonship. He puts a robe on him—a sign of honor. He puts a ring on his hand—a sign of authority. He puts sandals on his feet—a sign of free status, for servants went barefoot. He kills the fatted calf and hosts a celebration. The son who was dead is alive; the one who was lost is found. Relationship is not merely resumed but celebrated.

This parable reveals several dimensions of reconciliation. First, reconciliation requires the initiative of the wronged party. The father sees the son while he is still far off and runs to meet him. He does not wait for the son to reach the house, to prove himself, to complete his penance. He goes out to meet him, closing the distance, initiating the embrace.

Second, reconciliation requires acknowledgment of wrong. The son confesses his sin: "Father, I have sinned against heaven and before you, and am no longer worthy to be called your son." He does not minimize or excuse; he takes full responsibility. This acknowledgment opens the door to restoration.

Third, reconciliation involves restoration of relationship, not merely resumption of contact. The son is restored to sonship, not merely allowed back onto the property. He is given the symbols of belonging—robe, ring, sandals. He is welcomed into the celebration. The relationship is not merely tolerated but celebrated.

Fourth, reconciliation can be impeded by the attitudes of others. The elder son refuses to join the celebration, angry that his brother has been welcomed. His resentment threatens to exclude him from the very restoration he condemns. The father must go out to him as well, pleading with him to share in the joy.

This parable illustrates the restorative justice understanding of reconciliation. It is not enough to forgive; we must work toward restoration. It is not enough to release the debt; we must rebuild the relationship. This work takes time, requires effort, and depends on the willing participation of all parties. But when it is achieved, it is cause for celebration—the dead is alive, the lost is found.

The Relationship Between Forgiveness and Reconciliation

Understanding the relationship between forgiveness and reconciliation is crucial for restorative justice. The two are often conflated, leading to confusion and unrealistic expectations. Victims may be told they must reconcile with offenders when they are not ready, or they may be praised for forgiving when they have done nothing of the sort.

Forgiveness and reconciliation are distinct but related. Forgiveness is the release of the offender from the debt of guilt. It is a decision the victim can make unilaterally, regardless of the offender's response. Reconciliation is the restoration of relationship. It requires the willing participation of both parties, including the offender's repentance and commitment to change.

Forgiveness is necessary for reconciliation but not sufficient. Two parties can be reconciled only if the offense is acknowledged, responsibility taken, amends made, and trust rebuilt. Forgiveness opens the door to this process, but reconciliation requires walking through that door together.

In some cases, forgiveness may not lead to reconciliation. The offender may remain unrepentant, continuing in harmful behavior. The victim may forgive—releasing the offender from the debt of guilt—but cannot be reconciled because the offender refuses to change. In such cases, the victim is free to move forward, unburdened by resentment, while the relationship remains broken.

In other cases, reconciliation may be possible even if forgiveness is incomplete. The parties may come together, work through their issues, rebuild trust, and restore relationship, even if the victim's emotional forgiveness lags behind. The decision to forgive can be made even when feelings are still raw, and the process of reconciliation can actually facilitate the completion of forgiveness.

Restorative justice provides a structured framework for this process. Through victim-offender mediation, family group conferences, or circle processes, victims and offenders can come together in a safe, facilitated environment. Victims can express their pain, ask their questions, and share their needs. Offenders can acknowledge their responsibility, express remorse, and make commitments to amends. Together, they can work toward agreements that address the harm and rebuild trust.

This process does not guarantee reconciliation. Some victims will not be ready to meet offenders; some offenders will not be willing to take responsibility. But when both parties are willing, restorative justice creates the conditions in which forgiveness and reconciliation can occur. It does not force either but facilitates both.

The Theological Dimensions of Forgiveness and Reconciliation

Theologically, forgiveness and reconciliation are rooted in the character of God. The Scriptures consistently portray God as forgiving, merciful, and eager to restore relationship with His people. From the moment of the fall, when God seeks out Adam and Eve in the garden, to the call of Abraham, to the giving of the Law, to the sending of the prophets, to the ultimate revelation in Jesus Christ, God is shown as one who initiates reconciliation with wayward humanity.

The Old Testament is rich with images of God's forgiveness. When Moses intercedes for Israel after the golden calf incident, God reveals His character: "The Lord, the Lord God, merciful and gracious, longsuffering, and abounding in goodness and truth, keeping mercy for thousands, forgiving iniquity and transgression and sin" (Exodus 34:6-7). This self-revelation becomes a refrain throughout Scripture, the foundation of Israel's hope for forgiveness.

The psalmists celebrate this forgiveness: "Bless the Lord, O my soul, and forget not all His benefits: who forgives all your iniquities, who heals all your diseases, who redeems your life from destruction" (Psalm 103:2-4). "As far as the east is from the west, so far has He removed our transgressions from us" (Psalm 103:12). "He will again have compassion on us, and will subdue our iniquities. You will cast all our sins into the depths of the sea" (Micah 7:19).

The prophets proclaim God's willingness to forgive and restore. Through Isaiah, God declares: "Though your sins are like scarlet, they shall be as white as snow; though they are red like crimson, they shall be as wool" (Isaiah 1:18). Through Ezekiel, He promises: "I will sprinkle clean water on you, and you shall be clean; from all your filthiness and from all your idols I will cleanse you. I will give you a new heart and put a new spirit within you" (Ezekiel 36:25-26).

In the New Testament, this forgiveness becomes incarnate in Jesus Christ. He is the one who has authority on earth to forgive sins (Mark 2:10). He is the one who came to seek and to save the lost (Luke 19:10). He is the one who gave Himself as a ransom for many (Mark 10:45). Through His death and resurrection, He accomplished what the Old Testament sacrifices could only symbolize: the actual forgiveness of sins and the restoration of relationship with God.

The Apostle Paul articulates this theology of forgiveness and reconciliation most fully. In Romans, he writes that "all have sinned and fall short of the glory of God, being justified freely by His grace through the redemption that is in Christ Jesus" (Romans 3:23-24). In Colossians, he declares that God has "qualified us to be partakers of the inheritance of the saints in the light. He has delivered us from the power of darkness and conveyed us into the kingdom of the Son of His love, in whom we have redemption through His blood, the forgiveness of sins" (Colossians 1:12-14).

But Paul's most comprehensive statement on reconciliation comes in 2 Corinthians: "Therefore, if anyone is in Christ, he is a new creation; old things have passed away; behold, all things have become new. Now all things are of God, who has reconciled us to Himself through Jesus Christ, and has given us the ministry of reconciliation, that is, that God was in Christ reconciling the world to Himself, not imputing their trespasses to them, and has committed to us the word of reconciliation" (2 Corinthians 5:17-19).

This passage is foundational for understanding the Jesus Paradigm. It reveals that reconciliation is God's work—He is the one who reconciles us to Himself through Christ. It reveals that this reconciliation is based on God's decision not to count our trespasses against us—forgiveness that releases us from the debt of guilt. And it reveals that those who have received this reconciliation are entrusted with the ministry of reconciliation—called to extend to others what they have received.

The ministry of reconciliation is precisely what restorative justice seeks to embody. It is the work of bringing together those who have been separated by harm, facilitating acknowledgment and accountability, enabling forgiveness and restoration. It is not a human invention but a divine calling, not a social program but a spiritual practice. Those who practice restorative justice are participating in the very work of God, becoming ambassadors of Christ in a broken world.

The Psychological Process of Reconciliation

If forgiveness is a decision that can be made unilaterally, reconciliation is a process that requires the participation of both parties. Psychologically, this process involves several stages, each with its own challenges and opportunities.

The first stage is acknowledgment. The offender must acknowledge the harm they have caused, taking responsibility for their actions without excuse or minimization. This acknowledgment is not merely cognitive but emotional—an understanding of how the victim has been affected, an entering into their pain. Without this acknowledgment, reconciliation cannot begin.

The second stage is remorse. The offender must experience genuine sorrow for what they have done—not sorrow at being caught, not sorrow at consequences, but sorrow at the harm inflicted. This remorse may be expressed in apology, in tears, in changed behavior. It communicates to the victim that the offender understands the gravity of what they have done and is genuinely grieved by it.

The third stage is repentance. The offender must turn from their harmful behavior, making changes in their life that demonstrate a genuine commitment to change. This may involve seeking treatment for addiction, addressing underlying issues, removing themselves from harmful situations. Repentance is not merely words but actions—evidence that the offender is serious about transformation.

The fourth stage is restitution. The offender must make amends for the harm they have caused, to the extent possible. This may involve material restitution—repaying stolen money, repairing damaged property—but it also involves symbolic restitution—actions that communicate respect for the victim, commitment to change, desire to make things right.

The fifth stage is rebuilding trust. Trust is not restored automatically; it must be rebuilt over time through consistent, trustworthy behavior. The offender must demonstrate over an extended period that they have truly changed, that they can be relied upon, that the harm will not be repeated. This takes time and patience from both parties.

The sixth stage is reconciliation itself. When acknowledgment, remorse, repentance, restitution, and rebuilding have occurred, the relationship can be restored. The parties can come together in a new way, not pretending the past didn't happen but having worked through it, having addressed it, having grown through it. The relationship that emerges may be different from what it was before—often deeper, more honest, more resilient.

Throughout this process, the victim's journey is equally important. Victims must work through their own pain, anger, and grief. They must decide whether to forgive, whether to engage in the reconciliation process, whether to trust again. This journey cannot be forced; it must be honored. Restorative justice provides support for victims as they navigate this difficult terrain, offering counseling, advocacy, and community support.

The Legal Dimensions of Forgiveness and Reconciliation

The relationship between forgiveness, reconciliation, and the law is complex and often misunderstood. In legal contexts, forgiveness is not a concept that fits easily. The law deals in rights and obligations, in debts and damages, in guilt and punishment. Forgiveness seems to belong to a different realm—the realm of personal relationships, moral judgment, religious practice.

Yet forgiveness has legal implications. When a victim forgives an offender, they may choose not to press charges, not to seek maximum penalties, not to pursue civil damages. This decision is their right; the law cannot force them to seek vengeance. Restorative justice provides a framework within which such decisions can be made thoughtfully, with full information about the offender and the offense.

Restitution is a legal concept that bridges forgiveness and justice. When an offender makes restitution—repaying stolen money, repairing damaged property, compensating for losses—they are making amends in a tangible way. Restitution can be ordered by a court or agreed upon in a restorative process. It holds the offender accountable while also providing concrete benefit to the victim.

Reconciliation also has legal dimensions. In some cases, reconciliation between victim and offender may affect legal proceedings—leading to reduced charges, alternative sentencing, or dismissal of cases. Many jurisdictions now have restorative justice programs that operate alongside the conventional legal system, offering opportunities for victim-offender mediation, family group conferencing, and other restorative processes.

These programs do not replace the legal system but complement it. They operate within legal frameworks, respecting the rights of all parties while offering alternatives to purely punitive responses. They recognize that law alone cannot achieve justice; that healing requires more than punishment, that victims and offenders need opportunities that the conventional system does not provide.

The legal recognition of restorative justice is growing. The United Nations has adopted Basic Principles on the Use of Restorative Justice Programmes in Criminal Matters, encouraging member states to develop restorative approaches. Many countries have incorporated restorative justice into their legal systems, from New Zealand's family group conferences to

European victim-offender mediation programs to restorative justice provisions in various American jurisdictions.

This legal recognition is important, but it also raises questions. Can forgiveness be institutionalized? Can reconciliation be mandated? The answer is no—forgiveness and reconciliation are personal, voluntary, cannot be coerced. But the law can create space for them, can provide structures that facilitate them, can remove obstacles that impede them. This is what restorative justice seeks to do: not to force forgiveness and reconciliation but to make them possible.

Forgiveness and Justice: A Restorative Synthesis

One of the most persistent objections to forgiveness is that it undermines justice. If we forgive offenders, we let them off the hook. We fail to hold them accountable. We send a message that wrongdoing has no consequences. This objection has force, and it must be taken seriously.

But the objection rests on a misunderstanding of both forgiveness and justice. Forgiveness is not the absence of accountability; it is a particular form of accountability. It holds the offender responsible while releasing them from the debt of guilt. It acknowledges the wrong while choosing not to let it define the relationship. It seeks the good of the offender while also seeking healing for the victim.

Justice, rightly understood, is not opposed to forgiveness but fulfilled by it. Retributive justice seeks to balance the scales by inflicting pain on the offender. Restorative justice seeks to balance the scales by repairing harm, meeting needs, restoring relationships. Forgiveness is essential to this process because it releases the offender from the endless cycle of debt and payment, allowing genuine restoration to occur.

The parable of the unforgiving servant illustrates this relationship. The king's forgiveness of the astronomical debt was not unjust; it was super-just, going beyond what justice required to what mercy made possible. But when the servant refused to extend the same mercy, justice reasserted itself. He was handed over to the torturers until he should pay all that was due. Justice without mercy becomes condemnation; mercy without justice becomes license. True forgiveness holds them together.

Restorative justice embodies this synthesis. It does not ignore accountability; it redefines it. Accountability means taking responsibility for harm, making amends where possible, changing behavior to prevent future harm. This is a more demanding form of accountability than simply serving time. It requires offenders to face their victims, to acknowledge their wrongdoing, to work actively for restoration. This is accountability that leads to transformation, not merely punishment.

Forgiveness enables this accountability. When victims forgive, they release offenders from the fear of endless retaliation, creating space for genuine acknowledgment and amends. They communicate that the relationship is more important than the debt, that restoration is possible, that there is a future beyond the past. This forgiveness is not cheap; it costs the victim dearly. But it opens the door to the kind of accountability that heals.

The Challenge of Forgiveness in Difficult Cases

Forgiveness is never easy, but some cases present particular challenges. When the harm is severe—murder, rape, sustained abuse—forgiveness seems almost impossible. When the offender remains unrepentant, defiant, continuing in harmful behavior—forgiveness seems naive. When the victim is a child, vulnerable, unable to protect themselves—forgiveness seems to ask too much.

What does restorative justice say in such cases? It does not demand forgiveness. It does not pressure victims to forgive before they are ready. It does not suggest that forgiveness is always possible or always appropriate. It respects the victim's journey, honors their pain, supports them whatever they decide.

But it also holds open the possibility of forgiveness, even in the most difficult cases. There are remarkable stories of victims of terrible crimes who have found the strength to forgive—parents whose children were murdered, survivors of sexual assault, victims of torture. Their forgiveness does not minimize the crime or excuse the offender. It is a costly, hard-won victory over hatred and despair. And it often brings healing that nothing else could provide.

These stories do not prescribe what every victim should do. They witness to what is possible when grace triumphs over vengeance. They remind us that forgiveness is not weakness but strength, not capitulation but liberation. They point to the power of the human spirit, sustained by divine grace, to transcend even the worst that humans can do to one another.

Theologically, these stories reflect the cross. Jesus forgave His executioners even as they nailed Him to the tree. He did not minimize their sin; He prayed for their forgiveness. He did not wait for their repentance; He extended grace. His forgiveness was not a denial of justice but its deepest expression—the innocent one bearing the consequences of the guilty, opening the way for their restoration.

Restorative justice, in the most difficult cases, seeks to embody something of this costly grace. It does not pretend that easy answers exist. It does not offer formulas or guarantees. But it creates space for victims to tell their stories, to ask their questions, to receive support. And it holds open the possibility that even in the darkest places, light can dawn—that forgiveness can emerge, that reconciliation can occur, that healing can happen.

The Community's Role in Forgiveness and Reconciliation

Forgiveness and reconciliation are not merely private matters between individuals; they have communal dimensions. When harm occurs, the community is affected. Trust is damaged, relationships strained, the fabric of social life torn. The community has a stake in forgiveness and reconciliation, and it has a role to play in facilitating them.

In the parable of the prodigal son, the community is present. The servants are there, preparing the celebration. The friends and neighbors are called to rejoice. The elder son's refusal to participate threatens to mar the communal joy. The father goes out to him, seeking to draw him back into community. The restoration of the younger son is not complete until the elder son is also restored to the celebration.

In restorative justice, the community's role is essential. Community members participate in family group conferences, circle processes, and other restorative practices. They offer support to victims, holding them in care and providing practical assistance. They offer accountability to offenders, helping them see the impact of their actions and supporting their efforts to change. They help to create the conditions in which forgiveness and reconciliation can occur.

The community also benefits from forgiveness and reconciliation. When relationships are restored, trust is rebuilt, social cohesion strengthened. The community becomes safer, more resilient, more capable of preventing future harm. Restorative justice is not only about individual cases but about building the kind of community in which harm is less likely to occur and healing is more likely to happen when it does.

Churches, as communities of faith, have a particular calling in this regard. They are called to be communities of forgiveness and reconciliation—places where people can confess their sins, receive absolution, and be restored to fellowship. They are called to model restorative practices in their own life, addressing conflicts openly and honestly, working for reconciliation rather than division. And they are called to extend this ministry beyond their walls, advocating for restorative justice in the wider society, supporting victims and offenders, working for healing in the community.

This is not easy. Churches, like all human communities, struggle with conflict, division, and unforgiveness. They are not always places of grace. But they are called to be, and the gospel provides both the motivation and the means. The same forgiveness that reconciles us to God can reconcile us to one another. The same Spirit that raised Christ from the dead can raise broken relationships to new life. The same community that gathers around the Table can become the embodiment of restorative justice in the world.

The Practice of Forgiveness and Reconciliation

Understanding forgiveness and reconciliation is essential, but understanding alone is not enough. These concepts must be practiced, embodied, lived out in concrete situations. Restorative justice provides a framework for this practice, but the practice itself requires skill, commitment, and grace.

For victims, practicing forgiveness may begin with acknowledging the hurt. This is not easy; it means facing the pain, allowing oneself to feel it, giving voice to it. But acknowledgment is the first step toward release. Victims may then work through their anger, their grief, their questions. They may seek support from counselors, pastors, support groups. They may consider whether they are ready to forgive—to release the offender from the debt of guilt. If they are, they may do so in whatever way feels right—in prayer, in writing, in conversation with a trusted person, perhaps eventually in encounter with the offender.

For offenders, practicing repentance begins with acknowledgment. They must stop denying, minimizing, excusing. They must face the full reality of what they have done and its impact on others. This may require help—counseling, accountability partners, structured programs. They must then express remorse—not generic sorrow but specific grief over specific harms. They must make amends to the extent possible—restitution, service, changed behavior. And they must commit to the long work of rebuilding trust, demonstrating over time that they have truly changed.

For communities, practicing reconciliation means creating structures that support these processes. It means training facilitators who can guide restorative encounters. It means developing programs that provide support for victims and offenders. It means advocating for policies that enable restorative justice within the legal system. It means building a culture of forgiveness and reconciliation—teaching these values, modeling them in community life, celebrating them when they occur.

For all of us, practicing forgiveness and reconciliation means cultivating the inner dispositions that make them possible. It means developing the humility to recognize our own need for forgiveness. It means cultivating the empathy that enables us to understand others' pain. It means nurturing the hope that believes change is possible. It means opening our hearts to the grace that enables us to forgive as we have been forgiven.

Forgiveness and Reconciliation as the Heart of the Jesus Paradigm

As we conclude this exploration, we see that forgiveness and reconciliation are not peripheral to restorative justice but central. They are not optional extras for the especially virtuous but essential practices for all who would follow Jesus. They are not naive ideals for a perfect world but practical necessities for this broken one.

The Jesus Paradigm is, at its core, a paradigm of forgiveness and reconciliation. It begins with the forgiveness we receive from God—the unconditional, costly, transformative forgiveness that restores us to relationship with Him. It continues with the forgiveness we extend to others—the forgiveness that releases them from debt, opens the door to reconciliation, and heals our own hearts. And it culminates in the reconciliation of all things—the restoration of relationships, communities, and creation itself to the shalom for which they were made.

This paradigm challenges every assumption of the retributive mindset. It refuses to let offenders be defined by their worst acts. It refuses to let victims be defined by their suffering. It refuses to let communities be defined by their conflicts. It insists that there is always more—more to the person than their sin, more to the future than the past, more to justice than punishment.

This paradigm also challenges cheap grace. Forgiveness is not easy; it cost the cross. Reconciliation is not automatic; it requires the hard work of acknowledgment, repentance, restitution, rebuilding. Restorative justice is not a quick fix; it is a long journey. But it is a journey worth taking, for it leads to healing, to wholeness, to shalom.

The gospel of restorative justice is this: that in Jesus Christ, God has reconciled the world to Himself, not counting our trespasses against us. And He has entrusted to us the ministry of reconciliation—the privilege and responsibility of extending to others what we have received. This is our calling. This is our joy. This is the Jesus Paradigm, lived out in forgiveness and reconciliation, transforming harm into healing and estrangement into embrace.

CHAPTER 05

RESTORATIVE JUSTICE IN BIBLICAL CONTEXT AND IN THE CHURCH

The relationship between restorative justice and the Christian faith is not merely incidental or illustrative; it is foundational and organic. Restorative justice is not a secular concept that the church has adopted and adapted, but rather a framework for justice that is deeply embedded in the biblical narrative from Genesis to Revelation. When we speak of restorative justice in a biblical context, we are not imposing an external framework onto Scripture but rather excavating the rich seams of justice that run through the very fabric of God's revelation. And when we consider restorative justice in the church, we are not proposing an optional program for particularly progressive congregations but rather calling the people of God to embody the very justice that defines their identity and mission.

This chapter explores the profound integration of restorative justice with biblical faith and ecclesial practice. We will examine the theological foundations of restorative justice in Scripture, the principles that guide its practice, and the practical steps by which churches can become communities of restoration. We will see that restorative justice is not a departure from historic Christian teaching but its fullest expression, not a compromise with secular culture but a faithful witness to the gospel in a broken world.

The Biblical Foundation of Restorative Justice

Biblical restorative justice is a framework for justice that is grounded in the teachings of the Bible and emphasizes the importance of repairing harm caused by wrongdoing, reconciling relationships, and restoring wholeness to individuals and communities. It is based on the conviction that justice is not merely about punishing offenders but about healing and restoring both victims and offenders. This conviction runs throughout Scripture, from the laws of Moses to the teachings of the prophets to the life and ministry of Jesus to the writings of the apostles.

The foundational premise of biblical restorative justice is the creation account itself. Genesis 1:26-27 declares that humanity was created in the image of God—male and female, bearing the divine likeness, possessing inherent dignity and worth. This imago Dei is the bedrock of all biblical ethics and the cornerstone of restorative justice. Because every person bears God's image, every person possesses intrinsic value that cannot be erased by any action, no matter how heinous. The offender, no less than the victim, remains an image-bearer, deserving of dignity and capable of restoration.

This premise has profound implications for justice. If the offender's dignity is inviolable, then justice cannot be satisfied by degrading or dehumanizing punishment. If the victim's dignity is inviolable, then justice cannot ignore their suffering or sideline their needs. If both share the divine image, then justice must seek the restoration of both, the healing of the relationship between them, and the wholeness of the community that encompasses them.

The fall introduced rupture into this created goodness. Sin fractured relationships—between humanity and God, between humans and each other, within the human heart, and between humanity and creation. Justice, in the biblical vision, is the work of repairing these fractures, of restoring what was broken, of recovering what was lost. It is not merely the punishment of wrongdoers but the redemption of all that sin has damaged.

This restorative vision is evident in the laws given to Israel. While the Torah includes provisions for punishment, its dominant concern is restoration. When an ox is stolen, the law requires restitution—five oxen for one (Exodus 22:1). The goal is not merely to punish the thief but to restore the victim, to compensate for the loss, to make the victim whole. When property is damaged, the law requires repayment (Exodus 22:5-6). When a person is injured, the law requires compensation for loss of time and healing (Exodus 21:18-19). The legal system is designed not merely to adjudicate guilt but to repair harm.

Even the lex talionis—"eye for eye, tooth for tooth"—serves a restorative purpose. This principle was not a license for vengeance but a limit on it. In a world where retaliation could escalate into blood feuds that destroyed families and communities, the law of talion established proportionality: no more than an eye for an eye, no more than a tooth for a tooth. It restrained vengeance and created space for restoration.

The prophets amplified this restorative vision. They thundered against a justice system that favored the powerful and ignored the vulnerable. They called Israel to a justice that went beyond ritual observance to active care for the oppressed. Micah famously distilled God's requirements: "to do justly, to love mercy, and to walk humbly with your God" (Micah 6:8). Justice and mercy are not opposed but intertwined; walking humbly with God means walking justly and mercifully with others.

Isaiah envisioned a justice that would issue in peace—shalom, the flourishing of all creation under God's reign. "Justice will dwell in the wilderness and righteousness abide in the fruitful field. The work of righteousness will be peace, and the effect of righteousness, quietness and assurance forever" (Isaiah 32:16-17). Justice is not an end in itself but the path to peace, the condition for human flourishing, the foundation of a restored creation.

Hosea envisioned a covenant of peace that would embrace all creation: "In that day I will make a covenant for them with the beasts of the field, with the birds of the air, and with the creeping things of the ground. Bow and sword of battle I will shatter from the earth, to make them lie down safely" (Hosea 2:18). Justice extends beyond human relationships to encompass the whole created order, restoring the harmony that sin disrupted.

In the New Testament, this restorative vision finds its fullest expression in Jesus Christ. He is the one who came to seek and to save the lost (Luke 19:10). He is the one who proclaimed good news to the poor, freedom to the prisoners, recovery of sight to the blind, liberation to the oppressed (Luke 4:18). He is the one who touched lepers, forgave sinners, welcomed outcasts, and restored the marginalized to community. His entire ministry was a work of restoration.

The apostle Paul articulated the theological foundation of this restorative work. In 2 Corinthians 5, he declared that "God was in Christ reconciling the world to Himself, not imputing their trespasses to them, and has committed to us the word of reconciliation" (2 Corinthians 5:19). Reconciliation is God's work and the church's mission. Those who have been reconciled to God through Christ are called to be agents of reconciliation in the world.

This is the gospel of restorative justice: that the Creator of the universe is in the business of making all things new, of restoring what was broken, of healing what was wounded, of reconciling what was estranged. And this gospel comes with a commission: that those who have received this restoration should extend it to others, becoming ambassadors of reconciliation in every sphere of life.

Key Principles of Biblical Restorative Justice

Biblical restorative justice is built on several foundational principles that distinguish it from purely punitive approaches and align it with the character and purposes of God.

The first principle is the importance of community. Restorative justice is grounded in the belief that individuals are interconnected and that communities have an essential role in promoting justice and healing. This reflects the biblical understanding of humanity as created for relationship. We are not isolated atoms but members one of another, bound together in networks of mutual responsibility and care.

In the Old Testament, Israel was constituted as a covenant community. The laws were given not merely to regulate individual behavior but to shape a society in which all could flourish. When harm occurred, it was not just a private matter but a breach in the community's fabric. The entire community was implicated, and the entire community was involved in restoration.

In the New Testament, the church is described as the body of Christ—a living organism in which each member is connected to every other, and the health of the whole depends on the health of each part. When one member suffers, all suffer together; when one member is honored, all rejoice together (1 Corinthians 12:26). This organic unity means that harm to any member harms the whole, and restoration of any member blesses the whole.

Restorative justice honors this communal dimension. It brings together victims, offenders, and community members to address harm and work toward healing. It recognizes that crime is not merely an offense against the state but a wound in the community's life. It seeks not only to hold offenders accountable but to mobilize community resources for support, healing, and prevention.

The second principle is the value of relationships. Restorative justice emphasizes the importance of repairing relationships damaged by wrongdoing and seeks to create opportunities for dialogue and understanding between victims and offenders. This reflects the biblical emphasis on covenant relationship as the context for human flourishing.

The entire biblical narrative is a story of relationship—God's relationship with creation, with Israel, with the church, with each person. The law and the prophets call God's people to faithful relationship with God and with one another. Jesus teaches that love of God and love of neighbor are the greatest commandments, on which all the law and prophets hang (Matthew 22:36-40). Paul describes love as the bond of perfection, the virtue that unites all others and makes them meaningful (Colossians 3:14).

When harm occurs, relationships are damaged. Trust is broken, connection is severed, community is fragmented. Restorative justice seeks to repair these relationships, to rebuild trust, to restore connection. It does this by creating safe spaces for dialogue, by facilitating honest communication, by supporting the hard work of forgiveness and reconciliation.

The third principle is the need for accountability. Restorative justice recognizes the importance of holding offenders accountable for their actions while also providing them with opportunities to take responsibility for repairing the harm they have caused. This reflects the biblical understanding that accountability is essential for justice and for transformation.

In Scripture, accountability is woven into the fabric of human relationship. From the garden, where God calls Adam and Eve to account for their disobedience, to the prophets, who hold Israel accountable for covenant unfaithfulness, to Jesus, who calls individuals to account for their choices, accountability is a constant theme. But biblical accountability is not merely about assigning blame; it is about calling people to take responsibility, to acknowledge wrongdoing, to make amends, to change.

Restorative justice embodies this understanding. It holds offenders accountable not by inflicting pain but by requiring them to face the human consequences of their actions, to acknowledge the harm they have caused, to make amends to the extent possible, and to commit to changed behavior. This is a more demanding form of accountability than merely serving time. It requires offenders to engage actively in the work of restoration.

The fourth principle is the importance of healing and restoration. Restorative justice focuses on restoring wholeness to individuals and communities impacted by crime or conflict and seeks to promote healing, forgiveness, and reconciliation. This reflects the biblical vision of shalom—the peace, wholeness, and flourishing that God intends for all creation.

Throughout Scripture, God is revealed as healer. "I am the Lord who heals you," He declares to Israel (Exodus 15:26). The psalmists celebrate God's healing power: "He heals the brokenhearted and binds up their wounds" (Psalm 147:3). The prophets promise a day when healing will flow like a river: "The sun of righteousness shall arise with healing in its wings" (Malachi 4:2).

Jesus' ministry was characterized by healing—healing of bodies, minds, spirits, relationships. He touched lepers and made them clean. He forgave sinners and restored them to community. He cast out demons and liberated the oppressed. He raised the dead and comforted the grieving. His healing was holistic, addressing every dimension of human brokenness.

Restorative justice participates in this healing work. It seeks healing for victims, addressing their trauma, giving them voice, supporting their recovery. It seeks healing for offenders, addressing the underlying causes of their behavior, supporting their transformation, restoring them to community. It seeks healing for communities, repairing the social fabric torn by harm, rebuilding trust, strengthening relationships.

Implementing Biblical Restorative Justice

Implementing biblical restorative justice requires a commitment to its principles and values and a willingness to engage in processes that seek to repair harm, reconcile relationships, and restore wholeness. This implementation occurs at multiple levels—individual, congregational, community, and societal. It involves education, engagement, development, support, integration, and evaluation.

The first step is education and training. Individuals and communities must understand the principles and values of biblical restorative justice. This involves learning about the biblical foundations, the historical practices, the contemporary applications, and the practical skills required for restorative processes. Churches can offer classes, workshops, and seminars that introduce members to restorative justice concepts. They can invite speakers, show videos, distribute literature, and facilitate discussions. They can send members to training programs that equip them as facilitators, mediators, and advocates.

Education is not merely about information but about transformation. It involves helping people shift their mindset from punitive to restorative, from retributive to healing-centered. It means grappling with the hard questions: What does justice require? How do we balance accountability and mercy? How do we support victims while also seeking restoration for offenders? How do we create communities that prevent harm and promote healing?

The second step is engagement with the community. Restorative justice cannot be implemented in isolation; it requires building relationships and promoting a sense of shared responsibility for justice. Churches can reach out to local organizations, other congregations, community leaders, and government agencies to promote awareness of restorative justice principles and values. They can participate in community coalitions, join interfaith initiatives, and collaborate with secular partners who share similar goals.

This engagement is not merely about promoting restorative justice but about embodying it. Churches can demonstrate restorative values in their own interactions with the community—welcoming the stranger, caring for the vulnerable, advocating for the oppressed, working for reconciliation across divisions. They can become known as places where healing happens, where conflicts are resolved, where relationships are restored.

The third step is the development of restorative justice processes. Communities need structures and practices that enable restorative responses to harm. This may involve implementing victim-offender mediation programs, community conferencing, circle processes, or other forms of restorative justice that promote dialogue and understanding between victims and offenders. These processes must be appropriate for the specific community and the specific circumstances of each case.

Developing these processes requires careful planning. It involves identifying potential cases, recruiting and training facilitators, establishing protocols and procedures, ensuring safety and confidentiality, and creating mechanisms for follow-up and support. It may involve partnering with existing restorative justice programs or creating new ones from scratch. It requires ongoing attention to quality and effectiveness.

The fourth step is the establishment of support systems. Both victims and offenders need support as they navigate the restorative process. Victims may need counseling, advocacy, practical assistance, and ongoing care. Offenders may need mentorship, accountability, treatment for underlying issues, and assistance with reintegration. Churches can provide or connect people to these support services, creating networks of care that surround all those affected by harm.

Support systems are not optional add-ons but essential components of restorative justice. Without adequate support, victims may be re-traumatized, and offenders may lack the resources needed for genuine change. With support, both can find the strength and encouragement to engage in the difficult work of healing and restoration.

The fifth step is integration with the justice system. Restorative justice does not exist in a vacuum; it operates alongside and within broader systems of law and justice. Churches can collaborate with law enforcement, courts, corrections, and other justice system stakeholders to promote the use of restorative justice in appropriate cases. They can advocate for policies that enable restorative alternatives, provide training for justice system personnel, and offer restorative services as a complement to conventional processes.

This integration requires navigating complex relationships and respecting the boundaries of different systems. It means understanding the legal framework within which restorative justice operates and working within that framework to create space for restorative approaches. It means building trust with justice system officials and demonstrating the effectiveness of restorative practices.

The sixth step is evaluation and improvement. Restorative justice processes must be evaluated regularly to assess their effectiveness and identify areas for improvement. This involves monitoring outcomes such as victim satisfaction, offender recidivism rates, community relations, and other indicators of success. It means gathering feedback from participants, analyzing data, and making adjustments as needed.

Evaluation is not merely about accountability but about learning. It helps practitioners understand what works and what doesn't, what needs to be changed and what can be replicated. It builds a body of evidence that can inform practice, guide policy, and inspire others. It ensures that restorative justice remains dynamic, responsive, and effective.

Restorative Justice in the Church: Theological Foundation

In the church context, restorative justice is not merely a program or a practice but an expression of the church's identity and mission. The church is called to be a community of restoration—a place where the reconciling work of Christ is embodied and extended. This calling is rooted in the church's theological foundation, particularly in the teachings of the apostle Paul in his letter to the Romans.

The Book of Romans provides a rich theological basis for restorative justice. Paul's exposition of the gospel reveals a God who is in the business of reconciliation, forgiveness, transformation, and restoration. These themes, woven throughout the letter, shape the church's understanding of justice and its practice of restoration.

Reconciliation is the central theme of Romans. Paul declares that "while we were still sinners, Christ died for us" (Romans 5:8). He explains that "when we were enemies we were reconciled to God through the death of His Son" (Romans 5:10). Reconciliation is God's work, accomplished through Christ, extended to all who believe. Those who have been reconciled to God are called to be reconciled to one another, embodying in their relationships the grace they have received.

This reconciliation is not merely a private spiritual experience but a public, communal reality. It creates a new humanity, a new community in which divisions of race, class, and status are overcome. "There is no distinction between Jew and Greek, for the same Lord over all is rich to all who call upon Him" (Romans 10:12). The reconciled community is a sign and foretaste of God's intention for all creation.

Forgiveness is another key theme in Romans. Paul writes that "all have sinned and fall short of the glory of God, being justified freely by His grace through the redemption that is in Christ Jesus" (Romans 3:23-24). Justification is forgiveness—the declaration that the sinner is righteous, not because of their own merit but because of Christ's work. This forgiveness is the foundation of all Christian ethics, including the ethics of justice.

In Romans 12, Paul applies this forgiveness to human relationships. "Repay no one evil for evil. Have regard for good things in the sight of all men. If it is possible, as much as depends on you, live peaceably with all men. Beloved, do not avenge yourselves, but rather give place to wrath; for it is written, 'Vengeance is Mine, I will repay,' says the Lord. Therefore 'if your enemy is hungry, feed him; if he is thirsty, give him a drink; for in so doing you will heap coals of fire on his head.' Do not be overcome by evil, but overcome evil with good" (Romans 12:17-21).

This passage is a classic statement of restorative ethics. It prohibits revenge, commands peacemaking, and instructs believers to respond to evil with good. It recognizes that vengeance belongs to God, not to humans, and that our role is to seek the good even of our enemies. This is the ethic of restorative justice, applied to daily life.

Love and compassion are central to Paul's vision. In Romans 13, he writes that "love does no harm to a neighbor; therefore love is the fulfillment of the law" (Romans 13:10). Love is not merely a sentiment but a practice—the active pursuit of the neighbor's good. It is the principle that should govern all human relationships, including those affected by crime and conflict.

This love is not abstract but concrete. It takes specific form in actions that promote the well-being of others. It refuses to harm, seeks to help, and works for the flourishing of all. In restorative justice, love is the motivation for supporting victims, holding offenders accountable, and building community. It is the energy that sustains the hard work of healing and reconciliation.

Accountability is another theme in Romans. Paul writes that "each of us shall give account of himself to God" (Romans 14:12). This ultimate accountability shapes our accountability to one another. We are responsible for our actions, for their consequences, for their impact on others. We cannot evade this responsibility or transfer it to someone else.

Restorative justice honors this accountability. It calls offenders to face the consequences of their actions, to acknowledge the harm they have caused, to make amends to the extent possible.

It does not let them off the hook but holds them responsible in a way that promotes healing rather than merely inflicting pain.

Transformation is a key theme in Romans. Paul exhorts believers: "Do not be conformed to this world, but be transformed by the renewing of your mind, that you may prove what is that good and acceptable and perfect will of God" (Romans 12:2). Transformation is the work of God in the believer, renewing the mind, reshaping the character, reorienting the life.

Restorative justice seeks this transformation. It aims not merely to change behavior but to change hearts—to bring offenders to genuine repentance, to enable victims to forgive, to transform communities into places of healing and reconciliation. It is not satisfied with surface compliance but seeks deep, lasting change.

Justice and mercy are held together in Romans. Paul quotes God's word to Moses: "I will have mercy on whomever I will have mercy, and I will have compassion on whomever I will have compassion" (Romans 9:15). Mercy is not opposed to justice but transcends it. It is God's freedom to go beyond what justice requires, to show compassion to the undeserving, to extend grace to the guilty.

Restorative justice seeks to harmonize justice and mercy. It does not ignore the demands of justice but fulfills them in a way that makes mercy possible. It holds offenders accountable while also offering them the opportunity for restoration. It supports victims while also encouraging them to extend forgiveness. It upholds the law while also embodying grace.

Congregational Engagement in Restorative Justice

The church's engagement with restorative justice is not merely a matter of occasional programs or specialized ministries but of congregational culture and identity. When a church embraces restorative justice, it commits to becoming a community in which these principles are embodied in all aspects of its life.

Promoting understanding is the first task of congregational engagement. Members need to understand what restorative justice is, why it matters, and how it relates to their faith. This understanding can be cultivated through sermons that address biblical themes of justice and reconciliation, study groups that explore restorative justice literature, workshops that teach restorative practices, and testimonies from those who have experienced restorative processes.

A well-informed congregation is better equipped to support and implement restorative justice principles. When members understand the biblical foundations, they can ground their practice in faith. When they understand the practical applications, they can identify opportunities for restorative responses. When they understand the challenges and complexities, they can engage with wisdom and humility.

Creating a supportive environment is essential. The church community can become a safe and supportive space for those affected by harm or conflict. This means cultivating a culture of welcome, acceptance, and care—a culture in which people feel safe to share their struggles, to ask for help, to seek healing.

Congregational members can offer emotional and spiritual support to victims and offenders. They can listen without judgment, pray without ceasing, accompany without controlling. They can provide practical assistance—meals, transportation, childcare—to those in crisis. They can create small groups and support networks that sustain people through the long journey of healing.

Conflict resolution is a key area for congregational engagement. Churches, like all human communities, experience conflicts—disagreements over vision, disputes between members, tensions between leaders. These conflicts can divide congregations, damage relationships, and undermine witness. Restorative justice provides a framework for addressing these conflicts in a way that promotes healing rather than division.

When conflicts arise, church leaders can employ restorative principles. They can encourage open dialogue, creating safe spaces for all parties to express their perspectives. They can help parties understand the impact of their words and actions on others, fostering empathy and compassion. They can encourage accountability, calling each person to take responsibility for their part in the conflict. They can facilitate making amends, helping parties find ways to repair harm. And they can work toward reconciliation, seeking to restore relationships and rebuild trust.

Accountability is vital for congregational health. Churches must be communities in which people are held responsible for their actions, in which harmful behavior is addressed, in which consequences are clear. This accountability should be restorative rather than punitive—aimed at healing rather than hurting, at restoration rather than exclusion.

Churches can model accountability by establishing clear expectations for behavior, by creating processes for addressing complaints, by providing support for those who have been harmed, and by offering opportunities for those who have caused harm to make amends. They can demonstrate that accountability is not opposed to grace but is one of its expressions—that love sometimes means confronting, that care sometimes means correcting.

Reconciliation is the goal of all these efforts. The church is called to be a community of reconciliation—a place where broken relationships are mended, where estranged parties are brought together, where forgiveness is extended and received. This reconciliation is not merely a human achievement but a gift of the Spirit, a sign of God's reconciling work in Christ.

Congregations can actively promote reconciliation, both within the church and in the broader community. They can host reconciliation services, where people are invited to seek and extend forgiveness. They can offer mediation services, helping parties in conflict find resolution. They can build bridges across divisions of race, class, and culture, demonstrating that reconciliation is possible even in a fractured world.

Ministry and outreach extend restorative justice beyond the church's walls. The church is not called to be a closed community but a light to the world, a city on a hill, a sign of God's kingdom. Restorative justice provides a framework for this outward mission, guiding the church's engagement with societal issues.

Churches can support victims of crime, offering counseling, advocacy, and practical assistance. They can advocate for criminal justice reform, pushing for policies that emphasize rehabilitation and restoration rather than mere punishment. They can establish reentry programs, helping formerly incarcerated individuals rebuild their lives. They can engage in community-building initiatives, fostering relationships and trust among diverse groups. They can educate the public about restorative justice, raising awareness and building support. They can participate in social justice campaigns, addressing the root causes of crime and conflict.

Moral leadership is a crucial aspect of the church's engagement with restorative justice. The church, through its leaders and members, can provide a prophetic voice in the public square, advocating for a vision of justice that reflects God's character and purposes.

This moral leadership involves advocating for compassion in the criminal justice system, emphasizing the need to view offenders as individuals capable of healing and restoration rather than merely as wrongdoers deserving punishment. It means encouraging a shift from retribution to rehabilitation, from punishment to restoration. It means supporting victim-centered approaches that prioritize the healing and well-being of those who have been harmed. It means promoting reconciliation as a goal of justice, facilitating dialogue and forgiveness between offenders and victims. It means addressing systemic injustices, working to eliminate disparities and biases that disproportionately affect marginalized populations.

Victim Support in the Church

Victim support is imperative for restorative justice, and the church plays a vital role in this crucial aspect of the work. Victims of crime and conflict carry deep wounds—physical, emotional, psychological, spiritual. These wounds require care, and the church is uniquely positioned to provide it.

Compassion and empathy are the foundation of victim support. Restorative justice emphasizes empathy for those who have suffered harm, and the church, rooted in Christian teachings, exemplifies these values by extending care and support to victims. This compassion is not merely a feeling but a practice—a commitment to entering into another's suffering, to bearing their burden, to walking with them through pain.

When the church extends compassion to victims, it aligns with both Christian values and restorative justice principles. It acknowledges the reality of their pain, validates their experience, and communicates that they are not alone. This acknowledgment is itself healing, countering the isolation and invisibility that victims often feel.

Healing and restoration are the goals of victim support. Victims often go through traumatic experiences that leave lasting scars. The church can provide a safe space for victims to heal—a place where they can be honest about their pain, where they can seek counseling and support, where they can find comfort in their faith. This healing process is essential for restoring victims' well-being, in line with restorative justice's focus on repairing harm.

Healing takes time and often requires professional help. Churches can connect victims with counselors who specialize in trauma, support groups where they can share with others who have suffered similarly, and spiritual directors who can help them navigate the questions of faith that arise from suffering. They can provide practical assistance—help with daily tasks, financial support, advocacy with systems—that eases the burden and creates space for healing.

Dignity and worth are central to victim support. Restorative justice places strong emphasis on recognizing the inherent dignity and worth of every individual, and supporting victims in their journey to recovery is a practical way to affirm this dignity. The church's role in this process aligns with the Christian belief in the sanctity of human life—that every person is created in God's image and possesses infinite value.

When victims are treated with dignity, they are empowered to reclaim their sense of worth. When their voices are heard, their needs are addressed, their suffering is acknowledged, they are reminded that they matter. This restoration of dignity is essential for healing and for the prevention of future harm.

Rebuilding trust is a crucial aspect of victim support. Victims often feel a loss of trust in their community and the world at large. The church, through its consistent presence and faithful care, can contribute to rebuilding this trust. When victims experience the church as a safe and supportive community, they begin to trust again—not only in others but in the possibility of healing and restoration.

This restoration of trust is a fundamental aspect of restorative justice. It means that victims can again believe that the world is not entirely hostile, that others can be relied upon, that relationships can be safe. This trust enables them to reengage with community, to form new connections, to move forward with their lives.

Community and belonging are essential for victim support. The church serves as a community of faith and belonging, a place where people are known and loved. By providing support for victims, the church reinforces the idea that victims are not alone in their suffering. They are part of a body, members of a family, participants in a story larger than their own.

Restorative justice seeks to repair the social bonds that are strained by harm, and the church plays a key role in reestablishing a sense of community. When victims are embraced by the church, they experience belonging that counters the isolation of victimization. When they are surrounded by care, they find strength for the journey of healing.

Moral and ethical responsibility compels the church to support victims. For the church, extending support to victims is not optional but essential—a reflection of the Christian commitment to love, compassion, and helping those in need. This sense of responsibility resonates with the restorative justice principle of addressing the needs of those who have been harmed.

The church's support for victims is not charity but justice—not an optional extra but a core obligation. It flows from the conviction that every person matters, that suffering should not be ignored, that the wounded must be cared for. It is an expression of the love that lies at the heart of the gospel.

Promoting forgiveness and reconciliation is a delicate but important aspect of victim support. Restorative justice encourages processes of forgiveness and reconciliation, recognizing that these can be healing for victims as well as offenders. While forgiveness and reconciliation are personal journeys that cannot be forced, the church can offer guidance and a spiritual foundation for individuals seeking to forgive or reconcile with those who have caused harm.

This guidance must be offered with sensitivity and respect. Victims should never be pressured to forgive before they are ready or to reconcile when it is not safe. But they can be supported in exploring the possibility of forgiveness, in understanding what it means and what it does not mean, in discerning whether and when to extend it. The church can provide a safe space for this exploration, trusting the Spirit to lead each person in their own time and way.

Advocacy for victims is another aspect of the church's role. The church can advocate for the rights and needs of victims within the wider community and even in the criminal justice system. This advocacy is in alignment with the restorative justice principle of ensuring that victims have a voice in the process.

When the church advocates for victims, it speaks truth to power, challenging systems that sideline or silence those who have been harmed. It demands that victims be heard, that their needs be addressed, that their rights be protected. It works for policies and practices that support victim healing and prevent further victimization.

Promoting Reconciliation in the Christian Community

Promoting reconciliation within the Christian community involves the active participation of various individuals and groups. Reconciliation is not a solo project but a collaborative endeavor, requiring the engagement of the whole body of Christ.

Church leaders play a pivotal role in promoting reconciliation. Pastors, priests, elders, and other leaders set the tone for the entire congregation. When they prioritize reconciliation, when they model forgiveness, when they address conflicts openly and honestly, they create a culture in which reconciliation can flourish.

Leaders can provide guidance, counsel, and pastoral care to individuals and families in conflict. They can preach and teach on themes of forgiveness and reconciliation, grounding these practices in Scripture and tradition. They can establish structures and processes that support restorative responses to conflict. Their leadership is essential for creating a congregation that embodies restorative justice.

Church members are a significant part of the reconciliation process. The congregation itself is ideally positioned to model reconciliation for the broader society. When members support one another in times of conflict, offer forgiveness to those who have wronged them, and extend a helping hand to those in need, they demonstrate what reconciled community looks like.

This modeling is not merely for internal benefit but for external witness. When the world sees a community in which conflicts are resolved, relationships are restored, and forgiveness is practiced, it sees a sign of God's kingdom. The church's internal life becomes an advertisement for the gospel, an invitation to the reconciliation that God offers in Christ.

Counselors and mediators can be valuable resources within the church. Trained professionals can facilitate communication, help resolve disputes, and guide individuals and families toward reconciliation. Their expertise is especially important when conflicts involve complex dynamics when emotions are high, when communication has broken down, when past wounds complicate present disagreements.

Churches can invest in training members as mediators and counselors, building internal capacity for restorative work. They can also partner with outside professionals who can provide specialized services when needed. By making these resources available, churches demonstrate their commitment to healing and reconciliation.

Families are often at the heart of conflicts, and their involvement is essential for reconciliation. The church places strong emphasis on the importance of family, recognizing that families are the primary context for formation and relationship. When conflicts arise within families, the church can support parents, children, and extended family members as they work together to heal relational wounds and restore harmony.

This support might include pastoral counseling, family mediation, support groups for parents or children, and educational programs on communication and conflict resolution. It might involve helping families draw on their faith resources—prayer, Scripture, worship—as they navigate difficult situations. The goal is to strengthen families as units of healing and reconciliation.

Small groups and support networks provide intimate settings for reconciliation. Many churches organize small groups—Bible studies, prayer groups, fellowship gatherings—where members can share their struggles, receive emotional support, and explore ways to reconcile with one another. These groups create the trust and intimacy that make honest conversation possible.

When conflicts arise within small groups, leaders can employ restorative principles to address them. When members are struggling with relationships outside the group, the group can provide prayer, encouragement, and accountability. Small groups become laboratories of reconciliation, places where members practice the skills and dispositions that restorative justice requires.

Community engagement extends reconciliation beyond the church's walls. Churches can engage with the broader community to promote reconciliation in society at large. This can involve outreach programs that bring together diverse groups, community service that builds bridges across divides, and advocacy for peace and reconciliation in the public square.

When churches engage in this broader work, they demonstrate that reconciliation is not merely a private concern but a public good. They witness to the possibility of healing even in the most divided communities. They become agents of shalom, working for the peace and flourishing of the whole society.

Prayer and spiritual guidance are central to the Christian approach to reconciliation. The church community can come together in prayer to seek God's guidance and strength in the process of reconciliation. Prayer opens hearts to grace, softens resistance to forgiveness, and sustains hope when reconciliation seems impossible.

Spiritual guidance helps individuals navigate the inner dimensions of reconciliation—the anger, fear, and grief that must be addressed before forgiveness can be extended. Pastors, spiritual directors, and mature believers can walk with those who are struggling, helping them discern the Spirit's leading and find the strength to take the next step.

Restorative justice ministries are specialized expressions of the church's commitment to reconciliation. Some churches have dedicated ministries or teams focused on restorative justice. These groups address conflicts, promote healing, and actively practice restorative justice principles within the church and in the community.

These ministries might offer mediation services, facilitate victim-offender dialogues, support reentry programs, or advocate for criminal justice reform. They might train church members in restorative practices, develop resources for restorative responses, and build partnerships with community organizations. They become centers of expertise and energy for restorative justice within the church.

Youth and children play a significant role in fostering reconciliation. Younger members of the church can be shaped by restorative values from an early age. Youth groups and children's ministries can instill values of forgiveness, empathy, and conflict resolution, contributing to a culture of reconciliation in the future.

When children learn to apologize sincerely, to forgive generously, to resolve conflicts peacefully, they are being formed in restorative ways. When youth practice these skills in their relationships, they become witnesses to their peers. Investing in the next generation is investing in the future of restorative justice.

Outreach to the marginalized is a crucial aspect of promoting reconciliation. The church can engage with marginalized and vulnerable individuals and communities, offering reconciliation and healing to those who have been excluded or harmed by society. This outreach embodies the gospel's concern for the poor, the oppressed, and the outcast.

When the church reaches out to prisoners, refugees, the homeless, and others on the margins, it demonstrates that reconciliation is for everyone. It challenges the divisions that separate people and builds bridges across the deepest chasms. It becomes a sign of God's inclusive love, a foretaste of the reconciled humanity that God intends.

Reconciliation services provide structured opportunities for healing and unity. Some churches hold specific reconciliation services or events, where individuals are encouraged to come forward and seek forgiveness or reconciliation with others. These services can be powerful catalysts for healing and unity, creating sacred space for the hard work of reconciliation.

In these services, the church gathers as a community of confession and forgiveness. People are invited to name their sins, to seek and extend forgiveness, to celebrate restored relationships. The service may include Scripture readings, prayers, testimonies, and symbolic actions that embody reconciliation. It culminates in the sharing of peace and the celebration of Eucharist, the sacrament of unity.

Education and awareness are essential for promoting reconciliation. Churches can educate their members about the importance of reconciliation, forgiveness, and restorative justice. By raising awareness, they empower individuals to actively pursue reconciliation in their lives. Education can take many forms—sermons, classes, workshops, books, articles, videos, conferences.

When members understand the biblical foundations of reconciliation, they are grounded in faith. When they learn the practical skills of conflict resolution, they are equipped for action. When they hear stories of reconciliation, they are inspired to hope. Education creates the conditions for a culture of reconciliation to flourish.

Moral Leadership in Restorative Justice

Moral leadership in the context of restorative justice involves the church community and its leaders taking a principled and ethical stand in advocating for restorative practices in the criminal justice system. This leadership is rooted in the teachings of Jesus and the apostles, and it takes concrete form in various aspects of public engagement.

Advocating for compassion is a primary task of moral leadership. Moral leaders within the church promote compassion as a central value in the criminal justice system. They emphasize the need to view offenders as individuals in need of healing and restoration, rather than solely as wrongdoers deserving punishment. This compassionate perspective does not minimize the seriousness of crime but insists that offenders remain human beings, created in God's image, capable of change and worthy of dignity.

Compassion in criminal justice means treating offenders with respect, providing opportunities for rehabilitation, and supporting their reintegration into society. It means recognizing the humanity even of those who have committed terrible acts, refusing to reduce them to their worst deeds. This compassionate approach is not soft on crime but deep on humanity, recognizing that true justice must be just for all.

Rehabilitation over retribution is a key emphasis of moral leadership. Leaders advocate for a shift from retribution-focused approaches to rehabilitation-focused ones. They encourage policies and practices that prioritize the rehabilitation of offenders, aiming to address the root causes of their actions and prevent future harm. This shift reflects the restorative justice conviction that accountability should lead to transformation, not merely to punishment.

Rehabilitation addresses the underlying issues that contribute to criminal behavior—addiction, mental illness, poverty, trauma, lack of education or employment. It provides offenders with the tools they need to change, the support they need to sustain change, and the opportunities they need to build new lives. It invests in human flourishing rather than merely in incapacitation.

Supporting victim-centered approaches is another aspect of moral leadership. Moral leaders acknowledge the importance of supporting victims of crime and advocating for their needs. They work to ensure that restorative justice practices prioritize the healing and well-being of victims, allowing them to participate in the process and have their voices heard.

Victim-centered approaches recognize that victims have been directly harmed and that their needs should be central to any just response. They provide victims with information, support, and opportunities to participate. They respect victims' choices about whether and how to engage. They seek to restore victims' sense of dignity, safety, and control.

Promoting reconciliation is a core emphasis of moral leadership. The church's moral leaders emphasize the transformative power of reconciliation. They encourage criminal justice systems to incorporate restorative justice principles that facilitate dialogue, forgiveness, and the rebuilding of trust between offenders and victims.

Reconciliation does not mean that the harm is forgotten or minimized. It means that the parties find a way to move forward, to coexist, to build a future not defined by the past. It may involve apology and forgiveness, restitution and reparation, changed behavior and restored trust. It is a process, not an event, and it requires commitment from all parties.

Healing and restoration are the ultimate goals of moral leadership. Moral leaders advocate for the inclusion of healing and restoration as core components of the criminal justice process. They recognize that true justice involves not only addressing the harm caused by offenses but also helping individuals rebuild their lives in a positive and productive manner.

Healing addresses the wounds that crime inflicts—on victims, on offenders, on communities. Restoration seeks to make things right, to repair what was broken, to restore what was lost. This is a more demanding vision of justice than mere punishment, but it is also a more hopeful one. It believes that even the worst situations can be redeemed, that even the most broken people can be healed.

Addressing systemic injustices is a crucial aspect of moral leadership. Church leaders, as moral advocates, address systemic injustices within the criminal justice system. They work to eliminate disparities and biases that disproportionately affect marginalized and vulnerable populations. They recognize that restorative justice must be applied justly, not merely as another tool of the powerful.

Systemic injustices include racial disparities in arrest, conviction, and sentencing; economic inequalities that affect access to quality legal representation; and biases against immigrants, the mentally ill, and other marginalized groups. Addressing these injustices requires more than individual compassion; it requires structural change. Moral leaders advocate for this change, working for a justice system that treats all people fairly.

Educational initiatives are essential for moral leadership. Moral leaders within the church take an active role in educating their congregations and the broader community about the principles of restorative justice. They raise awareness of the potential for transformation and healing through these practices, and they equip others to become advocates and practitioners.

Education can take many forms—sermons, classes, workshops, conferences, publications, media. It can target different audiences—church members, community leaders, justice system professionals, policymakers. It can cover different topics—biblical foundations, practical skills, policy implications, personal stories. The goal is to build a movement of people informed and inspired to pursue restorative justice.

Prayer and spiritual guidance sustain moral leadership. Moral leaders engage in prayer and spiritual guidance to seek wisdom and strength in their advocacy for restorative justice. They encourage their congregations to pray for both victims and offenders, emphasizing the importance of spiritual support in the healing process.

Prayer connects advocacy to its deepest source—the God who loves justice and mercy. It reminds leaders that they are not alone, that they are part of a larger story, that ultimate success is in God's hands. It sustains hope when progress is slow and discouragement threatens. It opens hearts to the Spirit's guidance, discerning the next steps in the journey.

Community engagement extends moral leadership beyond the church's walls. Church leaders engage with the broader community—law enforcement agencies, policymakers, advocacy groups, other faith communities—to promote restorative justice principles and advocate for criminal justice reform. They build coalitions, forge partnerships, and amplify their voices through collaboration.

This engagement requires humility and respect. Church leaders must listen as well as speak, learn as well as teach, follow as well as lead. They must recognize that they do not have all the answers and that wisdom is found in many places. But their presence in the public square is essential, bearing witness to a vision of justice rooted in faith.

Policy and legislative advocacy is a practical expression of moral leadership. Moral leaders may engage in policy and legislative advocacy to bring about changes in the criminal justice system. They work with lawmakers to develop and support legislation that aligns with restorative justice principles. They mobilize their congregations to contact elected officials, to vote for just policies, to hold leaders accountable.

This advocacy requires political skill and strategic thinking. It involves understanding how laws are made, building relationships with key decision-makers, crafting effective messages, and mobilizing grassroots support. It requires patience and persistence, recognizing that policy change is often slow and incremental. But it is essential for translating restorative principles into systemic reality.

Nonviolent resistance may be necessary when systems are deeply unjust. Moral leaders may advocate for nonviolent resistance to oppressive or punitive measures within the criminal justice system. This can include peaceful protests, civil disobedience, and public awareness campaigns that challenge unjust laws and practices.

Nonviolent resistance follows in the tradition of the prophets, of Jesus, of the early church, of movements for justice throughout history. It refuses to cooperate with injustice while also refusing to use violence to oppose it. It seeks to awaken consciences, to change hearts, to transform systems through the power of truth and love.

Case Studies in Restorative Justice

Case studies are essential for understanding and advancing restorative justice. These real-life examples or stories illustrate the practical application of restorative justice principles within the Christian community. They serve multiple purposes in the work of education, advocacy, and practice.

Concrete illustration is the primary purpose of case studies. They provide tangible examples of how restorative justice is put into practice, giving readers a clear understanding of how the principles discussed in theory are applied in real-life situations. Abstract concepts become vivid when embodied in stories. Principles come alive when seen in action.

A case study might describe a victim-offender mediation session, showing how the facilitator created a safe space, how the victim expressed their pain, how the offender took responsibility, how an agreement was reached. It might tell the story of a church that used restorative circles to address a conflict, describing the process step by step and the outcome achieved. These concrete illustrations make restorative justice accessible and understandable.

Inspiration is another purpose of case studies. They can inspire individuals, churches, and communities to adopt restorative justice practices. When people see successful examples and positive outcomes, they are more likely to become motivated to implement similar approaches. Hope is contagious; stories of healing inspire others to believe that healing is possible.

A case study might describe a victim who found closure through meeting the offender, an offender whose life was transformed through restorative processes, a community that was strengthened by addressing conflict restoratively. These stories ignite imagination, sparking the question: Could this happen here? Could we do this? The answer, often, is yes.

Learning opportunities are provided by case studies. By examining case studies, readers can learn from both the successes and challenges faced by others. They can gain insights into what works well and what pitfalls to avoid when implementing restorative justice within a Christian context. Each story becomes a teacher, offering lessons that can be applied in new situations.

A case study might reveal the importance of thorough preparation, the challenges of working with resistant parties, the need for ongoing support after the formal process ends. It might show how cultural factors shaped the process, how theological resources were used, how the community was engaged. These lessons are invaluable for practitioners.

Contextual relevance is enhanced by case studies. They can be tailored to specific contexts, allowing readers to relate to situations and challenges that are similar to their own. A rural congregation might learn from another rural church's experience; an urban ministry might draw lessons from a similar urban setting. This contextual relevance makes the application of restorative justice more relatable and achievable.

Testimonials of transformation are powerful aspects of case studies. They often highlight stories of personal transformation, redemption, and reconciliation. These stories emphasize the positive impact of restorative justice and demonstrate that individuals can change and make amends. They bear witness to the power of grace to transform even the most broken lives.

A case study might tell of an offender who, through restorative processes, came to understand the harm they had caused, experienced genuine remorse, made amends to the victim, and went on to become a mentor to others. It might tell of a victim who, through meeting the offender, found healing from trauma, released years of anger, and discovered a new purpose in advocating for restorative justice. These testimonials are powerful evidence of restorative justice's potential.

Demonstration of Christian values is another purpose of case studies. They can showcase how restorative justice aligns with Christian values of love, forgiveness, and reconciliation. They demonstrate how the principles derived from the teachings of Romans and the Gospels can be put into action. They show that restorative justice is not merely a secular concept but a faithful expression of Christian faith.

Building support is facilitated by sharing successful case studies. They help build support for restorative justice initiatives within the church and the broader community. They serve as evidence of the effectiveness of these practices, countering skepticism and resistance. When people see that restorative justice works, they are more likely to support its implementation.

Challenging stereotypes is an important function of case studies. They can challenge stereotypes and preconceptions about offenders and victims. They humanize the individuals involved and show that everyone has the potential for healing and transformation. They reveal the complexity behind simple judgments, the humanity behind crime statistics.

Promoting accountability is highlighted in case studies. They often highlight the importance of accountability and making amends, emphasizing that justice can be achieved through actions that repair harm. They show that accountability is not opposed to mercy but is one of its expressions—that taking responsibility is the first step toward restoration.

Fostering dialogue is the final purpose of case studies. These real-life stories can foster dialogue and discussion within the church community, encouraging members to consider the practical application of restorative justice principles in their own lives. They create common reference points, shared narratives around which conversation can occur.

In the context of restorative justice in the church, case studies serve as powerful tools for both education and advocacy. They demonstrate that restorative justice is not just a theoretical concept but a practical and effective approach that can lead to healing, reconciliation, and transformation within the Christian community. They provide the evidence that inspires action, the examples that guide practice, and the stories that sustain hope.

As the church continues to embrace restorative justice, the collection of case studies will grow. Each successful process, each healed relationship, each transformed life becomes a chapter in an ongoing story. These stories are not merely records of the past but seeds for the future. They plant hope in new hearts, inspire new initiatives, and build the movement for restorative justice in the church and beyond.

CHAPTER 06

HISTORICAL PERSPECTIVE OF JUSTICE

The story of justice is the story of civilization itself. From the earliest human communities to the most complex modern societies, the question of how to respond to wrongdoing has shaped our laws, our institutions, and our collective identity. To understand restorative justice—and to appreciate its profound resonance with the teachings of Jesus—we must first understand where our conceptions of justice have come from, how they have evolved over millennia, and why the restorative paradigm represents not a departure from the past but a recovery of wisdom as old as humanity itself.

This chapter traces the historical arc of justice, from ancient codes etched in stone to the emergence of restorative practices in our own time. We will explore the legal systems of ancient civilizations, the philosophical contributions of Greece and

Rome, the theological frameworks of medieval Europe, the revolutionary ideas of the Enlightenment, the development of modern legal systems, and the social justice movements of the twentieth century. We will also examine the rich traditions of restorative justice that have existed for millennia in Africa and other indigenous cultures—traditions that challenge the assumption that punitive justice is the only or the most advanced form of responding to harm. And we will consider the biblical foundations of restorative justice, discovering that the Scriptures have always pointed toward a justice that heals, restores, and reconciles.

Ancient Civilizations: The Dawn of Codified Justice

The earliest human communities likely handled wrongdoing through informal means—family negotiations, tribal councils, blood feuds, or simple retaliation. But as societies grew more complex, the need for formal systems of justice became apparent. The great civilizations of the ancient Near East produced the first written law codes, establishing principles that would influence legal thinking for millennia to come.

The Code of Ur-Nammu, dating to approximately 2100-2050 BCE, is the oldest known law code surviving today. Composed in the Sumerian language and inscribed on clay tablets, this code from ancient Mesopotamia already reveals a sophisticated approach to justice. It prescribed monetary compensation for bodily injuries rather than the physical retaliation that would appear in later codes. For example, if a man cut off another man's foot, he was required to pay ten shekels of silver. This emphasis on restitution rather than retribution anticipates restorative principles that would reemerge thousands of years later.

The Laws of Eshnunna, dating to around 1930 BCE, continued this tradition. These laws, inscribed on two cuneiform tablets discovered in modern-day Iraq, prescribed specific monetary penalties for various offenses. They also addressed issues of restitution for stolen property and compensation for victims of crime. The underlying assumption was that harm created obligations—obligations that could be fulfilled through payment to the victim.

The most famous of these ancient codes is the Code of Hammurabi, composed around 1755-1750 BCE during the reign of the sixth king of Babylon's First Dynasty. Hammurabi united Mesopotamia and established a vast empire, and his law code was designed to unify and regulate his diverse realm. The code originally contained nearly three hundred legal judgments, inscribed on a stele that stood in a public place so that all could see the laws that governed them.

The Code of Hammurabi is best known for its formulation of the lex talionis—the law of retaliation. "If a man has destroyed the eye of another man, they shall destroy his eye. If he has broken a man's bone, they shall break his bone. If a man has knocked out the tooth of a man of his own rank, they shall knock out his tooth." This principle of proportional retaliation—"an eye for an eye, a tooth for a tooth"—has often been misunderstood as a license for vengeance. In fact, it was a limit on vengeance. Before such codes, retaliation could escalate without limit; a minor injury could trigger a blood feud that destroyed entire families. The lex talionis established proportionality: no more than an eye for an eye, no more than a tooth for a tooth.

But the Code of Hammurabi also contained restorative elements. Many offenses were addressed through monetary compensation rather than physical punishment. Victims were to be compensated for the harms they suffered. Offenders were required to make restitution. The code recognized that crime injured not only the social order but specific individuals, and that justice required addressing those individual injuries.

These ancient codes reveal that from the very beginning of recorded history, human societies grappled with the tension between retribution and restoration. They understood that wrongdoing demanded a response, but they also recognized that victims had legitimate claims to compensation and that communities had an interest in resolving conflicts rather than perpetuating cycles of vengeance. The seeds of restorative justice were present at the dawn of civilization.

Classical Antiquity: Philosophy and the Idea of Justice

The Greek and Roman philosophers transformed thinking about justice, moving beyond the codification of rules to profound reflections on the nature of justice itself. They asked not only what the laws required but what justice meant, what it demanded, and how it related to human flourishing.

Plato, in his dialogue the Republic, explored justice as a virtue of both individuals and societies. For Plato, justice was harmony—each part of the soul and each class of society performing its proper function in right relation to the whole. The just person was one in whom reason ruled, spirit supported, and appetite obeyed. The just society was one in which rulers governed wisely, warriors defended courageously, and workers provided diligently. Justice was not merely a matter of laws and punishments but of right order and proper relationship.

Aristotle developed these ideas further, distinguishing between different forms of justice. Distributive justice concerned the fair distribution of goods, honors, and resources within a society—giving each person their due based on merit or need. Corrective justice concerned the rectification of wrongs—restoring the equilibrium that had been disturbed by injury or injustice. Aristotle recognized that different situations called for different forms of justice and that a complete understanding required attention to both.

The Roman jurists built upon Greek philosophy, developing a sophisticated legal system that would influence Western law for two millennia. Roman law distinguished between public and private wrongs, between crimes that offended the state and delicts that injured individuals. For private wrongs, the emphasis was on compensation—the offender must make good the loss suffered by the victim. This Roman emphasis on restitution and compensation preserved elements of restorative justice within a formal legal framework.

The Roman philosopher Cicero, in his work On Duties, articulated a vision of justice grounded in natural law—universal principles that transcended particular legal systems. He argued that justice required not harming others, respecting property, and fulfilling obligations. He emphasized the social nature of humanity and the importance of maintaining community through fair dealing and mutual respect.

Yet classical antiquity also saw the development of more punitive approaches, particularly in criminal law. The Roman state increasingly asserted its authority to punish offenders as a matter of public interest, not merely private compensation. Crimes came to be seen as offenses against the state, deserving of punishment inflicted by the state. This shift laid the groundwork for the punitive systems that would dominate Western justice for centuries.

Biblical Foundations: Justice in the Old Testament

While the philosophers of Greece and Rome were developing their understandings of justice, another tradition was emerging in ancient Israel—a tradition rooted not in human reason alone but in divine revelation. The Hebrew Scriptures present a vision of justice that is deeply restorative, grounded in the character of God and the covenant relationship between God and His people.

The foundation of biblical justice is the creation of humanity in the image of God (Genesis 1:26-27). Every human being bears the divine likeness, possesses inherent dignity, and deserves to be treated with respect. This imago Dei means that no person can be reduced to their actions, no offender can be defined solely by their offense. The image of God, though marred by sin, is never erased. Restoration, not merely punishment, is always possible because the divine image remains.

The Law of Moses developed this foundational insight into a comprehensive legal system. While the Torah includes provisions for punishment, its dominant concern is restoration. When an ox is stolen, the law requires restitution—five oxen for one (Exodus 22:1). The goal is not merely to punish the thief but to restore the victim, to compensate for the loss, to make the victim whole. When property is damaged, the law requires repayment (Exodus 22:5-6). When a person is injured, the law requires compensation for loss of time and healing (Exodus 21:18-19).

The lex talionis—"eye for eye, tooth for tooth"—appears in this context. But as we have seen, this principle was not a license for vengeance but a limit on it. It established proportionality and prevented escalation. Moreover, its application was often commuted to monetary compensation. The Mishnah, the written record of Jewish oral tradition, specifies that physical penalties were rarely if ever actually inflicted; instead, offenders paid the value of the injured body part to the victim.

The Law also established cities of refuge where those who had caused accidental death could flee from the avenger of blood (Numbers 35:9-34). This provision recognized the difference between intentional and unintentional harm and created space for justice to be tempered with mercy. It acknowledged that even in cases of death, restoration—or at least protection—was possible.

The prophets amplified this restorative vision. They thundered against a justice system that favored the powerful and ignored the vulnerable. They called Israel to a justice that went beyond ritual observance to active care for the oppressed. Isaiah declared: "Learn to do good; seek justice, rebuke the oppressor; defend the fatherless, plead for the widow" (Isaiah 1:17). Jeremiah proclaimed: "Execute judgment and righteousness, and deliver the plundered out of the hand of the oppressor" (Jeremiah 22:3). Amos thundered: "Let justice run down like water, and righteousness like a mighty stream" (Amos 5:24).

Micah famously distilled God's requirements: "He has shown you, O man, what is good; and what does the Lord require of you but to do justly, to love mercy, and to walk humbly with your God?" (Micah 6:8). Justice and mercy are not opposed but intertwined. Walking humbly with God means walking justly and mercifully with others.

The prophets also envisioned a future in which justice would flourish and peace would prevail. Isaiah saw a day when "justice will dwell in the wilderness and righteousness remain in the fruitful field. The work of righteousness will be peace, and the effect of righteousness, quietness and assurance forever" (Isaiah 32:16-17). Hosea foresaw a covenant of peace that would embrace all creation: "In that day I will make a covenant for them with the beasts of the field, with the birds of the air, and with the creeping things of the ground. Bow and sword of battle I will shatter from the earth, to make them lie down safely" (Hosea 2:18).

This prophetic vision is summed up in the concept of shalom—the Hebrew word for peace that denotes far more than the absence of conflict. Shalom means wholeness, completeness, flourishing, right relationship. It is the condition of life as God intended it to be—harmony between God and humanity, between humans and each other, within the human heart, and between humanity and creation. Justice, in the biblical vision, is the work of restoring shalom when it has been broken by sin and harm.

The Teachings of Jesus: Restorative Justice Incarnate

In the teachings and life of Jesus, the restorative justice of the Old Testament finds its fullest expression. Jesus did not come to abolish the Law and the Prophets but to fulfill them (Matthew 5:17)—to bring to completion their deepest intentions, to embody in His own person the justice they envisioned.

Jesus consistently prioritized mercy over sacrifice, compassion over ritual, restoration over condemnation. When the Pharisees criticized Him for eating with tax collectors and sinners, He replied: "Those who are well have no need of a physician, but those who are sick. But go and learn what this means: 'I desire mercy and not sacrifice.' For I did not come to call the righteous, but sinners, to repentance" (Matthew 9:12-13). His mission was to heal the broken, to restore the lost, to reconcile the estranged.

In the Sermon on the Mount, Jesus taught a justice that transcended mere retaliation. "You have heard that it was said, 'An eye for an eye and a tooth for a tooth.' But I tell you not to resist an evil person. But whoever slaps you on your right cheek, turn the other to him also" (Matthew 5:38-39). This teaching is not a call to passivity but a call to break the cycle of violence, to refuse the logic of retaliation, to open the door to a different way of responding to harm.

Jesus also taught the importance of reconciliation before worship: "Therefore if you bring your gift to the altar, and there remember that your brother has something against you, leave your gift there before the altar, and go your way. First be reconciled to your brother, and then come and offer your gift" (Matthew 5:23-24). Right relationship with God requires right relationship with others. Reconciliation is not optional but essential.

In the parable of the Good Samaritan (Luke 10:25-37), Jesus illustrated what restorative justice looks like in practice. The Samaritan did not ask whether the wounded man deserved help, whether he was of the right ethnicity or religion, whether helping would be convenient or costly. He saw a person in need, was moved with compassion, and acted to restore him to wholeness. This is justice as love in action.

In the parable of the Prodigal Son (Luke 15:11-32), Jesus portrayed the heart of God as one that runs to meet the returning sinner, that restores without demanding penance, that celebrates the recovery of the lost. The father's response is not punitive but restorative—he welcomes, he restores, he celebrates. This is the model for all who would practice restorative justice.

In the encounter with Zacchaeus (Luke 19:1-10), Jesus demonstrated that restoration requires accountability. When Zacchaeus, a tax collector who had defrauded many, encountered Jesus, he declared: "Look, Lord, I give half of my goods to the poor; and if I have taken anything from anyone by false accusation, I restore fourfold." Jesus responded: "Today salvation has come to this house." Restitution was evidence of genuine repentance and the fruit of restored relationship.

On the cross, Jesus embodied the ultimate act of restorative justice. As the soldiers drove nails through His hands and feet, as the religious leaders mocked Him, as the crowds passed by and hurled insults, Jesus prayed: "Father, forgive them, for they do not know what they do" (Luke 23:34). He absorbed the worst that humanity could do and responded with forgiveness. He opened the way for reconciliation between God and humanity, between humans and each other. This is the gospel of restorative justice: that in Christ, God was reconciling the world to Himself, not counting their trespasses against them (2 Corinthians 5:19).

Medieval Europe: Justice and the Church

With the decline of the Roman Empire and the rise of Christianity as the dominant religion of Europe, the administration of justice underwent significant changes. The Church emerged as a major institution for resolving disputes and maintaining order, while feudal lords exercised authority over their territories.

Canon law—the law of the Church—developed as a sophisticated legal system governing not only ecclesiastical matters but many aspects of daily life. Church courts handled cases involving clergy, marriage, inheritance, and moral offenses. The Church emphasized penance and reconciliation, requiring offenders to perform acts of restitution and to be reconciled with the community. This penitential system preserved elements of restorative justice within a religious framework.

At the same time, secular justice under feudalism was often harsh and arbitrary. Lords exercised authority over their domains, dispensing justice according to local custom and personal discretion. Punishments could be severe—execution, mutilation, branding, whipping. The concept of crime as an offense against the king's peace (rather than merely against individuals or local lords) began to emerge, laying the groundwork for the modern state's monopoly on criminal justice.

The medieval period also saw the development of trial by ordeal and trial by combat—methods of determining guilt that seem primitive to modern sensibilities but reflected the belief that divine intervention would reveal the truth. A defendant might be required to carry a hot iron or be thrown into water; if the wound healed cleanly or they sank (considered innocent because the water, blessed, received them), they were acquitted. These practices gradually gave way to more rational methods of proof as the influence of Roman law and canon law grew.

Despite the harshness of much medieval justice, the influence of Christian theology moderated some tendencies toward pure retribution. The Church taught that even the worst sinners could repent and be forgiven. It provided sanctuary for those fleeing vengeance. It emphasized the duty of Christians to forgive one another. These teachings kept alive the restorative vision, even when practice fell short.

The Enlightenment: Reason, Rights, and the Social Contract

The Enlightenment of the seventeenth and eighteenth centuries revolutionized thinking about justice, law, and society. Philosophers began to ground justice not in divine revelation or ancient tradition but in human reason and natural rights. They imagined justice as emerging from a social contract—an agreement among free individuals to establish a system of laws for the common good.

Thomas Hobbes, in Leviathan (1651), portrayed the state of nature as a war of all against all, in which life was "solitary, poor, nasty, brutish, and short." To escape this condition, individuals surrendered their natural rights to a sovereign who would enforce laws and maintain order. Justice, for Hobbes, was whatever the sovereign commanded—a positivist view that divorced justice from any transcendent standard.

John Locke offered a more hopeful vision. In his Second Treatise of Government (1690), he argued that individuals in the state of nature possessed natural rights to life, liberty, and property. When these rights were violated, the offender incurred a debt to the victim—a debt that could be exacted through punishment. But Locke also emphasized that punishment must be proportionate and that the purpose of government was to protect rights, not merely to inflict pain.

Jean-Jacques Rousseau, in The Social Contract (1762), argued that legitimate political authority rests on the consent of the governed. Individuals surrender their natural freedom to the general will—the collective expression of the common good—and in return receive civil freedom and the protection of their rights. Justice, for Rousseau, is the expression of the general will, which aims at the good of all.

These social contract theorists laid the foundation for modern democratic governance and the rule of law. They emphasized that laws must be grounded in the consent of the governed, that government must be limited by the rights of individuals, and that justice requires fairness and impartiality. These principles would shape the development of modern legal systems.

But the Enlightenment also produced theories of punishment that emphasized retribution and deterrence. The most influential of these came from the German philosopher Immanuel Kant.

Immanuel Kant and Retributive Justice

Immanuel Kant, the great philosopher of the Enlightenment, developed a theory of punishment that has profoundly influenced Western thinking about justice. For Kant, the moral law—the categorical imperative—required that we treat persons as ends in themselves, never merely as means. This principle had profound implications for punishment.

Kant argued that punishment must be imposed because the offender deserves it—and for no other reason. Utilitarian justifications for punishment, such as deterrence or rehabilitation, treated the offender as a means to social ends, violating their dignity as a person. Only retribution—giving the offender what they deserve—respected them as moral agents capable of choosing their actions and responsible for their consequences.

For Kant, the severity of punishment must be proportionate to the gravity of the crime. This proportionality was not a matter of social utility but of moral necessity. The principle of lex talionis—"an eye for an eye"—provided the appropriate measure. Not because it satisfied vengeance but because it expressed the moral equivalence between crime and punishment.

Kant famously illustrated this with the example of an island society about to disband. Even if they were going to separate forever, he argued, they must first execute the last murderer in their prisons. Otherwise, they would all share in the guilt of the murder by failing to give the offender what they deserved. Punishment was not optional but obligatory, required by justice itself.

Kant's theory of retributive justice has been enormously influential. It underlies the common intuition that offenders must be punished because they deserve it—the principle of "just deserts." It shapes sentencing guidelines that seek to match punishment to crime. It justifies the infliction of suffering as a moral necessity, not merely a practical expedient.

But Kant's theory has also been subject to powerful critiques. Critics argue that it can lead to harsh and ineffective sentencing, that it ignores the social conditions that contribute to crime, that it offers nothing to victims, and that it fails to address the underlying causes of offending behavior. The exclusive focus on what offenders deserve leaves no room for mercy, for restoration, for the possibility of change.

Moreover, Kant's theory, for all its philosophical sophistication, stands in tension with the biblical vision of justice. The Scriptures do not deny that offenders deserve punishment—Paul writes that "the wages of sin is death" (Romans 6:23). But they insist that God's response to human sin is not merely to give us what we deserve but to offer us what we do not deserve—grace, forgiveness, reconciliation. The gospel announces that in Christ, God was reconciling the world to Himself, not counting our trespasses against us (2 Corinthians 5:19). This is a justice that transcends retribution, a justice that seeks not merely to give us what we deserve but to restore us to right relationship.

Modern Legal Systems: Due Process and the Rule of Law

The nineteenth and twentieth centuries saw the development of modern legal systems as we know them today. Democratic institutions, codified laws, professional judiciaries, and established procedures created frameworks for justice that aimed to be fair, consistent, and impartial.

Key principles emerged that now characterize modern legal systems. Due process requires that legal proceedings be conducted fairly, with notice and opportunity to be heard. The presumption of innocence holds that accused persons are considered innocent until proven guilty. The right to counsel ensures that even the poorest defendant has legal representation. The separation of powers distributes authority among legislative, executive, and judicial branches, preventing any single institution from becoming too powerful.

These principles represent significant advances in the administration of justice. They protect the rights of the accused, ensure fair treatment, and guard against arbitrary power. They reflect the Enlightenment commitment to human dignity and the rule of law.

Yet modern legal systems also have profound limitations. They are primarily adversarial, pitting prosecution against defense in a contest that often obscures truth and marginalizes victims. They are overwhelmingly punitive, focusing on punishment rather than restoration. They are expensive and inefficient, consuming vast resources while often failing to achieve their stated goals. And they are marked by deep disparities—racial, economic, and social—that undermine their claim to impartiality.

The prison, which emerged as the primary form of punishment in the nineteenth century, exemplifies these limitations. Originally promoted as a humane alternative to corporal and capital punishment, prisons were intended to reform offenders through discipline and labor. In practice, they have become places of violence, degradation, and despair—factories of crime rather than schools of virtue. Recidivism rates remain stubbornly high; about two-thirds of released prisoners are rearrested within three years. Prisons do not rehabilitate, do not deter, do not satisfy victims, and do not make communities safer. They simply incapacitate, at enormous cost.

The biblical witness offers a different vision. When Joseph was imprisoned in Egypt, the Lord was with him and showed him steadfast love (Genesis 39:21). When Peter was imprisoned by Herod, the church prayed earnestly for him, and an angel of the Lord set him free (Acts 12:5-11). When Paul and Silas were imprisoned in Philippi, they prayed and sang hymns to God, and their witness led to the conversion of their jailer (Acts 16:25-34). Prison could not contain the power of God or the witness of the faithful.

The Scriptures also speak to those who are imprisoned. To the guilty, they offer the possibility of forgiveness and new life through Christ. To the innocent, they offer patience, hope, and the assurance of God's presence. To all, they offer the promise that the day will come when prisoners will be freed, when captives will be released, when the chains of injustice will be broken (Isaiah 61:1).

Social Justice Movements: Expanding the Vision of Justice

The twentieth century witnessed the emergence of powerful social justice movements that expanded the understanding of justice beyond criminal law to encompass social and economic dimensions. These movements challenged the assumption that justice could be achieved simply through fair legal procedures, insisting that genuine justice must address systemic inequalities and structural oppression.

The civil rights movement in the United States confronted the brutal reality of racial injustice—segregation, discrimination, violence, and exclusion. Leaders like Martin Luther King Jr. drew on biblical prophecy and Gandhian nonviolence to demand not merely legal equality but genuine human dignity. King's vision of the "beloved community" envisioned a society in which all people could flourish, in which justice would roll down like waters and righteousness like an ever-flowing stream.

The feminist movement challenged patriarchal structures that excluded women from full participation in society. It demanded not only legal rights but social transformation—changes in attitudes, institutions, and relationships that would enable women to live with dignity and equality. The personal, feminists insisted, is political; justice must address the intimate as well as the public dimensions of life.

The human rights movement, emerging from the horrors of World War II, articulated a vision of universal rights belonging to every person simply by virtue of their humanity. The Universal Declaration of Human Rights (1948) proclaimed that "all human beings are born free and equal in dignity and rights" and enumerated rights to life, liberty, security, education, work, and participation in cultural life. This vision transcends national boundaries and legal systems, insisting on the inherent worth of every person.

Liberation theology, emerging from Latin America in the 1960s and 1970s, articulated a vision of justice rooted in God's preferential option for the poor. Theologians like Gustavo Gutiérrez argued that the gospel demands not merely charity toward the poor but solidarity with them in their struggle for justice. True justice requires transformation of the social structures that create and perpetuate poverty.

These movements have profoundly influenced restorative justice. They have insisted that justice cannot be reduced to legal procedures or criminal punishment. They have demonstrated that systemic injustices—racism, sexism, poverty, exclusion—are themselves forms of harm that must be addressed. They have shown that genuine justice requires not merely treating individuals fairly but transforming the conditions that produce and perpetuate harm.

Indigenous Traditions: Restorative Justice as Ancient Wisdom

While Western legal systems have been dominated by punitive approaches, many indigenous cultures around the world have maintained restorative traditions for millennia. These traditions are not primitive precursors to more advanced systems but sophisticated approaches to justice that embody wisdom Western societies are only now beginning to recover.

In Africa, restorative justice has deep historical roots that extend far back before European colonization. Scholars like Mangena (2011) have documented that the origins of restorative justice run deep across the continent, regardless of the nomenclature employed. These indigenous systems represent not a departure from tradition but a return to it—a recovery of practices that sustained communities for generations before colonial powers imposed foreign legal systems.

In Tanzania, the Kinga community of the southern highlands practiced restorative justice for millennia. When conflicts arose between family members or clans, the community gathered for reconciliation. Seated in a circular arrangement around a communal fire—a setting called Lugono that resembled a court—community members engaged in dialogue about the harm that had occurred. A complainant would recount the incident, and the defendant would respond to the accusations, presenting their defense.

The goal of these gatherings was not to determine who could make the most convincing case but to uncover the truth.

Through questioning and dialogue, the community assisted in unraveling the complexities of the problem and understanding its root causes. This pursuit of truth distinguished the restorative system from adversarial approaches that emphasize winning arguments rather than discovering what actually happened.

For the offender, truth-telling was essential. They had to voluntarily confess or acknowledge responsibility for their words, actions, or inaction that resulted in harm. Displaying genuine remorse was a prerequisite for reconciliation. Once the truth was revealed, accepted, and responsibility acknowledged, the path to restoration unfolded naturally. Repairing and restoring the fractured relationship became the central objective.

The reconciliation process reached its culmination with communal rituals that symbolized restored relationship. These included the sharing of locally brewed alcohol (ukupelanila ulupelo) and the consumption of roasted meat (okukatelanila inyama), in which disputants cut pieces of meat and each party consumed their share. A symbolic act of reconciliation occurred through the blowing of a special medicinal substance (ukupulilanila untuguva) into each individual's face. These rituals embodied the restoration of relationship, the healing of the breach, the rebuilding of community.

The approach varied based on the severity of the wrongdoing. Minor conflicts, such as insults, were typically left to the parties concerned for resolution. More serious offenses necessitated the engagement of clan members and the broader community. In all cases, the urgency of resolving conflicts quickly was recognized, as unresolved disputes could cause further harm and suffering.

In Nigeria, various communities embraced restorative practices with similar emphases. Omale (2006) underscores the significance of reconciliation and its ceremonial aspects: to ensure genuine reconciliation following dispute mediation, both parties might partake in shared activities such as eating from the same bowl, drinking palm wine or local gin from the same cup, and breaking and consuming kola nuts. These shared activities symbolized the restoration of unity, the rebuilding of trust, the healing of community.

African communities, guided by their collective wisdom, recognized that social cohesion rested on truth, understanding root causes, and practicing reconciliation. Unearthing the truth behind events and motives required the active involvement of all community members in candid discussions about specific wrongs, problems, and conflicts. Consequently, these mechanisms empowered ordinary people to freely participate in addressing disputes without interference from a centralized and distant state authority.

The colonial imposition of Western legal systems disrupted these indigenous practices. Post-independence African nations largely retained the legal systems of their colonizers—systems that have proven ill-suited to resolving the conflicts afflicting these nations. As Ndiaye (2012) notes, scholars and researchers have been prompted to revisit African traditional practices and their relevance in a post-colonial state. While indigenous justice systems are not flawless, discarding them entirely in favor of Western models risks erasing cultural practices and perpetuating the denigration of African ideas and values.

The Emergence of Modern Restorative Justice

The late twentieth century witnessed the emergence of restorative justice as a formal movement, drawing on these diverse historical streams—biblical tradition, indigenous wisdom, victim advocacy, and critique of punitive systems. Practitioners and scholars began to articulate a coherent framework for justice that prioritized healing over punishment, relationship over retribution, community over isolation.

The modern restorative justice movement has its roots in several developments. The Mennonite Central Committee, drawing on Anabaptist traditions of peacemaking and community, pioneered victim-offender reconciliation programs in Canada in the 1970s. These programs brought together victims and offenders in facilitated meetings, allowing them to address the harm and work toward resolution.

In New Zealand, the Children, Young Persons and Their Families Act of 1989 formally incorporated Maori restorative practices into the juvenile justice system. Family group conferences brought together victims, offenders, and their families to discuss the offense and develop plans for accountability and restoration. This model has been widely adopted and adapted around the world.

In the United States, restorative justice programs have proliferated at every level of the justice system—from school disciplinary programs to juvenile diversion initiatives to adult criminal cases. The United States Department of Justice has recognized the potential of restorative justice, funding programs and supporting research that demonstrates its effectiveness in reducing recidivism, increasing victim satisfaction, and doing so at lower cost than traditional incarceration.

The United Nations has endorsed restorative justice, adopting Basic Principles on the Use of Restorative Justice Programmes in Criminal Matters in 2002. These principles encourage member states to develop restorative approaches, establish standards for practice, and ensure that restorative processes respect the rights of all parties.

Today, restorative justice is practiced in diverse contexts around the world—from post-apartheid South Africa, where the Truth and Reconciliation Commission applied restorative principles to address massive human rights abuses, to the favelas of Brazil, where restorative circles have helped reduce violence and build community, to the schools of Australia, where restorative practices have transformed disciplinary culture and reduced bullying.

The Assumptions of Retributive Justice: A Critical Examination

Despite the growing influence of restorative justice, the dominant paradigm in most legal systems remains retributive. Understanding this paradigm—its assumptions, its logic, its limitations—is essential for appreciating what restorative justice offers.

When we identify something as a crime, a number of basic assumptions shape our responses. These assumptions are so deeply ingrained that they often go unexamined, yet they determine the entire shape of our justice system.

First, we assume that guilt must be assigned. Someone must be identified as the offender, held responsible for the crime. The question of guilt is the hub of the entire criminal justice process—everything else revolves around it. Elaborate rules govern how guilt may be legally established, designed to protect the rights of the accused, ensure fairness, prevent abuse of power, and maintain public confidence in the justice system.

These safeguards are essential. The presumption of innocence, the right to counsel, the requirement of proof beyond a reasonable doubt, the exclusion of illegally obtained evidence—these protections reflect our commitment to the principle that it is better to let the guilty go free than to convict the innocent. They are achievements of civilization that must be preserved.

But once guilt has been established, concern about procedural safeguards and rights diminishes. The focus shifts to the second assumption: that the guilty must receive their "just deserts." This principle—that punishment should be proportionate to the crime—has deep roots in human history and moral intuition. It reflects the sense that wrongdoers ought to suffer for their wrongdoing, that the scales of justice must be balanced by the infliction of pain.

The concept of "just deserts" has been used in English since at least the thirteenth century. Originally, it meant receiving what one deserved—whether reward or punishment. The similar principle that "the punishment should fit the crime" expresses the same intuition: the severity of penalty should be reasonable and proportionate to the severity of the offense.

Criminal justice officials see their job as meting out appropriate levels of punishment. They administer pain in the name of retribution, in the name of deterrence, sometimes even in the name of rehabilitation. The threat of pain has long been recognized as the basis of modern law—the assumption that people will obey the law only if they fear the consequences of disobeying.

But this focus on inflicting pain has profound consequences. Elaborate safeguards of offenders' rights are needed precisely because the consequences are so serious. These safeguards can make it difficult to get at the truth. Judges and jurors may become less likely to convict when the potential punishment is seen as very severe. The primary goal of the justice process becomes the determination of guilt and the infliction of pain.

The third assumption is that justice is measured by the process. Appeals are usually centered on whether correct procedures have been followed, not on whether the outcome was just or whether harm was repaired. Priority is given to equity of treatment as a test of justice—treating like cases alike, following the rules consistently. Yet due to the complexity of legal processes, approximate equity in outcome is usually not achieved.

The fourth assumption is that the breaking of the law defines the offense. The act of violating a legal statute triggers the justice process, not the damage done or the conflict created. The legal charge may seem to bear little relationship to the actual offense. The language of guilt or innocence may have little connection to what actually happened. When the legal charge sounds quite different from the actual offense, and the offender has been advised to plead "not guilty," many times the offender comes to believe that they are in fact not guilty.

In criminal law, the victim is defined as the state. Crime is considered an offense against the sovereign, against the people collectively, not merely against the individual who suffered harm. Therefore, criminal law pits offenders against the state. The relationship between victim and offender is not seen as an important problem. The state is so impersonal and abstract that forgiveness and mercy are nearly impossible to achieve.

These five assumptions shape our entire justice system: crime is essentially lawbreaking; when a law is broken, justice involves establishing guilt; so that just deserts can be meted out; by inflicting pain; through a process in which rules and intentions are placed above outcomes. This is essentially a retributive model of justice, and that model is at the root of many of our problems.

The limitations of this model are increasingly recognized. Studies of capital punishment have proven that the death penalty does not deter people from killing. The elaborate rules designed to protect rights can make it difficult to get at truth. The focus on process often obscures outcomes. The definition of crime as offense against the state sidelines victims. The impersonal nature of the system makes forgiveness and mercy nearly impossible.

Moreover, the model fails to address the complexity of human motivation and responsibility. The Apostle Paul captured this complexity in Romans 7:15: "I do not understand what I do. For what I want to do I do not do, but what I hate I do." Paul's problem was not lack of knowledge—he knew what the right thing was. His problem was lack of power to do it, a power that the law could not provide.

The Scriptures affirm both human freedom and the influence of circumstances. Moses set before Israel a choice: life and prosperity or death and destruction (Deuteronomy 30:15). Joshua declared: "Choose for yourselves this day whom you will serve... But as for me and my house, we will serve the Lord" (Joshua 24:15). These affirmations of free choice stand alongside recognition that background and circumstances shape decisions. A person raised in a violent environment may be more prone to violence. Social and economic factors influence behavior. Justice must hold offenders accountable while also taking into consideration the contexts that shaped their choices.

The legal process often discourages accountability by giving offenders the option of pleading "not guilty." This plea, which may simply mean "I want a trial" or "I need more time," can lead offenders to believe they are not guilty even when they are. The label of "guilty" sticks to a person for life, becoming part of their identity, regardless of whether they have changed.

The Resurgence of Restorative Justice

In recent decades, restorative justice has emerged as a powerful alternative to the retributive model. It is not a novel invention but a recovery of ancient wisdom, a return to traditional conflict resolution methods practiced around the world for millennia.

The resurgence of interest in restorative justice reflects growing recognition that punitive systems are failing. Prison populations have exploded without corresponding reductions in crime. Victims remain marginalized and unsatisfied. Offenders cycle through institutions without being transformed. Communities are excluded from the process of healing. The costs—financial, social, human—are unsustainable.

Restorative justice offers a different path. It reorients justice around the needs of victims, holding offenders accountable in meaningful ways, involving communities in the work of healing. It seeks not merely to punish but to repair, not merely to deter but to restore, not merely to incapacitate but to transform.

This approach is not soft on crime. It demands more of offenders than passive incarceration—it requires them to face their victims, acknowledge their harm, make amends to the extent possible, and commit to changed behavior. It provides victims with voice, answers, and opportunities for healing that the conventional system never offers. It engages communities in the hard work of supporting both victims and offenders, rebuilding trust, and addressing underlying conditions that contribute to crime.

The unification of retributive and restorative approaches has shown promise in reducing the harshness of contemporary sentencing while providing meaningful relief to crime victims. Through organized face-to-face meetings among all parties connected to a crime, restorative justice seeks to reach agreements on what offenders can do to repair harm rather than simply handing out punishment. Research demonstrates that these processes can reduce recidivism, increase victim satisfaction, and strengthen communities at lower cost than conventional incarceration.

Critics argue that restorative justice can create conflicts between its reconciliation objectives and the condemnatory objectives of retributive punishment. But this assumes that condemnation and reconciliation are necessarily opposed. The biblical witness suggests otherwise. Genuine repentance requires acknowledgment of wrongdoing—a form of self-condemnation that opens the door to forgiveness. Genuine reconciliation requires accountability—a recognition of harm that makes restoration possible. Condemnation and reconciliation, properly understood, are not opposites but stages in a single journey.

The Biblical Call: A Justice That Restores

Throughout this historical survey, one theme emerges with striking clarity: the biblical vision of justice is fundamentally restorative. From the laws of Moses to the teachings of the prophets to the life and ministry of Jesus to the writings of the apostles, Scripture consistently points toward a justice that heals, restores, and reconciles.

The Law provided for restitution, compensation, and restoration. The prophets thundered against empty ritual and called for justice that defended the vulnerable. Jesus embodied restorative justice in His healing, His teaching, His forgiveness, His death. The apostles proclaimed that God was in Christ reconciling the world to Himself and entrusting to us the ministry of reconciliation.

This biblical vision challenges every assumption of purely retributive justice. It insists that offenders are more than their crimes—they are image-bearers capable of change. It insists that victims are more than witnesses—they are wounded persons deserving care. It insists that communities are more than bystanders—they are essential participants in the work of healing.

The Bible offers numerous passages that highlight this restorative perspective. Forgiveness and reconciliation are central: "For if you forgive other people when they sin against you, your heavenly Father will also forgive you" (Matthew 6:14). "Bear with each other and forgive one another if any of you has a grievance against someone. Forgive as the Lord forgave you" (Colossians 3:13).

Restitution and repair are emphasized: "Anyone who steals must certainly make restitution" (Exodus 22:1). When Zacchaeus encountered Jesus, he declared: "If I have cheated anybody out of anything, I will pay back four times the amount" (Luke 19:8). Restitution was evidence of genuine repentance.

Reconciliation and healing are prioritized: "Therefore, if you are offering your gift at the altar and there remember that your brother or sister has something against you, leave your gift there in front of the altar. First go and be reconciled to them; then come and offer your gift" (Matthew 5:23-24). "Therefore confess your sins to each other and pray for each other so that you may be healed" (James 5:16).

Justice and compassion are intertwined: "He has shown you, O mortal, what is good. And what does the Lord require of you? To act justly and to love mercy and to walk humbly with your God" (Micah 6:8). "Learn to do right; seek justice. Defend the oppressed. Take up the cause of the fatherless; plead the case of the widow" (Isaiah 1:17).

These verses reflect the biblical principles of resolving conflicts, seeking restitution, and fostering reconciliation. They provide the foundation for a justice that aligns with the essence of restorative justice—a justice that emphasizes the transformative power of forgiveness, restitution, and reconciliation in the context of community relationships.

The Long Arc of Justice

The history of justice is long and complex, marked by both progress and regression, wisdom and folly, moments of great insight and periods of terrible cruelty. From the ancient codes of Mesopotamia to the philosophical reflections of Greece and Rome, from the theological frameworks of medieval Europe to the revolutionary ideas of the Enlightenment, from the development of modern legal systems to the emergence of restorative justice, humanity has continually grappled with the question of how to respond to wrongdoing.

Throughout this history, two competing visions have vied for dominance. One sees justice as primarily about punishment—giving offenders what they deserve, balancing the scales through the infliction of pain, deterring future wrongdoing through fear of consequences. The other sees justice as primarily about restoration—repairing harm, healing wounds, restoring relationships, rebuilding community.

The first vision has dominated Western legal systems for centuries. It has produced elaborate codes, sophisticated procedures, and massive institutions. It has also produced overcrowded prisons, marginalized victims, and communities fractured by crime and punishment. It has proven incapable of achieving its own goals—recidivism remains high, victim satisfaction low, public confidence shaky.

The second vision is as old as humanity itself. It has been preserved in indigenous traditions, embedded in biblical revelation, and practiced in communities around the world for millennia. It is now being recovered and articulated in the modern restorative justice movement. It offers a path beyond the failures of punitive systems—a path that leads to healing rather than hurting, restoration rather than isolation, reconciliation rather than estrangement.

The long arc of justice, it appears, is bending toward restoration. Not in a straight line—there are detours and setbacks, resistances and regressions. But the direction is clear. The growing recognition of restorative justice's effectiveness, the increasing integration of restorative practices into legal systems, the flourishing of restorative programs in schools, churches, and communities—all these point toward a future in which justice is measured not by how much punishment is inflicted but by how much harm is repaired, how many relationships are restored, how many lives are transformed.

This is the vision that the Scriptures have always proclaimed. This is the justice that Jesus embodied and taught. This is the hope that restorative justice offers to a world weary of punishment and hungry for healing. The history of justice is still being written, and we have the privilege—and the responsibility—of contributing to its next chapter.

CHAPTER 07

MODERN RESTORATIVE JUSTICE

The emergence of modern restorative justice represents one of the most significant developments in criminology and social ethics of the past half-century. It is not merely a set of techniques or programs but a fundamental reorientation of how we understand and respond to harm, conflict, and crime. In an era marked by mass incarceration, escalating costs, persistent racial disparities, and widespread dissatisfaction with conventional justice systems, restorative justice offers a path forward that is both practical and principled, evidence-based and value-driven.

This chapter explores the contemporary restorative justice movement in its full dimensions. We will examine its defining features, its contrast with punitive approaches, its diverse applications, its empirical foundations, and its global reach. We will also consider how modern restorative justice embodies the principles of the Jesus Paradigm—bringing healing to victims, accountability to offenders, and restoration to communities in ways that reflect the teachings and example of Christ.

The Nature of Modern Restorative Justice

Modern restorative justice is a contemporary approach to addressing harm, conflicts, and crimes that focuses on repairing the harm done to victims, reintegrating offenders into society, and involving the community in the resolution process. It represents a fundamental shift from the questions that have dominated Western justice systems for centuries—what law was broken, who broke it, and what punishment do they deserve—to a different set of inquiries: who has been harmed, what are their needs, whose obligations have arisen, and how can we make things right?

This reorientation is not merely semantic but profoundly consequential. It changes who participates in the justice process, what outcomes are sought, and how success is measured. It elevates the voices of those most affected by crime—victims, offenders, and community members—who have long been marginalized by systems that treat crime as an offense against the state and justice as a matter of abstract rules.

At its core, modern restorative justice is built on the recognition that crime is first and foremost an injury to people and relationships. The state has an interest in maintaining order and upholding laws, but the primary harm is suffered by specific individuals and communities. Justice, therefore, must begin by addressing that harm—acknowledging it, repairing it to the extent possible, and preventing its recurrence.

This recognition aligns deeply with biblical teaching. Throughout Scripture, God reveals Himself as one who hears the cry of the oppressed, who cares for the wounded, who seeks the restoration of the broken. The law of Moses provided for restitution to victims, not merely punishment of offenders. The prophets thundered against a justice system that ignored the vulnerable. Jesus consistently prioritized the needs of those who had been harmed—the leper, the paralytic, the woman caught in adultery, the grieving parent. Modern restorative justice, in its focus on victims and their healing, echoes this ancient wisdom.

Victim-Centered: Honoring the Wounded

The first and most distinctive feature of modern restorative justice is its victim-centered orientation. Unlike conventional systems that treat victims as witnesses to the state's case—sources of evidence rather than participants in justice—restorative justice places victims at the center of the process.

This victim-centered approach begins with the recognition that crime causes real harm to real people. Victims are not abstractions but human beings with feelings, memories, fears, and hopes. They have been directly affected by the harm caused, and their suffering demands recognition. Too often, in conventional legal proceedings, victims feel re-victimized by a system that treats them as means to an end. Their pain becomes evidence, their testimony becomes a tool for prosecution, and their ongoing needs—for answers, for acknowledgment, for a sense of closure—are systematically ignored.

Modern restorative justice seeks to change this entirely. It provides victims with a platform to express their feelings, to ask the questions that haunt them, and to have a meaningful say in how the offender can make amends. This is not about vengeance or extracting maximal concessions. It is about restoring to victims what the crime stripped from them: their voice, their agency, their sense of being seen and heard as persons of inherent worth.

The psychological dimensions of this victim-centered approach are profound and well-documented. Decades of research in victimology have revealed that the trauma of crime extends far beyond the immediate incident. Victims often experience a constellation of psychological wounds: hypervigilance and anxiety, depression and hopelessness, a persistent sense of violation and powerlessness. They are haunted by questions they cannot ask: Why me? What were you thinking? Do you have any idea what you took from me? Do you feel any remorse? These unanswered questions become a form of ongoing torment, a loop of rumination that prevents healing.

Restorative justice processes, particularly victim-offender mediation, create a structured and safe environment in which these questions can finally be asked and answered. When victims have the opportunity to confront the person who harmed them—to speak their truth, to express their pain, to receive answers—the psychological benefits can be transformative. Studies consistently show that victims who participate in restorative processes report significantly higher levels of satisfaction than those whose cases proceed through conventional channels. They are more likely to feel that justice has been done, that their needs have been addressed, and that they can begin the process of moving forward.

But the benefits extend beyond subjective satisfaction. Research has demonstrated that restorative processes can reduce symptoms of post-traumatic stress, decrease feelings of anger and desire for revenge, and restore a sense of safety and control. When victims see that the offender genuinely understands the harm caused and is taking concrete steps to make amends, the psychological grip of victimization begins to loosen. The victim is no longer defined solely by what was done to them; they become an active agent in their own healing.

This victim-centered approach resonates deeply with the teachings of Jesus. Throughout the Gospels, Jesus consistently prioritizes the needs of those who have been harmed. He touches lepers, restoring them not only to health but to community. He forgives the woman caught in adultery, restoring her dignity and calling her to a new life. He weeps with Mary and Martha at the death of Lazarus, sharing their grief before raising their brother. He hears the cry of blind Bartimaeus and restores his sight. In every encounter, Jesus sees the person behind the condition, the wounded human being deserving of compassion and care. Modern restorative justice, in its victim-centered orientation, reflects this same compassionate attention.

Offender Accountability: Responsibility and Transformation

While modern restorative justice is victim-centered, it is not soft on offenders. On the contrary, it demands a deeper, more demanding form of accountability than conventional punishment ever could. The question is not simply, "What punishment do you deserve?" but rather, "What can you do to make things right?"

This distinction is crucial and often misunderstood. Critics of restorative justice sometimes assume that it lets offenders off the hook, that it prioritizes the needs of wrongdoers over the rights of victims. Nothing could be further from the truth.

Restorative justice requires offenders to take genuine responsibility for their actions—to face the human consequences of their behavior, to acknowledge the harm they have caused, and to actively participate in making amends.

Consider what happens in a typical criminal proceeding. The offender is represented by counsel, whose job is to minimize consequences. The offender is advised to say as little as possible, to admit nothing beyond what the evidence forces, to portray themselves in the most favorable light. The entire process incentivizes denial, deflection, and minimization. The offender never has to look the victim in the eye, never has to hear the full extent of the pain they caused, never has to grapple with the human consequences of their actions. They serve their time—passively, often bitterly—and emerge from incarceration no more accountable than when they entered, and often far more damaged and alienated.

Restorative justice reverses this entire dynamic. Offenders are encouraged—indeed, required—to take genuine responsibility for their actions. They are confronted, not with an abstract charge, but with the living reality of the person they have harmed. They hear, in the victim's own words, the impact of their behavior. They are asked to explain themselves, to answer questions, to grapple with the consequences of their choices. And then they are given the opportunity—the profound privilege—of making amends.

This accountability process is not punitive in nature but restorative. Its goal is not to inflict pain but to repair harm. Offenders are invited to understand the harm they have caused, to feel genuine remorse, and to actively participate in making things right. This participation can take many forms: a sincere apology that acknowledges the specific harm done, restitution that compensates for material losses, community service that gives back to those affected, or other actions tailored to the particular circumstances of the case.

The psychological journey involved in this process is transformative. When offenders are shielded from the human consequences of their actions, they remain trapped in cycles of denial and self-justification. They can tell themselves that the victim deserved it, that they had no choice, that everyone does it, that the system is unfair. These rationalizations protect them from the painful truth of what they have done—but they also prevent any genuine change.

Restorative justice dismantles these defenses. When a victim looks an offender in the eye and describes, with tears, the ongoing impact of the crime, the walls of denial begin to crumble. The offender can no longer hide behind abstractions. They are confronted with a person—a person who is hurting because of choices they made. This confrontation evokes what the Apostle Paul called "godly sorrow"—a grief over wrongdoing that leads not to despair but to genuine repentance and transformation (2 Corinthians 7:10). This is sorrow that produces change, that motivates amends, that reorients a life.

Research consistently demonstrates the effectiveness of this approach. Offenders who participate in restorative justice programs have significantly lower recidivism rates than those processed through conventional channels. They are less likely to reoffend because they have undergone an internal transformation, not merely endured external punishment. They have faced the harm they caused, made amends where possible, and been welcomed back into community. They have experienced accountability not as something done to them but as something they actively participated in—a journey of taking responsibility and making things right.

This understanding of accountability aligns perfectly with biblical teaching. The Scriptures consistently call offenders to acknowledge their wrongdoing, to make restitution, and to change their behavior. When Zacchaeus encountered Jesus, he did not merely express remorse; he declared, "Look, Lord, I give half of my goods to the poor; and if I have taken anything from anyone by false accusation, I restore fourfold" (Luke 19:8). Jesus affirmed this response: "Today salvation has come to this house." Restitution was evidence of genuine repentance and the fruit of restored relationship.

The Apostle Paul, writing to the Corinthians, distinguished between worldly sorrow and godly sorrow: "For godly sorrow produces repentance leading to salvation, not to be regretted; but the sorrow of the world produces death" (2 Corinthians 7:10). Worldly sorrow is regret at being caught, at suffering consequences, at having one's desires frustrated. It leads to guilt, shame, despair, and ultimately more of the same. Godly sorrow is grief over the harm caused, over the violation of relationship, over the offense against God and neighbor. It leads to genuine change, to making amends, to new life. Restorative justice seeks to create the conditions for godly sorrow, for accountability that transforms.

Community Involvement: Collective Responsibility for Healing

The third defining feature of modern restorative justice is its emphasis on community involvement. Restorative justice recognizes that crime is not merely an offense against an individual or the state but a wound in the fabric of community life. Trust is damaged, relationships are strained, the sense of safety is eroded. For true healing to occur, the community must be actively involved in the process of repair.

In conventional justice systems, the community is largely absent. The state acts on behalf of "the people," but this representation is abstract and impersonal. Community members have no meaningful role in the process, no opportunity to contribute to resolution, no responsibility for supporting either victims or offenders. The result is a justice system that happens *to* communities rather than *with* them—a system that disempowers the very people most affected by crime and conflict.

Restorative justice restores the community to its rightful place. Communities play an active role in supporting both victims and offenders in their journey toward resolution. This support can take many forms: providing resources and assistance to victims, offering mentorship and accountability to offenders, creating structures of welcome for those returning from incarceration, and addressing the underlying social conditions that contribute to crime.

In restorative processes such as family group conferences and circle processes, community members participate directly in addressing harm and developing plans for repair. They bring their perspectives, their wisdom, their resources. They help victims feel supported and heard. They hold offenders accountable while also offering encouragement and hope. They become partners in the work of healing, not passive observers of a process controlled by others.

This community involvement creates a profound sense of shared responsibility and collective healing. When a crime occurs, it is not just an offense against an individual; it is a tear in the social fabric. The community itself is diminished, its trust eroded, its sense of safety compromised. For true healing to occur, the community must be actively involved in repairing that tear. This involvement communicates to victims that they are not alone, that their suffering matters to others, that the community stands with them. It communicates to offenders that they are still members of the community, that their restoration is a shared priority, that there is a place for them to return. And it communicates to all that justice is not something done by experts and officials but something the community collectively owns and pursues.

The biblical foundations of this community-centered approach run deep. Israel was constituted as a covenant community, bound together by shared relationship with God and mutual responsibility for one another. When harm occurred, it was not merely a private matter but a breach in the community's covenant relationship. The entire community was implicated, and the entire community was involved in restoration. The prophetic vision of shalom—of peace, wholeness, and right relationship—was always a communal vision, a picture of all creation dwelling together in harmony under God's reign.

In the New Testament, the church is described as the body of Christ—a living organism in which each member is connected to every other, and the health of the whole depends on the health of each part. When one member suffers, all suffer together. When one member is restored, all rejoice together (1 Corinthians 12:26). This is the theological reality that restorative justice seeks to embody: that we are created for relationship, that our lives are intertwined, and that our healing is inseparable from the healing of others.

Resolution and Healing: Beyond Punishment

Modern restorative justice aims to achieve resolution and healing rather than just punishment. It prioritizes the restoration of relationships and the repair of harm, which is often missing in punitive systems. This focus on healing distinguishes restorative justice from both retributive and rehabilitative approaches.

Retributive justice seeks to balance the scales by inflicting pain on the offender. The assumption is that suffering cancels debt, that punishment restores equilibrium. But this assumption is questionable. Punishment does nothing to repair the harm suffered by the victim. It does nothing to address the underlying causes of offending behavior. It does nothing to strengthen the community or rebuild trust. At best, it incapacitates the offender temporarily; at worst, it exacerbates the very problems that contributed to crime.

Rehabilitative justice seeks to change the offender through treatment, education, and training. This is an important goal, and restorative justice embraces it. But rehabilitation alone does not address the victim's needs or the community's wounds. The offender may be transformed, but the victim remains harmed, the community remains fractured. Healing requires more than individual change; it requires relational repair.

Restorative justice seeks both—the transformation of the offender and the healing of the victim and community. It recognizes that these are not separate processes but interconnected dimensions of a single journey. When victims are heard, when offenders take responsibility, when community members offer support, healing becomes possible for all.

This healing is multifaceted. For victims, it involves the acknowledgment of harm, the opportunity to express pain, the receipt of answers, the experience of seeing the offender take responsibility, and the possibility of forgiveness. For offenders, it involves facing the consequences of their actions, experiencing remorse, making amends, and being restored to community. For communities, it involves addressing the underlying conditions that contribute to crime, rebuilding trust, and strengthening social bonds.

The goal is not merely the absence of conflict but the presence of right relationship—shalom, in the biblical sense. Shalom is not simply peace as opposed to war; it is wholeness, flourishing, well-being in every dimension of life. It is the condition of creation as God intended it to be, the harmony of all things in right relationship. Restorative justice seeks to restore shalom when it has been disrupted by harm.

This vision of healing aligns with the ministry of Jesus. Throughout the Gospels, Jesus is portrayed as healer—healing the sick, the blind, the lame, the leprous, the demon-possessed. But His healing was never merely physical; it was always holistic, addressing the whole person and restoring them to community. When He healed the leper, He also restored him to religious and social life. When He forgave the paralytic, He also healed his body. When He cast out demons, He also liberated the oppressed from spiritual bondage. Jesus' healings were signs of the kingdom—foretastes of the time when all things would be made new, when every tear would be wiped away, when death and pain would be no more.

Modern restorative justice, in its focus on healing, participates in this same kingdom work. It is not merely a technique for resolving disputes but a practice of restoration that reflects God's own purposes for creation.

Diverse Applications: A Versatile Framework

One of the remarkable features of modern restorative justice is its versatility. While it emerged primarily in response to crime, its principles and practices have been applied across a wide range of contexts—from schools to workplaces, from families to communities, from civil disputes to international conflicts.

In criminal justice, restorative justice is used at every stage of the process—as diversion from prosecution, as a supplement to court proceedings, as part of sentencing, as a condition of probation, as a component of reentry. Victim-offender mediation, family group conferencing, circle processes, and restorative panels provide structured opportunities for dialogue, accountability, and repair. Research consistently demonstrates that these processes can reduce recidivism, increase victim satisfaction, and do so at lower cost than traditional incarceration.

In education, restorative practices are transforming school discipline. Rather than suspending or expelling students who misbehave—practices that disproportionately affect minority students and push them out of school—restorative approaches bring together those affected by misconduct to address harm, repair relationships, and reintegrate the offending student. Restorative circles, peer mediation, and restorative conferences create a school culture of respect, accountability, and care. Studies show that these practices reduce disciplinary incidents, improve school climate, and increase academic achievement.

In families, restorative principles are applied to address conflicts between parents and children, between siblings, between extended family members. Family group conferencing, originally developed in New Zealand for youth justice, has been adapted for child welfare cases, bringing together family members to develop plans for the care and protection of children. Restorative approaches help families resolve conflicts, heal wounds, and strengthen bonds.

In workplaces, restorative practices address conflicts between employees, between staff and management, between organizations and their communities. Restorative circles and conferences provide structured processes for addressing grievances, repairing relationships, and rebuilding trust. Organizations that embrace restorative principles report improved communication, increased morale, and reduced litigation.

In communities, restorative justice addresses neighborhood conflicts, disputes between groups, and tensions arising from crime and disorder. Community conferencing brings together those affected by conflict to develop solutions that meet everyone's needs. Restorative circles create spaces for dialogue across difference, building understanding and trust. Community justice initiatives build partnerships between residents and justice system stakeholders to address underlying conditions that contribute to crime.

In international contexts, restorative principles inform transitional justice processes in post-conflict societies. Truth and reconciliation commissions, such as South Africa's, have drawn on restorative principles to address massive human rights abuses, providing platforms for victims to tell their stories and perpetrators to acknowledge their wrongdoing. These processes seek not merely punishment but healing, not merely accountability but reconciliation.

This versatility reflects the fundamental nature of restorative justice. It is not a rigid program but a set of principles—encounter, inclusion, amends, reintegration—that can be adapted to diverse contexts. It is not a one-size-fits-all solution but a framework for crafting contextually appropriate responses to harm. It honors the particularity of each situation while embodying universal values.

The parable of the Good Samaritan illustrates this versatility. The Samaritan did not have a pre-packaged program for helping wounded travelers. He responded to the specific needs of the specific person in front of him—bandaging wounds, providing transport, arranging for ongoing care, covering costs. His response was tailored to the situation, yet it embodied the universal principle of love for neighbor. Modern restorative justice, in its diverse applications, follows this same pattern—adapting principles to contexts, responding to particular needs while embodying timeless values.

Structured Processes: Creating Space for Encounter

Modern restorative justice is not merely a set of principles but a practical discipline embodied in specific processes. These structured processes create safe spaces for encounter, dialogue, and resolution—making it possible for victims, offenders, and community members to engage with one another in ways that promote healing.

Victim-offender mediation is the most widely used and best-researched restorative process. In mediation, a trained facilitator brings together the victim and offender in a safe, structured setting. The victim has the opportunity to describe the impact of the crime, to ask questions, and to express their feelings. The offender has the opportunity to hear this impact directly, to explain their actions, and to take responsibility. Together, they work toward an agreement about what the offender will do to make amends.

Mediation differs fundamentally from traditional mediation. In conventional mediation, parties are presumed to have equal standing, each with legitimate interests to negotiate. In victim-offender mediation, there is clear recognition that harm has been done, that one party has caused injury to another. The process is not about finding a middle ground between competing claims but about addressing the harm, holding the offender accountable, and working toward restoration. This recognition of harm is essential to the integrity of the process.

Family group conferences extend this model to include the broader networks of support surrounding both victim and offender. Originally developed in New Zealand, drawing on Maori indigenous practices, these conferences bring together victims, offenders, and their respective families and supporters. Together, they discuss the harm that has occurred, the needs that have arisen, and the steps necessary for repair and reintegration. The presence of family and supporters creates a powerful context for accountability and healing—offenders must face not only their victims but also their own loved ones, who witness the consequences of their actions. And both victims and offenders receive the ongoing support of their communities as they move forward.

Circle processes represent another form of restorative practice, drawing on indigenous traditions from North America and elsewhere. Participants sit in a circle, symbolizing equality and mutual respect. A talking piece is passed from person to person, ensuring that each voice is heard without interruption. Circles can be used for a wide variety of purposes: addressing conflicts within communities, supporting victims and offenders, making decisions about sanctions and reparation, and celebrating successful reintegration. The circle creates a space of safety and respect in which even the most difficult conversations can occur.

Restorative panels or boards bring together trained community members to meet with offenders and, sometimes, victims. The panel engages the offender in dialogue about the offense, its impact, and what can be done to repair harm. Together, they develop a plan for accountability and restoration. Panels are often used in diversion programs, providing an alternative to formal prosecution for low-level offenses.

These processes are not rigid formulas but flexible frameworks that can be adapted to the specific circumstances of each case. They share common elements: preparation of participants, facilitation by trained neutral parties, structured dialogue, focus on harm and repair, and follow-up to ensure agreements are implemented. They create the conditions in which healing can occur.

The Apostle Paul, in his letter to Philemon, modeled this kind of restorative process. When Onesimus, a runaway slave, came to faith under Paul's ministry, Paul faced a delicate situation. Onesimus had wronged his master Philemon; justice required accountability. But Onesimus was now a brother in Christ. Paul could have commanded Philemon to forgive, but instead he orchestrated a restorative encounter. He sent Onesimus back to

Philemon—accompanied by a letter that acknowledged the harm, affirmed the relationship, offered to make amends, and appealed for reconciliation. He created the conditions for dialogue, accountability, and restoration. This is restorative justice, embodied in Scripture, centuries before the term was coined.

Evidence-Based Success: What Research Shows

Modern restorative justice is not merely a hopeful theory but an empirically validated approach. Decades of research have demonstrated its effectiveness across multiple dimensions—victim satisfaction, offender accountability, recidivism reduction, and cost-effectiveness.

Victim satisfaction is consistently high in restorative processes. Studies from around the world show that victims who participate in restorative justice report significantly higher levels of satisfaction than those whose cases proceed through conventional channels. They feel that they have been heard, that their needs have been addressed, and that justice has been done. They are more likely to receive apologies, to have their questions answered, and to feel a sense of closure. This satisfaction is not merely subjective; it reflects the genuine benefits that restorative processes provide.

Offender accountability is also enhanced. Restorative processes require offenders to face the human consequences of their actions—something conventional punishment rarely achieves. Offenders who participate in restorative justice are more likely to acknowledge their wrongdoing, to express genuine remorse, and to make amends. They understand the impact of their behavior in ways that abstract punishment cannot convey.

Recidivism reduction is one of the most striking findings of restorative justice research. Multiple meta-analyses have shown that restorative justice programs reduce reoffending rates compared to conventional processing. The effects are particularly strong for violent offenses and for cases involving personal victims. When offenders face those they have harmed, when they take responsibility and make amends, they are less likely to reoffend. They have undergone an internal transformation, not merely endured external punishment.

Cost-effectiveness is another demonstrated benefit. Restorative justice processes are significantly less expensive than incarceration. They reduce the burden on courts, prosecutors, defense attorneys, and correctional systems. They generate savings that can be reinvested in prevention, treatment, and community programs. They offer not only better outcomes but better value for public resources.

These findings are not limited to one country or context. Research from North America, Europe, Australia, New Zealand, and elsewhere consistently supports the effectiveness of restorative justice. The evidence base is robust and growing.

The United States Department of Justice has recognized this evidence. In 2014, its Office of Justice Programs launched the National Center for Restorative Justice, providing training and technical assistance to jurisdictions and organizations seeking to implement restorative justice programs. The Department has funded a variety of restorative justice initiatives, including victim-offender mediation programs and community conferencing programs. Several states and local jurisdictions have implemented restorative justice programs with support and encouragement from the Department. These programs have shown promising results in reducing recidivism rates and improving outcomes for victims and communities.

This empirical validation is important, but it is not the ultimate justification for restorative justice. Restorative justice is not merely a technique that happens to work; it is a moral vision rooted in fundamental values—respect for human dignity, commitment to healing, belief in the possibility of change. The evidence confirms what these values would lead us to expect: that treating people with respect, addressing harm, and involving community leads to better outcomes than inflicting pain and isolating offenders. But even if the evidence were less favorable, the moral claims of restorative justice would remain. We are called to do justice, love mercy, and walk humbly with God—not because it is effective but because it is right.

Global Reach: A Movement Without Borders

Modern restorative justice is not limited to one geographic region or cultural context. It has been implemented in diverse countries and cultures around the world, adapting to local circumstances while maintaining core principles. This global reach reflects the universal resonance of restorative values and the adaptability of restorative practices.

In New Zealand, restorative justice is embedded in the youth justice system through family group conferences, drawing on Maori indigenous traditions. These conferences bring together victims, offenders, and their families to discuss the offense and develop plans for accountability and restoration. The model has been widely adopted and adapted in other countries.

In Canada, restorative justice programs operate at every level of the justice system, from diversion to post-sentencing.

Indigenous healing circles, drawing on First Nations traditions, have been integrated into sentencing and corrections. The federal government has supported restorative justice through legislation, funding, and policy.

In Europe, restorative justice is widely practiced, particularly in juvenile justice systems. Victim-offender mediation is available in most European countries, often as a diversion from prosecution or as a component of sentencing. The Council of Europe has issued recommendations encouraging member states to develop restorative justice programs.

In Africa, restorative justice draws on deep indigenous traditions that predate colonial legal systems. Countries like South Africa have incorporated restorative principles into post-apartheid justice, most notably through the Truth and Reconciliation Commission. Community-based restorative practices continue to operate alongside formal legal systems.

In Latin America, restorative justice programs have been developed in countries such as Brazil, Argentina, and Chile. Restorative circles and mediation are used in criminal justice, education, and community settings. Indigenous communities have preserved restorative traditions that are now being recognized and supported.

In Asia, restorative justice practices draw on cultural values of harmony, relationship, and community. Countries like Japan, South Korea, and Singapore have incorporated restorative elements into their justice systems. Traditional practices of mediation and conciliation are being revitalized and adapted.

In the Pacific Islands, restorative justice builds on indigenous traditions of community justice. Family group conferencing, originally developed in New Zealand, has been adapted in countries like Fiji and Samoa, where extended family and community play central roles in addressing harm.

This global diversity is a strength of restorative justice. It demonstrates that restorative principles can be expressed in many cultural forms, that they are not bound to any particular legal system or cultural tradition. It also provides a rich source of learning, as practitioners and scholars share experiences across borders and adapt successful practices to new contexts.

The universal appeal of restorative justice reflects its alignment with fundamental human values—the desire to be heard when we are hurt, the need for accountability when we cause harm, the importance of community in healing. These values are not Western or Eastern, Northern or Southern; they are human. Restorative justice gives them expression in diverse cultural forms.

The Contrast with Punitive Justice

To appreciate modern restorative justice fully, it is helpful to contrast it with the punitive paradigm that has dominated Western legal systems for centuries. This contrast illuminates what restorative justice offers and why it is needed.

The primary focus of today's criminal justice system is punishing offenders for their crimes. This focus is not wrong in itself—offenders should be held accountable for their actions. But critics argue that the system often fails to address the underlying causes of criminal behavior and does little to help offenders face the impact of their crimes. Punishment alone is not enough to deter future offending, and it may actually contribute to a cycle of criminal behavior by exacerbating the social, economic, and psychological factors that lead to crime.

Under the current system, offenders are typically punished through incarceration, fines, or other legal penalties. While these penalties can serve as a deterrent, they may not address the underlying issues that led to the crime. The system may not offer enough support for offenders to reintegrate into society once their sentence is completed, leading to recidivism and further criminal behavior.

Moreover, the current system often neglects the needs and perspectives of victims and communities. Victims may feel ignored or disrespected by the justice system. Communities may experience a loss of trust in law enforcement and the broader justice system. The system processes cases, but it does not heal wounds or repair relationships.

An anecdote illustrates this failure: Many years ago, Texas prisons were called the Texas Department of Corrections, suggesting a mission of rehabilitation. But when an offender successfully sued the state over conditions, the prison system was renamed the Texas Department of Criminal Justice. The name change reflected a shift in philosophy—from correction to punishment, from rehabilitation to retribution. The system now punishes offenders without helping them face the impact of their crimes.

Restorative justice offers a different path. It focuses on repairing harm caused by crime, involving all stakeholders in the process of addressing harm and preventing future harm. Its goals include not only holding offenders accountable but also promoting healing and restoration for victims and communities, and addressing the underlying causes of criminal behavior.

The principles of restorative justice reflect this different orientation. It focuses on harm rather than rule-breaking. It is inclusive, involving all stakeholders. It seeks to empower victims and communities, giving them voice and agency. It emphasizes collaboration and problem-solving, finding solutions satisfactory to all. It holds offenders accountable while providing opportunities for rehabilitation and reintegration.

These principles offer a more inclusive, collaborative, and community-oriented approach to justice. They seek to promote healing and restoration while addressing the underlying causes of criminal behavior. They create common ground that accommodates the goals of many constituencies and provides a collective focus for the work of justice.

The primary stakeholders in restorative justice are the person who caused harm (the offender), the person harmed (the victim), and the affected community. The goal is to create healing by identifying and addressing the harms, needs, and obligations that result from wrongdoing. This focus on stakeholders, rather than on abstract legal categories, is what makes restorative justice humanizing and effective.

Why Restorative Justice Is Finding a Receptive Audience

Restorative justice has been finding a receptive audience because it offers a more inclusive and collaborative approach to justice that accommodates the goals of many constituencies and provides a collective focus.

Victims' advocates have long criticized the conventional system for sidelining victims, treating them as witnesses rather than participants. Restorative justice gives victims voice, agency, and the opportunity to have their needs addressed. It offers what victims consistently say they want: to be heard, to receive answers, to see the offender take responsibility, to have a say in the outcome.

Offender advocates have criticized the system for its failure to rehabilitate, its high recidivism rates, its damaging effects on offenders and their families. Restorative justice offers offenders the opportunity to take genuine responsibility, to make amends, to be restored to community. It addresses the underlying causes of offending behavior and supports genuine change.

Community advocates have criticized the system for excluding communities, for failing to address the conditions that produce crime, for eroding trust between residents and law enforcement. Restorative justice involves communities in the process of healing, builds partnerships between communities and justice system stakeholders, and addresses underlying conditions.

Justice system professionals—judges, prosecutors, defense attorneys, police, corrections officials—have become frustrated with a system that processes cases without producing satisfaction. Restorative justice offers a way to achieve meaningful outcomes, to see cases resolved in ways that actually address harm and promote healing.

Policymakers have become concerned about the costs of mass incarceration, the persistent racial disparities, the failure to achieve public safety goals. Restorative justice offers a cost-effective alternative that reduces recidivism, increases victim satisfaction, and builds community trust.

Faith communities have found in restorative justice an expression of their deepest values—forgiveness, reconciliation, healing, restoration. Restorative justice aligns with the teachings of Jesus and the prophets, offering a way to embody faith in response to harm.

This broad appeal reflects the fundamental wisdom of restorative justice. It is not a partisan program or a narrow interest but a framework that serves multiple goods—victim healing, offender accountability, community well-being, public safety, fiscal responsibility, moral integrity. It creates common ground where different constituencies can unite around shared goals.

The Jesus Paradigm and Modern Restorative Justice

As we consider modern restorative justice in all its dimensions, we see that it embodies the principles of the Jesus Paradigm. Its victim-centered orientation reflects Jesus' compassion for the wounded. Its emphasis on offender accountability echoes Jesus' call to repentance and transformation. Its involvement of community mirrors Jesus' formation of a reconciled people. Its focus on healing and restoration participates in Jesus' ministry of making whole. Its structured processes create space for the kind of encounter that Jesus facilitated—between the woman caught in adultery and her accusers, between Zacchaeus and those he had defrauded, between Peter and the risen Christ. Its empirical validation confirms what faith has always known: that love and truth, accountability and grace, community and healing are the paths to wholeness.

Modern restorative justice is not a secular alternative to Christian faith but a secular expression of Christian wisdom. Its principles, though articulated in non-religious language, resonate with the deepest truths of Scripture. Its practices, though developed in diverse contexts, reflect the pattern of Jesus' own ministry. Its promise, though expressed in terms of outcomes and evidence, points toward the shalom that God intends for all creation.

This does not mean that restorative justice is a disguised form of evangelism or that its practitioners must be Christians. Restorative justice stands on its own merits as a humane and effective approach to addressing harm. But for those who follow Jesus, restorative justice is more than a useful technique; it is a way of embodying the gospel, of participating in God's work of reconciliation, of bearing witness to the kingdom.

The Jesus Paradigm calls us to see in every harm an opportunity for healing, in every offender a potential for transformation, in every victim a dignity to be restored, in every community a capacity for collective restoration. Modern restorative justice provides the framework and practices for answering that call. It is not the kingdom fully realized—that awaits God's final renewal of all things. But it is a sign of the kingdom, a foretaste of the time when justice will roll down like waters and righteousness like an ever-flowing stream, when swords will be beaten into plowshares and nations will learn war no more, when God will wipe away every tear and death shall be no more.

This is the vision that animates restorative justice. This is the hope that sustains its practitioners. This is the promise that invites us all to become agents of healing in a wounded world. Modern restorative justice, in its principles, practices, and growing global movement, offers a path toward that vision—a path that is both practical and hopeful, evidence-based and value-driven, humanizing and transformative. It is a path worth walking, for the sake of victims, offenders, communities, and the God who calls us to justice, mercy, and humility.

CHAPTER 08

JESUS AS A MODEL FOR RESTORATIVE JUSTICE

Of all the figures who have shaped human history, none provides a more compelling and comprehensive model for restorative justice than Jesus of Nazareth. His life, teachings, death, and resurrection constitute the ultimate paradigm for how to respond to wrongdoing, heal broken relationships, and restore individuals and communities to wholeness. When we examine the Gospels through the lens of restorative justice, we discover that Jesus did not merely teach about reconciliation—He embodied it. He did not merely command forgiveness—He enacted it. He did not merely proclaim restoration—He accomplished it through the most costly act of love the world has ever known.

This chapter explores Jesus as the model for restorative justice in all its dimensions. We will examine how His compassion and mercy, His teaching on forgiveness, His ministry of reconciliation, His call to accountability, His engagement with community, His restoration of dignity, His healing and transformation, and His embodiment of justice as love in action provide a comprehensive paradigm for restorative practice. We will also consider the practical implications of this model for those who seek to follow Jesus in ministry to the incarcerated, the victimized, and the broken. In doing so, we will discover that restorative justice is not merely consistent with Christian faith but lies at its very heart.

Compassion and Mercy: The Foundation of Restorative Practice

The Gospels portray Jesus as one who was consistently moved with compassion. Again and again, we read that He saw the crowds and had compassion on them because they were harassed and helpless, like sheep without a shepherd (Matthew 9:36). He saw the hungry multitude and had compassion, feeding them with loaves and fish (Matthew 14:14). He saw the grieving widow of Nain, whose only son had died, and had compassion, raising the young man to life (Luke 7:13). He saw the leper, the blind, the lame, the demon-possessed, and was moved to heal and restore.

This compassion was not merely an emotion but a motivation for action. It moved Jesus to touch the untouchable, to speak to the outcast, to welcome the marginalized, to forgive the sinner. His compassion transcended social boundaries, religious restrictions, and cultural taboos. He touched lepers, though the Law declared them unclean. He spoke with Samaritan women, though Jews had no dealings with Samaritans. He ate with tax collectors and sinners, though the religious elite condemned such associations. He welcomed children, though disciples tried to send them away. His compassion knew no limits.

This compassion is foundational for restorative justice. Restorative practices begin with compassion for those who have been harmed—seeing their pain, acknowledging their suffering, validating their experience. Victims need to know that someone cares about what happened to them, that their wounds matter, that they are not alone. The church, following Jesus' example, is called to extend this compassion to victims, offering presence, support, and care.

But Jesus' compassion extended also to offenders. He did not condone their wrongdoing, but He saw beyond their sins to their humanity. He saw Zacchaeus up a tree and called him down, inviting Himself to his house—and Zacchaeus was transformed, promising restitution fourfold. He saw the woman caught in adultery, surrounded by accusers ready to stone her, and He did not condemn her—but neither did He condone her sin, calling her instead to leave her life of sin. He saw Peter, who had denied Him three times, and after the resurrection He sought him out, restored him, and commissioned him to feed His sheep.

This compassion for offenders is equally essential for restorative justice. Offenders are not monsters but human beings who have made harmful choices. They are created in God's image, bearing inherent dignity and worth. They are capable of change, of repentance, of making amends, of being restored. Restorative justice, following Jesus' example, seeks not to condemn offenders but to call them to accountability and transformation, offering them the opportunity to make things right and be restored to community.

The compassion of Jesus was not soft sentimentality but costly love. It cost Him His reputation, as He was called a friend of tax collectors and sinners. It cost Him His comfort, as He had no place to lay His head. It cost Him His life, as His compassion led Him to the cross. Restorative justice, likewise, is costly. It requires victims to extend compassion to those who have harmed them. It requires offenders to face the pain they have caused. It requires communities to invest time, energy, and resources in the work of healing. It requires all involved to embrace the way of the cross—the way of sacrificial love.

Forgiveness: The Heart of Restoration

If compassion is the foundation of restorative justice, forgiveness is its heart. And no one taught or modeled forgiveness more profoundly than Jesus.

In the Lord's Prayer, Jesus instructed His disciples to pray: "Forgive us our debts, as we forgive our debtors" (Matthew 6:12). This simple petition links divine forgiveness to human forgiveness in an inseparable bond. Those who receive forgiveness from God are called to extend forgiveness to others. Those who refuse to forgive others reveal that they have not truly received God's forgiveness. The prayer assumes that forgiveness is not optional but essential for those who follow Jesus.

After teaching the prayer, Jesus added a commentary that underscores the seriousness of this connection: "For if you forgive men their trespasses, your heavenly Father will also forgive you. But if you do not forgive men their trespasses, neither will your Father forgive your trespasses" (Matthew 6:14-15). These words are stark, even alarming. They seem to make divine forgiveness conditional on human forgiveness. Yet they are not a legal formula but a spiritual principle: an unforgiving heart cannot receive forgiveness because it is closed to the very reality of grace. To refuse forgiveness to others is to place ourselves outside the flow of forgiving love.

When Peter asked how often he must forgive his brother—suggesting seven times, which seemed generous—Jesus responded: "I do not say to you, up to seven times, but up to seventy times seven" (Matthew 18:21-22). The number is not literal but symbolic, indicating limitless forgiveness. There is no point at which we may cease to forgive, no number of offenses beyond which grace may be withheld. This teaching challenges every natural human inclination, every instinct for retribution, every desire to keep score. It calls us to a forgiveness that knows no bounds.

The parable of the unforgiving servant, which immediately follows this teaching, drives home the point with unforgettable force. A servant owes his king an astronomical debt—ten thousand talents, millions of dollars, a sum impossible to repay. When the servant pleads for mercy, the king forgives the entire debt. But that same servant, immediately upon leaving the king's presence, encounters a fellow servant who owes him a paltry sum—a hundred denarii, a few thousand dollars, a debt that could reasonably be repaid. He seizes the man by the throat, demands payment, and when the man pleads for patience, has him thrown into prison.

When the king hears of this, he is furious. "You wicked servant! I forgave you all that debt because you begged me. Should you not also have had compassion on your fellow servant, just as I had pity on you?" He delivers the unforgiving servant to the torturers until he should pay all that was due. And Jesus concludes: "So My heavenly Father also will do to you if each of you, from his heart, does not forgive his brother his trespasses" (Matthew 18:32-35).

This parable reveals several essential truths about forgiveness. First, the forgiveness we have received is immeasurably greater than any forgiveness we are called to extend. The staggering disproportion between the debts—the first incalculable, the second trivial—underscores the absurdity of refusing to forgive. If God has forgiven us the infinite debt of our sin against Him, how can we refuse to forgive the finite debts others owe us?

Second, forgiveness must be from the heart. Jesus specifies that forgiveness must be "from your heart"—not merely external compliance but internal transformation. The unforgiving servant went through the motions of pleading for mercy but did not internalize the mercy he received. His heart remained unchanged, and so he could not extend to others what had been extended to him. Restorative justice requires genuine heart change, not merely behavioral conformity.

Third, unforgiveness has consequences. The servant who refuses to forgive is delivered to the torturers—a vivid image of the inner torment that unforgiveness produces. Bitterness, resentment, and anger do not harm only those against whom they are directed; they torture the one who holds them. Research in psychology confirms this: unforgiveness is associated with higher levels of depression, anxiety, and stress; with poorer physical health; with damaged relationships. The torturers are real, and they work from within.

On the cross, Jesus exemplified the forgiveness He taught. As the soldiers drove nails through His hands and feet, as the religious leaders mocked Him, as the crowds passed by and hurled insults, Jesus prayed: "Father, forgive them, for they do not know what they do" (Luke 23:34). This is forgiveness without condition, without waiting for repentance, without requiring acknowledgment. It is the purest expression of divine mercy—forgiveness extended even to those who are actively engaged in crucifying the forgiver.

This prayer does not mean that repentance is unnecessary or that all will be automatically saved regardless of their response. It means that Jesus' heart toward sinners is forgiveness, that His disposition is mercy, that even in the moment of His deepest suffering He is pleading for those who inflict it. This is the model for all Christian forgiveness: a heart so saturated with grace that it continues to love even when wronged, continues to pray even when persecuted, continues to seek the good of those who seek its harm.

For restorative justice, this model of forgiveness is essential. Forgiveness creates the possibility of restoration. When victims forgive, they release offenders from the debt of guilt, opening the door to reconciliation. When offenders receive forgiveness, they are freed from the burden of shame, enabled to make amends and move forward. When communities practice forgiveness, they create the conditions in which healing can occur. Forgiveness is not the end of the restorative process but its beginning—the gate through which all must pass who seek restoration.

Reconciliation: The Goal of Restorative Justice

If forgiveness is the heart of restorative justice, reconciliation is its goal. And Jesus was the great peacemaker, the one who came to reconcile humanity to God and to one another.

In the Sermon on the Mount, Jesus pronounced a blessing on peacemakers: "Blessed are the peacemakers, for they shall be called sons of God" (Matthew 5:9). Peacemakers are not merely those who avoid conflict but those who actively work to resolve it, to reconcile divided parties, to restore broken relationships. They are agents of reconciliation, reflecting the character of the God who reconciles the world to Himself. The promise attached to this beatitude—that peacemakers shall be called sons of God—indicates that in their peacemaking, they manifest the family likeness, bearing witness to the divine Father who is the ultimate source of all reconciliation.

Jesus also taught that reconciliation takes priority even over worship. "Therefore if you bring your gift to the altar, and there remember that your brother has something against you, leave your gift there before the altar, and go your way. First be reconciled to your brother, and then come and offer your gift" (Matthew 5:23-24). Worship is unacceptable if offered by an unreconciled heart. The vertical relationship with God cannot be right if horizontal relationships are wrong. Reconciliation with others is prerequisite to acceptable worship.

This teaching has profound implications for restorative justice. It means that the work of reconciliation is not optional but essential, not secondary but primary. It means that our relationship with God is intimately connected to our relationships with others. It means that we cannot claim to love God whom we have not seen if we do not love our neighbor whom we have seen (1 John 4:20). Restorative justice, in seeking to reconcile those who have been estranged by harm, is not merely a social program but a spiritual practice—a way of preparing ourselves to meet God.

The parable of the prodigal son provides the most powerful illustration of reconciliation in all of Scripture. The father does not merely forgive his wayward son; he restores him to full sonship. He puts a robe on him—a sign of honor. He puts a ring on his hand—a sign of authority. He puts sandals on his feet—a sign of free status, for servants went barefoot. He kills the fatted calf and hosts a celebration. The son who was dead is alive; the one who was lost is found. Relationship is not merely resumed but celebrated.

This parable reveals several dimensions of reconciliation. First, reconciliation requires the initiative of the wronged party. The father sees the son while he is still far off and runs to meet him. He does not wait for the son to reach the house, to prove himself, to complete his penance. He goes out to meet him, closing the distance, initiating the embrace.

Second, reconciliation requires acknowledgment of wrong. The son confesses his sin: "Father, I have sinned against heaven and before you, and am no longer worthy to be called your son." He does not minimize or excuse; he takes full responsibility. This acknowledgment opens the door to restoration.

Third, reconciliation involves restoration of relationship, not merely resumption of contact. The son is restored to sonship, not merely allowed back onto the property. He is given the symbols of belonging—robe, ring, sandals. He is welcomed into the celebration. The relationship is not merely tolerated but celebrated.

Fourth, reconciliation can be impeded by the attitudes of others. The elder son refuses to join the celebration, angry that his brother has been welcomed. His resentment threatens to exclude him from the very restoration he condemns. The father must go out to him as well, pleading with him to share in the joy.

This parable illustrates the restorative justice understanding of reconciliation. It is not enough to forgive; we must work toward restoration. It is not enough to release the debt; we must rebuild the relationship. This work takes time, requires effort, and depends on the willing participation of all parties. But when it is achieved, it is cause for celebration—the dead is alive, the lost is found.

The Apostle Paul, drawing on the ministry of Jesus, articulated the theological foundation of reconciliation. In 2 Corinthians 5, he declared that "God was in Christ reconciling the world to Himself, not imputing their trespasses to them, and has committed to us the word of reconciliation" (2 Corinthians 5:19). Reconciliation is God's work and the church's mission. Those who have been reconciled to God through Christ are called to be agents of reconciliation in the world.

This is the gospel of restorative justice: that the Creator of the universe is in the business of making all things new, of restoring what was broken, of healing what was wounded, of reconciling what was estranged. And this gospel comes with a commission: that those who have received this reconciliation should extend it to others, becoming ambassadors of reconciliation in every sphere of life.

Accountability: Responsibility and Opportunity

While Jesus emphasized forgiveness and reconciliation, He did not minimize accountability. He held individuals responsible for their actions while also offering them opportunities for redemption. This balance between accountability and grace is essential to restorative justice.

In the encounter with the woman caught in adultery (John 8:1-11), Jesus demonstrated this balance perfectly. The scribes and Pharisees brought to Him a woman who had been caught in the act of adultery. They reminded Him that the Law of Moses commanded such women to be stoned. They were testing Jesus, hoping to trap Him between the demands of the law and His reputation for mercy.

Jesus responded by stooping down and writing in the dust with His finger. When they continued pressing Him, He straightened up and said: "He who is without sin among you, let him throw a stone at her first." Then He stooped down again and continued writing. One by one, beginning with the oldest, the accusers slipped away until only Jesus and the woman remained.

Jesus straightened up and asked her: "Woman, where are those accusers of yours? Has no one condemned you?" She replied, "No one, Lord." And Jesus said: "Neither do I condemn you; go and sin no more."

This encounter reveals several dimensions of restorative accountability. First, Jesus did not minimize the woman's sin. He did not say that adultery was acceptable or that the law was wrong. He acknowledged that she had done something worthy of condemnation. Accountability begins with acknowledgment of wrongdoing.

Second, Jesus challenged the self-righteousness of the accusers. By inviting the one without sin to cast the first stone, He exposed the hypocrisy of those who were eager to condemn while ignoring their own faults. Accountability must be administered with humility, recognizing that we all stand in need of grace.

Third, Jesus refused to condemn the woman. "Neither do I condemn you" are words of grace, releasing her from the penalty she deserved. But this grace was not cheap; it came with a command: "Go and sin no more." Forgiveness does not mean permission to continue in sin. It means a new beginning, an opportunity to live differently.

This balance between accountability and grace is essential for restorative justice. Offenders must be held accountable for their actions—they must acknowledge their wrongdoing, face the consequences, and make amends. But accountability should not be merely punitive; it should open the door to transformation. The goal is not to condemn but to restore, not to punish but to change, not to exclude but to reintegrate.

Jesus demonstrated this same balance in His encounter with Zacchaeus (Luke 19:1-10). Zacchaeus was a chief tax collector, wealthy and despised. When Jesus came to Jericho, Zacchaeus climbed a sycamore tree to see Him over the crowd. Jesus looked up and said, "Zacchaeus, make haste and come down, for today I must stay at your house." Despite the murmuring of the crowd—"He has gone to be a guest with a man who is a sinner"—Jesus went to Zacchaeus's house.

During this visit, Zacchaeus was transformed. He stood and said to the Lord, "Look, Lord, I give half of my goods to the poor; and if I have taken anything from anyone by false accusation, I restore fourfold." Jesus responded: "Today salvation has come to this house, because he also is a son of Abraham; for the Son of Man has come to seek and to save that which was lost."

Note what happened. Jesus did not demand that Zacchaeus make restitution; He simply extended grace by coming to his house. But that grace evoked a response of accountability. Zacchaeus voluntarily committed to making amends—giving half his possessions to the poor and restoring fourfold anyone he had defrauded. Grace did not eliminate accountability; it inspired it. And Jesus affirmed this response as evidence of salvation.

This encounter illustrates the restorative principle that accountability flows from grace, not from coercion. When offenders experience genuine acceptance and love, they are more likely to take responsibility for their actions and make amends. Punishment alone rarely produces this kind of transformation. Grace, properly received, evokes repentance and restitution.

The Apostle Paul also emphasized accountability within a framework of grace. In Romans 14:12, he wrote: "So then each of us shall give account of himself to God." This ultimate accountability to God shapes our accountability to one another. We are responsible for our actions, for their consequences, for their impact on others. We cannot evade this responsibility or transfer it to someone else.

Restorative justice honors this accountability. It calls offenders to face the consequences of their actions, to acknowledge the harm they have caused, to make amends to the extent possible. It does not let them off the hook but holds them responsible in a way that promotes healing rather than merely inflicting pain.

Community Involvement: The Body of Christ

Jesus did not minister in isolation. He called disciples, formed a community, and sent them out to continue His work. He engaged the community in His ministry of healing and reconciliation, and He taught that community is essential for the life of faith.

When Jesus healed the paralytic lowered through the roof (Mark 2:1-12), He responded to the faith of the four friends who brought him. Their determination and love moved Jesus to act. The man's healing was not an individual transaction but a community event—involving his friends, the crowd, the scribes, and ultimately the whole community that witnessed and glorified God.

When Jesus sent out the twelve (Matthew 10) and later the seventy (Luke 10), He sent them in pairs, not alone. They were to support one another, to witness together, to embody the community of the kingdom. Their mission was not individual but corporate, not private but public.

When Jesus taught about conflict resolution in the church (Matthew 18:15-20), He outlined a process that involves the community. First, go alone to your brother. If he does not listen, take one or two others. If he refuses to listen to them, tell it to the church. The community is involved in the process of accountability and restoration. And Jesus promised His presence where two or three gather in His name.

This emphasis on community is foundational for restorative justice. Crime and conflict are not merely individual matters but communal wounds. They affect not only direct victims but families, friends, neighbors, and the broader society. Healing, therefore, requires community involvement.

In restorative processes such as family group conferences and circle processes, community members participate directly in addressing harm and developing plans for repair. They bring their perspectives, their wisdom, their resources. They help victims feel supported and heard. They hold offenders accountable while also offering encouragement and hope. They become partners in the work of healing, not passive observers of a process controlled by others.

The community's involvement in restorative justice serves several essential functions. First, it helps to rebuild trust between victims, offenders, and the community. When the community comes together to address harm, it sends a powerful message of solidarity and support to both victim and offender. This can help to promote a sense of community and foster a sense of accountability for everyone involved.

Second, community involvement can promote healing and closure for victims. In traditional criminal justice systems, victims are often left feeling isolated and powerless. But when the community comes together to support the victim and hold the offender accountable, it can help the victim to regain a sense of control over their life and promote healing.

Third, community involvement can reduce recidivism. By providing the offender with support and guidance, the community can help to address the underlying issues that may have contributed to their criminal behavior. This can help to reduce the likelihood of future offenses and promote rehabilitation.

Fourth, community involvement strengthens the social fabric. When communities take responsibility for addressing harm, they become more cohesive, more resilient, more capable of preventing future harm. Restorative justice builds community even as it heals individuals.

The biblical vision of community as the body of Christ (1 Corinthians 12) provides a theological foundation for this restorative role. In the body, each member is connected to every other, and the health of the whole depends on the health of each part. When one member suffers, all suffer together. When one member is honored, all rejoice together. This organic unity means that harm to any member harms the whole, and restoration of any member blesses the whole. The community, therefore, has a vital stake in the work of healing and reconciliation.

Restoration of Dignity: Seeing the Image of God

Throughout His ministry, Jesus consistently sought to restore the dignity of those who had been marginalized, excluded, and dehumanized. He touched lepers, restoring them not only to health but to community. He spoke with Samaritan women, affirming their worth despite ethnic and gender barriers. He welcomed children, declaring that the kingdom of heaven belongs to such as these. He ate with tax collectors and sinners, treating them as honored guests rather than outcasts.

In every encounter, Jesus saw beyond the labels that society had placed on people—leper, sinner, Samaritan, woman, child—and saw the human being created in God's image. He addressed them with respect, treated them with compassion, and restored them to dignity. This restoration of dignity is essential to restorative justice.

Consider Jesus' encounter with the Samaritan woman at the well (John 4:1-42). She came to draw water at noon, the hottest part of the day, likely because her reputation made it uncomfortable to come when other women gathered. She was a Samaritan, despised by Jews. She was a woman, with whom Jewish men did not speak in public. She had a complicated marital history—five husbands and currently living with a man not her husband.

Jesus broke through every barrier. He spoke to her, asked her for a drink, engaged her in theological conversation, revealed His knowledge of her life, and ultimately disclosed that He was the Messiah. He treated her with dignity, addressing her as a person capable of deep thought and spiritual insight. She responded by becoming the first evangelist to the Samaritans, bringing many to faith.

This encounter illustrates the restorative principle that dignity must be restored before healing can occur. Jesus did not begin by confronting the woman about her sin. He began by treating her as a person of worth, engaging her in conversation, taking her seriously. Only after establishing relationship did He address the painful realities of her life—and He did so gently, without condemnation. The woman's dignity restored, she was able to receive His truth and share it with others.

Similarly, in His encounter with the woman caught in adultery, Jesus restored her dignity even as He refused to condemn her. The accusers had treated her as an object, a tool for trapping Jesus, a sinner deserving death. Jesus treated her as a person, speaking to her directly, protecting her from violence, releasing her with a word of grace. He restored her dignity, and with it, her possibility for a new life.

This restoration of dignity is essential for restorative justice. Victims of crime have been degraded, violated, dehumanized. They need not only practical assistance but the restoration of their sense of worth. They need to know that they matter, that their suffering is acknowledged, that they are seen as persons, not cases.

Offenders, too, have been degraded—by their own actions, by societal stigma, by the justice system that often treats them as less than human. They need the restoration of dignity to become capable of genuine change. They need to see themselves as persons created in God's image, capable of good, worthy of respect, able to make amends and be restored.

The community also needs restoration of dignity. Communities affected by crime often feel violated, fearful, ashamed. They need to recover their sense of identity, their confidence in one another, their capacity for trust. Restorative justice, by involving the community in healing, helps to restore communal dignity.

The biblical doctrine of the imago Dei—that every human being is created in the image of God—provides the theological foundation for this restoration of dignity. Because we bear God's image, our worth is inherent, not earned. It cannot be erased by any action, no matter how heinous. The offender, no less than the victim, remains an image-bearer, deserving of dignity and capable of restoration. Restorative justice, in seeking to restore dignity to all, reflects this foundational truth.

Healing and Transformation: The Ministry of Wholeness

Jesus' ministry was fundamentally a ministry of healing and transformation. He healed the sick, gave sight to the blind, made the lame walk, cleansed lepers, cast out demons, raised the dead. But His healing was never merely physical; it was always holistic, addressing the whole person and restoring them to community.

When Jesus healed the leper (Mark 1:40-45), He did more than cure a disease. He restored a man who had been excluded from community, cut off from family and worship, forced to live alone and cry "Unclean!" to warn others away. By touching him—an act that would have made Jesus ceremonially unclean—He communicated that this man was worthy of contact, deserving of compassion, fit for community. The healing restored not only his body but his place in society.

When Jesus healed the paralytic lowered through the roof (Mark 2:1-12), He first declared, "Son, your sins are forgiven." This announcement addressed the man's deepest need—reconciliation with God—before addressing his physical condition. Only after establishing this spiritual restoration did Jesus heal his body. The healing was holistic, addressing the whole person.

When Jesus cast out Legion from the Gerasene demoniac (Mark 5:1-20), He liberated a man who had been bound by countless demons, living among the tombs, cutting himself, crying out night and day. After the demons were cast out, the man was found "sitting, clothed and in his right mind." Jesus then sent him back to his community to tell what the Lord had done for him. The healing restored not only his sanity but his role as a witness, his place in community, his purpose in life.

This holistic healing is the model for restorative justice. Crime causes harm in multiple dimensions—physical, emotional, psychological, relational, spiritual. Healing, therefore, must address all these dimensions. Victims need not only practical assistance but emotional support, psychological care, spiritual comfort. Offenders need not only accountability but transformation, addressing the underlying issues that led to their behavior. Communities need not only safety but restoration of trust, rebuilding of relationships, strengthening of social bonds.

Restorative justice, following Jesus' example, seeks this holistic healing. It brings together those affected by harm to address the full impact of what has happened. It provides opportunities for victims to express their pain, for offenders to acknowledge their responsibility, for communities to offer support. It seeks not merely to resolve disputes but to transform lives, not merely to settle cases but to heal wounds.

The Apostle Paul described this transformation in Romans 12:2: "Do not be conformed to this world, but be transformed by the renewing of your mind, that you may prove what is that good and acceptable and perfect will of God." Transformation is the renewal of the mind, the reorientation of the heart, the reshaping of the life. It is what happens when people encounter the healing power of God's love.

Restorative justice seeks this transformation for all involved. Victims can be transformed from wounded to healed, from bitter to forgiving, from isolated to connected. Offenders can be transformed from guilty to accountable, from ashamed to repentant, from broken to restored. Communities can be transformed from fractured to united, from fearful to trusting, from passive to engaged. This transformation is the goal of restorative justice, and it is made possible by the healing power of God's love, mediated through the practices of encounter, accountability, and repair.

Justice as Love in Action

Jesus' teachings on love are the foundation of His vision of justice. When asked about the greatest commandment, He replied: "You shall love the Lord your God with all your heart, with all your soul, and with all your mind. This is the first and great commandment. And the second is like it: You shall love your neighbor as yourself. On these two commandments hang all the Law and the Prophets" (Matthew 22:37-40).

Love, for Jesus, is not merely a sentiment but a practice, not merely a feeling but an action. It is the fulfillment of the law, the sum of all that God requires. And it is the measure of justice. Justice, rightly understood, is love distributed—love for the neighbor, love for the stranger, love for the enemy, love for the marginalized, love for the oppressed.

In the Sermon on the Mount, Jesus taught a love that goes beyond natural affection. "You have heard that it was said, 'You shall love your neighbor and hate your enemy.' But I say to you, love your enemies, bless those who curse you, do good to those who hate you, and pray for those who spitefully use you and persecute you" (Matthew 5:43-44). This is not love as attraction but love as action—seeking the good of even those who wish us ill.

This love for enemies is the ultimate expression of restorative justice. It refuses to be defined by the harm received, refuses to return evil for evil, refuses to perpetuate cycles of violence. Instead, it seeks the good of the offender, hoping for their transformation, working for their restoration. This is the love that Jesus embodied on the cross, praying for those who crucified Him.

The Apostle Paul, drawing on Jesus' teaching, wrote in Romans 13:10: "Love does no harm to a neighbor; therefore love is the fulfillment of the law." Love is not merely one commandment among many; it is the sum of all commandments, the principle from which all specific duties flow. Whatever harms a neighbor is forbidden; whatever helps a neighbor is required. Justice, then, is love made practical, love applied to the complexities of human relationship.

Restorative justice embodies this love in action. It seeks the good of victims by addressing their needs, giving them voice, supporting their healing. It seeks the good of offenders by holding them accountable, calling them to repentance, offering them restoration. It seeks the good of communities by involving them in healing, rebuilding trust, strengthening relationships. Restorative justice is love distributed to all affected by harm.

This understanding of justice as love in action has profound implications for how we respond to crime and conflict. It means that our primary question should not be, "What punishment does this offender deserve?" but rather, "What does love require for the victim, the offender, and the community?" It means that our goal should not be the infliction of pain but the restoration of relationship. It means that our measure of success should not be how many offenders we punish but how many lives we heal, how many relationships we restore, how many communities we strengthen.

The Mandate for Prison Ministry

Jesus explicitly commanded His followers to minister to those in prison. In the parable of the sheep and the goats (Matthew 25:31-46), He identified Himself with the imprisoned and made care for them a criterion of judgment. "I was in prison and you came to Me," He says to the righteous. And when they ask when they saw Him in prison, He replies: "Assuredly, I say to you, inasmuch as you did it to one of the least of these My brethren, you did it to Me."

This identification of Jesus with prisoners is remarkable. He does not say that visiting prisoners is like visiting Him; He says it is visiting Him. The prisoner represents Christ. To care for the prisoner is to care for Jesus Himself. To neglect the prisoner is to neglect Jesus. This teaching elevates prison ministry from optional charity to essential worship.

The author of Hebrews reinforces this mandate: "Remember the prisoners as if chained with them—those who are mistreated—since you yourselves are in the body also" (Hebrews 13:3). This remembrance is not merely cognitive but empathetic—as if chained with them, sharing their suffering, bearing their burden. It recognizes that we are all in the body, all subject to suffering, all in need of solidarity.

Throughout Scripture, God's concern for prisoners is evident. The prophet Isaiah proclaimed that the Messiah would "proclaim liberty to the captives, and the opening of the prison to those who are bound" (Isaiah 61:1). Jesus announced that this prophecy was fulfilled in Him (Luke 4:18-19). His mission included freeing prisoners—not only spiritually but physically, not only metaphorically but actually.

The early church took this mandate seriously. When Peter was imprisoned by Herod, the church prayed earnestly for him (Acts 12:5). When Paul and Silas were imprisoned in Philippi, they prayed and sang hymns to God, and their witness led to the conversion of their jailer and his family (Acts 16:25-34). Prison could not contain the power of God or the witness of the faithful.

This mandate for prison ministry raises important questions for the church. What specific actions should the church take to fulfill this mandate? How can the church balance its role as a spiritual institution with the practical aspects of criminal justice ministry? How can the church work collaboratively with the criminal justice system while also advocating for systemic change? What types of support and resources are necessary for the church to effectively carry out its mandate? How can the church ensure that its criminal justice ministry is inclusive and equitable, and does not perpetuate systemic biases or discrimination? How can the church help to address the root causes of crime, such as poverty, inequality, and lack of access to education and employment opportunities? How can the church support both victims and offenders in the restorative justice process, while also upholding the principles of accountability and justice?

These questions challenge the church to move beyond token gestures toward sustained engagement. Visiting prisoners is essential, but it is not enough. The church must also advocate for criminal justice reform, support reentry programs, address underlying causes of crime, and promote restorative justice practices. The mandate is comprehensive, calling the church to be agents of transformation in every dimension of criminal justice.

The Ministry of Reconciliation

Restorative justice is grounded in the biblical call to the ministry of reconciliation. The Apostle Paul, in 2 Corinthians 5:18-19, articulates this foundation: "All this is from God, who reconciled us to himself through Christ and gave us the ministry of reconciliation: that God was reconciling the world to himself in Christ, not counting people's sins against them. And he has committed to us the message of reconciliation."

This passage reveals several essential truths. First, reconciliation is God's work. It is God who reconciles us to Himself through Christ. We do not achieve reconciliation by our own efforts; we receive it as a gift. This gift is the foundation of all restorative justice.

Second, reconciliation is accomplished through Christ. His death and resurrection made possible the restoration of relationship between God and humanity. In Christ, God was reconciling the world to Himself, not counting our trespasses against us. This is the gospel—the good news that God has acted to restore what sin had broken.

Third, those who have received this reconciliation are entrusted with the ministry of reconciliation. They are called to extend to others what they have received. They are to be ambassadors of Christ, as though God were pleading through them: "Be reconciled to God" (2 Corinthians 5:20). The ministry of reconciliation is not optional for believers; it is their identity and mission.

This ministry of reconciliation requires that we view people through the eyes of Jesus, not as the world views them. Jesus made this clear in John 3:17: "God did not send His Son into the world to condemn the world, but that the world through Him might be saved." His mission was not condemnation but salvation. His purpose was not to judge but to restore. Until He comes again in judgment, we must remember that humanity is so important to Jesus that He died for them (John 3:16).

The world often views individuals based on their actions or social status. It stigmatizes and marginalizes those who have been involved in the criminal justice system. It labels them as criminals, offenders, felons—reducing them to their worst acts. This creates a cycle of shame and despair that can hinder their ability to make positive changes and reintegrate into society.

The restorative justice paradigm, following Jesus' example, shifts the focus from punishment and retribution to healing and restoration. It requires us to see individuals not just as perpetrators of crime, but as human beings who have the potential to change and be restored to their communities. It recognizes that they too are made in God's image and are in need of His love and mercy.

By viewing individuals through the eyes of Jesus and embracing the restorative justice paradigm, we can promote healing, reconciliation, and transformation for all those impacted by crime. We can become agents of the ministry of reconciliation, extending to others the grace we have received.

The Theological Foundation: Sin, Redemption, and Restoration

The biblical story provides the theological foundation for restorative justice. It begins with creation, when humanity was made in the image of God, placed in right relationship with God, with each other, and with creation. This original shalom—peace, wholeness, flourishing—is God's intention for all creation.

But sin entered the world through Adam's disobedience. As a result of his sin, Adam passed on to the human race physical and spiritual death. The Apostle Paul explains that "through one man sin entered the world, and death through sin, and thus death spread to all men, because all sinned" (Romans 5:12). This state of sinfulness, often called original sin, means that all human beings are born with a natural tendency toward sin and a predisposition to rebel against God. This sin nature affects every aspect of human life—thoughts, emotions, and actions.

Death has three distinct manifestations: spiritual death or separation from God (Ephesians 2:1-2; 4:18); physical death (Hebrews 9:27); and eternal death, also known as the second death, which includes not only eternal separation from God but eternal torment in the lake of fire (Revelation 20:11-15). This is the terrible consequence of sin.

Yet God, in His love and mercy, provided a way for humans to be reconciled to Him through the sacrifice of His Son Jesus Christ. "All have sinned and fall short of the glory of God" (Romans 3:23), and "the wages of sin is death" (Romans 6:23). But "God demonstrates His own love toward us, in that while we were still sinners, Christ died for us" (Romans 5:8). Through His death and resurrection, Jesus paid the penalty for sin and opened the way for forgiveness and restoration.

In this sense, Jesus brings restorative justice to the earth. Rather than condemning the world, "God was in Christ reconciling the world to Himself, not imputing their trespasses to them" (2 Corinthians 5:19). The new justice of God is not retributive but redemptive. As Paul describes in Titus 2:14, Jesus "gave Himself for us, that He might redeem us from every lawless deed and purify for Himself His own special people." God's justice seeks to redeem, to purify, to restore.

This redemptive justice brings healing to relationships with God and with the community of humanity. Through Jesus' death and resurrection, it is possible for humanity to be reconciled to God and to one another. This reconciliation is not simply a matter of forgiving sins and moving on, but of restoring broken relationships and building new ones based on love, trust, and mutual respect.

The restorative justice paradigm, grounded in this theology, views crime as an injury to God, individuals, relationships, and the community—not just a violation of laws and rules. It emphasizes repairing the harm done to victims and restoring relationships between offenders, victims, and the community. It recognizes that crime also injures the criminal, considering the opportunity costs associated with choosing illegal rather than productive activities.

The goal of restorative justice, therefore, is to repair the harm caused by crime, promote healing for the victim and community, and hold the offender accountable while giving them an opportunity to make amends and reintegrate into society. It focuses on addressing the root causes of crime and finding ways to prevent future harm, rather than just punishing the offender. It seeks to restore relationships and promote reconciliation between the parties involved, and to empower individuals and communities to take an active role in resolving conflicts and repairing harm.

The Lesson of Job: Trusting God's Justice

The book of Job provides profound insights into the nature of God's justice and the proper human response to suffering. Job was a righteous man who experienced immense suffering and loss—his children killed, his property destroyed, his health devastated. Throughout the book, Job struggles to understand why he is suffering and questions the justice of God.

Job's friends offer various theories, including that Job must have sinned and brought his misfortune upon himself. But Job maintains his innocence, insisting that he has not done anything to deserve such suffering. He demands an explanation from God, wanting to understand why the righteous suffer while the wicked prosper.

In the end, God responds to Job out of a whirlwind (Job 38-41). He does not answer Job's questions directly or explain the reasons for his suffering. Instead, He reveals His power, wisdom, and sovereignty—His control over creation, His knowledge beyond human comprehension, His purposes beyond human understanding.

In Job 40:8, God asks two penetrating questions: "Would you discredit my justice? Would you condemn me to justify yourself?" These questions suggest that Job had a limited understanding of God's justice and that he had been trying to justify himself rather than trust in God's wisdom and sovereignty.

The first question, "Would you discredit my justice?" implies that Job may have been questioning the fairness or goodness of God's justice. His suffering seemed to contradict his understanding of how God should treat the righteous. God's question challenges Job to trust in His justice, even when it is difficult to understand.

The second question, "Would you condemn me to justify yourself?" suggests that Job may have been trying to justify his own righteousness in the face of his suffering. He had maintained his innocence, and he may have been tempted to criticize God's justice in order to make his own case. God's question challenges Job to trust in His righteousness and sovereignty, even when it challenges his own sense of justice.

In chapter 42, Job responds to God's revelation with humility and submission: "I know that you can do all things, and that no purpose of yours can be thwarted... I had heard of you by the hearing of the ear, but now my eye sees you" (Job 42:2,5). Job confesses that he had spoken without understanding and repents in dust and ashes.

When Job saw the righteousness of God, he also saw the justice of God. He recognized that God's justice is not necessarily based on human understanding of fairness and punishment. Instead, God's justice is rooted in His ultimate plan and purpose, which is beyond human comprehension. Job's experience leads him to a deeper appreciation of God's justice, which is not simply about rewarding the righteous and punishing the wicked, but is rooted in God's wisdom, sovereignty, and goodness.

This lesson from Job is essential for restorative justice. It reminds us that God's ways are not our ways, that His justice transcends our understanding, that we must trust Him even when we cannot comprehend. It also reminds us that suffering is not always a consequence of sin, that the innocent may suffer, that we must be careful not to judge others based on their circumstances. Restorative justice, grounded in humility before God's mystery, seeks to restore without presuming to know all the answers.

The Unity of God's Attributes

It is important to know that God's attributes are one. In Christian theology, God's attributes are described as being unified or inseparable. Each attribute—love, mercy, justice, righteousness—is not separate or distinct but interconnected, flowing from God's essential nature.

God's justice, therefore, is not arbitrary or separate from His love and mercy. It is grounded in His love and works in harmony with mercy. God's justice is not punitive but restorative, seeking to bring about the healing and redemption of individuals and society. Similarly, God's righteousness is not separate from His justice but flows from it, providing the standard by which justice is measured.

In Scripture, Jesus is spoken of as both the justice and righteousness of God. He embodies these attributes in His teachings and actions. He taught about the importance of justice and how it should be carried out with compassion and mercy. He challenged corrupt authorities and defended the marginalized and oppressed. He lived a life of perfect righteousness, obeying God's laws and fulfilling the prophecies of the Old Testament.

Through His death and resurrection, Jesus provided a way for humanity to be reconciled with God and receive salvation. This act was both just and righteous, fulfilling the requirement of justice for sin while demonstrating God's love and mercy for His creation. When justice came to the nations in the person of Jesus Christ, it brought the righteousness of God, which reconciles those who receive Him as Savior.

The unity of God's attributes means that restorative justice is not opposed to God's justice but is its fullest expression. God's justice is not satisfied by punishment alone but by restoration.

His righteousness is not content with condemnation but seeks redemption. His love is not passive but active, working to heal and reconcile. Restorative justice, grounded in these unified attributes, reflects the character of God Himself.

The Responsibility of Every Believer

Second Corinthians 5:18 states, "All this is from God, who reconciled us to himself through Christ and gave us the ministry of reconciliation." This verse highlights the responsibility of every believer to be involved in the ministry of reconciliation.

The passage emphasizes that it is God who initiated reconciliation through Jesus Christ. As believers, we have received this gift of reconciliation and are now called to extend it to others. This involves actively participating in the work of bringing people into a restored relationship with God and with one another.

The phrase "ministry of reconciliation" means that believers are called to be ambassadors of Christ, working towards the restoration of relationships and the healing of brokenness. This can take many forms: sharing the gospel with others, seeking to reconcile broken relationships, working for social justice, and demonstrating love and compassion towards others.

The responsibility of every believer is not just to receive the gift of reconciliation but to actively participate in extending it to others. This requires a commitment to living out our faith in practical ways, both individually and collectively as the body of Christ. It is a call to be agents of change in a broken world, working towards the restoration of all things through the power of the Holy Spirit.

As ambassadors for Christ, we have the responsibility of bringing others to Christ so they can reconcile with God. But this reconciliation with God is inseparable from reconciliation with others. The vertical and horizontal dimensions of reconciliation are intertwined. We cannot claim to be reconciled to God while remaining unreconciled to our brothers and sisters. The ministry of reconciliation encompasses both.

Restoration in the Law and the Gospel

Restoration is reflected in the Law that was given in the Old Testament and the new commandment Jesus gave in the New Testament. In the Old Testament, the Law included provisions for restitution and restoration for victims of crime. For example, Exodus 22:1 states, "If a man steals an ox or a sheep and slaughters it or sells it, he must pay back five head of cattle for the ox and four sheep for the sheep." This shows that the offender had to not only return the stolen property but also provide additional compensation for the harm caused to the victim.

These provisions for restitution were not merely punitive but restorative. They sought to make the victim whole, to compensate for loss, to repair harm. They held offenders accountable while also providing a path to restoration. The Law, in this sense, was a schoolmaster pointing toward the restorative justice that would be fully revealed in Christ.

In the New Testament, Jesus gave a new commandment to His disciples: "A new commandment I give to you, that you love one another: just as I have loved you, you also are to love one another" (John 13:34). This commandment emphasizes the importance of love and forgiveness in relationships, and is reflected in the principles of restorative justice which aim to repair harm and restore relationships.

The purpose of the Law, as Paul explains in Galatians 3:24, was to serve as a schoolmaster or tutor to bring us to Christ. The Law revealed God's standards of righteousness and demonstrated humanity's inability to perfectly keep them. It exposed the need for a Savior and pointed toward Jesus Christ, who fulfilled the Law and made a way for justification by faith.

When the Word of God became flesh and lived among us, the consummation of the justice of God in the earth yielded righteousness. Jesus Christ, through His life, death, and resurrection, reconciled humanity to God and made it possible for people to experience the righteousness of God. The justice of God finds its ultimate fulfillment in Him.

The law of lex talionis—"an eye for an eye, a tooth for a tooth"—was given to limit the revenges of a people without Christ. It sought to limit revenge by instituting proportionate punishment, preventing individuals from taking excessive vengeance on others. But it was limited in its ability to address underlying issues and restore relationships.

With the coming of Christ, the concept of justice was transformed from retribution to restoration. Jesus taught that revenge was not part of God's justice and that punishment did not yield righteousness. Instead, He called for forgiveness and reconciliation, teaching that the greatest commandment was to love God and love our neighbors as ourselves.

Jesus came not to abolish the Law but to fulfill it (Matthew 5:17). He provided the perfect example of righteousness and obedience to God's will, serving as the ultimate sacrifice for the forgiveness of sins and offering a path to true restoration. Through faith in Jesus, believers can experience reconciliation with God and the transformation necessary to live a life of righteousness.

Furthermore, Jesus elevated the concept of restoration beyond physical or material compensation to include emotional and spiritual healing. In the Sermon on the Mount, He taught that those who have been wronged should not seek revenge but rather seek to love and serve their enemies (Matthew 5:43-48). He emphasized the importance of forgiveness, instructing His followers to forgive others as they have been forgiven by God (Matthew 6:14-15).

In this way, Jesus provided a higher standard of justice and restoration that goes beyond mere legalistic compliance with the Law. He showed that true restoration involves not only the settling of debts and the restoration of relationships but also the healing of emotional and spiritual wounds. Through faith in Him, believers can experience the transformative power of God's love and grace, leading to true restoration and righteousness.

Romans 6:23 describes two inexorable absolutes: spiritual death is the paycheck for every man's sin, and eternal life is a loving free gift God gives undeserving sinners who believe in His Son. The fulfillment of justice was not intended to give offenders what they deserved, but to move them towards restoration through the power of love. Jesus demonstrated this approach in His teachings and actions, offering forgiveness and restoration rather than condemnation.

The Goal of Restorative Justice Ministry

The goal of restorative justice ministry is to promote healing, reconciliation, and restoration for all parties affected by crime or harm. This approach recognizes that crime is not just a violation of law but a violation of relationships and the community. Restorative justice ministry seeks to repair the harm caused by crime by bringing together the victim, the offender, and the community to address the needs of all involved.

Most ministries today do not address all the parties affected by crime. They either focus on the offender while neglecting the victim and community, or they focus only on the victim. Complete healing and restoration only occur when the injuries to all parties are addressed. Restorative justice ministry aims to shift the focus from punishment to restoration, offering a more holistic approach to justice that takes into account the emotional, psychological, and spiritual needs of all parties involved.

This involves creating a safe space for open dialogue, empathy, and understanding, and facilitating a process of healing and transformation that leads to greater accountability, responsibility, and meaningful restitution. The goal is not just to resolve conflicts but to promote social justice and community well-being, addressing the root causes of crime and working towards systemic change that promotes equity, fairness, and respect for all individuals.

Restorative justice ministry also seeks to empower individuals and communities to take an active role in shaping the justice system and promoting a more compassionate and restorative approach to justice. It fosters healing, reconciliation, and restoration for all involved, promoting a more just and peaceful society.

Love as the Foundation

God requires that we love one another as Jesus loved us, and to love our neighbor as ourselves. This commandment is derived from two key teachings of Jesus. In John 13:34-35, Jesus says, "A new commandment I give to you, that you love one another: just as I have loved you, you also are to love one another. By this all people will know that you are my disciples, if you have love for one another." This commandment to love one another is rooted in Jesus' own love for His disciples, which was selfless, sacrificial, and unconditional.

The second teaching comes from Mark 12:31, where Jesus answers a question about the most important commandment. He replies that the first is to love God with all one's heart, soul, mind, and strength, and the second is this: "You shall love your neighbor as yourself." There is no commandment greater than these.

Together, these teachings call us to love others with the same love that God has shown us, and to love our neighbors as ourselves. This love is not based on merit or worthiness but is a reflection of the unconditional love that God has for all people. As Christians, we are called to live out this love in our relationships with others, seeking to show kindness, compassion, and forgiveness to all, regardless of their background, beliefs, or actions.

Our neighbor includes the prisoner who offended, the victim who is brokenhearted, and the community which was blinded by a need for revenge. When we show love and compassion to those who have offended, we fulfill this commandment and demonstrate the love of Christ. When we show love and support to victims as they heal from trauma, we fulfill this commandment. When we involve the community in addressing harm and developing solutions that promote healing and prevention, we fulfill this commandment.

Restorative justice ministry recognizes that all people are created in the image of God and have inherent dignity and worth. By loving our neighbor—including those who have offended, those who have been victimized, and the wider community—we can work towards a more just and compassionate society.

Biblical Justice as Restoration

Biblical justice is restoration through righteousness to all who receive Christ. Paul described this view in Romans 3:22: "the righteousness of God, through faith in Jesus Christ, to all and on all who believe." Biblical justice can be defined as the restoration of what is broken or wrong, to bring about righteousness in all aspects of life.

The ultimate source of justice is God, and He has revealed His perfect standard of justice in the Bible. God desires justice for all people, including both the victim and the offender. Restoration is the key to biblical justice. When a wrong has been committed, restoration involves making things right between the offender and the victim, and also between the offender and God. This restoration is made possible through the sacrifice of Jesus Christ, who paid the penalty for our sins and made it possible for us to reconciled to God.

Restorative justice ministry seeks to bring about this restoration through various means such as restitution, reconciliation, and rehabilitation. It seeks to involve all parties affected by the crime—the offender, the victim, and the community. The goal is not only to hold offenders accountable for their actions but also to bring about healing and reconciliation for all involved. It aims to address the root causes of crime and to provide opportunities for offenders to take responsibility for their actions, make amends, and move towards a better future.

The Epistle to Philemon: A Case Study in Restorative Justice

Paul's letter to Philemon serves as a fine example of restorative justice. In this brief but powerful epistle, Paul writes to Philemon, a slave owner, regarding his slave Onesimus who had run away and then come to faith in Christ through Paul's ministry. Paul writes to appeal to Philemon to receive Onesimus back not just as a slave but as a brother in Christ.

Paul could have simply ordered Philemon to release Onesimus, or could have taken legal action against him for mistreating his slave. Instead, Paul takes a restorative justice approach by appealing to Philemon's Christian values and urging him to do what is right, not just what is legally required.

In his letter, Paul acknowledges that Onesimus had wronged Philemon and offers to make things right by paying for any damage caused by his escape. He also reminds Philemon that they are brothers in Christ, and that he should receive Onesimus back as he would receive Paul himself. This approach emphasizes reconciliation and restoration rather than punishment and retribution.

The concepts found in this epistle demonstrate the principles of restorative justice. Rehabilitation is evident in Paul's description of Onesimus as his son (verse 10) and as a beloved brother (verse 16). Onesimus had been transformed through his encounter with Paul and with Christ. Restoration is evident in Paul's appeal to Philemon to receive Onesimus as he would receive Paul (verse 17). Restitution is evident in Paul's offer to pay whatever Onesimus owed (verses 18-19).

Paul's leadership in this situation is remarkable. He leaves the decision completely up to Philemon, not trampling on his rights as the slave's owner. Yet he arranges things so it would be very difficult for Philemon to say no without losing face among his brothers and sisters in Christ. The letter demonstrates forgiveness, reconciliation, restitution, healing, and community involvement—all principles of restorative justice.

The crime Onesimus committed against Philemon was stealing from his master and running away. Under Roman law, he could face the death penalty. Yet Paul recommended that Onesimus return to Philemon to make amends, urging Philemon to welcome him back not as a slave but as a brother in Christ. Paul's message was that true restoration and justice can only be achieved through forgiveness and reconciliation, rather than punishment and retribution.

The epistle is Paul's plea that Onesimus no longer be viewed as a runaway slave but as a brother beloved. In the ancient Roman world, slavery was a common institution, and it was not uncommon for slaves to run away. But Paul recognized that Onesimus was now a brother in Christ and encouraged Philemon to see him in the same light. In this relationship as brothers and not slaves, Paul effectively abolished the sting of the master-slave relationship.

The Way of the Cross

While the world pursues power and glory, Christians are to pursue the way of the Cross—the way of forgiveness, restoration, and love. The way of the Cross, as exemplified by Jesus Christ, is a way of sacrificial love and humility. It is a path that goes against the values of the world, which often prioritize power, prestige, and personal gain. Instead of seeking these things, Christians are called to imitate Christ by putting the needs of others before their own and seeking restoration and reconciliation rather than revenge.

Forgiveness is a key aspect of the way of the Cross. Just as Christ forgave those who crucified Him, Christians are called to forgive those who have wronged them. This does not mean that justice should not be sought or that wrongs should be ignored, but that forgiveness should be extended even to those who do not deserve it. In this way, forgiveness can lead to restoration and healing, both for the individual who forgives and for the one who is forgiven.

Restoration is also a crucial aspect of the way of the Cross. Rather than seeking revenge or punishment, Christians are called to seek restoration and reconciliation with those who have wronged them. This means working towards repairing relationships and restoring the dignity of those who have been hurt. Restoration requires humility and a willingness to admit fault and seek forgiveness.

Love is the foundation of the way of the Cross. Christ's sacrificial love on the Cross is the ultimate example of love in action, and Christians are called to love others in the same way. This means seeking the good of others, even at personal cost, and putting the needs of others before one's own desires. Love is a transformative force that can bring healing, restoration, and reconciliation.

No matter what a person has done in the past, God calls them to Himself and offers them the hope of restorative justice. Paul recognized this fact when he wrote in 1 Timothy 1:15: "Christ Jesus came into the world to save sinners, of whom I am chief." Paul had been a persecutor and murderer of the followers of Christ, but God called him to Himself and offered him the hope of restorative justice.

The message of the gospel is one of hope and redemption. God loves us despite our failures and sins and desires to restore us to a right relationship with Him. This hope is available to all people, no matter what they have done in the past. Throughout the Bible, we see examples of individuals who were given a second chance by God—David, who committed adultery and murder but was forgiven and restored; Paul, who persecuted Christians but became the greatest evangelist in history.

The forgiveness granted by God and by others is what makes restoration possible. Forgiveness is an essential component of restorative justice because it allows for healing and reconciliation to take place. When someone has wronged another person, the relationship is damaged, and forgiveness is necessary for that relationship to be restored. Without forgiveness, the wronged person may hold onto anger, bitterness, and resentment, preventing any chance of restoration.

God's forgiveness is offered freely to all who come to Him in repentance. This forgiveness is not based on our own merit or worthiness but on God's grace and love for us. Similarly, when someone wrongs us, forgiving them is an act of grace and love, based on our desire to restore the relationship and move forward in love and reconciliation.

In restorative justice, forgiveness allows both the offender and the victim to move towards healing and restoration. The offender can acknowledge wrongdoing, seek forgiveness, and work towards making amends and rebuilding trust. The victim can choose to forgive and release anger and bitterness, allowing them to move forward in healing and reconciliation. Forgiveness is crucial for restoration and healing for all parties involved.

Jesus Christ, then, stands as the perfect model for restorative justice. His compassion and mercy, His teaching on forgiveness, His ministry of reconciliation, His call to accountability, His engagement with community, His restoration of dignity, His healing and transformation, and His embodiment of justice as love in action provide a comprehensive paradigm for restorative practice. Those who follow Him are called to embody this same restorative justice in their own lives and ministries, becoming agents of reconciliation in a broken world.

CHAPTER 09

RESTORATIVE JUSTICE IN CHRISTIAN COMMUNITIES

The Christian community, the body of Christ, the church—these terms describe a people called out of the world to be a sign and foretaste of God's redemptive purposes for all creation. The church is not merely an institution or a gathering of like-minded individuals; it is a new humanity, a reconciled people, a community in which the dividing walls of hostility have been broken down and the peace of Christ reigns. As such, the church is uniquely positioned to embody and practice restorative justice. Indeed, it is difficult to imagine a community more naturally suited to restorative principles than one founded on forgiveness, reconciliation, and the restoration of broken relationships.

This chapter explores the application of restorative justice within Christian communities. We will examine how churches can draw on their biblical foundations to address conflicts and harm, how they can support both victims and offenders, how they can engage the broader community in the work of healing, and how they can become centers of restorative practice in a broken world. We will also consider the challenges and opportunities that arise when churches seek to embody restorative justice, and we will discover that the church, at its best, is a living demonstration of the restorative justice that God intends for all humanity.

Biblical Foundations: The Church as a Restorative Community

The church's engagement with restorative justice is not an innovation but a recovery of its own deepest identity. From its earliest days, the Christian community understood itself as a place where forgiveness was practiced, relationships were restored, and the marginalized were welcomed. The New Testament letters are filled with exhortations to pursue reconciliation, to forgive one another, and to bear with one another in love.

The Apostle Paul, in his letter to the Colossians, captures this vision: "Therefore, as the elect of God, holy and beloved, put on tender mercies, kindness, humility, meekness, longsuffering; bearing with one another, and forgiving one another, if anyone has a complaint against another; even as Christ forgave you, so you also must do" (Colossians 3:12-13). Forgiveness is not optional but essential, grounded in the forgiveness we have received from Christ. The community is to be characterized by tender mercies, kindness, humility, meekness, and patience—precisely the qualities that restorative justice requires.

Paul also provides practical guidance for conflict resolution within the community. In 1 Corinthians 6, he expresses dismay that believers are taking their disputes before secular courts rather than resolving them within the church. "Dare any of you, having a matter against another, go to law before the unrighteous, and not before the saints?" (1 Corinthians 6:1). He assumes that the community has the wisdom and authority to adjudicate disputes among its members, to hold members accountable, and to restore relationships. The church is to be a place where justice is done, not by external authorities but by the community itself.

The letter to the Ephesians proclaims that Christ "has broken down the middle wall of separation" between Jews and Gentiles, creating "one new man from the two, thus making peace" (Ephesians 2:14-15). The church is the embodiment of this reconciliation—a community in which former enemies become brothers and sisters, in which historic divisions are overcome, in which the peace of Christ reigns. This reconciled community is itself a proclamation of the gospel, a sign that in Christ, all things can be made new.

The letter to the Hebrews exhorts believers to "pursue peace with all people, and holiness, without which no one will see the Lord" (Hebrews 12:14). The pursuit of peace is not optional but essential, not peripheral but central to the life of faith. And this peace is not merely the absence of conflict but the presence of right relationship—shalom, the flourishing of community under God's reign.

The first letter of John insists that love for God and love for neighbor are inseparable. "If someone says, 'I love God,' and hates his brother, he is a liar; for he who does not love his brother whom he has seen, how can he love God whom he has not seen?" (1 John 4:20). The vertical relationship with God is manifested in horizontal relationships with others. A community that claims to love God must demonstrate that love through mutual care, forgiveness, and reconciliation.

These biblical foundations provide the theological rationale for restorative justice in Christian communities. The church is called to be a place where forgiveness is practiced, where conflicts are resolved, where relationships are restored, where the marginalized are welcomed, where the peace of Christ reigns. Restorative justice is not an add-on to the church's mission but an expression of its very nature.

Confession and Repentance: The Path to Restoration

Christian communities have always emphasized the importance of confession and repentance. From the ministry of John the Baptist, who called people to "repent, for the kingdom of heaven is at hand" (Matthew 3:2), to Jesus' own proclamation that "repentance and remission of sins should be preached in His name to all nations" (Luke 24:47), to the apostles' call to "repent and be converted, that your sins may be blotted out" (Acts 3:19), the message is clear: restoration begins with acknowledgment of wrongdoing and a turning toward God.

In restorative justice, confession and repentance play an equally essential role. Offenders are encouraged to acknowledge their wrongdoing, to take responsibility for the harm they have caused, and to seek forgiveness from those they have wronged. This is not merely a matter of external compliance but of internal transformation. The goal is not simply to go through the motions of confession but to experience genuine repentance—a change of heart and mind that leads to changed behavior.

The Apostle Paul distinguishes between two kinds of sorrow: worldly sorrow and godly sorrow. "Godly sorrow produces repentance leading to salvation, not to be regretted; but the sorrow of the world produces death" (2 Corinthians 7:10). Worldly sorrow is regret at being caught, at suffering consequences, at having one's desires frustrated. It leads to guilt, shame, despair, and ultimately more of the same. Godly sorrow is grief over the harm caused, over the violation of relationship, over the offense against God and neighbor. It leads to genuine change, to making amends, to new life.

In a restorative justice context, the offender's journey begins with this godly sorrow. The offender must recognize the harm they have caused, experience genuine remorse, and take responsibility for their actions. This recognition often comes through a process of deep reflection and self-examination. The offender may be encouraged to acknowledge the full extent of the harm they have caused, and to understand how their actions have affected not only their victim but also their family, their community, and themselves. Through this process, the offender comes to understand the gravity of their actions and the need for accountability.

This recognition and remorse lead to genuine repentance, which involves not only feeling sorry for one's actions but taking concrete steps to make things right. This can include making restitution to the victim, participating in counseling or treatment programs to address underlying issues that led to the offense, and engaging in community service or other activities to make amends for the harm caused. Repentance is not merely a feeling but a decision—a decision to change behavior, attitudes, and beliefs that are not in agreement with the Word of God.

The church, as a community of grace, provides the context for this repentance. It offers a safe space where offenders can confess their sins without fear of condemnation. It offers support and accountability as they work toward change. It offers the assurance of forgiveness when repentance is genuine. And it offers the possibility of restoration—full reintegration into the community of faith.

This emphasis on confession and repentance is not unique to Christian communities. Research in psychology confirms that acknowledgment of wrongdoing and expression of remorse are essential for healing relationships. When offenders take responsibility for their actions and express genuine sorrow, victims are more likely to forgive and to experience closure. When offenders make amends and demonstrate changed behavior, trust can be rebuilt. The church's ancient practices of confession and repentance anticipate what modern psychology has discovered: that healing requires acknowledgment, remorse, and change.

Forgiveness and Reconciliation: The Heart of Christian Community

The Christian ethos of forgiveness and reconciliation is central to restorative justice. Jesus taught His disciples to pray, "Forgive us our debts, as we forgive our debtors" (Matthew 6:12), linking divine forgiveness to human forgiveness in an inseparable bond. He taught that forgiveness must be limitless—"seventy times seven" (Matthew 18:22)—and illustrated this teaching with the parable of the unforgiving servant, who was condemned not for his original debt but for his refusal to forgive.

In Christian communities, forgiveness is not optional but essential. It is the air we breathe, the water we drink, the bread we eat. We gather each week to confess our sins and receive absolution. We pray the prayer that Jesus taught us, asking for forgiveness as we forgive. We share the peace, extending to one another the reconciliation we have received from God. We come to the Table, where Christ gives Himself for the forgiveness of sins and invites us to be one body, one spirit in Him.

This culture of forgiveness creates the conditions for restorative justice. When conflicts arise, forgiveness is the default expectation, not the exception. When harm occurs, reconciliation is the goal, not merely resolution. When offenders repent, restoration is the outcome, not exclusion. Forgiveness opens the door to healing; reconciliation walks through that door.

But forgiveness is not cheap. It does not mean pretending that harm didn't happen or that it doesn't matter. It means acknowledging the harm fully and then choosing to release the offender from the debt of guilt. It means opening the door to reconciliation while recognizing that reconciliation requires the willing participation of both parties. It means extending grace while also holding accountable.

Reconciliation, in the Christian vision, is even more costly. It requires the offender to acknowledge wrongdoing, to express genuine remorse, to make amends to the extent possible, and to demonstrate changed behavior. It requires the victim to extend forgiveness, to release resentment, to open the door to renewed relationship. It requires the community to support both parties, to hold them accountable, and to celebrate restoration when it occurs.

The parable of the prodigal son illustrates this costly reconciliation. The father runs to meet his wayward son, embracing him before he can complete his confession. He restores him to full sonship—robe, ring, sandals, celebration. But the son's journey home was costly: he had to hit bottom, to come to himself, to acknowledge his sin, to return in humility. The father's forgiveness was costly: he had to absorb the pain of rejection, to run in undignified haste, to welcome one who had squandered his inheritance. Reconciliation was costly for both, but it was also joyful—the dead was alive, the lost was found.

Christian communities, following this model, are called to be places where costly forgiveness and reconciliation are practiced. This means creating a culture in which people feel safe to acknowledge their failures, to seek forgiveness, and to extend it to others. It means equipping members with the skills and dispositions needed for restorative conversations. It means celebrating restoration when it occurs, and supporting those who are still on the journey.

Church-Based Mediation: Structures for Restoration

Many Christian communities have established mediation and reconciliation ministries to facilitate restorative justice processes. These ministries draw on the biblical call to peacemaking and provide trained mediators who work with individuals involved in conflicts or harm to find resolution.

Mediation, in the church context, is not merely a technique for resolving disputes but a spiritual practice grounded in prayer, scripture, and the presence of Christ. Mediators are not neutral third parties in the secular sense but brothers and sisters in Christ who seek to embody the love and wisdom of God. They create safe spaces for dialogue, help parties express their feelings and perspectives, facilitate understanding, and guide the process toward reconciliation.

The mediator's role is multifaceted. They prepare parties for the encounter, explaining the process and setting expectations. They create a safe environment, ensuring that all participants can speak freely without fear. They facilitate communication, helping parties express themselves clearly and listen attentively. They manage the process, keeping conversations focused and productive. They help parties identify the harm that has been done, the needs that have arisen, and the steps necessary for repair. They assist in developing agreements that address the harm and restore relationships. And they provide follow-up support to ensure that agreements are implemented and relationships continue to heal.

Mediation in the church context is informed by biblical principles. Mediators draw on scripture to ground the process in God's purposes. They pray with and for the parties, inviting God's presence and guidance. They remind parties of their identity in Christ—forgiven sinners called to forgive, reconciled people called to reconcile. They point to the example of Jesus, who broke down dividing walls and made peace through the cross.

Mediation is particularly appropriate for conflicts within the church—disagreements between members, disputes between leaders, tensions between groups. These conflicts, if unresolved, can divide congregations, damage witness, and hinder mission. Mediation offers a way to address them constructively, to restore relationships, and to strengthen community.

But mediation can also be used for more serious harms—cases of abuse, betrayal, or criminal behavior. In these cases, mediation must be handled with great care, ensuring the safety and well-being of all parties. Trained professionals should be involved, and the process should be conducted in coordination with legal authorities. But even in these difficult cases, mediation can offer a path to healing that purely punitive approaches cannot provide.

The church's mediation ministries are not limited to internal conflicts. They can also serve the wider community, offering restorative processes for families, neighborhoods, and organizations. By making these services available, the church demonstrates its commitment to the common good and bears witness to the restorative justice of God.

Accountability: Responsibility Within Grace

Restorative justice in Christian communities places importance on holding individuals accountable for their actions. It recognizes that repentance and forgiveness can be accompanied by accountability, that grace does not eliminate responsibility, and that love sometimes requires confronting.

Accountability in the church context is not punitive but restorative. Its goal is not to inflict pain but to promote healing, not to exclude but to restore, not to condemn but to transform. It is accountability within grace—accountability that flows from love and aims at restoration.

The New Testament provides numerous examples of this kind of accountability. When Peter denied Jesus three times, he was confronted by the risen Christ, who asked him three times, "Do you love Me?" (John 21:15-17). This confrontation was not punitive but restorative. It gave Peter the opportunity to reaffirm his love and to receive a new commission: "Feed My sheep." Accountability led to restoration.

When the church in Corinth tolerated a case of sexual immorality, Paul called them to accountability. "Deliver such a one to Satan for the destruction of the flesh, that his spirit may be saved in the day of the Lord Jesus" (1 Corinthians 5:5). This severe language reflects the seriousness of the situation, but the goal is ultimately restorative—the salvation of the offender's spirit. Later, when the offender repented, Paul urged the church to forgive and comfort him, "lest perhaps such a one be swallowed up with too much sorrow" (2 Corinthians 2:7). Accountability was followed by restoration.

When a member of the church sins, Jesus provides a process for accountability. "If your brother sins against you, go and tell him his fault between you and him alone. If he hears you, you have gained your brother. But if he will not hear, take with you one or two more, that by the mouth of two or three witnesses every word may be established. If he refuses to hear them, tell it to the church. But if he refuses even to hear the church, let him be to you like a heathen and a tax collector" (Matthew 18:15-17). This process moves from private conversation to small group mediation to community involvement. The goal is always to "gain your brother"—to restore the relationship. Even the final step, treating the unrepentant member as a heathen and tax collector, is not about exclusion but about redefining the relationship in hopes of eventual restoration. Jesus Himself ate with heathens and tax collectors, seeking to bring them to repentance.

This process embodies the restorative principle of accountability within community. It recognizes that sin affects relationships and that restoration requires addressing the harm. It provides multiple opportunities for resolution, escalating only as necessary. It involves the community in the process of accountability and restoration. And it keeps the door open for eventual reconciliation.

In restorative justice ministry, this biblical model informs how churches hold offenders accountable. Offenders are encouraged to acknowledge their wrongdoing, to face the consequences of their actions, to make amends to the extent possible. They are supported by the community as they work toward change. And they are welcomed back when repentance is genuine and amends are made.

Community Involvement: The Body of Christ in Action

Christian communities emphasize the involvement of the broader faith community in restorative processes. This communal approach to justice aligns with restorative justice's emphasis on community support and healing. It reflects the biblical understanding that we are members one of another, that the health of the whole depends on the health of each part, and that healing requires the participation of all.

The Apostle Paul's image of the body of Christ is particularly apt. "For as the body is one and has many members, but all the members of that one body, being many, are one body, so also is Christ" (1 Corinthians 12:12). Each member has a role to play, each is essential to the functioning of the whole. When one member suffers, all suffer together; when one member is honored, all rejoice together (1 Corinthians 12:26). This organic unity means that harm to any member harms the whole, and restoration of any member blesses the whole.

In restorative justice, this understanding translates into active community involvement. Community members participate in restorative processes, offering support to victims and offenders alike. They provide resources and assistance to those in need. They hold offenders accountable while also offering encouragement and hope. They celebrate restoration when it occurs and continue to support those on the journey.

Community involvement serves several essential functions. First, it helps to rebuild trust between victims, offenders, and the community. When the community comes together to address harm, it sends a powerful message of solidarity and support to both victim and offender. This can help to promote a sense of community and foster a sense of accountability for everyone involved.

Second, community involvement can promote healing and closure for victims. In traditional criminal justice systems, victims are often left feeling isolated and powerless. But when the community comes together to support the victim and hold the offender accountable, it can help the victim to regain a sense of control over their life and promote healing.

Third, community involvement can reduce recidivism. By providing the offender with support and guidance, the community can help to address the underlying issues that may have contributed to their criminal behavior. This can help to reduce the likelihood of future offenses and promote rehabilitation.

Fourth, community involvement strengthens the social fabric. When communities take responsibility for addressing harm, they become more cohesive, more resilient, more capable of preventing future harm. Restorative justice builds community even as it heals individuals.

In the church context, community involvement takes many forms. Prayer teams intercede for victims, offenders, and all affected by crime. Support groups provide emotional and practical assistance to those in need. Mentors walk alongside offenders, offering guidance and accountability. Restorative circles bring together those affected by harm to discuss the impact and work toward resolution. Celebration events mark the restoration of relationships and the reintegration of offenders into community.

This communal approach reflects the church's identity as the body of Christ. It recognizes that we are not isolated individuals but members one of another, bound together in mutual responsibility and care. It embodies the truth that when one suffers, all suffer, and when one is restored, all rejoice.

Restorative Practices: Circles and Conferences

Restorative justice practices like peacemaking circles find resonance in Christian communities. These practices provide a structured way to address harm, encourage communication, and promote healing. They draw on ancient wisdom—both biblical and indigenous—and adapt it to contemporary contexts.

Peacemaking circles bring together those affected by harm in a structured, facilitated conversation. Participants sit in a circle, symbolizing equality and mutual respect. A talking piece is passed from person to person, ensuring that each voice is heard without interruption. The circle creates a space of safety and respect in which even the most difficult conversations can occur.

Circles can be used for a wide variety of purposes. Healing circles bring together victims, offenders, and supporters to address the impact of crime and work toward restoration. Conflict circles help parties in dispute to understand each other's perspectives and find resolution. Support circles surround individuals in crisis with care and assistance. Celebration circles mark milestones of healing and restoration.

The circle process reflects several key values. Equality: in the circle, all participants are equal; there is no hierarchy, no privileged position. Respect: each person's voice is valued; each person's story is heard. Inclusivity: all affected parties are invited to participate; no one is excluded. Transparency: the process is open and honest; there are no hidden agendas. Accountability: participants are expected to take responsibility for their actions and to follow through on commitments.

These values align closely with Christian understandings of community. In Christ, there is no Jew nor Greek, slave nor free, male nor female (Galatians 3:28)—all are one. Each member of the body is valued; each has a contribution to make. The community is called to bear one another's burdens, to confess sins to one another, to pray for one another. The circle provides a structure for living out these commitments.

Family group conferences, another restorative practice, bring together victims, offenders, and their respective families and supporters. Originally developed in New Zealand, drawing on Maori indigenous practices, conferences provide a forum for discussing the harm, addressing needs, and developing plans for repair and reintegration. The presence of family and supporters creates a powerful context for accountability and healing—offenders must face not only their victims but also their own loved ones, who witness the consequences of their actions. And both victims and offenders receive the ongoing support of their families as they move forward.

In Christian communities, conferences can be adapted for a variety of situations—conflicts within families, disputes between church members, cases of harm involving young people. They draw on the church's understanding of the family of God, in which all members are brothers and sisters, responsible for one another's well-being.

Victim-offender mediation, the most widely used restorative practice, brings together victims and offenders in a safe, structured setting. A trained facilitator guides the conversation, helping parties to express their feelings, ask questions, and work toward agreement. Mediation can be used for a wide range of offenses, from minor property crimes to serious violent crimes, when both parties are willing and it is safe to do so.

In the church context, mediation can be informed by biblical principles of forgiveness and reconciliation. Mediators can draw on scripture to ground the process in God's purposes. They can pray with and for the parties, inviting God's presence and guidance. They can remind parties of their identity in Christ—forgiven sinners called to forgive, reconciled people called to reconcile.

These restorative practices are not merely techniques but embodiments of gospel values. They create space for truth-telling, for acknowledgment of harm, for expression of emotion, for accountability, for making amends, for forgiveness, for reconciliation. They reflect the pattern of Jesus' own ministry—His willingness to engage with sinners, His call to repentance, His offer of forgiveness, His restoration of the broken.

Teaching and Preaching: Forming a Restorative Culture

Clergy and religious leaders play a crucial role in forming a restorative culture within Christian communities. Through their teaching and preaching, they shape how congregants understand justice, forgiveness, reconciliation, and restoration. They interpret scripture, applying its ancient wisdom to contemporary challenges. They model restorative values in their own interactions and leadership.

Preaching on restorative justice is not merely about advocating for a particular social program but about proclaiming the gospel itself. The good news is that God, in Christ, was reconciling the world to Himself, not counting our trespasses against us (2 Corinthians 5:19). This reconciliation is the heart of the gospel, and it has implications for how we relate to one another. Those who have been reconciled to God are called to be ministers of reconciliation, extending to others the grace they have received.

Preaching can explore the biblical foundations of restorative justice—the justice of the prophets, the teachings of Jesus, the practices of the early church. It can illuminate the parables that embody restorative principles—the Good Samaritan, the Prodigal Son, the Unforgiving Servant. It can connect these ancient texts to contemporary issues—mass incarceration, racial injustice, family conflict, community violence. It can challenge congregants to examine their own attitudes and practices, to consider how they might become agents of restoration in their spheres of influence.

Teaching on restorative justice can take many forms. Bible studies can explore passages that address justice, forgiveness, and reconciliation. Sunday school classes can examine restorative principles and practices. Workshops can train congregants in conflict resolution, mediation, and restorative communication. Seminars can bring in experts to share research and best practices. Small groups can provide opportunities for members to practice restorative skills in a safe environment.

Teaching and preaching also address the questions that restorative justice raises. What is God's view of justice? How does it differ from the world's view? What does God expect of us in response to harm? How should we view offenders—as enemies to be punished or as brothers and sisters to be restored? Does biblical justice include something other than punishment? How do we minister through a biblical paradigm of justice? These questions are explored in light of scripture, tradition, reason, and experience.

Teaching and preaching also address the practical challenges of restorative ministry. How can we respond to harm within our faith community in a way that promotes accountability, healing, and reconciliation? How can we address the root causes of injustice in our society and work toward systemic change? How can we create a culture of empathy, compassion, and forgiveness within our faith community? How can we support those who have experienced trauma and help them find healing and wholeness? How can we engage in dialogue with those who hold different beliefs or have been harmed by our community? How can we integrate restorative justice principles into our worship and spiritual practices? How can we work toward repairing harm caused by historical injustices? How can we support individuals impacted by the criminal justice system? How can we promote a restorative approach to conflict resolution in our faith community and in wider society? How can we collaborate with other organizations and faith communities to promote restorative justice?

Through teaching and preaching, clergy and religious leaders form a restorative imagination in their congregations. They help members see the world through the lens of God's reconciling love. They equip them with the skills and dispositions needed for restorative practice. They inspire them to become agents of healing in a broken world.

Redemption and Reintegration: The Hope of Restoration

Christian communities believe in the potential for redemption and reintegration. This belief is rooted in the gospel itself—the good news that in Christ, all things can be made new, that even the worst sinners can be forgiven and transformed, that no one is beyond the reach of God's grace.

The Scriptures are filled with stories of redemption. David, who committed adultery and murder, repented and was restored, becoming the ancestor of the Messiah. Peter, who denied Jesus three times, repented and was restored, becoming the leader of the early church. Paul, who persecuted the church, was converted and became its greatest missionary. These stories are not exceptions but illustrations of the gospel's central claim: that God specializes in redeeming the lost, restoring the broken, and transforming the worst into the best.

Restorative justice ministry embraces this hope. It recognizes that offenders are not defined by their worst acts but are human beings created in God's image, capable of change, worthy of restoration. It offers them a path to redemption through acknowledgment of wrongdoing, genuine repentance, making amends, and changed behavior. And it welcomes them back into community when that path is followed.

Reintegration is the goal of this process. Offenders who have made amends and demonstrated changed behavior are restored to full participation in the community. They are no longer labeled by their past offenses but welcomed as brothers and sisters. They are given opportunities to contribute, to serve, to use their gifts for the common good. They are supported in their ongoing journey of growth and transformation.

This reintegration is not merely a matter of policy but of practice. It requires the community to overcome its fears and suspicions, to extend trust even when trust has been broken, to welcome even those who have caused harm. It requires the community to create structures of support—mentoring, accountability, assistance—that help returning individuals succeed. It requires the community to celebrate restoration when it occurs, to rejoice that the dead is alive, the lost is found.

The church, as a community of grace, is uniquely positioned to offer this reintegration. It can provide a spiritual home for returning individuals, a place where they can worship, grow, and serve. It can offer relationships that support and sustain them. It can give them opportunities to use their gifts and to contribute to the community's life. It can bear witness to the power of God's grace to transform even the most broken lives.

But reintegration is not only for offenders. Victims also need to be reintegrated into community. Crime often isolates victims, leaving them feeling alone, afraid, and disconnected. The church can provide a community of support, surrounding victims with care, listening to their stories, helping them heal. It can help them find their place again, to feel safe again, to trust again. Reintegration is for all affected by crime—victims, offenders, and the community itself.

Restorative Approaches to Conflicts

Intra-church disputes or conflicts within Christian communities can be addressed through restorative practices rather than adversarial or punitive methods. Conflicts are inevitable in any human community, but how they are handled makes all the difference. Adversarial approaches—litigation, formal complaints, public accusations—tend to escalate conflict, damage relationships, and divide communities. Restorative approaches—dialogue, mediation, circles—tend to de-escalate conflict, heal relationships, and strengthen community.

Restorative approaches to conflict begin with open dialogue. Parties are given the opportunity to express their perspectives, to share their feelings, to articulate their needs. This dialogue is facilitated in a way that ensures safety, respect, and mutual understanding. The goal is not to determine who is right and who is wrong but to understand what has happened and what is needed to move forward.

Restorative approaches emphasize understanding the impact of the conflict. Parties are encouraged to consider how their words and actions have affected others, to develop empathy for those who have been hurt, to acknowledge the harm that has been done. This understanding is essential for genuine resolution and healing.

Restorative approaches encourage accountability. Parties are invited to take responsibility for their part in the conflict, to acknowledge their contributions to the harm, to express remorse where appropriate. This accountability is not about blame but about ownership—recognizing one's role and committing to change.

Restorative approaches facilitate making amends. Parties work together to identify what needs to be done to repair the harm, to restore relationships, to rebuild trust. This may involve apologies, restitution, changed behavior, or other actions that demonstrate commitment to restoration.

Restorative approaches seek reconciliation as their ultimate goal. The aim is not merely to settle the dispute but to restore relationship, to rebuild trust, to renew community. This reconciliation may take time and may not always be fully achieved, but it remains the guiding purpose of the process.

Restorative approaches involve the wider community. In conflicts within the church, this may mean seeking advice or mediation from church leaders, elders, or congregation members who can support the resolution efforts. It may mean involving the community in the process of healing and restoration. It may mean celebrating reconciliation when it occurs.

Restorative approaches seek to restore dignity. All parties are treated with respect, their worth as individuals created in God's image is affirmed. Even when behavior is condemned, the person is valued. This restoration of dignity is essential for healing.

Restorative approaches encourage transformation and renewal. Conflict, handled restoratively, can become an opportunity for growth—for individuals to change, for relationships to deepen, for community to be strengthened. The goal is not just to resolve the conflict but to emerge from it better than before.

Restorative approaches emphasize forgiveness and repentance. These are not forced or demanded but encouraged and supported. The community creates the conditions in which forgiveness and repentance can occur, trusting that God's grace is at work in the process.

By applying these restorative principles, church leaders and members can effectively resolve conflicts, promote healing, and maintain unity within the church community. These principles offer a pathway to address disputes in a way that reflects the teachings of Jesus, fostering a culture of understanding, forgiveness, and reconciliation.

Ministry and Outreach: Extending Restoration Beyond the Walls

The church's involvement in restorative justice extends beyond its own walls. It plays a role in addressing broader societal issues, such as supporting those affected by crime, advocating for criminal justice reform, and promoting healing and reconciliation in the community. This ministry and outreach are expressions of the church's mission to be salt and light in the world, to bear witness to God's restorative justice in every sphere of life.

Supporting victims is a crucial aspect of this outreach. Churches can provide vital support for individuals who have been victims of crime—counseling, emotional support, practical assistance. Restorative justice encourages empathy and care for those who have suffered harm, aligning with the Christian values of compassion and love. By walking with victims through their pain, the church embodies the love of Christ and bears witness to the hope of healing.

Advocating for criminal justice reform is another important dimension. Restorative justice principles emphasize a shift from punitive to restorative measures. Churches can engage in advocacy efforts for criminal justice reform, pushing for policies that emphasize rehabilitation, reintegration, and addressing the root causes of crime. This advocacy can take many forms—letters to elected officials, public statements, participation in coalitions, support for reform organizations. By raising their voices for justice, churches fulfill their prophetic calling to speak truth to power.

Reentry programs support individuals reintegrating into society after serving time in the criminal justice system. Churches can establish reentry programs that provide resources, mentorship, and a supportive community for those looking to rebuild their lives. These programs align with restorative justice's emphasis on transformation and renewal, offering practical assistance and spiritual support to returning individuals. They also help to reduce recidivism, making communities safer for everyone.

Community building is essential to restorative justice. Restorative justice is about repairing harm and building stronger, more harmonious communities. Churches can engage in community-building initiatives, fostering relationships, trust, and unity among their members and the broader community. These initiatives might include neighborhood events, community gardens, youth programs, and other activities that bring people together and strengthen social bonds.

Restorative practices can be incorporated within the church's own community and extended to the community at large. Churches can use restorative circles or mediation to address conflicts and promote healing. They can offer these services to the wider community, helping to resolve disputes and foster reconciliation. By modeling restorative practices, churches demonstrate their commitment to healing and restoration.

Restorative justice education empowers individuals and communities. Churches can educate their congregations and the community about restorative justice principles, their biblical foundations, and their practical applications. This education can empower individuals to engage in restorative practices in their own lives and to support them in wider society. It can also build a constituency for restorative justice, creating pressure for systemic change.

Social justice initiatives address the root causes of crime. Addressing societal injustices is a fundamental aspect of restorative justice. Churches can initiate and support social justice campaigns that tackle issues such as poverty, inequality, racism, and discrimination. These efforts align with the principles of addressing harm and promoting equity, working to prevent crime before it occurs.

Prison ministry provides spiritual and emotional support to incarcerated individuals. It can also be a platform for sharing restorative justice principles, offering hope for personal transformation and redemption. Many churches have long traditions of prison visitation, following Jesus' command to visit those in prison (Matthew 25:36). This ministry can be deepened and extended by incorporating restorative principles and practices.

Victim-offender dialogue can be part of outreach efforts. Encouraging victim-offender dialogue and reconciliation processes can help both victims and offenders find closure and healing. These dialogues, carefully facilitated, provide opportunities for victims to express their pain and receive answers, and for offenders to take responsibility and make amends. They embody the restorative principle that healing requires encounter.

Refugee and migrant support is another form of restorative outreach. Churches can actively support refugees and migrants, helping them find shelter, resources, and community. Restorative justice principles emphasize empathy and hospitality, which align with the support needed by those forced to leave their homes. By welcoming the stranger, churches embody the love of Christ and bear witness to the inclusive welcome of God's kingdom.

In all these ministries, the church extends the principles of restorative justice to create a more just, compassionate, and reconciled society. It becomes a sign and foretaste of God's restorative purposes, a community that embodies the healing and reconciliation that God intends for all creation.

Victim Support: The Church's Call to Care

Victim support is imperative for restorative justice, and the church plays a vital role in this crucial aspect of the work. Victims of crime and conflict carry deep wounds—physical, emotional, psychological, spiritual. These wounds require care, and the church is uniquely positioned to provide it.

Compassion and empathy are the foundation of victim support. Restorative justice emphasizes empathy for those who have suffered harm, and the church, rooted in Christian teachings, exemplifies these values by extending care and support to victims. This compassion is not merely a feeling but a practice—a commitment to entering into another's suffering, to bearing their burden, to walking with them through pain. When the church extends compassion to victims, it aligns with both Christian values and restorative justice principles, acknowledging the reality of their pain, validating their experience, and communicating that they are not alone.

Healing and restoration are the goals of victim support. Victims often go through traumatic experiences that leave lasting scars—emotional, psychological, and sometimes physical. The church can provide a safe space for victims to heal—a place where they can be honest about their pain, where they can seek counseling and support, where they can find comfort in their faith. This healing process is essential for restoring victims' well-being, in line with restorative justice's focus on repairing harm. Healing takes time and often requires professional help. Churches can connect victims with counselors who specialize in trauma, support groups where they can share with others who have suffered similarly, and spiritual directors who can help them navigate the questions of faith that arise from suffering. They can provide practical assistance—help with daily tasks, financial support, advocacy with systems—that eases the burden and creates space for healing.

Dignity and worth are central to victim support. Restorative justice places strong emphasis on recognizing the inherent dignity and worth of every individual, and supporting victims in their journey to recovery is a practical way to affirm this dignity. The church's role in this process aligns with the Christian belief in the sanctity of human life—that every person is created in

God's image and possesses infinite value. When victims are treated with dignity, they are empowered to reclaim their sense of worth. When their voices are heard, their needs are addressed, their suffering is acknowledged, they are reminded that they matter. This restoration of dignity is essential for healing and for the prevention of future harm.

Rebuilding trust is a crucial aspect of victim support. Victims often feel a loss of trust in their community and the world at large. The church, through its consistent presence and faithful care, can contribute to rebuilding this trust. When victims experience the church as a safe and supportive community, they begin to trust again—not only in others but in the possibility of healing and restoration. This restoration of trust is a fundamental aspect of restorative justice, enabling victims to reengage with community, to form new connections, to move forward with their lives.

Community and belonging are essential for victim support. The church serves as a community of faith and belonging, a place where people are known and loved. By providing support for victims, the church reinforces the idea that victims are not alone in their suffering. They are part of a body, members of a family, participants in a story larger than their own. Restorative justice seeks to repair the social bonds that are strained by harm, and the church plays a key role in reestablishing a sense of community. When victims are embraced by the church, they experience belonging that counters the isolation of victimization. When they are surrounded by care, they find strength for the journey of healing.

Moral and ethical responsibility compels the church to support victims. For the church, extending support to victims is not optional but essential—a reflection of the Christian commitment to love, compassion, and helping those in need. This sense of responsibility resonates with the restorative justice principle of addressing the needs of those who have been harmed. The church's support for victims is not charity but justice—not an optional extra but a core obligation. It flows from the conviction that every person matters, that suffering should not be ignored, that the wounded must be cared for. It is an expression of the love that lies at the heart of the gospel.

Promoting forgiveness and reconciliation is a delicate but important aspect of victim support. Restorative justice encourages processes of forgiveness and reconciliation, recognizing that these can be healing for victims as well as offenders. While forgiveness and reconciliation are personal journeys that cannot be forced, the church can offer guidance and a spiritual foundation for individuals seeking to forgive or reconcile with those who have caused harm. This guidance must be offered with sensitivity and respect. Victims should never be pressured to forgive before they are ready or to reconcile when it is not safe. But they can be supported in exploring the possibility of forgiveness, in understanding what it means and what it does not mean, in discerning whether and when to extend it. The church can provide a safe space for this exploration, trusting the Spirit to lead each person in their own time and way.

Advocacy for victims is another aspect of the church's role. The church can advocate for the rights and needs of victims within the wider community and even in the criminal justice system. This advocacy is in alignment with the restorative justice principle of ensuring that victims have a voice in the process. When the church advocates for victims, it speaks truth to power, challenging systems that sideline or silence those who have been harmed. It demands that victims be heard, that their needs be addressed, that their rights be protected. It works for policies and practices that support victim healing and prevent further victimization.

The Offender's Family: Invisible Victims

One aspect of criminal justice ministry that could easily be listed with the victims of crime is the offender's family and loved ones. They too suffer from the offender's criminal behavior. Even the sanctions levied against the offender, as a result of their crime, are felt by their family and loved ones. These invisible victims are often overlooked, yet their suffering is real and deserving of attention.

Incarceration produces what has been dubbed a prison widow or widower, and the prison orphan. The partners of incarcerated individuals may experience a sense of loneliness, isolation, and loss while their loved one is in prison. They may struggle to maintain relationships, raise children, and manage the responsibilities of daily life while their partner is incarcerated. Children who have one or both parents incarcerated may experience emotional distress, academic challenges, and financial hardship. They may face stigma and social exclusion due to their parent's status. The impact of incarceration on family members can be profound and long-lasting, contributing to cycles of intergenerational poverty, trauma, and social exclusion.

As the offender's family waits on them, they need help spiritually, emotionally, and financially. Spiritually, family members may experience a sense of guilt or shame, as well as a sense of disconnection from their faith community. They may struggle to reconcile their love for their incarcerated family member with their own sense of moral values and beliefs. Emotionally, they may experience anxiety, depression, anger, and grief. They may feel a sense of loss, isolation, and shame, as well as a sense of responsibility for their loved one's actions. Financially, incarceration can impose significant costs on families, including legal fees, travel expenses, and loss of income. This can lead to economic hardship, debt, and financial insecurity.

Criminal justice ministries and other support systems can play an important role in helping families of incarcerated individuals. This can include providing emotional and spiritual support, counseling services, and financial assistance. It can also involve working with families to help them stay connected to their incarcerated loved one, such as through visitation programs or letter writing campaigns. By addressing the spiritual, emotional, and financial needs of families, we can help to mitigate the negative impacts of incarceration and promote healing, restoration, and community engagement.

There is a great need for marriage seminars that could save literally hundreds of offender marriages, and, as a result, break the generational cycle of crime and brokenness in these families. Approximately ninety percent of all marriages end in divorce when the incarceration period exceeds one year. If the offender can come home to a loving, waiting, Christian family, they have a greater chance of avoiding crime and staying out of prison in the future.

Marriage seminars can be a powerful tool for addressing the needs of families affected by incarceration and breaking the cycle of crime and brokenness that can be passed down from generation to generation. When a family member is incarcerated, it can have significant impacts on their relationships, including their marriage or intimate partner relationships. The stress, trauma, and financial strain associated with incarceration can strain these relationships and lead to divorce or separation.

By providing marriage seminars that address the unique needs of families affected by incarceration, criminal justice ministries and other support systems can help to strengthen relationships, promote healthy communication and conflict resolution skills, and provide a sense of hope and healing to families who may be struggling. These seminars can also help to address the specific challenges faced by families of incarcerated individuals, such as financial strain and emotional distress.

By promoting healthy relationships and strengthening families, marriage seminars can also help to break the cycle of crime and brokenness that can be passed down from generation to generation. Research has shown that children of incarcerated parents are at higher risk for involvement in criminal behavior themselves. By addressing the needs of families affected by incarceration, we can help to prevent future offending behavior and promote a more just and peaceful society for all.

Ministering to Criminal Justice Professionals

One of the most difficult aspects of criminal justice ministry is working with offenders who are resistant to change or who are struggling with addiction, mental health issues, or other challenges that make it difficult for them to fully engage in the restorative justice process. These individuals may be deeply entrenched in patterns of behavior and may not be receptive to taking responsibility or making amends. Working with them requires patience, compassion, and persistence.

But another challenging aspect is ministering to criminal justice professionals themselves—the police officers, corrections staff, judges, prosecutors, and others who work within the system. Theirs is not an easy job. They work in highly stressful and challenging environments that can take a toll on their mental and emotional well-being. They face danger, trauma, and moral complexity on a daily basis. They are often misunderstood and unappreciated by the communities they serve. They need support, encouragement, and care.

The first step in ministering to a criminal justice professional is the building of relationships. By building relationships with these individuals, criminal justice ministries can provide them with a sense of support, connection, and community that can help to mitigate the effects of stress and promote greater resilience. Building relationships can help to break down barriers and build trust between these individuals and the broader community. Many criminal justice professionals may feel isolated or misunderstood by the communities they serve, and building relationships with them can help to bridge this divide and promote greater understanding and collaboration. Building relationships can also help to promote the values of restorative justice and community engagement within the criminal justice system. By demonstrating the importance of building relationships and promoting healing and restoration, criminal justice ministries can help to shift the focus of the criminal justice system away from punitive measures and towards a more restorative and community-centered approach.

Establishing a relationship requires much patience because correctional staff in many ways is a closed community that shuns outsiders. Correctional staff work in a highly stressful and challenging environment, where their safety and the safety of those in their care is a constant concern. This can create a sense of isolation and distrust, leading them to view outsiders as a potential threat or interference to their work. To build relationships, it is important to approach them with respect, sensitivity, and an understanding of the challenges they face daily. Trust and rapport are built slowly over time. Seeking opportunities for collaboration and partnership—offering training or support, working together to identify areas where restorative justice principles could be integrated—can help. It is also important to be mindful of the boundaries and limitations of the correctional setting and to work within the constraints of the system.

Because of varying work hours, a church should be willing to schedule special activities and develop programs to include these unique individuals. Criminal justice professionals may have difficulty participating in traditional church activities and programs. To include them, churches should offer flexible scheduling for worship services and other activities, such as Bible studies or prayer groups. This might involve offering multiple service times or scheduling events on different days of the week. Churches can also develop specialized programs designed specifically for criminal justice professionals, such as support groups for those who work in the correctional system or specialized training programs that address the unique challenges of this work. It is also important for churches to be intentional about creating a welcoming and supportive environment for criminal justice professionals, developing specialized outreach efforts or partnering with organizations that work directly with them.

The Offender's Journey: From Harm to Healing

To the degree possible, offenders should attempt to reconcile the damages they have caused to those affected by their crime. Restorative justice emphasizes the importance of offenders taking responsibility for their actions and attempting to make amends for the harm they have caused. Reconciliation can take many forms, depending on the circumstances of the crime and the needs of the victim(s) and their community. In some cases, it may involve a direct apology or a face-to-face meeting between the offender and the victim, where the offender can express remorse and take steps to make things right. In other cases, reconciliation may involve the offender making restitution to the victim, such as paying for damages or providing financial support. This can be particularly important in cases where the victim has suffered financial or material losses as a result of the crime. Reconciliation can also involve efforts to address the root causes of the offender's behavior and to prevent future offenses, such as participation in counseling or rehabilitation programs, or making efforts to address the social and environmental factors that contributed to the offender's criminal behavior.

James 5:16 provides two prerequisites to healing: confession and prayer. "Therefore, confess your sins to each other and pray for each each other so that you may be healed. The prayer of a righteous person is powerful and effective." Confession involves acknowledging and taking responsibility for our actions, as well as seeking forgiveness from those we have wronged. This act of humility and repentance can be a powerful step towards healing and reconciliation. Prayer demonstrates our care and concern for each other's well-being and invites God's healing power into our lives. These two prerequisites to healing move both the victim and offender toward restoration. In many cases, lasting friendships are also developed.

An offender also needs to understand how his/her crime has affected the community. When an offender commits a crime, the harm caused is not limited to just the victim(s). The wider community can also be affected, either directly or indirectly. For example, a violent crime may cause fear and anxiety in the community, leading to a sense of insecurity and distrust. Understanding the impact of the crime on the community is an important aspect of restorative justice. It helps the offender to see the wider consequences of their actions beyond the immediate victim(s), and to take responsibility for their role in causing harm. By understanding the impact of their crime on the community, the offender can begin to see the need for repairing the harm and making amends. Once the offender understands how their crime has affected the community, they will begin to see how they contribute to its stability. As a result, they will take measures to change.

Every time an offense occurs in a community, the trust level between people decreases and the element of fear increases. When an offense occurs, it can have a significant impact on the level of trust between individuals. This is particularly true when the offense is violent or involves a breach of trust, such as theft or fraud. When people feel like they cannot trust those around them, it can lead to a breakdown in community cohesion and a sense of isolation. Offenses can also increase the level of fear within a community. When people are afraid, they may avoid certain areas or activities, leading to a further breakdown in community cohesion. Both the decrease in trust and the increase in fear can have negative consequences for a community. Restorative justice can help to address these issues by promoting healing, reconciliation, and forgiveness. By bringing together victims, offenders, and community members to discuss the impact of the offense and to work towards repairing the harm caused, restorative justice can help to rebuild trust and promote a sense of community.

As people become increasingly suspicious of others, they may begin to secure their homes with extra lights, locks, sturdier fences, or even purchase firearms. They may avoid interactions, check up on people, question others' motives, become secretive, isolate themselves, guard their possessions, and become increasingly vigilant. In severe cases, they may experience paranoia or scelerophobia—the fear of burglars, bad men, or crime in general. For those with this phobia, many normal things become difficult. Restorative justice offers a path to address these fears at their source, by addressing the harm that caused them and rebuilding the trust that fear has eroded.

When offenders are encouraged to address the harm that results from their crime, they can begin to see that their actions are not isolated, and that their families, as well as friends and neighbors, suffer from their crime. When offenders see how their crime has impacted their families, friends, and neighbors, they can begin to recognize that their actions do not just affect themselves, but have a ripple effect throughout the community. They may see that their loved ones have been hurt by their behavior, and that their relationships with others have been damaged as a result. This realization can be a powerful motivator for offenders to make changes in their lives and work towards making amends.

When the offender focuses on the ills of the prison system rather than address the harm that resulted from his crime, the offender is not held accountable for the damage they have caused. By deflecting attention away from their behavior and onto the prison system, offenders may fail to take responsibility for their actions and the harm they have caused. This can hinder the healing process for victims and the community. If offenders do not address the harm they caused, they may not be held accountable for their actions, leading to a sense of injustice for victims and undermining the legitimacy of the justice system. By focusing solely on the prison system, offenders may fail to address the root causes of their behavior. They forget that what they have done harmed others, and avoid feeling accountable for the harm they have caused.

A Christian offender needs to be willing to confront the pain he has caused, and discover a way to rebuild the trust that was destroyed by his actions. This requires a willingness to face the consequences of their behavior and work towards making amends. To rebuild trust, the offender must first acknowledge the harm they have caused and express genuine remorse for their actions. This involves taking responsibility for their behavior and recognizing the impact it has had on others. The offender must be willing to listen to the victim and other affected parties, and take their feelings and needs into account. The offender must be committed to making things right, which may involve making restitution, participating in restorative justice programs, and taking steps to prevent future harm. The offender may also need to seek counseling or therapy to address any underlying issues that contributed to their behavior.

The Goal: Restoration of All

Ministry, using the restorative justice paradigm, ends in the restoration of both the victim and the offender back into the community. Restorative justice seeks to repair harm and restore relationships between those who have been affected by crime. This approach involves bringing together the victim, the offender, and the community to work towards a shared goal of healing and reconciliation. In a ministry context, this paradigm aligns with Christian values of forgiveness, compassion, and love.

The goal is to restore both the victim and the offender back into the community. This involves providing support and resources to both parties as they work towards healing and reconciliation. The victim may receive counseling or other forms of support to help them cope with the trauma they have experienced. The offender may receive counseling or other forms of support to help them address the underlying issues that contributed to their behavior. Restorative justice ministry involves community involvement, including support groups, mentoring programs, and other forms of community engagement. By involving the broader community in the restoration process, both the victim and the offender can feel supported and valued.

The Church, as an accepting community, can help with the issues of restoration, and facilitate reintegration for both the victim and the offender back into the community. The Church can play a significant role in promoting restoration and facilitating reintegration. As an accepting and supportive community, the Church can provide a safe and nurturing space for those affected by crime to heal and find support. For victims of crime, the Church can offer pastoral care, counseling, and other forms of support to help them cope with the trauma they have experienced. The Church can also offer a supportive community where victims can connect with others who have had similar experiences and find comfort and healing. For offenders, the Church can offer a space for confession, repentance, and redemption. Through pastoral counseling, mentoring, and other forms of support, the Church can help offenders address the underlying issues that contributed to their behavior and find a path toward rehabilitation and restoration. The Church can play a role in facilitating the reintegration of both the victim and the offender back into the community through community outreach programs, support groups, and other forms of community engagement.

What is required of a ministry, in order to be holistic? It must consider both the offender and victim; it attempts to meet the spiritual as well as the physical and emotional needs of those involved; and it addresses the offender in prison, as well as after they are released back to the community. Putting it in simple terms, you must cover all the bases in order to be holistic. A holistic ministry addresses the needs of the whole person—body, mind, and spirit. This approach recognizes that people have complex and interconnected needs, and that addressing one area of need can have a positive impact on other areas of their life. A holistic ministry must take into account the diverse needs of the people it serves, providing support and resources in spiritual, emotional, physical, social, and financial areas. By addressing the diverse needs of the people it serves, a holistic ministry can help to promote healing, growth, and transformation in the lives of those it serves. This approach recognizes the interconnectedness of our physical, emotional, and spiritual needs and provides a framework for supporting the whole person.

The church, then, is called to be a holistic restorative community—a place where victims are supported, offenders are held accountable, families are cared for, professionals are encouraged, and all are welcomed into the process of healing and restoration. This is not an easy calling, but it is a faithful one. It reflects the heart of God, who is in the business of making all things new. And it bears witness to the gospel, which announces that in Christ, God was reconciling the world to Himself and has entrusted to us the ministry of reconciliation. May the church embrace this calling, embody this ministry, and become a sign and foretaste of the restorative justice that God intends for all creation.

CHAPTER 10

CHALLENGES AND CRITIQUES

The path of restorative justice, like any transformative movement, is not without its obstacles and detractors. To present restorative justice as a panacea, a simple solution to the complex problems of crime and conflict, would be both dishonest and counterproductive. The Jesus Paradigm, for all its profound wisdom and transformative power, must be examined with clear eyes, acknowledging the challenges that arise when attempting to apply its principles in a fallen world. This chapter engages honestly with the critiques and obstacles that restorative justice faces, particularly when grounded in a biblical framework. We will explore these challenges not to discourage but to equip, not to undermine but to strengthen. For only by understanding the difficulties can we hope to overcome them.

The challenges are real and multifaceted. They range from theological disagreements among Christians to institutional resistance within legal systems, from resource limitations to questions of participant willingness, from societal skepticism to concerns about equity, from difficulties in measuring outcomes to the lack of legal frameworks. Each of these challenges deserves careful consideration, for each represents a potential barrier to the implementation of restorative justice. Yet each also represents an opportunity for growth, refinement, and deeper understanding.

Theological Differing Interpretations

One of the most fundamental challenges in applying restorative justice within a biblical framework lies in the diverse interpretations of biblical teachings across Christian denominations and faith traditions. Restorative justice principles may not align with every theological perspective, and theological debates can arise over the scriptural basis and interpretation of reconciliation and redemption. These debates have the potential to hinder the widespread acceptance of restorative justice within the Christian community.

Theological diversity is not a weakness of Christianity but a reflection of its global reach and historical depth. From the Orthodox churches of the East to the Roman Catholic Church of the West, from the mainline Protestant denominations to the evangelical and Pentecostal movements, from the ancient traditions of Oriental Orthodoxy to the independent churches of Africa and Asia, Christianity encompasses a breathtaking range of theological perspectives. Each tradition brings its own emphases, its own interpretations, its own understandings of key biblical concepts.

This diversity becomes significant when considering restorative justice. Different denominations may have distinct doctrines regarding the nature of justice, the purpose of punishment, the meaning of atonement, and the relationship between God's justice and God's mercy. For example, traditions that emphasize the penal substitutionary view of the atonement—the idea that Christ suffered the punishment due for sin in our place—may have a more retributive understanding of justice. They may see punishment as essential to satisfying the demands of divine justice and may therefore be more sympathetic to punitive approaches in human justice systems.

Other traditions may emphasize the restorative dimensions of the atonement—the idea that Christ's work reconciles us to God and restores us to right relationship. These traditions may be more naturally aligned with restorative justice, seeing in the cross not merely the satisfaction of justice but the demonstration of God's love and the opening of a path to reconciliation. They may be more inclined to view human justice through the lens of restoration rather than retribution.

These doctrinal variations are not merely academic; they shape how Christians understand and respond to crime and conflict. A congregation that emphasizes God's wrath and the necessity of punishment may be more likely to support harsh sentencing and punitive measures. A congregation that emphasizes God's mercy and the possibility of restoration may be more likely to embrace restorative practices. These differences can create challenges when seeking to implement restorative justice across denominational lines or within diverse faith communities.

Scriptural emphasis also varies among traditions. Different denominations may place varying degrees of emphasis on different sections of the Bible. Passages that are central to one tradition's understanding of restorative justice may not hold the same significance for another. For example, a tradition that emphasizes the prophetic calls for justice—Amos's demand that "justice roll down like waters" (Amos 5:24) or Micah's insistence on doing justice, loving mercy, and walking humbly with God (Micah 6:8)—may find strong biblical support for restorative principles. A tradition that emphasizes the Pauline emphasis on justification by faith may focus more on individual salvation than on communal restoration.

The theological framework within which a denomination operates can significantly influence its interpretation of biblical principles. Traditions shaped by the legal categories of Roman law or the philosophical categories of Greek thought may approach justice differently than those shaped by Hebraic concepts of shalom and covenant. Traditions influenced by Reformation debates about law and gospel may have different understandings of the relationship between God's justice and God's mercy than those formed in other contexts.

Historical context also plays a role. The historical circumstances in which a particular denomination or faith tradition was formed can impact its interpretation of biblical passages. Denominations that emerged from periods of persecution may have different perspectives on justice than those that developed in times of cultural dominance. Traditions shaped by experiences of oppression may read biblical texts about justice differently than those formed in contexts of privilege. Historical events and theological debates throughout the centuries have contributed to the development of specific theological positions that continue to influence how justice is understood.

Denominational leadership further shapes interpretation. The stance of religious authorities within a tradition can influence how certain principles are applied. When church leaders speak on issues of crime and punishment, when they advocate for or against restorative justice, when they model restorative practices in their own ministries, they shape how their congregations understand and respond to these issues. Leadership matters, and differences in leadership can create differences in practice.

Interfaith dialogue adds another layer of complexity. As restorative justice is increasingly practiced in interfaith contexts, theological differences among religious traditions become relevant. Jewish, Muslim, Buddhist, Hindu, and other faith communities have their own understandings of justice, forgiveness, and reconciliation. These understandings may align with or diverge from Christian perspectives in various ways. Engaging in interfaith restorative justice requires navigating these theological differences with respect and humility.

Theological debates that stem from these differing interpretations can be a challenge when attempting to apply restorative justice within a biblical framework. Some Christians may argue that restorative justice is not biblical enough—that it fails to take seriously the demands of divine justice or the reality of human sin. Others may argue that it is too biblical—that it imposes religious categories on a secular system or that it reflects a particular theological tradition rather than a universally accessible approach. These debates can be divisive, creating obstacles to cooperation and implementation.

Yet theological diversity need not be a barrier to restorative justice. It can also be a source of enrichment, bringing multiple perspectives to bear on complex questions. The key is to engage in respectful dialogue, seeking common ground while acknowledging differences. This means recognizing that no single tradition has a monopoly on biblical truth, that our understandings are always partial and provisional, and that we have much to learn from one another. It means focusing on the core convictions that unite us—the belief that every person is created in God's image, that forgiveness is possible, that reconciliation is worth pursuing—while respecting the distinctive emphases of different traditions. It means approaching theological differences not as obstacles to be overcome but as opportunities for deeper understanding.

The Apostle Paul's words in Ephesians 4 provide guidance for this kind of dialogue: "I, therefore, the prisoner of the Lord, beseech you to walk worthy of the calling with which you were called, with all lowliness and gentleness, with longsuffering, bearing with one another in love, endeavoring to keep the unity of the Spirit in the bond of peace" (Ephesians 4:1-3). Lowliness, gentleness, patience, bearing with one another in love—these are the qualities needed for navigating theological differences. They are also the qualities that restorative justice seeks to cultivate. In this sense, the process of engaging with theological diversity itself embodies restorative principles.

Institutional Resistance

Institutional resistance represents one of the most formidable obstacles to the implementation of restorative justice. The criminal justice system, legal structures, and established correctional institutions are often deeply resistant to significant changes. Those who have spent their careers working within punitive systems may be skeptical of alternative approaches. Institutions develop cultures, practices, and vested interests that resist disruption. Overcoming this resistance requires sustained effort, strategic thinking, and patient persistence.

The current punitive approach is deeply embedded in most criminal justice systems. For centuries, Western legal systems have focused on punishment and retribution as the primary responses to wrongdoing. Laws are written in punitive terms. Court procedures are designed around adversarial contest. Correctional institutions are built to confine and control. Legal professionals are trained to think in terms of guilt and punishment. This entire apparatus is so familiar, so established, so taken for granted that it seems like the natural order of things.

Introducing restorative justice, which emphasizes reconciliation, restoration, and healing, represents a fundamental departure from this punitive model. It challenges deeply ingrained assumptions about what justice is and how it should be achieved. It asks professionals to think differently about their roles and responsibilities. It requires new skills, new procedures, new ways of measuring success. This shift challenges the status quo and can face resistance from individuals comfortable with the current approach.

The mindset and culture within these institutions often reinforce punitive practices. Law enforcement officers are trained to catch criminals, not to facilitate healing. Prosecutors are evaluated by conviction rates, not by victim satisfaction. Judges are expected to impose sentences, not to oversee restorative processes. Correctional officers are responsible for security and control, not for supporting rehabilitation and reintegration. These institutional cultures are not easily changed. They are reinforced by training, by peer pressure, by reward systems, by deeply held beliefs about the nature of justice.

Skepticism and opposition naturally arise when restorative justice is proposed. Individuals within the system may doubt its effectiveness, questioning whether it can really hold offenders accountable or protect public safety. They may worry about its impact on legal procedures, concerned that it might undermine due process or create inconsistencies in sentencing. They may fear that it will be seen as soft on crime, damaging public confidence in the justice system. These concerns are not unreasonable; they deserve to be taken seriously and addressed thoughtfully.

Resource allocation presents another dimension of institutional resistance. Implementing restorative justice often requires additional resources—funding for training, for facilitators, for community programs. In an era of tight budgets and competing priorities, securing these resources can be challenging. Institutions may resist allocating funds to restorative initiatives, especially if they perceive them as unproven or unnecessary. The allocation of resources is always a political process, and proponents of restorative justice must be prepared to make their case effectively.

Lack of awareness within institutions can also contribute to resistance. Many criminal justice professionals have never been exposed to restorative justice principles or practices. They may not understand what restorative justice is, how it works, or what benefits it can offer. This lack of awareness can lead to skepticism, suspicion, or outright opposition. Education and training are essential to addressing this challenge.

Overcoming institutional resistance requires a multi-faceted approach. Education is essential—helping professionals understand what restorative justice is, how it works, and what evidence supports its effectiveness. Training is crucial—equipping practitioners with the skills they need to facilitate restorative processes. Collaboration is key—building partnerships between restorative justice advocates and key stakeholders within the system. Demonstration projects can help—showing, through successful implementation, that restorative justice can work in practice, not just in theory.

Highlighting successful case studies can also help mitigate skepticism. When judges, prosecutors, and corrections officials see concrete examples of restorative justice working—victims satisfied, offenders accountable, communities strengthened—they may become more open to the approach. Personal testimony from those who have participated in restorative processes can be particularly powerful.

The Apostle Paul's approach to institutional engagement offers a model. When Paul stood before the Roman authorities, he did not simply denounce the system or demand its overthrow. He engaged with it respectfully, explaining his beliefs, appealing to his rights as a Roman citizen, and using the structures of the system to advance his mission. He understood that change often comes through patient engagement rather than revolutionary confrontation. Those who seek to introduce restorative justice into existing institutions would do well to follow his example.

Resource Limitations

Resource limitations pose a significant challenge to the effective implementation of restorative justice. Restorative processes demand resources that may not always be readily available, making application difficult, particularly in areas with limited access to such support. These resource constraints operate at multiple levels and affect various aspects of restorative practice.

Trained facilitators are essential for restorative justice processes. Victim-offender mediation, family group conferences, circle processes, and other restorative practices require skilled facilitators who can guide dialogue, manage emotions, ensure safety, and help parties reach meaningful agreements. These facilitators need comprehensive training in restorative principles, communication skills, conflict resolution, trauma awareness, and cultural sensitivity. They need ongoing supervision and support to maintain quality and prevent burnout.

Training and maintaining a pool of qualified facilitators is resource-intensive. It requires investment in training programs, curriculum development, and experienced trainers. It requires ongoing professional development to keep skills current and address emerging challenges. It requires systems for supervision, quality assurance, and accountability. In many communities, particularly those with limited resources, these investments may be difficult to make.

Counselors and support services are also essential. Restorative justice often involves addressing the emotional and psychological needs of victims, offenders, and affected parties. Victims may be dealing with trauma, anxiety, depression, and other mental health challenges. Offenders may be struggling with addiction, mental illness, or other issues that contributed to their behavior. Family members may need support as they navigate the impact of crime and incarceration.

Access to counseling and support services is essential to help individuals cope with these challenges and work towards healing. However, providing these services can strain existing mental health and support resources. Many communities already face shortages of mental health professionals, long waiting lists for services, and limited funding for treatment. Adding restorative justice to the mix can exacerbate these strains.

Community support is vital for restorative justice. Engaging the community in restorative processes requires community members who are willing to participate as volunteers, provide support to victims and offenders, and create safe spaces for dialogue. This kind of community engagement takes time to develop and sustain. It requires outreach, education, and relationship-building. It requires community members who are committed to the work and willing to invest their time and energy.

Limited community involvement and support can hinder the application of restorative justice, especially in areas with fewer resources or where community engagement is not readily available. In some communities, social capital may be depleted by poverty, violence, or historical trauma. In others, there may be cultural barriers to the kind of open dialogue that restorative processes require. Building the community infrastructure for restorative justice takes time and effort.

Economic constraints affect restorative justice programs at every level. Programs need funding for administrative costs, facilities, materials, and personnel. They need resources for outreach and education, for training and supervision, for evaluation and research. They need sustainable funding streams that can support long-term operation. Economic constraints can limit the ability of organizations and institutions to establish and maintain restorative justice programs, particularly in economically disadvantaged areas.

Geographic disparities compound these challenges. Resource limitations may be more pronounced in rural or economically disadvantaged areas, where access to trained facilitators, counselors, and community support may be even scarcer. This can result in unequal access to restorative justice services, which goes against the principle of equitable justice. Urban areas with more resources may be able to offer robust restorative programs, while rural areas may have few or none. This disparity raises questions of justice in access to justice.

Time and administrative costs add another layer. Implementing restorative justice takes time—time for preparation, for facilitation, for follow-up. It requires administrative coordination—scheduling meetings, managing cases, tracking outcomes. These administrative tasks require dedicated personnel and financial resources. In systems already stretched thin, finding the time and resources for restorative justice can be challenging.

Overcoming resource limitations requires a multi-faceted approach. Seeking funding and support from government agencies, private organizations, and community partners is essential. Grant funding, foundation support, and government appropriations can provide the resources needed to establish and sustain restorative programs. Training and capacity-building programs can help develop a pool of skilled facilitators and support personnel. Investing in local capacity reduces dependence on outside experts and builds sustainable infrastructure.

Exploring innovative approaches can help expand access. Online platforms, for example, can facilitate restorative processes in areas where in-person meetings are difficult. Virtual mediation, video conferencing, and other technologies can connect participants across distances and reduce travel costs. While technology cannot replace the power of face-to-face encounter, it can extend the reach of restorative justice to underserved communities.

Collaboration among multiple stakeholders is essential. Government agencies, non-profit organizations, community groups, and faith communities all have roles to play. By working together, pooling resources, and coordinating efforts, they can achieve more than any single entity could alone. Partnerships can leverage complementary strengths, avoid duplication of effort, and create comprehensive systems of support.

The early church faced similar resource challenges. When a need arose, believers pooled their resources, sharing what they had so that no one was in need (Acts 2:44-45; 4:32-35). They did not wait for outside funding or government support; they created their own systems of mutual aid. This model of community-based resource sharing offers inspiration for restorative justice advocates today. By mobilizing the resources of the community—time, talent, treasure—we can overcome resource limitations and build sustainable restorative practices.

Victim and Offender Willingness

The success of restorative justice hinges on the willingness of both victims and offenders to engage in the process. This voluntariness is foundational to the principles of empowerment and self-determination that underlie restorative practice. Yet securing this willingness can be challenging. Some victims may be hesitant to face their offenders, fearing retraumatization. Some offenders may not be open to taking responsibility for their actions. The lack of participant willingness can pose a substantial hurdle to effective implementation.

Voluntary participation is essential for several reasons. Restorative justice aims to empower victims by giving them a voice and a role in the process. If participation is coerced, this empowerment is undermined. Victims may feel pressured, manipulated, or controlled rather than empowered. Offenders, similarly, need to choose to take responsibility and make amends; coercion produces compliance, not genuine accountability. The voluntary nature of restorative justice is not a practical inconvenience but a philosophical necessity.

Healing and recovery depend on willingness. Victims who are not ready to face their offenders may experience further trauma if forced into restorative processes. The encounter can be emotionally challenging, even under the best circumstances. Victims need to engage at their own pace, when they feel prepared and supported. Their willingness is crucial for the potential healing that restorative justice can offer. When victims are ready to confront their offenders and seek resolution, they are more likely to experience positive outcomes.

Accountability and responsibility require willingness from offenders. Offenders who are unwilling to take responsibility for their actions may not genuinely engage in the process. They may go through the motions without experiencing the transformation that restorative justice seeks. Willingness on the part of the offender signifies a sincere commitment to making amends and addressing the harm caused. Without this commitment, the process is unlikely to produce meaningful results.

Outcome effectiveness depends on participant investment. Restorative justice is most effective when participants are genuinely invested in the process and its outcomes. Willing participants are more likely to engage openly, honestly, and constructively. They are more likely to listen, to empathize, to take responsibility, to make amends. This engagement leads to more meaningful resolutions and greater satisfaction for all involved.

Avoiding re-traumatization is a critical concern. For victims, particularly in cases of serious harm, facing an offender can be emotionally challenging. Even with careful preparation and skilled facilitation, the encounter may trigger painful memories and intense emotions. Willing participation allows victims to engage at their own pace and when they feel emotionally prepared, minimizing the risk of re-traumatization. Forcing participation could cause additional harm.

Building trust in the process requires willing participation. When victims and offenders choose to engage in restorative justice, they demonstrate confidence in the process. This confidence can be contagious, encouraging others to participate and building trust in restorative approaches within the broader community. Coerced participation would have the opposite effect, undermining trust and confidence.

Several factors can affect willingness. Victims may fear facing their offenders, worrying about their safety or emotional stability. They may doubt that the process will benefit them, believing that offenders will not be genuine or that nothing will change. They may feel pressure from others—family, friends, advocates—to participate or not to participate. They may have cultural or religious beliefs that influence their willingness.

Offenders may resist taking responsibility, clinging to denial, minimization, or blame. They may fear the consequences of admitting guilt—legal repercussions, social stigma, damaged relationships. They may doubt their ability to make amends or to change. They may be struggling with addiction, mental illness, or other issues that impair their judgment and motivation.

To overcome challenges related to participant willingness, practitioners must prioritize informed consent. Victims and offenders need clear information about what restorative justice involves, what they can expect, and what their options are. They need time to consider their decision and opportunities to ask questions. They need assurance that their participation is voluntary and that they can withdraw at any time.

Creating a safe and respectful environment is essential. Participants need to feel that the process will protect their safety, respect their dignity, and honor their needs. Facilitators must be trained to create this environment, to manage power imbalances, and to respond appropriately to emotional distress. When participants feel safe and respected, they are more likely to engage willingly.

Acknowledging and addressing concerns is crucial. Victims and offenders may have legitimate worries about the process. These concerns should be heard, validated, and addressed to the extent possible. Sometimes, simply acknowledging the concern and discussing how it will be managed can increase willingness.

Supporting participants throughout the process builds confidence. Pre-meeting preparation, ongoing support, and post-meeting follow-up help participants feel cared for and valued. Knowing that support is available can increase willingness to engage.

The example of Jesus with the woman caught in adultery (John 8:1-11) illustrates the importance of willingness and respect. Jesus did not force the woman to participate in a process of accountability and restoration. He protected her from those who would condemn her, spoke to her with respect, and invited her into a new way of living. He created conditions in which she could respond freely. This model of respectful invitation, not coercive imposition, should guide restorative practitioners.

Societal Skepticism

Restorative justice challenges the conventional understanding of justice, which often centers on punitive measures. It may face skepticism from the broader society, which may question the efficacy of this approach. Overcoming this skepticism and educating the public about the benefits of restorative justice is a persistent challenge that requires sustained effort and strategic communication.

Lack of familiarity contributes to skepticism. Most people have grown up with the punitive model of justice. They have seen it portrayed in countless movies and television shows. They have heard politicians talk about being tough on crime. They have absorbed cultural messages about the need for punishment and retribution. Restorative justice, by contrast, is unfamiliar. People may not understand what it is, how it works, or why it might be preferable. This lack of familiarity breeds skepticism.

Concerns about public safety are legitimate and must be addressed. Some members of the public worry that restorative justice places too much emphasis on the needs and rights of offenders, potentially at the expense of public safety. They may fear that offenders will not be adequately punished, that they will reoffend, that the community will be less safe. These concerns are not unreasonable; they reflect genuine worries about safety and security. Restorative justice advocates must take these concerns seriously and demonstrate how restorative approaches can enhance public safety by reducing recidivism and addressing underlying causes of crime.

Perception of leniency is another source of skepticism. Restorative justice is sometimes perceived as being softer on offenders than traditional punitive measures. This perception can lead to skepticism, especially among those who believe that offenders should face severe consequences for their actions. The reality is that restorative justice is not lenient; it demands more of offenders than passive incarceration. It requires them to face their victims, to acknowledge harm, to make amends, to change. But this reality is not always understood by the public. Communicating the demanding nature of restorative accountability is essential.

Lack of trust in offenders also fuels skepticism. Some individuals doubt that offenders can genuinely change or that they will follow through on commitments made in restorative processes. They may have had negative experiences with offenders or absorbed stereotypes about criminals. They may believe that "once a criminal, always a criminal." Overcoming this distrust requires demonstrating, through evidence and personal testimony, that change is possible and that many offenders do, in fact, make amends and transform their lives.

Misconceptions and misinformation about restorative justice abound. Some people think it means letting offenders off without consequences. Others think it is only for minor offenses or first-time offenders. Others think it ignores the needs of victims or fails to hold offenders accountable. These misconceptions can be powerful barriers to acceptance. Correcting them requires clear, consistent, accessible information about what restorative justice actually is and how it works.

Cultural and value differences influence how restorative justice is perceived. In some cultures, punitive justice is deeply ingrained, seen as the only appropriate response to wrongdoing. Restorative approaches may be viewed with suspicion as foreign or untraditional. In other cultures, restorative values may be more familiar, resonating with communal traditions and practices. Understanding these cultural dynamics is essential for effective communication.

Overcoming societal skepticism requires proactive efforts to educate the public. Public awareness campaigns can introduce restorative justice concepts and principles to broad audiences. These campaigns might use traditional media, social media, community events, and other channels to reach diverse groups. The goal is to increase familiarity and understanding, laying the groundwork for acceptance.

Community outreach is essential. Engaging with community groups, faith communities, schools, and neighborhood organizations creates opportunities for dialogue and education. When people have the chance to ask questions, express concerns, and learn from those with experience, skepticism can give way to understanding. Personal connections build trust in ways that abstract information cannot.

Sharing success stories and case studies is powerful. When people hear about actual restorative justice processes—about victims who found healing, offenders who took responsibility, communities that were strengthened—they can see the approach in action. These stories humanize the process and demonstrate its potential. They counter abstract skepticism with concrete evidence.

Engaging in open and respectful dialogue with skeptics is crucial. Rather than dismissing concerns or becoming defensive, restorative justice advocates should listen carefully, acknowledge legitimate worries, and respond thoughtfully. Skeptics may have valid points that need to be addressed. Engaging with them respectfully can build bridges and create openings for understanding.

The Apostle Paul's approach in Athens (Acts 17) offers a model for engaging skeptical audiences. Paul did not simply proclaim the gospel; he engaged with the philosophers, acknowledged their religious sensibilities, and built bridges from their own cultural expressions. He found points of connection and used them to introduce new ideas. This approach of respectful engagement, cultural sensitivity, and thoughtful communication is essential for overcoming societal skepticism about restorative justice.

Ensuring Equity

A significant critique of restorative justice lies in its potential to perpetuate systemic inequities. Critics argue that it may not adequately address structural issues like racism or economic disparities. There is a need for rigorous attention to ensuring that restorative justice processes are equitable and accessible to all, regardless of social, economic, or racial backgrounds.

Addressing systemic inequities is essential. Restorative justice must be mindful of the systemic issues that underlie many forms of harm and wrongdoing. Crime does not occur in a vacuum; it is shaped by social, economic, and political conditions. Poverty, racism, inequality, lack of opportunity, historical trauma—these factors contribute to criminal behavior and shape how crime is experienced and responded to. Restorative justice that ignores these systemic dimensions risks becoming a Band-Aid on a deep wound, addressing individual harm while leaving structural causes untouched.

Failing to address systemic inequities can result in overlooking the root causes of conflicts, perpetuating inequality, and failing to provide meaningful justice for marginalized communities. If restorative justice is applied only to privileged offenders who can afford to make amends, while marginalized offenders face punitive sanctions, inequity is reinforced. If restorative processes are not culturally accessible to diverse communities, they may be used primarily by dominant groups. These outcomes would be deeply problematic, contradicting the values of justice and equity that restorative justice seeks to embody.

Preventing reinjury requires attention to equity. Failing to consider equity in restorative justice processes can risk reinjuring already marginalized individuals or communities. If systemic issues like racism or economic disparities are not addressed, the harm can continue, and individuals or communities may not experience genuine healing and reconciliation. A restorative process that ignores the racism that shaped a conflict may leave participants feeling unheard and invalidated. A process that does not address economic disparities may result in agreements that are impossible for marginalized offenders to fulfill.

Community trust and buy-in depend on equity. Ensuring that restorative processes are fair and accessible to all members of the community can help foster confidence in the system and its ability to provide just outcomes. When marginalized communities see restorative justice as another tool of oppression, they will not trust it. When they experience it as genuinely equitable, they may embrace it as a path to healing. Building this trust requires demonstrated commitment to equity, not just rhetorical affirmation.

An ethical imperative demands attention to equity. Equity is a fundamental principle of justice itself, essential for upholding the values of fairness, dignity, and respect for all individuals. Restorative justice that is not equitable is not truly just. Those who practice restorative justice have an ethical obligation to ensure that their practices do not perpetuate the very inequities they seek to address.

Effectiveness is enhanced by equity. Ensuring that marginalized individuals have equal access to and representation in restorative processes can result in more meaningful resolutions, better compliance with agreements, and stronger community cohesion. When all participants feel heard, respected, and fairly treated, they are more likely to engage genuinely and follow through on commitments. Equity is not just a moral imperative but a practical necessity.

To ensure equity in restorative justice, several steps are essential. Addressing structural inequities must be a priority. Restorative justice programs should acknowledge and actively work to address structural issues like racism, economic disparities, and discrimination that can contribute to harm and wrongdoing. This may involve partnering with organizations working on these issues, advocating for policy changes, and incorporating awareness of systemic factors into facilitator training.

Community engagement is crucial. Engaging with affected communities and involving them in the design and implementation of restorative justice programs helps ensure that processes are culturally sensitive and relevant. Community members know their own needs and contexts better than outside experts. Their participation is essential for creating programs that truly serve their communities.

Cultural competency training for facilitators and practitioners is necessary to address the diverse needs of participants. Facilitators need to understand how cultural factors may influence communication styles, conflict resolution preferences, and perceptions of justice. They need to be able to adapt their approaches to different cultural contexts. Ongoing training and supervision can help develop and maintain these competencies.

Accessible support services must be available. Ensuring that individuals, particularly those from marginalized backgrounds, have access to support services to address emotional, psychological, or material needs is essential. This may involve partnering with community-based organizations, providing transportation or childcare, offering services in multiple languages, or other accommodations. Accessibility is not just about physical access but about removing barriers to participation.

Evaluation and monitoring of equity are essential. Continuously evaluating and monitoring the equity of restorative justice programs can identify disparities and inform adjustments. Data on participant demographics, outcomes, and satisfaction should be collected and analyzed to identify patterns of inequity. When disparities are found, programs should be modified to address them. This ongoing process of evaluation and improvement is essential for maintaining equity.

The biblical prophets consistently called for equity and justice for the marginalized. Amos thundered against those who "trample the head of the poor into the dust of the earth" (Amos 2:7). Isaiah condemned those who "turn aside the needy from justice" (Isaiah 10:2). Jeremiah proclaimed that knowing God meant doing justice for the poor and needy (Jeremiah 22:16). These prophetic calls remind us that authentic justice must be equitable, that God's concern extends especially to the marginalized, and that any justice system that ignores the poor and oppressed stands under divine judgment. Restorative justice, to be faithful to this prophetic tradition, must prioritize equity.

Measuring Outcomes

Measuring the effectiveness of restorative justice programs and their long-term impact can be challenging. Traditional justice systems often rely on quantitative measures like recidivism rates, whereas the outcomes of restorative justice are multifaceted and may not be easily quantifiable. Developing appropriate evaluation frameworks and methods is essential for demonstrating effectiveness, improving practice, and building support for restorative approaches.

Accountability and transparency require outcome measurement. Measuring outcomes ensures that restorative justice programs are held accountable for their effectiveness.

Funders, policymakers, and the public need to know whether programs are achieving their goals. This transparency is crucial for maintaining trust and support. Without evidence of effectiveness, restorative justice may be dismissed as well-meaning but unproven.

Continuous improvement depends on evaluation. By understanding what works and what doesn't, practitioners can refine their methods and enhance the quality of services. Evaluation provides feedback that informs practice. It helps identify strengths to build on and weaknesses to address. Programs that do not evaluate are flying blind, unable to learn from experience or adapt to changing circumstances.

Evidence-based practices emerge from rigorous evaluation. Measuring outcomes provides the opportunity to identify practices that have the most positive impact on participants and communities. This evidence can guide program development, ensuring that resources are directed toward approaches that work. It can also inform training and technical assistance, spreading effective practices to new contexts.

Participant satisfaction is a crucial outcome. Understanding participant satisfaction and the perception of fairness is vital. High levels of participant satisfaction often correlate with successful outcomes, as they indicate that individuals feel their needs and concerns have been adequately addressed. Measuring satisfaction provides insight into the quality of the process, not just its outcomes.

Restitution and repair outcomes need assessment. Measuring outcomes helps assess the success of restitution and repair efforts. Evaluating whether offenders have made genuine efforts to make amends for their actions and whether victims have experienced healing and resolution is essential. These outcomes are central to restorative justice; they must be measured.

Community impact is another important dimension. Restorative justice can have broader community impacts beyond individual cases. It may affect community cohesion, trust in institutions, perceptions of safety, and social capital. Measuring these impacts can help demonstrate the value of restorative justice in building stronger, more cohesive communities. It can also identify unintended negative consequences that need to be addressed.

Resource allocation decisions benefit from outcome data. Resources are often limited, and measuring outcomes helps in making informed decisions about resource allocation. It ensures that resources are directed toward practices and programs that yield the best results. Programs that cannot demonstrate effectiveness may lose funding; those that show strong outcomes may receive additional support.

Policy and advocacy efforts rely on outcome data. Outcomes data can be valuable in advocating for restorative justice at a policy level. It provides evidence of the effectiveness of restorative practices and can be used to advocate for broader implementation and support. Policymakers want to know what works; outcome data provides answers.

To effectively measure outcomes in restorative justice, appropriate evaluation frameworks and methods must be developed. These may include a combination of qualitative and quantitative data. Surveys, interviews, and statistical analysis can provide a comprehensive view of outcomes. Qualitative data captures the richness of participant experiences; quantitative data provides measurable indicators of impact.

Longitudinal studies are important for tracking long-term impact. Restorative justice aims for lasting change—healing that endures, relationships that are restored, behavior that is transformed. Measuring these outcomes requires following participants over time. Longitudinal studies can help determine whether the benefits of restorative justice are sustained.

Feedback and participant surveys provide direct input from those most affected. Gathering feedback from victims, offenders, and affected parties about their experiences and perceptions of the process is essential. This feedback can identify what is working well and what needs improvement. It can also provide powerful testimony about the value of restorative justice.

Comparative analysis can provide insights into effectiveness. Comparing the outcomes of restorative justice cases with those processed through traditional justice systems can help demonstrate the relative effectiveness of restorative approaches. This comparison should account for differences in case characteristics, participant demographics, and other factors that might influence outcomes.

Cultural sensitivity in measurement tools is crucial. Ensuring that measurement tools are culturally sensitive and relevant to diverse communities is essential for accurately capturing outcomes. Tools developed for one population may not work for another. Adapting measures to local contexts and involving community members in the evaluation process can help ensure cultural appropriateness.

The parable of the sower (Matthew 13:3-9, 18-23) offers insight into the challenges of measuring outcomes. The same seed produced different results in different soils. Some yielded a hundredfold, some sixty, some thirty. The outcome depended on many factors—the condition of the soil, the care of the sower, the influence of weeds and birds. Measuring the success of the sowing required attention to these multiple factors and recognition that outcomes would vary. So too with restorative justice: outcomes must be measured with attention to context, complexity, and variation. Simple metrics will not capture the full story.

Lack of Legal Framework

In some jurisdictions, restorative justice may lack a robust legal framework or legislative support. This can lead to inconsistencies in its application and hinder its acceptance and legitimacy within the legal system. Developing appropriate legal frameworks is essential for the sustainable growth of restorative justice.

Inconsistent application is a primary challenge. Without a clear legal framework, the application of restorative justice may vary widely. Different practitioners or jurisdictions may interpret and implement restorative practices in various ways, leading to inequities in access and outcomes. Some offenders may have access to restorative options while others do not. Some victims may receive the benefits of restorative processes while others are excluded. This inconsistency undermines the principle of equal justice.

Legitimacy and trust depend on legal recognition. A well-established legal framework can enhance the legitimacy and trust in restorative justice processes. It provides a clear mandate for the use of restorative practices, making them more acceptable to the public, victims, and offenders. When restorative justice operates outside the legal framework, it may be viewed as unofficial, informal, or less legitimate than conventional processes.

Standardization is facilitated by legal frameworks. A legal framework can standardize restorative justice practices, ensuring that they meet specific criteria and adhere to best practices. This consistency is essential for the effectiveness and reliability of restorative processes. Standards can address facilitator qualifications, participant protections, procedural requirements, and outcome measures. Without such standards, quality may vary unpredictably.

Procedural safeguards are often included in legal frameworks. Legal frameworks typically include safeguards that protect the rights and interests of all parties involved. These may include requirements for informed consent, provisions for legal counsel, protections against self-incrimination, and mechanisms for appeal. Without these safeguards, there may be concerns about due process and fairness. Participants may be vulnerable to coercion or manipulation.

Accountability is enhanced by legal frameworks. A legal framework provides a mechanism for holding practitioners and facilitators accountable for their actions. It sets out the expectations and responsibilities of those involved in restorative justice processes. It may include provisions for oversight, complaint procedures, and disciplinary actions. This accountability helps maintain public trust and ensures ethical practice.

Enforceability of agreements is supported by legal frameworks. Legal support can make the outcomes of restorative justice processes more enforceable. Agreements reached through restorative practices may have legal weight, providing added incentives for compliance. When agreements are legally binding, parties are more likely to follow through. When they are not, enforcement may be difficult or impossible.

Public funding often depends on legal recognition. Legal recognition can facilitate the allocation of public funds to support restorative justice programs. Government funding is essential for the sustainability and growth of many restorative initiatives. Without legal recognition, programs may struggle to secure public support and may rely on unstable private funding.

Participant confidence is bolstered by legal frameworks. Victims and offenders may have greater confidence in the process when it operates within a legal framework. They may be more willing to participate if they know that their rights and interests are protected by law. Legal recognition provides assurance that the process is legitimate and that outcomes will be respected.

Consistent ethical standards are promoted by legal frameworks. Legal frameworks often include ethical standards that practitioners must adhere to. These standards help ensure that restorative justice processes are conducted ethically and responsibly. They address issues of confidentiality, impartiality, competence, and integrity. Without such standards, ethical practice may vary.

To address the lack of a legal framework for restorative practices, efforts can be made to advocate for legislative support. This may involve working with lawmakers, legal experts, and community stakeholders to create and implement legislation that supports the principles and practices of restorative justice while ensuring due process and fairness. Advocacy can take many forms: educating legislators about restorative justice, building coalitions to support reform, drafting model legislation, and mobilizing public support.

Developing legal guidelines can also help. Even without comprehensive legislation, guidelines issued by courts, bar associations, or professional organizations can provide direction for restorative practice. These guidelines can establish standards, clarify expectations, and promote consistency. They can also serve as stepping stones toward more formal legal frameworks.

Building relationships with legal system stakeholders is essential. Prosecutors, judges, defense attorneys, and court administrators can become allies in developing restorative justice within the legal system. Their support can help legitimize restorative practices and create opportunities for integration. Working collaboratively with these stakeholders can build trust and create momentum for legal recognition.

The relationship between law and grace in Scripture offers a model for thinking about legal frameworks. The law provided structure, guidance, and accountability; grace offered mercy, forgiveness, and restoration. Neither was sufficient alone. The law without grace became harsh and condemning; grace without law became license and chaos. Together, they pointed toward the fullness of God's justice. So too with restorative justice and legal frameworks: restorative principles need legal structures to ensure fairness and accountability; legal structures need restorative principles to achieve healing and restoration. The challenge is to hold them together in creative tension.

Navigating the Challenges with Faith and Wisdom

These challenges are real and significant. Theological differences, institutional resistance, resource limitations, participant willingness, societal skepticism, equity concerns, measurement difficulties, and legal gaps all pose obstacles to the implementation of restorative justice. Yet none of these challenges is insurmountable. With faith, wisdom, and persistence, they can be navigated.

Theological differences can be addressed through respectful dialogue and a focus on common ground. Institutional resistance can be overcome through patient engagement and demonstration of effectiveness. Resource limitations can be mitigated through creative partnerships and community mobilization. Participant willingness can be nurtured through careful preparation and support. Societal skepticism can be countered through education and testimony. Equity can be prioritized through intentional design and ongoing evaluation. Outcomes can be measured through thoughtful, multi-faceted evaluation. Legal frameworks can be developed through advocacy and collaboration.

The biblical wisdom literature offers guidance for navigating challenges. Proverbs speaks repeatedly of the importance of wisdom, understanding, and discernment. "Wisdom is the principal thing; therefore get wisdom. And in all your getting, get understanding" (Proverbs 4:7). Navigating the challenges of restorative justice requires this wisdom—the ability to see clearly, to understand complexities, to discern right paths.

Ecclesiastes reminds us that there is a time for everything—a time to plant and a time to uproot, a time to tear down and a time to build, a time to scatter stones and a time to gather them (Ecclesiastes 3:1-8). Implementing restorative justice requires discernment about timing—knowing when to push forward and when to wait, when to speak and when to listen, when to act and when to reflect.

James encourages believers to consider it pure joy when they face trials of various kinds, because the testing of faith produces perseverance (James 1:2-3). The challenges of restorative justice can be seen not as obstacles to be avoided but as opportunities for growth. They test our commitment, refine our practices, deepen our understanding. They produce perseverance, which is essential for the long work of transformation.

The Apostle Paul, who faced countless challenges in his ministry—imprisonment, beatings, shipwreck, opposition, betrayal—offers this perspective: "We are hard pressed on every side, yet not crushed; we are perplexed, but not in despair; persecuted, but not forsaken; struck down, but not destroyed" (2 Corinthians 4:8-9). The challenges of restorative justice may press us hard, but they need not crush us. They may perplex us, but they need not drive us to despair. With faith in the God who raised Jesus from the dead, we can face these challenges with hope and perseverance.

Ultimately, the challenges and critiques of restorative justice serve a valuable purpose. They keep us humble, reminding us that our approaches are imperfect and our understanding incomplete. They push us to improve, to refine our practices, to address our blind spots. They protect us from the arrogance that assumes we have all the answers. And they invite us into deeper engagement with those who question, doubt, and resist—engagement that can lead to mutual learning and unexpected growth.

The journey of restorative justice is not a sprint but a marathon. It requires patience, persistence, and perseverance. It demands willingness to learn, adapt, and grow. It calls for faith in the ultimate triumph of God's justice, even when present realities seem discouraging. But for those who are called to this work, the challenges are not reasons to turn back but invitations to press on. For in facing these challenges, we become more fully the people God calls us to be—agents of healing, instruments of peace, ministers of reconciliation in a broken but beloved world.

CHAPTER 11

OVERCOMING THE OBSTACLES

The challenges to restorative justice, while significant, are not insurmountable. Throughout history, transformative movements have faced resistance, skepticism, and obstacles that seemed overwhelming at the time. Yet through persistent effort, strategic thinking, and unwavering commitment to their principles, these movements have prevailed. The abolition of slavery, the extension of civil rights, the recognition of women's suffrage—each of these advances faced opposition that appeared immovable, yet each was achieved through the dedicated work of those who refused to accept injustice as inevitable.

The same can be true for restorative justice. The obstacles we have examined—theological differences, institutional resistance, resource limitations, participant unwillingness, societal skepticism, equity concerns, measurement difficulties, and legal gaps—can all be addressed through thoughtful strategies and sustained effort. This chapter explores the pathways to overcoming these obstacles, drawing on insights from law, psychology, philosophy, theology, and practical experience. We will examine strategies for education and training, standardization, legal protections, victim support, community engagement, evaluation and research, legislation, collaboration, cultural sensitivity, resource development, public awareness, and conflict prevention. We will also explore the contemporary relevance of restorative justice, its role in community healing, conflict resolution, truth and reconciliation, education, victim support, and its global applications. Through this exploration, we will see that restorative justice is not merely a theoretical ideal but a practical possibility, capable of transforming individuals, communities, and systems.

Education and Training: The Foundation for Change

The first and most fundamental strategy for overcoming obstacles to restorative justice is comprehensive education and training. Change begins with understanding. People cannot support what they do not know; they cannot practice what they have not learned. Providing thorough education and training for all stakeholders—judges, lawyers, law enforcement, community members, and participants in restorative justice processes—is essential for building the knowledge, skills, and commitment that restorative justice requires.

Education about restorative justice must begin with its principles and values. Stakeholders need to understand what restorative justice is and what it is not. They need to grasp its core commitments: repairing harm, involving stakeholders, transforming relationships, addressing root causes. They need to see how these principles align with their own values and professional responsibilities. For Christian communities, this education includes exploring the biblical foundations of restorative justice, connecting its practices to the teachings of Jesus and the witness of Scripture.

Education must also address the evidence base for restorative justice. Stakeholders need to know what research has demonstrated about the effectiveness of restorative approaches—reduced recidivism, increased victim satisfaction, cost savings, community benefits. They need to see that restorative justice is not merely a hopeful theory but a proven practice, supported by decades of research from around the world. This evidence can help overcome skepticism and build confidence in restorative approaches.

Training for practitioners is essential. Facilitators, mediators, circle keepers, and other restorative practitioners need comprehensive training in restorative principles, communication skills, conflict resolution, trauma awareness, cultural sensitivity, and ethical practice. They need opportunities to practice their skills under supervision, to receive feedback, and to continue learning throughout their careers. They need support systems that prevent burnout and promote ongoing growth.

Training for system stakeholders—judges, lawyers, law enforcement, corrections officials—is equally important. These professionals need to understand how restorative justice can complement their work, how to identify appropriate cases for referral, how to support restorative processes, and how to integrate restorative outcomes into their decisions. They need to see restorative justice not as a threat to their roles but as an enhancement of their ability to achieve justice.

Training for community members builds the grassroots support that sustains restorative programs. Community members need to understand how they can participate in restorative processes—as supporters, as circle participants, as volunteers. They need to develop the skills for constructive engagement in difficult conversations. They need to see restorative justice as something they do, not something done to them.

The Apostle Paul's method of teaching provides a model for restorative education. Paul did not simply proclaim truth; he reasoned with his hearers, engaged with their questions, addressed their concerns, and built bridges from their existing knowledge to new understanding (Acts 17:2-3; 18:4). He adapted his approach to different audiences—Jews, Greeks, philosophers, rulers—finding points of connection and speaking in ways they could understand. Restorative education requires this same flexibility, this same commitment to engagement, this same respect for the learner.

Jesus' method of teaching through parables also offers guidance. He used stories that were accessible, memorable, and provocative—stories that invited hearers into new ways of thinking without imposing conclusions. Restorative education can use stories—case studies, testimonials, narratives—to bring principles to life and engage hearts as well as minds. Stories of victims who found healing, offenders who were transformed, communities that were strengthened—these narratives can do what abstract arguments cannot.

Standardization: Consistency and Quality

The development and promotion of standardized practices and guidelines for restorative justice processes can help ensure consistency and fairness in how cases are handled. Standardization does not mean rigid uniformity; restorative justice must remain flexible enough to adapt to diverse contexts and individual circumstances. But core standards can provide a framework within which flexibility operates, ensuring that all restorative processes meet basic requirements of quality and fairness.

Standardization addresses several challenges. It helps ensure that all participants receive the same protections and opportunities, regardless of where they live or which program handles their case. It provides clear expectations for practitioners, promoting accountability and professional development. It gives policymakers and funders confidence that restorative programs meet recognized standards. It facilitates research and evaluation by providing consistent definitions and measures.

What should be standardized? Core principles should be articulated and promoted: voluntary participation, informed consent, safety, respect, accountability, restoration. Procedural standards should be established: preparation of participants, facilitation qualifications, confidentiality protections, agreement formalization, follow-up procedures. Ethical standards should be codified: impartiality, confidentiality, competence, integrity, respect for participants. Outcome measures should be defined: participant satisfaction, agreement completion, recidivism, healing indicators.

Who should develop these standards? The process should be inclusive, bringing together practitioners, researchers, policymakers, community representatives, and others with relevant expertise. International bodies like the United Nations have developed basic principles that can inform national and local standards. Professional associations can develop standards for their members. Government agencies can incorporate standards into funding requirements and regulatory frameworks. The goal is not to impose standards from above but to develop them through inclusive processes that build ownership and commitment.

The biblical concept of "measuring line" (Zechariah 2:1-5; Revelation 11:1) offers a metaphor for standardization. The measuring line establishes boundaries, defines spaces, ensures that construction proceeds according to plan. Without it, building is haphazard and unstable. With it, structures are sound and secure. Standards for restorative justice serve a similar function: they establish the boundaries within which restorative processes operate, ensuring that they are built on firm foundations and produce reliable results.

Yet the measuring line must be used with wisdom. In Zechariah's vision, the measuring line is followed by a declaration that Jerusalem will be "a city without walls" because of the multitude of people within it. The walls that defined the city also limited it; the absence of walls symbolized expansion and inclusion. Standards for restorative justice must similarly balance definition with flexibility—providing structure without creating barriers, ensuring quality without preventing innovation.

Legal Protections: Safeguarding Rights

Maintaining strong legal protections within restorative justice processes is essential for safeguarding the rights of both victims and offenders. Restorative justice operates within legal systems, not outside them. Participants must be assured that their legal rights are protected, that participation is truly voluntary, and that outcomes are fair and enforceable.

Voluntary participation is fundamental. Victims and offenders must choose to engage in restorative processes freely, without coercion or pressure. This requires clear information about what participation involves, what alternatives exist, and what rights they retain. It requires assurance that declining to participate will not result in negative consequences. It requires ongoing consent—the freedom to withdraw at any point without penalty.

Informed consent depends on adequate information. Participants need to understand the process, the potential benefits and risks, the roles of facilitators, the possible outcomes, and the implications of agreements. They need opportunities to ask questions and receive answers. They need time to consider their decision without pressure. Facilitators have a responsibility to ensure that participants are fully informed before consenting.

Procedural safeguards protect against abuse. Restorative processes should include protections against coercion, manipulation, and exploitation. Power imbalances between participants must be recognized and addressed. Confidentiality must be maintained, with clear limits explained in advance. Participants should have access to support persons, advocates, or legal counsel if desired. These safeguards are not obstacles to restorative justice but essential components of ethical practice.

Legal counsel can play an important role. Offenders, in particular, may need advice about the legal implications of participation—how statements made in restorative processes might affect their legal position, how agreements might be enforced, what rights they retain. Some restorative programs make counsel available to participants; others encourage participants to consult counsel independently. Ensuring access to legal information protects participants and builds confidence in the process.

Enforceability of agreements requires legal clarity. Restorative agreements may include provisions for restitution, community service, counseling, or other actions. Participants need to know whether these agreements are legally binding, how they will be enforced, and what consequences follow from non-compliance. Clear legal frameworks for restorative agreements protect all parties and ensure accountability.

The biblical tradition's emphasis on justice and righteousness includes concern for legal protections. The Law of Moses established numerous safeguards for the accused—requirements for multiple witnesses, protections against false testimony, limitations on punishment, provision for cities of refuge. These protections recognized that even the guilty retain rights, that procedures matter, that justice must be done fairly. Restorative justice, in maintaining strong legal protections, stands in this tradition.

Victim Support Services: Addressing Needs

Enhancing support services for victims is essential for addressing concerns about re-victimization and retaliation. Victims must have access to information, counseling, and legal advocacy throughout the restorative process and beyond. Their needs and perspectives must be central to restorative practice.

Information empowers victims. Victims need to understand the restorative process, their options for participation, the potential outcomes, and their rights. They need to know what to expect before, during, and after restorative encounters. They need information about available support services and how to access them. Providing clear, accessible information helps victims make informed decisions and reduces anxiety about the unknown.

Counseling supports healing. Many victims carry deep emotional and psychological wounds from crime. Professional counseling can help them process these wounds, develop coping strategies, and work toward recovery. Some victims may benefit from trauma-informed therapy, support groups, or spiritual care. Access to appropriate counseling services should be available throughout the restorative process and beyond.

Legal advocacy protects victims' rights. Victims may need assistance navigating the legal system, understanding their rights, and advocating for their interests. Victim advocates can provide this support, accompanying victims to meetings, explaining legal procedures, and ensuring that victims' voices are heard. Advocates can also help victims access compensation, restitution, and other forms of support.

Safety planning is essential for victims who fear retaliation. Some victims may have legitimate concerns about their safety if they engage in restorative processes. These concerns must be taken seriously and addressed through appropriate safety measures—secure meeting locations, separate entrances and exits, presence of support persons, safety plans for after the process. No victim should be asked to participate in ways that compromise their safety.

Ongoing support recognizes that healing takes time. The impact of crime does not end when a restorative process concludes. Victims may need continued support—counseling, advocacy, community connection—as they navigate the long journey of healing. Restorative programs should provide or connect victims to ongoing support services, checking in periodically and responding to emerging needs.

The biblical tradition's concern for victims is evident throughout Scripture. God is described as one who "heals the brokenhearted and binds up their wounds" (Psalm 147:3). Jesus consistently reached out to those who were suffering—the leper, the paralytic, the bleeding woman, the grieving parents. The early church cared for widows and orphans, the most vulnerable victims of their society. Victim support in restorative justice continues this tradition of compassionate care for the wounded.

Community Engagement: Building Ownership

Fostering community engagement and involvement in restorative justice is essential for addressing disparities in access and creating a stronger sense of community responsibility. Restorative justice is not something done to communities but something done with them and by them. Community ownership is essential for sustainability and effectiveness.

Community engagement begins with listening. Before designing programs or implementing practices, restorative justice advocates must listen to community members—their experiences, their needs, their concerns, their hopes. What does justice mean in this community? What harms are most pressing? What resources exist? What barriers must be overcome?

Listening builds trust and ensures that programs respond to actual community needs.

Community involvement in design and governance ensures relevance and ownership. Community members should participate in planning restorative programs, serving on advisory boards, and making decisions about how programs operate. This involvement draws on local knowledge, builds commitment, and ensures that programs reflect community values. It also creates accountability—programs that are governed by the community are responsive to the community.

Community members as participants are essential. Restorative processes depend on community members to serve as supporters, circle participants, mentors, and volunteers. Recruiting and training community members for these roles builds capacity and spreads restorative values throughout the community. It also creates opportunities for community members to experience restorative justice firsthand, deepening their understanding and commitment.

Community organizations as partners extend reach. Schools, faith communities, neighborhood associations, social service agencies, and other community organizations can become partners in restorative justice. They can host restorative processes, provide support services, recruit participants, and promote restorative values. Partnerships leverage existing resources and networks, extending the reach of restorative programs.

Community education builds understanding and support. Public awareness campaigns, community forums, school programs, and media engagement can educate community members about restorative justice. When people understand what restorative justice is and how it works, they are more likely to support it and participate in it. Education also counters misinformation and addresses skepticism.

The biblical vision of community as the body of Christ (1 Corinthians 12) provides a theological foundation for community engagement. In the body, each member has a role, each contribution matters, each person is valued. The health of the whole depends on the participation of all. Community engagement in restorative justice reflects this vision, recognizing that justice is not the work of experts alone but the responsibility of the whole community.

Evaluation and Research: Building Evidence

Investing in rigorous research and evaluation of restorative justice programs is essential for assessing their effectiveness, identifying areas for improvement, and building evidence of their impact. Evaluation serves multiple purposes: accountability, learning, advocacy, and improvement.

Accountability requires evaluation. Funders, policymakers, and the public need to know whether restorative justice programs are achieving their goals. Are victims satisfied? Are offenders being held accountable? Are communities being strengthened? Is recidivism being reduced? Evaluation provides answers to these questions, demonstrating the value of restorative programs and justifying continued investment.

Learning depends on evaluation. By studying what works and what doesn't, practitioners can refine their methods and improve their practice. Evaluation identifies successful strategies that can be replicated and challenges that need to be addressed.

It generates knowledge that benefits the entire field, not just individual programs.

Advocacy is strengthened by evidence. When restorative justice advocates can point to research demonstrating effectiveness, they are more persuasive with policymakers, funders, and the public. Evidence counters skepticism, builds credibility, and supports efforts to expand restorative programs. The more robust the evidence base, the stronger the case for restorative justice.

Improvement is guided by evaluation. Regular evaluation helps programs identify strengths to build on and weaknesses to address. It provides feedback that informs training, supervision, and program development. Programs that evaluate continuously are better able to adapt to changing circumstances and emerging challenges.

What should be evaluated? Multiple dimensions matter: participant satisfaction, procedural fairness, agreement completion, recidivism, victim healing, community impact, cost-effectiveness. Both quantitative measures (recidivism rates, satisfaction scores) and qualitative data (participant narratives, case studies) are valuable. Long-term follow-up is important for assessing lasting impact.

Who should conduct evaluation? Independent evaluators bring objectivity and credibility. Partnerships between programs and researchers combine practical knowledge with research expertise. Participatory evaluation involving community members ensures relevance and responsiveness. Multiple perspectives enrich understanding.

The wisdom literature's emphasis on testing and discernment applies to evaluation. Proverbs encourages testing words to see if they are true (Proverbs 18:17). Paul urges believers to "test all things; hold fast what is good" (1 Thessalonians 5:21). Evaluation is a form of testing—examining restorative practices to see what is good, what works, what should be held fast. It is an expression of wisdom, not skepticism.

Restorative Justice Legislation: Creating Frameworks

Encouraging the development and implementation of restorative justice legislation that outlines its role within the criminal justice system and ensures proper support and funding is essential for sustainability and growth. Legislation provides a foundation on which restorative programs can be built and maintained.

Legislation establishes legitimacy. When restorative justice is recognized in law, it gains official standing within the justice system. This recognition enhances its credibility with judges, lawyers, law enforcement, and the public. It signals that restorative justice is not an alternative to the system but an integral part of it.

Legislation provides structure. Laws can define restorative justice, establish standards, and create procedures for its use. They can specify which cases are appropriate for restorative processes, how referrals are made, what rights participants have, and how agreements are enforced. This structure promotes consistency and protects participants.

Legislation secures funding. Laws can authorize funding for restorative programs, creating sustainable financial support. They can establish mechanisms for allocating resources, ensuring that programs have the capacity to operate effectively. Funding stability allows programs to plan for the long term, invest in training, and serve more participants.

Legislation protects rights. Laws can include provisions that safeguard the rights of victims and offenders in restorative processes—requirements for informed consent, protections against coercion, access to counsel, confidentiality provisions. These protections build confidence in restorative justice and ensure that it operates ethically.

Legislation promotes accountability. Laws can establish oversight mechanisms, reporting requirements, and quality standards for restorative programs. They can create processes for complaints and grievances, ensuring that participants have recourse if problems arise. This accountability maintains public trust and program integrity.

Developing restorative justice legislation requires collaboration among diverse stakeholders—practitioners, researchers, victims' advocates, offenders' advocates, legal professionals, policymakers, community representatives. The process of developing legislation can itself build understanding and support for restorative justice. Model legislation developed by experts can guide state and national efforts.

The biblical tradition's understanding of law as a gift from God that orders community life and promotes justice offers a framework for thinking about restorative legislation. The Law of Moses established structures for justice, including provisions for restitution, protection of the vulnerable, and limitation of vengeance. Restorative justice legislation serves similar purposes: creating structures within which healing and restoration can occur.

Collaboration: Building Bridges

Promoting collaboration between traditional justice systems and restorative justice programs can help address resistance and ensure that restorative justice is integrated effectively into existing systems. Collaboration builds bridges, creates understanding, and leverages the strengths of both approaches.

Collaboration begins with relationships. Building trust between restorative practitioners and system professionals—judges, prosecutors, defense attorneys, law enforcement, corrections officials—is essential. This requires regular communication, shared training, joint projects, and opportunities for informal interaction. Relationships built on respect and understanding can overcome institutional barriers.

Collaboration requires mutual understanding. System professionals need to understand what restorative justice offers and how it can complement their work. Restorative practitioners need to understand the constraints and pressures under which system professionals operate. Cross-training, joint workshops, and shared learning opportunities build this understanding.

Collaboration creates referral pathways. When system professionals understand restorative justice and trust its practitioners, they are more likely to refer appropriate cases. Clear referral protocols, screening procedures, and communication channels facilitate smooth transitions between systems. Collaboration ensures that cases are handled efficiently and appropriately.

Collaboration enables integration. Restorative justice can be integrated at multiple points in the justice process—as diversion before charges, as a condition of pretrial release, as part of sentencing, as a component of probation, as part of reentry planning. Integration requires coordination between restorative programs and system actors at each point. Collaboration makes this coordination possible.

Collaboration addresses resistance. When system professionals are involved in developing restorative programs, they become stakeholders in their success rather than opponents of their implementation. Their concerns can be addressed directly, their expertise can inform program design, their support can be enlisted. Collaboration turns potential opponents into partners.

The Apostle Paul's practice of collaboration offers a model. Paul worked with a network of coworkers—Timothy, Titus, Silas, Priscilla and Aquila, and many others—each contributing their gifts to the common mission. He maintained relationships with the Jerusalem church even when they disagreed. He built bridges between Jewish and Gentile believers, between different communities, between diverse perspectives. Collaboration was essential to his ministry. Restorative justice requires similar collaborative spirit.

Cultural Sensitivity: Respecting Diversity

Adapting restorative justice practices to respect and incorporate the cultural values and norms of diverse communities is essential for ensuring that the approach is sensitive to local contexts. Restorative justice is not a one-size-fits-all model but a framework that must be embodied in culturally appropriate forms.

Cultural sensitivity begins with recognition. Every community has its own ways of addressing harm, resolving conflict, and restoring relationships. These traditional practices embody wisdom accumulated over generations. Restorative justice advocates must recognize and respect this wisdom, seeing themselves as learners as well as teachers.

Cultural adaptation involves listening. Before introducing restorative practices, practitioners must listen to community members about their values, their traditions, their concerns. What matters to this community? How do they understand justice? What practices already exist? What would they find helpful? Listening builds trust and ensures that programs are relevant.

Cultural integration draws on existing resources. Many communities already have restorative practices embedded in their traditions—indigenous healing circles, family conferences, community mediation, religious reconciliation rituals. Restorative justice programs can build on these existing resources, strengthening rather than supplanting them. Integration honors tradition while incorporating new insights.

Cultural competence requires training. Facilitators and practitioners need training in cultural awareness—understanding how culture shapes communication, conflict, and healing. They need to recognize their own cultural assumptions and biases. They need skills for working across cultural differences. Ongoing training and supervision support cultural competence.

Cultural humility goes beyond competence. Competence suggests mastery; humility recognizes that we never fully understand another's culture. Humble practitioners approach each encounter as learners, open to being taught by participants. They acknowledge the limits of their understanding and rely on participants to guide them.

The diversity of the early church offers a model for cultural sensitivity. The Jerusalem council (Acts 15) wrestled with how to include Gentiles without requiring them to become Jews. The decision—to require only essential things and respect differences—established a principle of cultural accommodation. Paul's practice of becoming "all things to all people" (1 Corinthians 9:22) reflects this same sensitivity. Restorative justice, in adapting to diverse cultures, follows this apostolic example.

Resources and Funding: Ensuring Sustainability

Advocating for adequate resources and funding for restorative justice programs is essential for their sustainability and capacity to operate effectively. Restorative justice cannot be done on a shoestring; it requires investment in people, training, facilities, and support services.

Funding supports personnel. Restorative programs need coordinators, facilitators, trainers, and support staff. These positions require compensation that attracts and retains qualified people. Volunteer programs can supplement paid staff but cannot replace them. Sustainable funding ensures that programs have the human resources they need.

Funding supports training. Facilitators need initial training and ongoing professional development. Trainers need compensation for their time. Curriculum development requires investment. Training infrastructure—facilities, materials, technology—requires funding. Programs that cannot invest in training cannot maintain quality.

Funding supports facilities. Restorative processes need appropriate spaces—safe, accessible, comfortable, neutral. Meeting spaces, offices, and community gathering places require funding for rent, utilities, maintenance. Virtual options require technology investments. Adequate facilities support participant comfort and program professionalism.

Funding supports support services. Victims and offenders may need counseling, advocacy, transportation, childcare, and other supports to participate. These services cost money. Programs that cannot provide or connect to support services limit access and effectiveness.

Funding supports evaluation and research. Programs need to assess their effectiveness, learn from experience, and demonstrate their value. Evaluation requires expertise, time, and resources. Research partnerships may require funding. Investment in evaluation builds knowledge and credibility.

Funding sources are diverse. Government appropriations at local, state, and federal levels can provide stable support. Foundation grants can fund innovation and expansion. Private donations from individuals and businesses demonstrate community support. Fee-for-service arrangements with courts or agencies can generate revenue. A diverse funding base provides stability and reduces dependence on any single source.

The early church's practice of sharing resources (Acts 2:44-45; 4:32-35) offers a model for funding restorative justice. Believers pooled their resources, ensuring that no one was in need. This communal sharing was not compelled but voluntary, flowing from shared commitment. Funding restorative justice similarly requires shared commitment from diverse sources, each contributing according to its capacity.

Public Awareness: Building Understanding

Increasing public awareness and understanding of restorative justice through public campaigns, educational initiatives, and outreach efforts is essential for building the political and social support that restorative programs need. Public awareness counters skepticism, corrects misconceptions, and builds demand for restorative approaches.

Public awareness campaigns use multiple channels. Traditional media—newspapers, radio, television—can reach broad audiences. Social media—Facebook, Twitter, Instagram, YouTube—can engage specific communities. Public events—forums, workshops, screenings—can create opportunities for direct engagement. Printed materials—brochures, newsletters, reports—can provide detailed information. Multiple channels reinforce messages and reach diverse audiences.

Educational initiatives target specific groups. Schools can incorporate restorative justice into curricula, teaching students about conflict resolution and peacemaking. Faith communities can include restorative justice in sermons, study groups, and adult education. Professional associations can offer continuing education on restorative approaches. Each initiative builds understanding within a specific community.

Outreach efforts engage directly with communities. Restorative practitioners can speak at community meetings, participate in neighborhood events, and build relationships with community leaders. They can offer workshops and training to community groups. They can be present in communities, listening and learning as well as teaching. Outreach builds trust as well as understanding.

Messaging matters. Public awareness efforts should emphasize what restorative justice is—healing, accountability, community—not just what it is against. They should tell stories that illustrate restorative principles in action—victims who found healing, offenders who were transformed, communities that were strengthened. They should address common concerns honestly, acknowledging limitations while highlighting benefits. Effective messaging connects with values, engages emotions, and provides information.

Partnerships extend reach. Collaborating with community organizations, faith groups, schools, and businesses multiplies the impact of public awareness efforts. Partners bring their own networks, credibility, and resources. They can amplify messages and reach audiences that restorative practitioners alone cannot.

The prophetic tradition's public proclamation offers a model for awareness efforts. Isaiah did not whisper his message; he cried aloud, sparing not his voice (Isaiah 58:1). Jeremiah did not hide his prophecy; he stood in the temple courts and proclaimed it to all who would hear (Jeremiah 7:2). John the Baptist preached in the wilderness, and crowds came out to hear him. Public awareness for restorative justice requires similar courage, similar visibility, similar persistence.

Conflict Prevention: Extending the Vision

Expanding the use of restorative justice in conflict prevention, education, and other areas beyond the criminal justice system can foster a culture of dialogue and understanding that prevents harm before it occurs. Restorative principles are not only for responding to crime but for building the kind of communities where crime is less likely to happen.

Conflict prevention through restorative education teaches children and youth the skills they need to resolve conflicts constructively. Restorative practices in schools—classroom circles, peer mediation, restorative conversations—help students learn to communicate, to listen, to empathize, to take responsibility. These skills prevent conflicts from escalating and build a positive school culture.

Conflict prevention through restorative parenting helps families address issues before they become crises. Restorative approaches to discipline—focusing on harm and repair rather than punishment—teach children accountability and empathy. Family meetings create spaces for addressing concerns and strengthening relationships. These practices prevent the kind of family breakdown that can lead to more serious problems.

Conflict prevention through restorative workplaces addresses tensions before they disrupt productivity and relationships. Restorative approaches to conflict resolution—mediation, circles, facilitated conversations—help colleagues address issues constructively. Restorative culture—open communication, mutual respect, shared responsibility—prevents conflicts from arising. Workplaces that practice restorative justice are more harmonious and productive.

Conflict prevention through restorative communities builds social cohesion that reduces crime. When neighbors know each other, when community organizations work together, when there are opportunities for dialogue across differences, communities are more resilient. Restorative practices can build this cohesion—neighborhood circles, community dialogues, collaborative problem-solving. Strong communities prevent crime.

Conflict prevention through restorative institutions—government agencies, nonprofit organizations, faith communities—models the values that prevent harm. When institutions practice restorative justice internally—addressing conflicts openly, treating employees fairly, responding to complaints constructively—they demonstrate that restorative values are possible. This modeling influences the broader culture.

The vision of shalom in the Hebrew prophets includes prevention as well as healing. Isaiah envisioned a time when "they shall beat their swords into plowshares and their spears into pruning hooks; nation shall not lift up sword against nation, neither shall they learn war anymore" (Isaiah 2:4). This vision is not only about ending conflict but about preventing it—transforming the instruments of violence into tools of peace. Restorative justice, extended into prevention, participates in this prophetic vision.

Contemporary Relevance: Addressing Today's Crises

Restorative justice plays a crucial role in ongoing efforts for criminal justice reform. The contemporary criminal justice system faces a range of challenges, and restorative justice principles, inspired by the teachings of Romans, offer valuable alternatives and solutions to these issues.

Over-incarceration is a pressing problem. The United States incarcerates more people than any other country in the world—nearly two million individuals behind bars. This mass incarceration has not made communities safer; recidivism rates remain high, and the costs—financial, social, human—are staggering. Restorative justice promotes a more balanced and proportional response to offenses. Instead of lengthy prison sentences for non-violent and low-level offenses, restorative justice offers ways to address harm without incarceration. Diversion programs, community-based sanctions, and restorative processes can reduce prison populations while still holding offenders accountable. This approach can help alleviate the crisis of over-incarceration, which has strained prison systems and disproportionately affected communities of color.

Racial disparities are deeply embedded in the criminal justice system. African Americans and Hispanics are incarcerated at rates far higher than whites, often for similar offenses. These disparities reflect systemic racism—in policing, prosecution, sentencing, and parole. Restorative justice principles prioritize fairness, equity, and addressing the root causes of crime. By focusing on understanding and repairing harm, restorative justice can help reduce racial disparities by addressing underlying issues rather than perpetuating systemic bias. Restorative processes can also create spaces for dialogue about race and justice, building understanding across racial lines.

Recidivism remains stubbornly high. About two-thirds of released prisoners are rearrested within three years; half return to prison. The current system fails to address the underlying causes of criminal behavior—addiction, mental illness, poverty, trauma, lack of education and employment. Restorative justice places strong emphasis on accountability and addressing these underlying causes. By involving offenders in the process of repairing harm and taking responsibility for their actions, restorative justice can contribute to reducing recidivism and promoting rehabilitation. Offenders who understand the harm they have caused, who make amends, and who receive support from community are less likely to reoffend.

Healing and reintegration are neglected in punitive systems. Traditional justice focuses on punishment, not healing. Victims are sidelined, offenders are isolated, communities are excluded. Restorative justice offers a holistic approach that recognizes the importance of addressing harm to victims, helping offenders take responsibility, and facilitating their successful reintegration into community. This approach benefits individuals and contributes to safer, more cohesive communities. Victims who experience restorative processes report higher satisfaction and better emotional outcomes. Offenders who are restored to community are less likely to reoffend. Communities that practice restorative justice are stronger and more resilient.

Community engagement is essential for public safety. The current system excludes communities from the work of justice, treating them as passive recipients of services rather than active participants. Restorative justice actively involves community in resolving conflicts and reintegrating offenders. This engagement fosters a sense of ownership and responsibility for addressing crime and its consequences. It encourages collective efforts to create a more just and compassionate society. When communities are engaged, they can address the conditions that produce crime and support those affected by it.

Restorative justice provides a promising avenue for addressing these pressing issues. It shifts the focus from punitive measures to healing, accountability, and reintegration, aligning with principles of fairness, compassion, and reconciliation inspired by the teachings of Romans. While it may not replace traditional criminal justice entirely, it offers a valuable and transformative complement that contributes to criminal justice reform efforts and paves the way for a more just and equitable system.

Community and Social Healing: Mending the Fabric

Community and social healing refer to the process of mending and revitalizing relationships, trust, and cohesion within a community that may have been strained or damaged by conflicts, divisions, or various forms of harm. In today's interconnected world, communities grapple with multiple challenges that restorative justice can address.

Conflicts within communities—between individuals, groups, or institutions—can lead to division, mistrust, and breakdown of social bonds. Restorative processes bring together conflicting parties to address harm, understand perspectives, and find resolution. These processes can heal relationships and rebuild trust, restoring community cohesion.

Prejudice and discrimination divide communities. Racism, sexism, religious intolerance, and other forms of bias create social divisions and exclusion. Restorative dialogues can create spaces where people from different backgrounds can share experiences, address misunderstandings, and build relationships. These dialogues do not eliminate prejudice overnight, but they can begin the process of healing and understanding.

Social divisions arising from economic disparities, political differences, and cultural diversity can fragment communities.

Restorative practices can build bridges across these divisions, creating opportunities for dialogue and collaboration. Community circles, intergroup dialogues, and collaborative problem-solving can bring diverse groups together around shared concerns.

The principles of reconciliation and restoration from Romans can play a pivotal role in community healing. Reconciliation involves bringing together individuals or groups in conflict, helping them understand each other's perspectives, and finding common ground. Romans emphasizes reconciliation with God and among people, offering a model for addressing conflicts within communities. Restoration entails repairing and revitalizing relationships and trust within a community. Romans highlights the value of restoration in personal transformation and healing, which can extend to the broader community. Healing addresses emotional, psychological, and social wounds caused by conflicts, divisions, and harm. The principles from Romans underscore the significance of healing and renewal at individual and community levels. Mending social rifts through community-based initiatives can create a sense of unity, shared purpose, and social cohesion.

Community and social healing are vital for fostering resilient and harmonious communities. By drawing inspiration from the principles of reconciliation and restoration found in Romans, communities can work towards resolving conflicts, addressing prejudice, and bridging social divisions, ultimately building more inclusive and compassionate societies.

Conflict Resolution and Peacebuilding: Global Applications

Conflict resolution and peacebuilding are essential processes aimed at resolving conflicts and promoting peace, both at local and global levels. In an increasingly interconnected world, various conflicts—from local disputes to international tensions—demand effective approaches to de-escalate and address these issues. Restorative justice, inspired by the principles of Romans, offers a valuable framework for these processes.

Conflict resolution through restorative justice encourages all parties to engage in dialogue, understand root causes, and work together to find mutually agreeable solutions. This process can be applied to interpersonal disputes, community conflicts, and even larger-scale conflicts, helping to prevent escalation and fostering resolution. The structured approach of restorative justice—acknowledgment of harm, accountability, repair—provides a template for addressing conflicts at any scale.

Dialogue and understanding are central to restorative justice. Open and meaningful dialogue creates an environment where all parties have the opportunity to express their perspectives and concerns. Through this process, individuals can develop deeper understanding of the motivations and needs of others involved in the conflict. Romans' teachings on reconciliation and forgiveness align with the aim of promoting empathy and understanding, crucial elements in any conflict resolution process.

Reconciliation is a strong emphasis in restorative justice. Reconciliation is the process of repairing and restoring relationships damaged by conflict. Romans highlights the importance of reconciling with one another, emphasizing forgiveness and healing. This concept is integral to peacebuilding efforts, as it fosters the re-establishment of trust and cooperation among parties in conflict.

Conflict prevention can be supported by restorative principles. While often applied after conflict has occurred, restorative justice principles can also contribute to preventing conflict. By addressing underlying causes and promoting understanding, individuals and communities can work proactively to reduce tensions and prevent conflicts from escalating.

Peacebuilding as a long-term process aims to establish and maintain peace in the aftermath of conflicts. Restorative justice, inspired by Romans, aligns with this goal by focusing on repairing harm, promoting accountability, and fostering positive relationships. It contributes to sustainable peace by addressing the root causes of conflict.

International diplomacy can draw on restorative principles. The principles of accountability, dialogue, and reconciliation offer valuable tools for resolving international conflicts, bridging divides, and promoting lasting peace. Truth commissions, peace negotiations, and post-conflict reconstruction can all benefit from restorative approaches.

Restorative justice, inspired by the teachings of Romans, provides a framework for conflict resolution and peacebuilding that emphasizes dialogue, understanding, and reconciliation. This approach is valuable not only in addressing conflicts but also in preventing them and contributing to lasting peace within communities and on a global scale.

Truth and Reconciliation: Addressing Historical Wrongs

Truth and reconciliation are integral components of transitional justice in post-conflict societies. Restorative justice principles, rooted in accountability and reconciliation, align closely with the goals of truth and reconciliation commissions.

Uncovering past wrongs is a primary function of truth commissions. These bodies aim to uncover and document past wrongs, including human rights abuses and crimes committed during conflicts or oppressive regimes. They create a platform for victims and perpetrators to share their experiences and for society to confront its history. Restorative justice principles emphasize acknowledging wrongdoing and the need for truth as a foundation for accountability. Truth commissions embody this principle on a national scale.

Accountability is underscored in restorative justice. Restorative justice emphasizes holding individuals accountable for their actions. Truth and reconciliation commissions serve a similar purpose by identifying those responsible for human rights violations and ensuring they face appropriate consequences, whether through legal proceedings or alternative forms of accountability. Restorative justice processes within these commissions can include acknowledgment of wrongdoing and sincere expressions of remorse.

Victim-centered approaches are prioritized in restorative justice. Restorative justice places victims at the center of the process, ensuring their voices are heard and their needs addressed. Truth and reconciliation commissions similarly prioritize the experiences and needs of victims, providing a space for them to share their stories and seek acknowledgment and reparations. Both approaches recognize that healing requires victims to be heard.

Healing and reconciliation are promoted by restorative justice. Restorative justice seeks to promote healing and reconciliation not only between individuals but within communities and society at large. Truth and reconciliation commissions aim to facilitate national healing by acknowledging past wrongs, fostering understanding, and promoting reconciliation. Both approaches recognize the significance of addressing the emotional and psychological wounds left by conflicts.

Preventing recurrence is a shared goal. Both restorative justice and truth and reconciliation commissions aim to prevent the recurrence of violence and injustice. They do so by addressing the root causes of conflict, exposing the consequences of past wrongdoing, and establishing a framework for building a just and peaceful society. This forward-looking orientation distinguishes restorative approaches from purely retributive ones.

Public acknowledgment is emphasized in restorative justice. Restorative justice emphasizes public acknowledgment of wrongdoing, and truth and reconciliation commissions provide a forum for this acknowledgment on a national scale. This acknowledgment is critical for both individual and societal healing and for breaking cycles of denial and impunity.

Truth and reconciliation commissions and restorative justice principles share a common objective in addressing the legacy of violence and injustice in post-conflict societies. They aim to uncover past wrongs, foster accountability, promote healing, and prevent the recurrence of conflict. The principles of acknowledgment, accountability, and reconciliation are central to both approaches, making them complementary in transitional justice processes.

Restorative Practices in Education: Transforming Schools

Restorative practices in schools, while highly beneficial, are not as common as they should be. These practices, inspired by principles found in Romans, can play a significant role in addressing bullying and school violence, as well as in creating a safe and inclusive learning environment. Understanding factors that limit implementation and strategies to overcome them is essential.

Lack of awareness among educators and administrators is a primary barrier. Many educators are not fully aware of restorative practices and their potential benefits. Awareness and education are crucial to encouraging adoption. Professional development, workshops, and training programs can introduce restorative concepts and demonstrate their relevance to school settings.

Traditional disciplinary approaches are deeply ingrained. The punitive approach to discipline—suspensions, expulsions—has been the norm in many schools. Transitioning to restorative practices requires a shift in mindset and a willingness to explore alternative methods of addressing behavioral issues. This shift can be supported by presenting evidence of restorative practices' effectiveness and by showcasing successful implementations in other schools.

Resistance to change is common. Implementing restorative practices may face opposition from those comfortable with the status quo or hesitant to try new approaches. Building buy-in through inclusive planning processes, addressing concerns directly, and demonstrating early successes can overcome resistance.

Training and resources are often lacking. Effective implementation requires proper training and resources for educators and school staff. Many schools lack the funding needed to provide this training. Advocacy for dedicated funding, partnerships with community organizations, and creative use of existing resources can address this gap.

Measuring outcomes can be challenging. School systems often focus on quantifiable outcomes like test scores and may hesitate to invest in restorative practices with less easily measurable outcomes. Developing appropriate evaluation frameworks that capture both quantitative and qualitative benefits can demonstrate the value of restorative practices.

Complexity of implementation can deter adoption. Restorative practices involve complex interpersonal dynamics and require deep understanding of the principles involved. Ongoing support, coaching, and professional learning communities can help educators develop the skills and confidence needed for effective implementation.

Time and commitment are required. Restorative practices demand time and commitment from both educators and students. Concerns about time investment must be addressed by demonstrating that restorative practices can actually save time in the long run by reducing disciplinary incidents and improving school climate.

Despite these challenges, restorative practices hold great promise in addressing bullying and school violence. These practices encourage dialogue, empathy, and accountability, creating an environment where students feel a sense of belonging and are more likely to address and resolve conflicts constructively. By promoting the principles of Romans—

acknowledgment, responsibility, and reconciliation—restorative practices have the potential to create safer and more inclusive learning environments in schools, making them a valuable investment in the well-being of students and the overall school community.

Victim Support: Integrating Restorative Principles

Victims of crime require comprehensive support to navigate the physical, emotional, and psychological impact of their experiences. Modern victim support services can greatly benefit from integrating restorative justice principles to empower victims, address their needs, and facilitate their healing journey.

Empowerment is a key principle. Restorative justice emphasizes empowering victims, giving them a voice and a role in the process. Victim support services can integrate this principle by providing victims with opportunities to express their feelings, needs, and preferences. Empowering victims helps them regain a sense of control over their lives and their recovery. This empowerment can be transformative, countering the powerlessness that victims often feel.

Acknowledgment and validation are crucial. Restorative justice encourages acknowledgment of the harm done to victims. Support services can use this principle to validate victims' experiences and provide a safe space for them to share their stories. This acknowledgment can be a crucial step in the healing process, confirming that what happened to them matters and that they are believed.

Individualized support meets unique needs. Restorative justice promotes tailoring the response to the specific circumstances of each case. Victim support services can adopt this individualized approach, recognizing that each victim's experience is unique and requires personalized care. One-size-fits-all approaches are inadequate for the complexity of victim needs.

Healing-centered approaches focus on recovery. Restorative justice focuses on healing and reconciliation, not only for offenders but also for victims. Victim support services can incorporate these healing-centered approaches by offering counseling, therapy, and resources that promote emotional and psychological recovery. Healing is the goal, not just managing symptoms.

Restitution and compensation are restorative concepts. Restorative justice principles include restitution and making amends. Victim support services can help victims access compensation, financial support, or restitution when applicable, ensuring they receive fair and just reparations for their losses. This practical support complements emotional care.

Restorative justice programs offer options for participation. Some victim support services are involved in restorative justice programs where victims have the option to participate in processes involving dialogue with offenders. These programs allow victims to ask questions, seek answers, and find closure, contributing to their emotional recovery. Participation is voluntary and carefully facilitated.

Education and awareness inform victims. Victim support services can educate victims about restorative justice principles and processes, allowing them to make informed decisions about their involvement in legal proceedings and restorative practices. Informed victims are empowered victims.

Long-term support recognizes ongoing needs. Restorative justice principles recognize that the impact of harm can be long-lasting. Victim support services should also provide long-term support, as needed, to help victims as they continue on their healing journey. Healing is not linear and does not follow a fixed timeline.

Incorporating restorative justice principles into victim support services can significantly enhance the quality of care and assistance provided to victims. By empowering victims, acknowledging their experiences, and promoting healing, these services can better address the complex and multifaceted needs of victims of crime, ultimately contributing to their recovery and well-being.

Global Relevance: Adapting Across Cultures

The global relevance of restorative justice principles is evident in their adaptability to diverse regions and cultures. Examples from various parts of the world demonstrate how these principles have been embraced to address local and global challenges.

South Africa's Truth and Reconciliation Commission, chaired by Archbishop Desmond Tutu, employed restorative justice principles to address the legacy of apartheid. It allowed victims and perpetrators to come forward, acknowledge wrongdoings, and work towards reconciliation. This approach served as a model for post-conflict societies worldwide, demonstrating that restorative principles can address massive, systemic injustice.

Canada's Indigenous communities have applied restorative justice principles in their justice systems. These principles are incorporated into sentencing, emphasizing community involvement and restoration of harmony. Indigenous healing circles draw on traditional practices while addressing contemporary challenges. This integration honors indigenous wisdom while advancing restorative goals.

Scandinavian countries like Norway and Sweden have implemented restorative justice practices in their criminal justice systems. They focus on rehabilitation and reintegration rather than punitive measures, resulting in lower recidivism rates and safer communities. These nations demonstrate that restorative approaches can work at the system level, not just in isolated programs.

The Middle East has seen organizations like the Sulha Peace Project use restorative justice principles to promote dialogue and reconciliation in conflict-ridden areas. They facilitate encounters between people of different backgrounds and encourage communication to build bridges across deep divides. Restorative principles offer hope in regions long torn by conflict.

Australia has widely used restorative justice practices in schools to address issues like bullying and student conflicts. These practices create more inclusive and respectful learning environments, demonstrating that restorative approaches can transform educational settings.

Brazil's favelas have seen implementation of restorative circles, a community-based approach to resolving conflicts and promoting social cohesion. These circles have helped reduce violence and improve community relations in some of the world's most challenging urban environments.

The Balkans region, which experienced violent conflicts in the 1990s, has seen initiatives drawing from restorative justice principles to promote reconciliation and healing among different ethnic groups. Restorative approaches offer pathways to healing in regions where ethnic violence has created deep divisions.

United States restorative justice programs have been introduced in various states, particularly within the juvenile justice system. These programs aim to divert young offenders from traditional justice systems and provide opportunities for rehabilitation. Growing evidence supports their effectiveness.

International tribunals, such as the International Criminal Court, draw on restorative justice principles when determining sentences for individuals found guilty of war crimes, crimes against humanity, and genocide. Restorative considerations can inform even the most serious international proceedings.

Community-based initiatives worldwide have adopted restorative justice practices to address local disputes, build trust, and promote reconciliation. From rural villages to urban neighborhoods, restorative principles are being adapted to local contexts and needs.

The global adoption of restorative justice principles reflects their adaptability and effectiveness in addressing a wide range of challenges, from post-conflict reconciliation to school bullying. These principles provide a framework for dialogue, acknowledgment, accountability, healing, and the promotion of a just and inclusive society, making them relevant and applicable on a global scale.

Interfaith and Interdisciplinary Dialogues: Enriching Understanding

Interfaith and interdisciplinary dialogues are crucial for leveraging restorative justice principles. These dialogues bring together diverse perspectives, enriching understanding and advancing practice.

Diversity of perspectives enriches understanding. Interfaith dialogues bring together representatives from different faith traditions, fostering a rich exchange of perspectives on restorative justice. This diversity helps create a more comprehensive and inclusive understanding of how these principles can be applied. Each tradition brings unique insights that can illuminate different dimensions of restorative practice.

Shared values emerge through dialogue. Many faith traditions share common values related to justice, forgiveness, and reconciliation. By engaging in interfaith dialogues, practitioners and scholars can identify these shared values and work towards a collective understanding of restorative justice. This common ground can support collaboration across religious boundaries.

Interdisciplinary collaboration draws from multiple fields. Restorative justice is inherently interdisciplinary, drawing from law, psychology, sociology, theology, and other disciplines. Interdisciplinary dialogues enable experts from various fields to collaborate and develop a holistic approach to restorative justice that considers multiple dimensions. This collaboration produces richer understanding and more effective practice.

Conflict resolution insights are sharpened through dialogue. Restorative justice is often applied in conflict resolution contexts. Interfaith and interdisciplinary dialogues can provide insights and strategies for applying these principles to manage conflicts effectively and promote peace. Diverse perspectives generate creative approaches to persistent challenges.

Global perspectives are valuable. Restorative justice has global relevance, and international perspectives are valuable. Engaging in interfaith and interdisciplinary dialogues with a global focus allows for the exchange of practices, lessons, and innovations from various parts of the world. This exchange accelerates learning and adaptation.

Ethical considerations are deepened through dialogue. Restorative justice is deeply rooted in ethical considerations. Interfaith dialogues can contribute to ethical discussions, helping to define common ethical principles that underpin restorative justice practices. Shared ethical frameworks strengthen practice across diverse contexts.

Education and advocacy benefit from dialogue. Interfaith and interdisciplinary dialogues can play a role in educating communities and advocating for the adoption of restorative justice principles in various settings, including schools, criminal justice systems, and conflict resolution programs. Diverse voices speaking together are more persuasive than isolated voices.

Practical applications emerge from dialogue. By bringing together individuals from diverse backgrounds and disciplines, these dialogues can result in practical strategies and guidelines for implementing restorative justice in real world situations. Dialogue generates actionable knowledge.

Overcoming misconceptions is facilitated by dialogue. Restorative justice may have misconceptions or biases associated with it. Interfaith and interdisciplinary dialogues can help dispel these misconceptions and foster a more accurate and informed understanding of the approach. Dialogue corrects errors and builds accurate understanding.

Community building results from dialogue. These dialogues can promote community building and strengthen bonds between faith communities, academics, practitioners, and policymakers, all of whom play a role in advancing restorative justice. Relationships built through dialogue sustain ongoing collaboration.

Interfaith and interdisciplinary dialogues not only enrich understanding of restorative justice but also offer platforms for collaboration, advocacy, and development of practical applications. They provide spaces where shared values, ethical considerations, and diverse perspectives converge to advance the cause of justice, healing, and reconciliation, as inspired by the teachings of Romans and embraced by a global and diverse community.

The Way Forward: Persistence and Hope

Overcoming the obstacles to restorative justice requires persistence and hope. The challenges are real, but they are not insurmountable. With thoughtful strategies, sustained effort, and commitment to core principles, restorative justice can become more effective and widely applicable.

The strategies outlined in this chapter—education and training, standardization, legal protections, victim support, community engagement, evaluation and research, legislation, collaboration, cultural sensitivity, resources and funding, public awareness, and conflict prevention—provide a roadmap for addressing obstacles and advancing restorative justice. Each strategy addresses specific challenges while contributing to the overall goal of making restorative justice accessible and effective for all who need it.

The contemporary relevance of restorative justice is clear. In a world of mass incarceration, racial disparities, high recidivism, and unmet needs for healing and reintegration, restorative principles offer hope. They provide alternatives to punitive approaches that have failed, frameworks for community healing that have been neglected, and pathways to reconciliation that have been ignored. Restorative justice is not a luxury but a necessity for creating a more just and compassionate world.

The global adoption of restorative principles demonstrates their adaptability and effectiveness. From South Africa to Canada, from Scandinavia to the Middle East, from Australia to Brazil, from the Balkans to the United States, restorative justice is being embraced in diverse contexts to address diverse challenges. This global movement testifies to the universal appeal of restorative values and the practical effectiveness of restorative practices.

Interfaith and interdisciplinary dialogues enrich restorative justice, bringing diverse perspectives to bear on common challenges. As people of different faiths and disciplines come together around restorative principles, they discover shared values and collaborative possibilities. These dialogues build the relationships and understanding needed for restorative justice to flourish across boundaries.

The way forward is not easy. Obstacles remain, resistance persists, challenges continue. But the way forward is also hopeful. Every successful restorative process, every healed relationship, every transformed life demonstrates what is possible. Every educator trained, every policy changed, every program funded builds the infrastructure for more. Every person who learns about restorative justice becomes a potential advocate, participant, practitioner.

The biblical vision of shalom—peace, wholeness, flourishing—inspires this hope. It promises a day when swords will be beaten into plowshares, when nations will not learn war anymore, when every tear will be wiped away. Restorative justice participates in this vision, offering glimpses of shalom in the midst of a broken world. It is not the full realization of God's peace, but it is a sign of that peace, a foretaste of what will be.

As we continue the work of overcoming obstacles and advancing restorative justice, we do so with persistence and hope. We persist because the work is worth doing, because people are being healed, because communities are being strengthened. We hope because we trust that God's restorative purposes will ultimately prevail, that love is stronger than hate, that grace is more powerful than sin, that reconciliation is possible even in the most divided places. With this persistence and hope, we press on toward the goal of a more just and compassionate world, where restorative justice is not an exception but the norm, not a novelty but the foundation of how we respond to harm and pursue healing.

CHAPTER 12

RESTORATIVE JUSTICE AND HEALING

The connection between restorative justice and healing is not incidental but essential. Restorative justice is, at its core, a philosophy and practice oriented toward healing—healing of wounds caused by harm, healing of relationships fractured by conflict, healing of communities torn by crime. Unlike punitive systems that focus primarily on the infliction of pain as a response to pain, restorative justice asks a different question: How can we make things whole? How can we restore what has been damaged? How can we heal what has been broken?

This chapter explores the intimate relationship between restorative justice and healing. We will examine how restorative processes contribute to healing for victims, for offenders, and for communities. We will consider the psychological dimensions of healing—the acknowledgment of harm, the empowerment of victims, the accountability of offenders, the power of apology and forgiveness, the significance of reparations, the role of community support, the prevention of recidivism, the resolution of trauma, the humanization of all parties, the catalyst for personal growth, the structure of healing circles, and the experience of catharsis and closure. Through this exploration, we will see that restorative justice is not merely an alternative method of conflict resolution but a comprehensive approach to human flourishing, grounded in the recognition that healing is possible even in the aftermath of profound harm.

Acknowledgment of Harm: The Foundation of Healing

Restorative justice begins with acknowledgment of the harm that has been done. This recognition is essential for the healing process, as it validates the pain and suffering experienced by the victim. Before healing can occur, the wound must be named, seen, and acknowledged. Hidden wounds fester; acknowledged wounds can be treated.

For victims, acknowledgment is a form of validation. When someone has been harmed, they need to know that what happened to them matters—that their pain is real, that their suffering is recognized, that they are not alone. The criminal justice system often fails to provide this validation. The focus is on the offender, on the law that was broken, on the state's interest in punishment. The victim becomes a witness, a source of evidence, a means to an end. Their pain is incidental to the proceedings.

Restorative justice reverses this dynamic. The first question is not "What law was broken?" but "Who has been harmed?" The victim's experience becomes central. They are given the opportunity to describe what happened, how it affected them, what they have suffered. This telling is not merely informational but therapeutic. It communicates that their experience matters, that their pain is real, that they are seen.

Acknowledgment also benefits offenders. When offenders hear directly from victims about the impact of their actions, they can no longer maintain the abstractions and rationalizations that protected them from the truth. They are confronted with the human reality of the harm they have caused. This confrontation can be the beginning of genuine remorse and the motivation for change.

The biblical tradition is rich with examples of acknowledgment. The Psalms are filled with lament—honest, raw expressions of pain, suffering, and complaint. The psalmists do not hide their wounds or pretend that everything is fine. They cry out to God, naming their pain, demanding attention, seeking healing. This lament is a form of acknowledgment, and it is the precondition for the praise and thanksgiving that follow.

Jesus Himself acknowledged suffering. In the Garden of Gethsemane, He did not pretend to be unafraid or untroubled. He confessed His distress to His disciples, prayed in anguish, sweat drops of blood. On the cross, He cried out in lament: "My God, my God, why have You forsaken Me?" (Matthew 27:46). This acknowledgment of suffering was not a lack of faith but an expression of it—a trust that even in the depths of pain, God could be addressed.

The healing miracles of Jesus often began with acknowledgment. He asked the blind man, "What do you want Me to do for you?" (Mark 10:51). He invited the lame man to tell his story. He listened to the bleeding woman's account of her suffering (Mark 5:33). This acknowledgment was the first step toward healing.

Psychological research confirms the importance of acknowledgment. Trauma survivors need to have their experiences validated. When others deny, minimize, or ignore their pain, the wound deepens. When others listen, believe, and affirm, healing becomes possible. Acknowledgment is not merely a nice gesture but a therapeutic necessity.

In restorative justice, acknowledgment is built into the process. Victims are invited to tell their stories. Offenders are asked to listen. The community witnesses and affirms. This acknowledgment creates the conditions for all that follows.

Empowerment: Restoring Agency

Restorative justice gives victims a voice, allowing them to express their feelings, concerns, and needs. This empowerment can be a crucial part of the healing journey, as victims regain a sense of control over their lives. Crime often leaves victims feeling powerless—their autonomy violated, their agency stripped, their sense of control shattered. Restorative justice seeks to restore what was taken.

In conventional justice systems, victims are often passive participants. They may testify if called, but the process is controlled by lawyers, judges, and other professionals. Decisions about charges, pleas, sentences, and outcomes are made by others. The victim's role is largely symbolic. This passivity can compound the powerlessness experienced through crime.

Restorative justice offers a different experience. Victims are active participants, not passive observers. They decide whether to participate, how to prepare, what to say, what questions to ask, what outcomes to seek. They are consulted about agreements and have a voice in determining what will happen. This participation restores a measure of control, countering the helplessness that crime inflicted.

Empowerment takes many forms. In victim-offender mediation, victims choose what to say and how to say it. They ask questions that have haunted them: Why me? What were you thinking? Do you have any idea what you took from me? They receive answers—sometimes inadequate, sometimes transformative. They express their feelings—anger, fear, grief—in a setting where they will be heard.

In family group conferences, victims are surrounded by supporters who amplify their voice and validate their experience. They are not alone but part of a community that stands with them. This communal support further empowers, reminding victims that they are not isolated in their suffering.

In circle processes, victims participate as equals, their voice carrying the same weight as every other. The circle structure—no hierarchy, no privileged position embodies the equality that empowers. Every person's voice matters; every person's perspective is valued.

This empowerment aligns with psychological understandings of trauma recovery. Trauma overwhelms the individual's capacity to cope, leaving them feeling helpless and out of control. Recovery requires restoring a sense of agency—the ability to make choices, to take action, to influence outcomes. Restorative justice provides opportunities for this agency to be exercised.

The biblical narrative affirms human agency. God creates humans with the capacity to choose, to respond, to participate in shaping their lives. Even after the fall, this agency is not revoked. Throughout Scripture, God invites human participation—Abraham's dialogue, Moses' negotiation, David's repentance, Esther's courage. Victims of harm are not reduced to passive recipients of divine action but are invited into active partnership in their own healing.

Jesus consistently empowered those He encountered. He did not heal people against their will or without their participation. He asked questions, invited responses, honored choices. To the man at the pool of Bethesda, He said, "Do you want to be made well?" (John 5:6). To the woman caught in adultery, He asked, "Has no one condemned you?" and invited her response (John 8:10-11). To the blind man, He applied mud and then sent him to wash—requiring his participation (John 9:6-7). This empowerment honored the dignity of those He healed.

Restorative justice, in empowering victims, follows this example. It treats victims not as objects of pity or sources of evidence but as agents of their own healing. It restores what crime took—voice, choice, control—and in doing so, contributes to genuine recovery.

Offender Accountability: Validation Through Responsibility

Restorative justice encourages offenders to take responsibility for their actions and the harm they've caused. This acknowledgment can be a significant step toward healing, as it validates the victim's experience. When an offender acknowledges wrongdoing, the victim receives confirmation that what happened was real, that they were not to blame, that their suffering matters.

Accountability in restorative justice is not the same as punishment. Punishment is about inflicting pain; accountability is about taking responsibility. Punishment is passive—something done to the offender; accountability is active—something the offender does. Punishment focuses on the past; accountability looks toward the future. Punishment seeks to balance scales through suffering; accountability seeks to repair harm through action.

When offenders take responsibility, several things happen. They acknowledge that their actions were wrong and that they caused harm. They validate the victim's experience, confirming that the victim's suffering is real and justified. They begin the process of making amends, taking steps to repair what they have damaged. They commit to change, working to address the underlying issues that led to their behavior.

This accountability benefits victims. Knowing that the offender acknowledges responsibility can bring a sense of validation and closure. Victims no longer have to wonder whether the offender understands what they did, whether they feel any remorse, whether they might do it again. The acknowledgment provides answers.

Accountability also benefits offenders. Taking responsibility is the first step toward change. As long as offenders deny, minimize, or blame others, they remain stuck in patterns that led to harm. Acknowledgment opens the door to genuine remorse, which can lead to transformation. Offenders who take responsibility are more likely to make amends, to seek help, to change.

The biblical tradition emphasizes accountability. From the garden, where God calls Adam and Eve to account for their disobedience, to the prophets, who hold Israel accountable for covenant unfaithfulness, to Jesus, who calls individuals to account for their choices, accountability is a constant theme. But biblical accountability is not merely about assigning blame; it is about calling people to take responsibility, to acknowledge wrongdoing, to make amends, to change.

David's response to Nathan's parable illustrates this accountability. When Nathan confronts David with his sin against Uriah and Bathsheba, David does not deny, deflect, or make excuses. He says simply, "I have sinned against the Lord" (2 Samuel 12:13). This acknowledgment opens the door to forgiveness and restoration. David's subsequent psalm of repentance (Psalm 51) expresses the depth of his remorse and his commitment to change.

Zacchaeus provides another example. When Jesus comes to his house, Zacchaeus does not wait to be confronted. He volunteers, "Look, Lord, I give half of my goods to the poor; and if I have taken anything from anyone by false accusation, I restore fourfold" (Luke 19:8). This proactive accountability flows from his encounter with Jesus and demonstrates genuine repentance.

Psychological research supports the importance of accountability for healing. When offenders acknowledge responsibility, victims are more likely to forgive and to experience closure. When offenders make amends, victims receive tangible evidence that their suffering matters. When offenders change, communities are safer and trust can be rebuilt. Accountability is not opposed to healing but essential to it.

Apology and Forgiveness: The Healing Exchange

In many restorative justice processes, offenders offer genuine apologies to their victims. Victims, in turn, have the opportunity to forgive. This exchange can be deeply healing, allowing both parties to let go of anger and resentment. Apology and forgiveness are not required in restorative justice—participation is voluntary, and outcomes are determined by participants—but when they occur, they can be transformative.

A genuine apology is more than saying "I'm sorry." It involves several elements: acknowledgment of wrongdoing, expression of remorse, acceptance of responsibility, commitment to change, and offer of repair. A genuine apology names the specific harm caused, communicates understanding of its impact, expresses sincere regret, and commits to making things right. Such an apology is costly—it requires vulnerability, humility, and honesty.

When victims receive a genuine apology, several things happen. They feel heard and validated. They know that the offender understands what they did and why it was wrong. They see that the offender is taking responsibility and is committed to change. This can reduce feelings of anger and desire for revenge, opening space for healing.

Forgiveness is the victim's response to apology. Forgiveness is not forgetting, excusing, or condoning. It is not reconciliation, which requires the offender's participation. Forgiveness is the victim's decision to release the offender from the debt of guilt, to let go of resentment, to relinquish the right to revenge. It is an act of grace that benefits the forgiver as much as the forgiven.

When victims forgive, they are not doing the offender a favor; they are freeing themselves. Research demonstrates that forgiveness reduces depression, anxiety, and anger; improves physical health; enhances relationships; and promotes overall well-being. Forgiveness breaks the cycle of rumination that keeps victims trapped in the past, allowing them to move forward.

The biblical tradition is rich with teaching on apology and forgiveness. Jesus taught His disciples to pray, "Forgive us our debts, as we forgive our debtors" (Matthew 6:12), linking divine and human forgiveness. He taught that forgiveness must be limitless—"seventy times seven" (Matthew 18:22). He illustrated this teaching with the parable of the unforgiving servant, who received forgiveness but refused to extend it, and was condemned for his hardheartedness.

On the cross, Jesus modeled ultimate forgiveness: "Father, forgive them, for they do not know what they do" (Luke 23:34). This forgiveness was extended to those who were actively crucifying Him—soldiers who nailed His hands, religious leaders who mocked Him, crowds who shouted for His death. It was forgiveness without condition, without waiting for repentance, without requiring acknowledgment. It was the purest expression of divine mercy.

The story of Joseph and his brothers illustrates the power of forgiveness. After years of suffering—sold into slavery, falsely accused, imprisoned—Joseph is finally in a position to exact revenge. His brothers, who had mistreated him, come begging for food, not knowing they are dealing with the brother they wronged. Joseph could have punished them severely. Instead, he forgives them, acknowledging that God used their evil for good (Genesis 50:20). This forgiveness heals not only Joseph but his brothers and the entire family.

Psychological research confirms the healing power of apology and forgiveness. Apologies reduce anger and promote reconciliation. Forgiveness reduces stress and improves mental health. The combination—genuine apology met with genuine forgiveness—can transform relationships and promote profound healing.

Restorative justice creates conditions in which apology and forgiveness can occur. It does not force them; they cannot be forced. But it brings victims and offenders together in settings where genuine encounter is possible. It provides support and facilitation that make these exchanges more likely. And it honors the choices that participants make, whether to apologize, to forgive, or not.

Reparations and Restitution: Tangible Healing

Restorative justice often includes actions aimed at making amends, such as restitution. These actions can help repair the tangible harm caused and provide a sense of closure to victims. While emotional healing is essential, practical repair also matters. Victims who have suffered material losses need those losses addressed. Offenders who have caused damage need to make it right.

Restitution takes many forms. It may involve returning stolen property, paying for damaged goods, covering medical expenses, or compensating for lost wages. It may involve community service that benefits those affected by the crime. It may involve symbolic actions—planting a tree, creating a memorial, volunteering with victims' organizations. Whatever form it takes, restitution is about making things right.

For victims, restitution provides tangible evidence that their suffering matters. When an offender pays for damages, it is not just about money; it is about acknowledgment. The payment says, "I caused this loss, and I am responsible for making it right." This acknowledgment can be as healing as any apology.

Restitution also has practical benefits. Victims who have suffered financial losses need those losses addressed. Without restitution, they may struggle with debt, medical bills, or other burdens. Restorative justice ensures that offenders, not victims, bear these costs to the extent possible.

For offenders, restitution is an act of accountability. It requires them to take responsibility in concrete ways, not just in words. It costs them something—time, money, effort—and that cost reinforces the seriousness of their actions. It also provides an opportunity to do good, to contribute positively, to make amends. This can be transformative, turning offenders from takers into givers.

The biblical tradition emphasizes restitution. The Law of Moses includes numerous provisions for making amends. If someone steals an ox or a sheep, they must repay five oxen for the ox and four sheep for the sheep (Exodus 22:1). If property is damaged, the offender must make restitution (Exodus 22:5-6). If someone is injured, the offender must compensate for loss of time and healing (Exodus 21:18-19). Restitution is not optional but required.

Zacchaeus exemplifies this principle. When he encounters Jesus, he does not merely express remorse; he commits to restitution: "If I have taken anything from anyone by false accusation, I restore fourfold" (Luke 19:8). This commitment goes beyond what the law required, demonstrating the depth of his repentance. Jesus affirms this response: "Today salvation has come to this house."

Restitution also appears in the teachings of Jesus about reconciliation. In the Sermon on the Mount, He advises: "Agree with your adversary quickly, while you are on the way with him, lest your adversary deliver you to the judge, the judge hand you over to the officer, and you be thrown into prison" (Matthew 5:25). This practical advice recognizes that unresolved disputes have consequences and that making things right is preferable to suffering those consequences.

Psychological research supports the importance of restitution. Victims who receive restitution report higher satisfaction with justice processes. They feel that their losses have been acknowledged and addressed. They are more likely to experience closure and to move forward. Restitution is not a substitute for emotional healing but a complement to it.

Restorative justice integrates restitution with other healing elements. In victim-offender mediation, restitution agreements are developed collaboratively, with input from victims about what would make things right. In family group conferences, families support offenders in fulfilling restitution commitments. In circle processes, community members may contribute resources to help offenders make amends. Restitution becomes part of a comprehensive approach to healing.

Community Support: The Healing Network

Restorative justice frequently involves the broader community in the process, providing a support network for victims and offenders. Community support can be instrumental in the healing journey. No one heals in isolation; healing requires connection, support, and belonging.

For victims, community support counters the isolation that crime often produces. Victims may feel alone, cut off from others, unable to trust. When the community surrounds them with care—listening, helping, affirming—they begin to feel connected again. They are reminded that they are not alone, that others care about what happened to them, that they belong.

Community support can take many forms. Family and friends may accompany victims to restorative processes, providing emotional support and practical assistance. Support groups bring together victims who have had similar experiences, creating spaces for sharing and healing. Faith communities offer prayer, pastoral care, and practical help. Neighborhood organizations provide resources and advocacy. Each form of support contributes to healing.

For offenders, community support is equally important. Offenders often feel isolated, ashamed, and cut off from community. This isolation can reinforce patterns of behavior that led to crime. When the community offers support—mentoring, accountability, encouragement—offenders are more likely to change. They are reminded that they are still valued, that change is possible, that they have a place.

Community support for offenders also benefits victims. When offenders are supported in changing, they are less likely to reoffend, reducing the risk of future harm to victims and others.

When offenders make amends and are restored to community, victims can see that something positive came from their suffering. This can contribute to healing.

The community itself heals through involvement. When communities take responsibility for addressing harm, they become stronger, more cohesive, more resilient. Trust is rebuilt, relationships are strengthened, social capital increases. Communities that practice restorative justice are not just helping individuals; they are transforming themselves.

The biblical vision of community is central to healing. Israel was constituted as a covenant community, bound together by shared relationship with God and mutual responsibility. The early church understood itself as a body, each member connected to every other, the health of the whole depending on the health of each part. When one suffered, all suffered; when one was honored, all rejoiced (1 Corinthians 12:26). This organic unity meant that healing was never individual but always communal.

The practice of mutual confession and prayer in James illustrates community's role in healing: "Confess your trespasses to one another, and pray for one another, that you may be healed" (James 5:16). Healing requires confession—acknowledgment of wrongdoing—and prayer—communal intercession. It is not a private transaction between the individual and God but a communal practice involving the whole body.

Jesus Himself was supported by community. He had disciples who traveled with Him, women who provided for Him, friends like Mary, Martha, and Lazarus who welcomed Him into their home. In Gethsemane, He asked His disciples to watch and pray with Him. On the cross, His mother and beloved disciple stood nearby. Even in His darkest hour, He was not alone.

Psychological research confirms the importance of social support for healing. Victims with strong support networks recover more quickly and completely from trauma. Offenders with positive social connections are less likely to reoffend. Communities with high social capital are more resilient in the face of challenges. Support matters.

Restorative justice mobilizes this support. It brings together natural networks—family, friends, faith communities—and connects them with victims and offenders. It creates new networks—support groups, mentoring relationships, community partnerships. It strengthens the social fabric that sustains healing.

Preventing Recidivism: Healing Through Prevention

By addressing the underlying issues that lead to criminal behavior, restorative justice can contribute to preventing repeat offenses, further promoting healing for victims and reducing the potential for future harm. Prevention is itself a form of healing—healing of the conditions that produce crime, healing of the cycles that perpetuate harm.

Recidivism is a persistent problem in conventional justice systems. About two-thirds of released prisoners are rearrested within three years; half return to prison. This revolving door undermines public safety, wastes resources, and causes continuing harm to victims and communities. Punishment alone does not prevent reoffending; something more is needed.

Restorative justice addresses the underlying causes of criminal behavior. Through dialogue with victims, offenders come to understand the impact of their actions. Through accountability and restitution, they take responsibility for making amends. Through support from community, they gain resources for change. Through attention to root causes—addiction, mental illness, poverty, trauma—they receive help for the issues that drove their behavior.

This comprehensive approach reduces recidivism. Research consistently shows that restorative justice programs produce lower reoffending rates than conventional processing. Offenders who participate in restorative processes are less likely to commit new crimes. They have undergone internal transformation, not merely external punishment.

For victims, knowing that offenders are less likely to reoffend contributes to healing. Victims may fear that the offender will harm them again or that others will suffer as they did. When restorative justice reduces recidivism, these fears are diminished. Victims can feel safer, knowing that something has been done to prevent future harm.

For communities, reduced recidivism means greater safety and well-being. Fewer crimes mean fewer victims, less fear, stronger social bonds. Communities that practice restorative justice become places where people can live without constant threat of harm. This safety is itself a form of healing.

The biblical vision includes prevention as well as repair. The prophets envisioned a time when "they shall not hurt nor destroy in all My holy mountain" (Isaiah 11:9). This vision is not only about responding to harm after it occurs but about creating conditions in which harm does not occur. Restorative justice, in addressing root causes and preventing recidivism, participates in this prophetic vision.

Jesus' ministry included both healing and teaching. He healed those who were sick and taught those who were healthy how to live. He addressed not only immediate suffering but underlying conditions—sin, ignorance, hardness of heart. His parables and teachings were designed to prevent future harm by transforming hearts and minds.

Psychological research on desistance—the process of ceasing criminal behavior—identifies several factors that promote change. These include developing empathy for victims, taking responsibility for actions, making amends, building positive relationships, finding meaningful work, and experiencing hope for the future. Restorative justice addresses each of these factors, creating conditions in which desistance can occur.

Preventing recidivism is not only about protecting potential future victims but about healing offenders. Offenders who stop committing crimes are able to live productive, fulfilling lives. They can contribute to their communities, build healthy relationships, and experience the satisfaction of making things right. This transformation is healing for them and for everyone connected to them.

Resolution of Trauma: From Victim to Survivor

For many victims, restorative justice offers a means to address and resolve trauma. The healing journey often involves a shift from being a victim to being a survivor. This shift is not about denying what happened but about reclaiming identity and agency in the aftermath of harm.

Trauma is the psychological wound caused by overwhelming experience. It disrupts normal functioning, producing symptoms like hypervigilance, avoidance, intrusive memories, and emotional numbing. It can shatter assumptions about safety, trust, and meaning. It leaves victims feeling powerless, isolated, and broken.

Healing from trauma requires several elements. Safety must be established—the threat must be past or manageable. The traumatic experience must be processed—remembered, grieved, integrated. Meaning must be reconstructed—new understandings of self, others, and world must be developed. Connection must be restored—relationships rebuilt, trust renewed, community reengaged.

Restorative justice can contribute to each of these elements. It provides a safe setting for processing the experience. It allows victims to tell their stories, to express their feelings, to ask their questions. It provides acknowledgment and validation from offenders and community. It offers opportunities for empowerment and agency. It facilitates connection with supportive others.

For some victims, confronting the offender in a restorative setting is a crucial part of trauma resolution. The offender represents the source of their suffering; facing that source can be empowering. Hearing the offender acknowledge responsibility can validate their experience. Receiving answers to questions can resolve uncertainty. Making decisions about outcomes can restore agency.

For other victims, restorative justice may not be appropriate or may need to be approached differently. Trauma must be respected; victims must be ready and willing to engage.

Preparation and support are essential. Alternative forms of participation—writing a statement, having a surrogate speak, participating in a circle without the offender—may be options. The goal is to support healing, not to force it.

The biblical narrative includes many stories of trauma and healing. Job suffers devastating losses—children, property, health—and wrestles with meaninglessness and despair. His journey through lament, protest, and encounter with God leads to a new understanding and ultimately to restoration. He emerges not as the same person he was but as someone transformed by suffering.

The Psalms give voice to trauma. Psalm 88 ends with no resolution, no happy ending—only the raw cry of one who has suffered and found no relief. This psalm validates the experience of those whose healing is incomplete, whose suffering continues. It reminds us that healing is not always linear or complete.

Jesus' own suffering and death represent the ultimate trauma—innocent suffering, violent death, apparent abandonment by God. Yet the resurrection transforms this trauma, demonstrating that even death does not have the final word. Those who follow Jesus are invited to trust that their own suffering can be transformed, that healing is possible even when it seems impossible.

Psychological research on post-traumatic growth identifies positive changes that can result from struggling with trauma. These include greater appreciation of life, improved relationships, increased personal strength, recognition of new possibilities, and spiritual deepening. Restorative justice can facilitate this growth by providing opportunities for meaning-making, connection, and empowerment.

Resolution of trauma does not mean forgetting or pretending that harm didn't happen. It means integrating the experience into one's life story in a way that allows moving forward. It means reclaiming identity—no longer defined by what happened but by who one is becoming. It means finding meaning in suffering—not that suffering was good but that good can come from it. Restorative justice supports this resolution.

Humanization: Seeing Beyond Roles

Restorative justice processes humanize both victims and offenders. They allow individuals to see each other as more than just the roles they've played in a criminal act, promoting empathy and understanding. This humanization is essential for healing.

Crime dehumanizes. Victims are reduced to targets, objects, means to an end. Their humanity is ignored in the pursuit of the offender's goals. Offenders are reduced to criminals, monsters, evildoers. Their humanity is obscured by the horror of their actions. Both are diminished by this dehumanization.

Restorative justice reverses this. In restorative processes, victims and offenders meet as human beings. They see each other's faces, hear each other's voices, learn each other's stories. They discover that the other is not a monster or a target but a person—complex, flawed, capable of good and evil, worthy of respect.

For victims, seeing the offender as human can be challenging but healing. It may be easier to think of the offender as a monster, someone fundamentally different from oneself. But this dehumanization keeps victims trapped in anger and fear. Recognizing the offender's humanity—seeing them as a person who made terrible choices but remains a person—can open the door to empathy, forgiveness, and release.

For offenders, seeing the victim as human is transformative. As long as victims remain abstractions, offenders can maintain distance and denial. Meeting the victim face to face, hearing their story, witnessing their pain—this breaks through abstractions and forces confrontation with reality. Offenders can no longer hide behind "it was just a crime" or "they probably deserved it." They must see the person they harmed.

This humanization promotes empathy. Empathy is the capacity to understand and share another's feelings. It is the opposite of the callousness that enables harm. When offenders develop empathy for victims, they are less likely to harm again. When victims develop empathy for offenders, they are more likely to forgive and heal. Empathy benefits both.

The biblical doctrine of the imago Dei—that every human being is created in God's image—provides the theological foundation for humanization. Because we bear God's image, our worth is inherent, not earned. It cannot be erased by any action, no matter how heinous. The offender, no less than the victim, remains an image-bearer, deserving of dignity and capable of restoration. This truth undergirds restorative justice's commitment to humanization.

Jesus consistently humanized those who were dehumanized by society. He touched lepers, whom others avoided as unclean. He spoke with Samaritan women, whom Jews despised as half-breeds. He ate with tax collectors and sinners, whom religious people condemned as outcasts. He welcomed children, whom disciples tried to send away. In every encounter, He saw beyond labels to the human being created in God's image.

The good Samaritan parable illustrates humanization. The priest and Levite see the wounded man but do not truly see him—they see a problem, a risk, an inconvenience. The Samaritan sees a human being in need, and that seeing moves him to action. Humanization leads to compassion; compassion leads to healing.

Psychological research confirms the importance of humanization for healing. When we dehumanize others, we become more capable of harming them and less capable of empathizing with them. When we humanize others, we become more compassionate and more connected. Humanization is essential for healthy relationships and communities.

Restorative justice creates conditions for humanization. It brings people together in settings where they can see each other as human beings. It provides opportunities for sharing stories, expressing feelings, and developing understanding. It promotes empathy and connection. In doing so, it contributes to healing for all involved.

Personal Growth: Transformation Through Accountability

For some offenders, participating in restorative justice processes can be a catalyst for personal growth and change. This transformation contributes to healing, not only for themselves but also for their communities. Growth is possible even for those who have caused great harm.

Personal growth involves change in multiple dimensions. It may include developing empathy for others, understanding the impact of one's actions, taking responsibility for behavior, making amends for harm, addressing underlying issues, building positive relationships, and finding new purpose. Each of these changes represents growth.

Restorative justice promotes growth by creating conditions in which it can occur. Confronting victims face to face breaks through denial and forces acknowledgment of harm. Hearing victims' stories develops empathy and understanding. Taking responsibility and making amends builds accountability and integrity. Receiving support and encouragement from community provides resources for change. Experiencing forgiveness and restoration offers hope for the future.

This growth benefits not only offenders but everyone connected to them. Victims benefit when offenders change and are less likely to harm again. Families benefit when offenders become responsible members. Communities benefit when former offenders contribute positively. Growth ripples outward, touching many lives.

The biblical narrative includes many stories of personal transformation. Saul of Tarsus was a persecutor of the church, consenting to the death of Stephen, hunting Christians to imprison them. After his encounter with the risen Christ, he became Paul the apostle, the greatest missionary in church history, author of much of the New Testament. His transformation was dramatic and complete.

Peter denied Jesus three times, yet after the resurrection he was restored and became the leader of the early church. His failure did not define him; his growth did. David committed adultery and murder, yet after repentance he was restored and became the ancestor of the Messiah. His sin was not the end of his story.

These transformations were not automatic or easy. They involved confrontation with wrongdoing, genuine remorse, acceptance of consequences, and commitment to change. They were supported by community—Ananias ministering to Paul, the apostles welcoming Peter, Nathan confronting David. They were sustained by grace—God's willingness to forgive and restore.

Psychological research on change identifies stages through which individuals progress. Precontemplation is denial or unawareness of problem. Contemplation is awareness and consideration of change. Preparation is commitment and planning. Action is implementing change. Maintenance is sustaining change over time. Relapse is common but not final. Restorative justice can move offenders from precontemplation to contemplation and action, supporting them through subsequent stages.

Growth is not guaranteed. Some offenders will resist, deny, and refuse to change. Restorative justice cannot force transformation; it can only create conditions in which it is possible. But for those who are open to change, restorative processes can be powerfully transformative.

Healing Circles: Structured Support for Healing

Restorative justice practices like healing circles provide a structured environment for participants to express their feelings and experiences. These circles can be instrumental in the healing process, creating safe spaces for the kind of honest communication that healing requires.

Healing circles bring together those affected by harm in a structured, facilitated conversation. Participants sit in a circle, symbolizing equality and mutual respect. A talking piece is passed from person to person, ensuring that each voice is heard without interruption. The circle creates a space of safety and respect in which even the most difficult conversations can occur.

The circle structure serves several healing functions. Equality—no one is above or below, no position is privileged—counters the powerlessness that victims may feel. Respect—each voice is valued—affirms the worth of every participant. Inclusivity—all affected parties are invited—ensures that no one is left out. Transparency—the process is open and honest—builds trust. Accountability—participants are expected to take responsibility—promotes growth.

In healing circles, participants can express feelings that might otherwise remain buried. Victims can speak their pain, anger, fear, and grief. Offenders can express remorse, shame, and hope for change. Community members can share their concern, support, and commitment. This expression, in a safe and respectful setting, is itself healing.

Circles can be used for multiple purposes. Healing circles address the impact of specific harms, bringing together victims, offenders, and supporters to work toward restoration. Support circles surround individuals in crisis with care and assistance. Conflict circles help parties in dispute understand each other and find resolution. Celebration circles mark milestones of healing and restoration.

The circle process draws on ancient wisdom. Indigenous peoples around the world have used circles for healing, decision-making, and community building for millennia. These traditions recognize that sitting in a circle, speaking and listening in turn, creates conditions for genuine communication and connection. Restorative justice has adapted these practices for contemporary contexts.

The biblical tradition includes circle-like practices. The early church gathered in circles for worship, teaching, and fellowship. The Last Supper was likely a circle—reclining around a table, sharing bread and wine, speaking and listening. The apostles gathered in council to discern God's will (Acts 15). These gatherings embodied values of equality, participation, and mutual respect.

Jesus often taught in circles. When He sat on the mountainside to teach the Beatitudes, the crowds gathered around Him—a natural circle. When He was in houses, people filled the space, surrounding Him. His teaching was not monologue but dialogue, inviting response and engagement. The circle was His context.

Psychological research supports the effectiveness of circle processes. Group settings that provide safety, respect, and structure can facilitate healing that individual therapy alone cannot achieve. The presence of others who have had similar experiences normalizes suffering and reduces shame. The opportunity to help others builds meaning and purpose. Circles leverage these therapeutic factors.

Healing circles are not a panacea. They require skilled facilitation, careful preparation, and ongoing support. They may not be appropriate for all situations or all participants. But when used appropriately, they can be powerfully healing.

Catharsis and Closure: The Healing Release

Restorative justice processes can offer catharsis, emotional release, and a sense of closure for both victims and offenders. This closure is an essential component of the healing journey. It does not mean forgetting or pretending that harm didn't happen. It means reaching a point where the past no longer dominates the present, where life can move forward.

Catharsis is the release of strong or repressed emotions. In restorative processes, participants may experience catharsis as they express feelings that have been bottled up—anger that has festered, grief that has been denied, fear that has paralyzed. This release can be intensely freeing, like lancing a wound to let out infection.

For victims, catharsis may come through telling their story, confronting the offender, expressing their pain, or receiving acknowledgment. For offenders, catharsis may come through admitting guilt, expressing remorse, making amends, or receiving forgiveness. For community members, catharsis may come through supporting victims, holding offenders accountable, or participating in restoration.

Closure is the sense of resolution that follows catharsis. It is not that everything is fixed or that all questions are answered. It is that the event is now in the past, no longer controlling the present. The victim can think about the future without being haunted by the past. The offender can move forward without being defined by their worst act. The community can rebuild without being paralyzed by fear.

Closure is not the same as completion. Healing is ongoing; closure is a milestone, not a destination. But reaching a point of closure—where the harm is acknowledged, addressed, and integrated—is essential for moving forward.

The biblical tradition includes moments of catharsis and closure. The Psalms often move from lament to praise, from complaint to thanksgiving. The psalmist pours out grief, anger, and fear, then arrives at a place of trust and hope. This movement is cathartic, providing release and resolution.

Job's story ends with a kind of closure. After his long struggle, after God's revelation, after his repentance, Job is restored—his health, his wealth, his family. The story does not explain his suffering or justify it. But it provides closure, a sense that his story has reached a meaningful end.

Jesus' death and resurrection provide the ultimate catharsis and closure for Christian faith. The cross is the place of ultimate suffering, where all the pain and evil of the world converge. The resurrection is the victory over death, the promise that suffering does not have the final word. For believers, this story provides catharsis—identification with Christ's suffering—and closure—hope of resurrection.

Psychological research on closure identifies several factors that contribute to it. Acknowledgment of harm by others validates the victim's experience. Accountability of offenders confirms that wrong was done. Making amends provides tangible repair. Forgiveness releases resentment. Community support provides belonging. Each of these factors can contribute to a sense of closure.

Restorative justice provides opportunities for each of these factors to be present. Acknowledgment occurs through victim-offender dialogue. Accountability occurs through offender responsibility. Amends occur through restitution and repair. Forgiveness occurs through victim choice. Community support occurs through involvement of family and friends. Together, these elements can produce catharsis and closure.

Not everyone will experience catharsis and closure through restorative justice. Some victims may find that facing the offender is too painful; some offenders may remain in denial. Restorative justice cannot guarantee outcomes; it can only create conditions in which healing is possible. But for many who participate, these processes provide the release and resolution they have been seeking.

The Healing Journey: A Holistic Vision

Restorative justice and healing are intimately connected. Restorative processes aim to facilitate healing for all affected by harm—victims, offenders, and communities. This healing is not merely the absence of symptoms but the presence of well-being—physical, emotional, psychological, relational, spiritual.

The healing journey is different for everyone. For victims, it may involve acknowledging harm, expressing feelings, receiving validation, experiencing empowerment, hearing apology, extending forgiveness, receiving restitution, and finding closure. For offenders, it may involve acknowledging responsibility, expressing remorse, making amends, addressing underlying issues, receiving support, and being restored to community. For communities, it may involve acknowledging collective responsibility, addressing systemic issues, supporting victims and offenders, and rebuilding trust.

This healing is holistic. It addresses the whole person—body, mind, spirit. It recognizes that harm affects every dimension of human existence and that healing must therefore address every dimension. It is not satisfied with surface fixes but seeks deep transformation.

This healing is relational. It recognizes that we are created for connection and that harm damages connection. Healing, therefore, requires restoring connection—with self, with others, with God. Restorative processes facilitate this restoration by bringing people together in settings of safety and respect.

This healing is communal. It recognizes that individuals do not heal in isolation; they heal in community. Communities provide support, accountability, and belonging. Communities themselves need healing—from the divisions, fears, and wounds that crime produces. Restorative justice addresses communal as well as individual healing.

This healing is possible. Not guaranteed, not easy, but possible. Countless victims have found healing through restorative processes. Countless offenders have been transformed. Countless communities have been strengthened. The evidence is there, in research and in testimony.

The biblical vision of shalom encompasses this holistic healing. Shalom is peace—not just absence of conflict but presence of well-being. It is wholeness—every dimension of life flourishing. It is right relationship—with God, with others, with self, with creation. Shalom is what God intends for all creation, and restorative justice participates in bringing shalom to birth.

Jesus embodied this healing vision. He healed the sick, gave sight to the blind, made the lame walk, cleansed lepers, cast out demons, raised the dead. But His healing was never merely physical; it was always holistic, restoring people to community, to dignity, to purpose. He touched the untouchable, spoke to the outcast, welcomed the marginalized. His healing was restorative.

The Gospel of Restorative Justice is this: that in Christ, God is healing the world. Not counting our trespasses against us, but reconciling us to Himself. Entrusting to us the ministry of reconciliation. Inviting us to participate in the healing of all things.

This is the hope that animates restorative justice. This is the vision that sustains its practitioners. This is the promise that invites us all to become agents of healing in a wounded world. Restorative justice, in its attention to acknowledgment, empowerment, accountability, apology, forgiveness, restitution, community support, prevention, trauma resolution, humanization, personal growth, healing circles, and catharsis and closure, offers a comprehensive approach to healing that reflects the very heart of God.

CHAPTER 13

RESTORATIVE JUSTICE AND CRIMINAL JUSTICE

The relationship between restorative justice and the conventional criminal justice system is one of the most important and contested questions in contemporary criminology and legal philosophy. Are these two approaches fundamentally opposed, representing incompatible visions of how society should respond to wrongdoing? Or can they coexist, complementing each other and offering different paths to different ends? Is restorative justice a replacement for criminal justice, an alternative to be used in some cases, or a supplement that can enrich and humanize existing systems? These questions have profound implications for policy, practice, and the lives of countless individuals who come into contact with the justice system.

This chapter explores the relationship between restorative justice and criminal justice, comparing their key principles, practices, and underlying philosophies. We will examine the punitive focus of criminal justice, its government-led processes, its adversarial nature, the role of victims as witnesses, the limited participation of victims, and the emphasis on sentencing proportional to crime. We will contrast these with restorative justice's focus on repairing harm, its community-led processes, its collaborative approach, the central role of victims, extensive victim participation, and emphasis on restitution and reintegration. We will also consider how these two approaches can coexist, the ways in which restorative justice is being integrated into criminal justice systems around the world, and the theological and philosophical foundations that support this integration. Through this exploration, we will see that restorative justice offers not a rejection of criminal justice but a transformation of it—a way of holding systems accountable to their deepest purposes and of humanizing processes that have become mechanical and dehumanizing.

The Nature of Criminal Justice: Punishment and Retribution

Criminal justice systems, as they have developed in Western societies over the past several centuries, are primarily focused on punishing offenders through incarceration, fines, probation, or other punitive measures. The emphasis is on retribution—giving offenders what they deserve—and deterrence—preventing future crimes through fear of punishment. This punitive focus is so deeply ingrained that it often seems like the natural and inevitable purpose of justice.

The philosophical foundations of this approach were most clearly articulated by Immanuel Kant, who argued that punishment must be imposed because the offender deserves it—and for no other reason. Utilitarian justifications like deterrence or rehabilitation, Kant insisted, treated the offender as a means to social ends, violating their dignity as a person. Only retribution—giving the offender what they deserve—respected them as moral agents capable of choosing their actions and responsible for their consequences.

For Kant, the severity of punishment must be proportionate to the gravity of the crime. The principle of lex talionis—"an eye for an eye"—provided the appropriate measure, not because it satisfied vengeance but because it expressed the moral equivalence between crime and punishment. Kant famously illustrated this with the example of an island society about to disband: even if they were going to separate forever, they must first execute the last murderer in their prisons. Otherwise, they would all share in the guilt of the murder by failing to give the offender what they deserved.

This retributive philosophy has shaped criminal justice systems in profound ways. Sentences are designed to be proportionate to offenses. Punishment is seen as an end in itself, not merely a means to other ends. The focus is on the past—what the offender did—rather than the future—what can be made right. The state's interest in punishing wrongdoing takes precedence over the needs of victims or the possibilities of restoration.

The biblical tradition includes elements that support this retributive understanding. The lex talionis appears in the Law of Moses: "life for life, eye for eye, tooth for tooth, hand for hand, foot for foot" (Deuteronomy 19:21). This principle was given to limit vengeance, to ensure that punishment did not exceed the offense. In a world where personal vendettas could escalate into blood feuds that destroyed families and communities, this principle represented a significant advance in justice. It said, in effect: you may take only one life for a life, not two; you may extract only one eye for an eye, not the offender's life.

But the biblical vision of justice extends far beyond retribution. The same Law that includes lex talionis also mandates restitution, requiring offenders to compensate victims for losses. The prophets call for justice that defends the vulnerable and restores the oppressed. Jesus teaches forgiveness, reconciliation, and love for enemies. The apostle Paul proclaims that God in Christ was reconciling the world to Himself, not counting our trespasses against us. The biblical witness is not simply retributive but profoundly restorative.

Contemporary criminal justice, however, has often lost sight of these restorative dimensions. The focus on punishment has become so dominant that other purposes—restitution, rehabilitation, restoration—are marginalized or forgotten. Prisons have become warehouses for the poor and marginalized, doing little to change behavior or repair harm. Victims are sidelined, their needs ignored. Communities are excluded, their role in justice reduced to passive observation. The system processes cases, but it does not heal wounds.

Government-Led Processes: The State as Victim

In criminal justice systems, the state takes the central role in investigations, prosecutions, and adjudications. Crime is defined as an offense against the state, against the sovereign, against the people collectively. The state, representing the abstract entity of "the people," prosecutes the offender. The victim, ironically, becomes a witness for the state—a source of evidence rather than a participant in justice.

This government-led approach has several consequences. First, it abstracts crime from its concrete human impact. The state's interest in maintaining order and upholding laws is important, but it is not the same as the victim's interest in healing and restoration. When the state takes over, the victim's experience becomes secondary, their needs incidental.

Second, it centralizes power in the hands of professionals—police, prosecutors, judges, corrections officials. These professionals make decisions that profoundly affect the lives of victims, offenders, and communities, but they are not directly accountable to those most affected. Their incentives—conviction rates, caseload clearance, institutional efficiency—may not align with the needs of those they serve.

Third, it excludes the community from meaningful participation. The community is represented by the state, but this representation is abstract and impersonal. Community members have no role in the process, no opportunity to contribute to resolution, no responsibility for supporting victims or offenders. Justice happens to communities, not with them.

The biblical tradition offers a different model. In ancient Israel, justice was administered at the community level—at the city gate, where elders gathered to hear disputes and render judgments (Ruth 4:1-12; Amos 5:10-15). The community was directly involved in the process, witnessing proceedings, supporting parties, and ensuring that justice was done. This communal approach kept justice close to those most affected by it.

The New Testament church also practiced communal accountability. When conflicts arose, they were to be addressed within the community, not taken before secular courts (1 Corinthians 6:1-8). The community was responsible for holding members accountable, for restoring the repentant, for maintaining unity. This was not justice imposed from above but justice practiced from within.

Restorative justice, in emphasizing community involvement, recovers this biblical vision. It recognizes that crime wounds communities and that communities must therefore be involved in healing. It brings together those most affected by harm—victims, offenders, families, supporters—to address what happened and what needs to be done. The state may play a supportive role—providing resources, ensuring safety, enforcing agreements—but it is not the sole decision-maker.

Adversarial Process: Contest Rather Than Conversation

The criminal justice process is fundamentally adversarial. Prosecution and defense present their cases in court, each seeking to persuade the judge or jury of their version of events. The prosecution seeks to prove guilt; the defense seeks to raise reasonable doubt. The process is structured as a contest, with winners and losers.

This adversarial approach has deep roots in Western legal tradition. It reflects a commitment to protecting the rights of the accused, ensuring that the state cannot simply impose its will on individuals. The presumption of innocence, the right to counsel, the requirement of proof beyond a reasonable doubt—these safeguards are essential protections against tyranny.

But the adversarial process also has significant limitations. It tends to obscure truth rather than reveal it. Each side presents evidence favorable to its case, while suppressing or minimizing evidence that might help the other side. Witnesses are examined and cross-examined, not to understand their experience but to score points. The goal is not to understand what happened but to win.

The adversarial process also exacerbates conflict. By pitting parties against each other, it deepens divisions and makes reconciliation more difficult. Victims and offenders become opponents rather than human beings trying to address harm. The process itself becomes an obstacle to healing.

Restorative justice offers a fundamentally different approach. Rather than adversarial, it is collaborative. Rather than contest, it is conversation. Rather than winners and losers, it seeks outcomes that satisfy all parties. The goal is not to determine who is right and who is wrong but to understand what happened and what needs to be done.

In restorative processes, victims and offenders come together in dialogue, not confrontation. They speak and listen, share and receive. They work toward agreement about how harm can be repaired. The facilitator's role is not to judge but to guide, not to decide but to support. The process is cooperative, not competitive.

This collaborative approach reflects biblical values. Jesus taught His followers to be peacemakers, not combatants (Matthew 5:9). He instructed them to settle matters quickly with their adversaries, rather than letting disputes escalate (Matthew 5:25). He modeled dialogue and engagement, not adversarial confrontation. The early church resolved its conflicts through council and conversation, not litigation (Acts 15).

The Apostle Paul appeals to Philemon not through legal coercion but through relational persuasion. He does not command; he requests. He does not demand; he appeals. He creates space for Philemon to respond freely, guided by love rather than law. This is collaboration, not adversarial contest.

The Victim as Witness: Sidelined Suffering

In criminal justice systems, victims are typically treated as witnesses to the crime. Their main role is to provide evidence for the prosecution—to testify about what happened, to identify the offender, to describe their injuries. Beyond that, they have little involvement in the process.

This treatment of victims has been widely criticized. Victims often feel re-victimized by a system that uses them as means to its ends. Their pain becomes evidence; their testimony becomes a tool for prosecution; their ongoing needs—for answers, for acknowledgment, for a sense of closure—are systematically ignored. They are present at the trial but not truly participants in justice.

Research confirms these concerns. Victims consistently report feeling ignored, disrespected, and frustrated by the criminal justice process. They want information about their case, but often don't receive it. They want to be heard, but feel silenced. They want their suffering acknowledged, but find that the system cares more about the offender's rights than their needs.

The biblical tradition offers a different vision. Throughout Scripture, God is portrayed as one who hears the cry of the oppressed, who cares for the suffering, who defends the vulnerable. The Law includes provisions for protecting victims and ensuring they receive restitution. The prophets thunder against those who ignore the needs of the wounded. Jesus consistently prioritizes the needs of those who have been harmed—the leper, the paralytic, the bleeding woman, the grieving parent.

In restorative justice, victims are not witnesses but central participants. Their needs, feelings, and desires take precedence. They have an active role in shaping the outcome. They decide whether to participate, how to prepare, what to say, what questions to ask. They are consulted about agreements and have a voice in determining what will happen. This is not using victims as means but honoring them as ends.

This victim-centered approach aligns with the biblical emphasis on the dignity and worth of every person. Because victims are created in God's image, they deserve to be treated with respect, to have their suffering acknowledged, to participate in decisions that affect their lives. Restorative justice embodies this respect.

Limited Victim Participation: Passive Rather Than Active

Related to the treatment of victims as witnesses is the limited participation they are allowed in criminal justice processes. Victims may testify, but the process is controlled by lawyers and judges. They may submit victim impact statements, but these often have little effect on outcomes. They may observe proceedings, but they are not active participants.

This limited participation has several consequences. Victims feel powerless, their agency stripped away by a process that treats them as passive objects rather than active subjects. They have no opportunity to ask the questions that haunt them, to express the feelings that consume them, to shape the outcomes that affect them. The system processes their case, but it does not serve their needs.

Research shows that victims want more participation. They want information about their case, to be sure, but they also want to be heard, to have their views considered, to have a say in what happens. They want to know that their suffering matters, that their voice counts, that they are not just a means to someone else's ends.

Restorative justice offers extensive victim participation. Victims have the opportunity to express their feelings, concerns, and needs. They can ask questions of the offender and receive answers. They can describe the impact of the crime in their own words, not through the filter of legal proceedings. They can participate in developing agreements about restitution and repair. They can choose whether to accept apologies and extend forgiveness.

This participation is not merely symbolic; it is substantive. Victims' input shapes outcomes. Their needs are addressed in agreements. Their voices are heard and honored. They are active agents in their own healing, not passive recipients of others' decisions.

The biblical narrative affirms this active participation. The psalmists do not passively accept suffering; they cry out to God, protest their circumstances, demand attention. Job does not silently endure; he argues, questions, challenges. The woman with the hemorrhage does not wait to be noticed; she reaches out and touches Jesus' garment. These are active participants in their own healing, models of the agency that restorative justice seeks to restore.

Sentencing: Proportional Punishment

Sentencing in criminal justice systems is typically determined by legal guidelines and statutes, with an emphasis on proportionality to the crime. The goal is to ensure that the punishment fits the offense—that more serious crimes receive more severe sentences, that like cases are treated alike.

This emphasis on proportionality reflects important values. It prevents arbitrary or excessive punishment. It ensures that offenders are not punished more harshly than they deserve. It provides predictability and consistency in sentencing. These are genuine achievements of modern legal systems.

But proportionality has limitations. It focuses on the offense, not the offender's needs or potential for change. It looks backward, not forward. It measures justice in terms of pain inflicted, not harm repaired. A sentence of five years in prison may be proportional to a crime, but it does nothing to address the victim's losses, the offender's underlying issues, or the community's wounds.

Restorative justice takes a different approach to outcomes. Rather than focusing on proportional punishment, it seeks restitution, apologies, and plans for reintegration. The goal is not to inflict pain but to repair harm. Outcomes are tailored to the specific circumstances of each case, not determined by rigid guidelines.

A restorative agreement might include restitution to compensate the victim for losses. It might include community service that benefits those affected by the crime. It might include counseling or treatment to address underlying issues. It might include a sincere apology and a commitment to changed behavior. These outcomes are not measured in years of incarceration but in actions that make things right.

This approach does not ignore proportionality entirely. Restitution should be proportionate to losses. Community service should be proportionate to harm. But the focus is on repair, not punishment—on making things right, not making the offender suffer.

The biblical tradition supports this restorative approach to outcomes. The Law of Moses required restitution, not imprisonment, for most offenses. An offender who stole an ox had to repay five oxen (Exodus 22:1)—proportionate, certainly, but focused on repair, not punishment. Zacchaeus, when he encountered Jesus, committed to restoring fourfold anything he had taken by fraud (Luke 19:8). His response was not about punishment but about making things right.

The Restorative Alternative: Healing and Reintegration

In contrast to criminal justice's punitive focus, restorative justice aims to repair the harm caused by the offense. The emphasis is on reconciliation, healing, and reintegration. This is not merely a different method but a different vision of what justice is for.

Repairing harm means addressing the wounds that crime inflicts. For victims, this means acknowledging their suffering, addressing their needs, and supporting their healing. For offenders, this means holding them accountable in ways that promote understanding, remorse, and change. For communities, this means involving them in the process of healing and strengthening the social bonds that crime weakens.

Reconciliation means restoring relationships that have been damaged by harm. This is not always possible or appropriate; some relationships cannot be restored, and some victims do not wish to reconcile. But when reconciliation is possible, it is a profound good—the restoration of trust, the rebuilding of connection, the renewal of community.

Reintegration means welcoming offenders back into community after they have made amends. This is not about ignoring what they have done but about believing that they can change and that they deserve a chance to contribute positively. Reintegration reduces recidivism, strengthens communities, and embodies the hope that even those who have caused harm can become forces for good.

This restorative vision aligns deeply with biblical values. The God of Scripture is portrayed as one who heals the brokenhearted, who reconciles the estranged, who restores the outcast. The ministry of Jesus was characterized by healing, reconciliation, and restoration. The early church understood itself as a community of reconciliation, called to embody God's restorative purposes in the world.

Community-Led Processes: Justice With the People

Restorative justice processes often involve community members, mediators, and other stakeholders in addressing harm. The state may play a supportive role—providing resources, ensuring safety, enforcing agreements—but it is not the sole decision-maker. Justice is done with the community, not to it or for it.

This community involvement has several benefits. It brings local knowledge and wisdom to bear on complex situations. It mobilizes resources and support that formal systems cannot provide. It builds trust between community members and justice processes. It creates a sense of shared responsibility for addressing harm and preventing its recurrence.

Community involvement also addresses the limitations of government-led processes. When communities are engaged, justice is more responsive to local needs and values. When communities are responsible, they are more invested in outcomes. When communities participate, they are strengthened by the experience.

The biblical tradition supports community involvement in justice. In ancient Israel, justice was administered at the city gate, where elders and community members gathered to hear disputes and render judgments (Ruth 4; Deuteronomy 21:18-21). The community was present, witnessing proceedings, holding parties accountable, ensuring that justice was done. This communal approach kept justice close to those most affected.

The New Testament church practiced communal accountability. When a member sinned, the community was involved in addressing the situation—first through private conversation, then with witnesses, then before the whole assembly (Matthew 18:15-20). The goal was always restoration, and the community's involvement was essential to achieving it.

Restorative justice, in emphasizing community involvement, recovers this biblical vision. It recognizes that justice cannot be delegated entirely to professionals and institutions; it must be owned by communities. It brings together those most affected by harm to address what happened and what needs to be done. It builds community even as it heals individuals.

Collaborative Process: Dialogue and Consensus

Restorative justice processes are collaborative, involving open dialogue between victims and offenders. Outcomes are often determined through consensus, not imposed by third parties. This collaboration is essential to the healing that restorative justice seeks.

Dialogue allows parties to express their perspectives, share their feelings, and understand each other's experiences. Victims can describe the impact of the crime; offenders can explain their actions. This exchange, facilitated by trained mediators, creates understanding that is impossible in adversarial proceedings.

Consensus ensures that outcomes are owned by those who must implement them. When victims and offenders agree on what should be done—how restitution should be made, what apologies should be offered, what steps should be taken to prevent future harm—they are more likely to follow through. Agreements imposed by courts are often resented and resisted; agreements reached through consensus are embraced and fulfilled.

This collaborative approach reflects biblical values. Jesus taught His followers to seek agreement with their adversaries, to settle matters out of court (Matthew 5:25). He modeled dialogue and engagement, not imposition and coercion. The early church made decisions through council and consensus, not hierarchical decree (Acts 15).

The Apostle Paul's approach to the situation with Onesimus and Philemon exemplifies collaboration. Paul does not command Philemon to forgive or to release Onesimus. He appeals, persuades, and creates space for Philemon to respond freely. He involves the church in supporting the process. The outcome is not imposed but chosen, not coerced but embraced. This is collaboration, not control.

Victim as Central: Honoring the Wounded

In restorative justice, victims are central to the process, with their needs, feelings, and desires taking precedence. They have an active role in shaping the outcome. This centrality is not merely a procedural preference but a fundamental recognition of the victim's dignity and worth.

Victims are central because they have been directly harmed. Their suffering demands attention. Their needs must be addressed. Their voices must be heard. A justice system that sidelines victims is not truly just; it serves the interests of the state, the professionals, the system itself, but not those who have been most affected.

Victims are central because their participation is essential to healing. When victims are able to express their feelings, ask their questions, and shape outcomes, they are more likely to experience closure and recovery. When they are ignored or excluded, their wounds fester. Justice that heals requires victim participation.

Victims are central because their dignity requires it. Every person is created in God's image and deserves to be treated with respect. Victims, no less than anyone else, have inherent worth that must be honored. A justice system that treats them as means to others' ends violates this dignity.

The biblical tradition consistently affirms the centrality of victims. God is described as one who hears the cry of the oppressed (Exodus 3:7), who defends the cause of the vulnerable (Psalm 10:17-18), who executes justice for the oppressed (Psalm 146:7). Jesus consistently prioritized the needs of those who had been harmed—healing them, restoring them, welcoming them. The early church cared for widows and orphans, the most vulnerable victims of their society.

Restorative justice, in placing victims at the center, embodies this biblical concern. It honors their dignity, addresses their needs, and supports their healing. It treats them not as means but as ends, not as witnesses but as participants, not as objects but as subjects.

Extensive Victim Participation: Agency and Voice

Restorative justice provides extensive opportunities for victim participation. Victims have the chance to express their feelings, ask questions, and participate in decision-making. This participation is not tokenistic but substantive; it shapes outcomes and contributes to healing.

Victims can express their feelings in their own words, not through the filter of legal proceedings. They can describe the impact of the crime—the fear, the anger, the grief, the ongoing struggles. They can name what they have lost—not just property but sense of safety, trust, well-being. This expression validates their experience and communicates its reality to others.

Victims can ask questions that have haunted them. Why me? What were you thinking? Do you have any idea what you took from me? Are you sorry? Will you do it again? These questions, unanswered in conventional proceedings, can be addressed directly to the offender. The answers, when genuine, can bring closure and peace.

Victims can participate in developing agreements about restitution and repair. They can say what would make things right—compensation for losses, community service, apologies, changed behavior. Their input shapes outcomes, ensuring that agreements address their actual needs.

This extensive participation empowers victims. It restores a sense of agency and control that crime stripped away. It counters the helplessness and passivity that victims often feel. It affirms that they matter, that their voice counts, that they are not just objects of others' decisions.

The biblical narrative affirms this agency. The psalmists do not passively accept suffering; they cry out, protest, demand. Job does not silently endure; he argues, questions, challenges. The woman with the hemorrhage does not wait to be noticed; she reaches out and touches Jesus' garment. These are active participants in their own healing, models of the agency that restorative justice seeks to restore.

Restitution and Reintegration: Making Things Right

Outcomes in restorative justice can include restitution, apologies, and plans for the reintegration of the offender into the community. The focus is on repairing relationships and addressing the root causes of the offense. These outcomes are not alternatives to accountability but expressions of it.

Restitution addresses the tangible harm caused by crime. Offenders may return stolen property, pay for damages, cover medical expenses, or compensate for lost wages. Restitution is not about punishment but about repair—making the victim whole to the extent possible. It communicates that the offender is responsible for the consequences of their actions.

Apologies address the relational harm caused by crime. A genuine apology acknowledges wrongdoing, expresses remorse, accepts responsibility, and commits to change. It communicates to victims that their suffering is recognized and that the offender is genuinely sorry. Apologies can be profoundly healing for both parties.

Reintegration addresses the future. Plans for reintegration may include counseling, treatment, education, employment, mentorship, and community support. These plans address the underlying issues that contributed to the offense and support the offender in building a new life. Reintegration is not about letting offenders off the hook but about helping them become productive, responsible members of community.

These outcomes reflect a holistic understanding of accountability. Accountability is not just about accepting punishment but about taking responsibility for harm, making amends, and changing behavior. It is not backward-looking only but forward-looking as well. It addresses the needs of victims, offenders, and communities together.

The biblical tradition supports this holistic accountability. Zacchaeus, when he encountered Jesus, did not simply express remorse; he committed to restitution and changed behavior (Luke 19:8). The prodigal son, when he returned home, did not simply apologize; he accepted the consequences of his actions and was restored to relationship (Luke 15:11-32). The woman caught in adultery was not condemned but called to "go and sin no more" (John 8:11). Accountability and restoration are not opposed but intertwined.

The Coexistence of Criminal and Restorative Justice

Criminal justice and restorative justice are not mutually exclusive. They can coexist, and many justice systems integrate restorative practices as an alternative or complement to traditional punitive measures. This integration recognizes that different cases, different offenders, and different victims may require different responses.

Restorative justice can be used at multiple points in the criminal justice process. As diversion, restorative processes can keep low-level offenders out of the formal system, avoiding the harms of prosecution and incarceration. As a supplement to prosecution, restorative outcomes can be incorporated into plea agreements or sentencing recommendations. As part of sentencing, restorative requirements can be included in probation conditions. As part of reentry, restorative processes can support offenders returning to community after incarceration.

Restorative justice can be used for a wide range of offenses. It is most commonly used for juvenile offenses and minor adult crimes, but it has also been used successfully for serious violent crimes, including rape and murder. In these cases, restorative processes must be handled with great care, ensuring the safety and well-being of all participants. But even in the most serious cases, restorative justice can offer opportunities for healing that purely punitive responses cannot.

Restorative justice can be used in various settings. It is used in criminal justice systems around the world, from New Zealand's family group conferences to European victim-offender mediation programs to restorative justice initiatives in the United States. It is used in schools, workplaces, faith communities, and neighborhoods. Its principles are adaptable to diverse contexts.

The coexistence of criminal and restorative justice reflects the complexity of human response to wrongdoing. Punishment may be necessary in some cases—to protect public safety, to express society's condemnation, to uphold the rule of law. But punishment alone is not enough. Victims need healing. Offenders need transformation. Communities need restoration. Restorative justice addresses these needs that punitive systems neglect.

The biblical tradition holds together justice and mercy, accountability and grace. The Law provided for punishment, but also for restitution and restoration. The prophets proclaimed judgment, but also hope for redemption. Jesus taught about the demands of discipleship, but also about the extravagance of grace. The apostles called for accountability, but also for forgiveness and reconciliation. Criminal justice and restorative justice, held together in creative tension, reflect this biblical complexity.

Humanizing the Justice System

Restorative justice is often seen as a way to humanize the justice system. It offers healing to victims, promotes accountability and rehabilitation for offenders, and involves communities in the work of justice. In doing so, it addresses the dehumanizing aspects of conventional criminal justice.

Conventional criminal justice can be deeply dehumanizing. Victims are reduced to witnesses, their humanity incidental to the state's case. Offenders are reduced to criminals, their humanity obscured by their worst acts. Communities are reduced to bystanders, their humanity irrelevant to proceedings that profoundly affect them. The system processes cases, but it does not honor persons.

Restorative justice reverses this dehumanization. Victims are honored as persons, their suffering acknowledged, their needs addressed. Offenders are seen as more than their crimes, capable of change, worthy of restoration. Communities are engaged as partners, their wisdom valued, their participation essential. The system serves persons rather than using them.

This humanization reflects the biblical understanding of human dignity. Every person is created in God's image, possessing inherent worth that cannot be erased by any action. Victims, no less than anyone else, bear this image and deserve to be treated with respect. Offenders, no less than anyone else, bear this image and deserve the opportunity for restoration. Communities, as collections of image-bearers, deserve to be involved in the work of justice.

Jesus consistently humanized those who were dehumanized by society. He touched lepers, whom others avoided as unclean. He spoke with Samaritan women, whom Jews despised as half-breeds. He ate with tax collectors and sinners, whom religious people condemned as outcasts. He welcomed children, whom disciples tried to send away. In every encounter, He saw beyond labels to the human being created in God's image.

Restorative justice, in humanizing the justice system, follows this example. It sees victims, offenders, and community members as persons, not cases. It treats them with respect, honors their dignity, and supports their healing. It embodies the love that lies at the heart of the gospel.

Accountability and Rehabilitation

Restorative justice promotes accountability and rehabilitation for offenders in ways that conventional punishment often fails to achieve. This is not because restorative justice is softer but because it is smarter—it addresses the root causes of behavior and engages offenders in their own transformation.

Accountability in restorative justice means taking responsibility for harm, not just accepting punishment. Offenders must acknowledge what they did, understand its impact, and take steps to make amends. This is a more demanding form of accountability than simply serving time. It requires offenders to face their victims, to hear their pain, to answer their questions, to make things right.

Rehabilitation in restorative justice means addressing the underlying issues that led to criminal behavior. Offenders may need treatment for addiction, counseling for trauma, education for employment, support for mental health. Restorative processes connect offenders with these resources and provide ongoing support for change. This is rehabilitation that sticks, not just programs that process.

Research supports the effectiveness of this approach. Offenders who participate in restorative justice programs have lower recidivism rates than those processed through conventional systems. They are less likely to reoffend because they have undergone internal transformation, not merely endured external punishment. They have faced the harm they caused, made amends where possible, and been welcomed back into community.

The biblical tradition supports this integration of accountability and rehabilitation. The prophets called Israel to account for its sins, but they also promised restoration and renewal. Jesus called sinners to repentance, but He also offered forgiveness and new life. Paul confronted wrongdoing, but he also nurtured growth and transformation. Accountability and rehabilitation are not opposed but complementary.

The Gospel of Restorative Justice

As we consider the relationship between restorative justice and criminal justice, we see that restorative justice offers not a rejection of criminal justice but a transformation of it. It calls the system to remember its deepest purposes—to do justice, to protect the innocent, to hold the guilty accountable. But it also calls the system to expand its vision—to heal the wounded, to restore the broken, to reconcile the estranged.

This transformative vision is rooted in the gospel itself. The good news is that in Christ, God was reconciling the world to Himself, not counting our trespasses against us (2 Corinthians 5:19). This reconciliation is not cheap; it cost the cross. But it is also not merely punitive; it is restorative. God's justice is satisfied, but

God's love is also expressed. The offender is held accountable, but the offender is also restored.

Those who have received this reconciliation are called to be ministers of it. We are to be ambassadors of Christ, as though God were pleading through us: be reconciled to God (2 Corinthians 5:20). This ministry of reconciliation extends to every sphere of life, including the justice system. We are called to embody restorative justice in our own lives, to advocate for it in our communities, to work for it in our institutions.

The Gospel of Restorative Justice is this: that healing is possible, that relationships can be restored, that even the deepest wounds can be transformed. It is not a naive optimism that ignores the reality of evil or the seriousness of harm. It is a hope grounded in the resurrection, a confidence that God's restorative purposes will ultimately prevail.

Criminal justice and restorative justice need not be enemies. They can be partners, each contributing what the other lacks. Criminal justice provides structure, accountability, and protection. Restorative justice provides healing, restoration, and hope. Together, they can create a justice system that is both just and merciful, both firm and compassionate, both punitive and restorative.

This is the vision toward which we strive. It is not fully realized in any system, any program, any practice. But it is the goal that guides us, the hope that sustains us, the promise that calls us forward. In the meantime, we work—for restorative justice in criminal justice, for healing in the midst of harm, for reconciliation in a broken world. And we trust that the God who began this good work in us will bring it to completion at the day of Christ Jesus.

CHAPTER 14

RESTORATIVE JUSTICE IN THE GLOBAL CONTEXT

Restorative justice is not a Western invention imposed on other cultures, nor is it a modern innovation disconnected from ancient wisdom. It is a universal human response to harm that has emerged independently in diverse cultures throughout history, finding expression in indigenous traditions, religious communities, and contemporary social movements across the globe. The principles of restorative justice—acknowledgment of harm, accountability of offenders, involvement of community, healing of victims, restoration of relationships—resonate with fundamental human values that transcend cultural boundaries. This universal appeal explains why restorative justice has gained recognition and adoption in various parts of the world, adapting to local contexts while maintaining core principles.

This chapter explores restorative justice in the global context, examining how it manifests in different cultural settings, legal frameworks, and community initiatives around the world. We will consider the diverse adaptations of restorative practices, the integration of restorative justice into legal systems, the role of community-based organizations, the alignment with indigenous practices, the application in conflict resolution and peacebuilding, the support of international organizations, the intersection with human rights concerns, the potential for cross-border applications, the emphasis on victims' rights, the contribution to conflict prevention, and the importance of community engagement. We will also examine inspiring examples from South Africa, Canada, Rwanda, Scandinavia, New Zealand, and other regions that demonstrate the global relevance of restorative principles. Finally, we will envision a restorative society—a world in which healing, accountability, empathy, and reconciliation are not occasional exceptions but the norm.

Cultural Adaptations: Universal Principles, Local Expressions

Restorative justice is adapted to fit the cultural contexts of various regions. Practices may vary significantly from one place to another, but the core principles of addressing harm, promoting reconciliation, and involving stakeholders remain consistent. This adaptability is one of restorative justice's greatest strengths, allowing it to take root in diverse soils while bearing fruit that is recognizably restorative.

In Africa, restorative justice draws on deep indigenous traditions that predate colonial legal systems. The concept of Ubuntu—"I am because we are"—expresses a communal understanding of personhood that undergirds restorative approaches. When harm occurs, it is not just an individual matter but a wound in the community's fabric. Healing requires the participation of all affected, the restoration of relationships, the reintegration of offenders. African traditional courts, family conferences, and community gatherings have embodied these principles for centuries.

In Asia, restorative justice resonates with cultural values of harmony, relationship, and community. Confucian emphasis on right relationship, Buddhist teaching on compassion, and Islamic principles of reconciliation all support restorative approaches. Countries like Japan, South Korea, and Singapore have incorporated restorative elements into their justice systems, often drawing on traditional practices of mediation and conciliation.

In Latin America, restorative justice has been embraced in countries such as Brazil, Argentina, and Chile, often in response to the failures of punitive systems and the legacy of political violence. Restorative circles, community mediation, and victim-offender dialogues address crime and conflict while building social cohesion. Indigenous communities have preserved restorative traditions that are now being recognized and supported.

In the Pacific Islands, restorative justice builds on indigenous traditions of community justice. Family group conferencing, originally developed in New Zealand, draws on Maori practices and has been adapted in countries like Fiji and Samoa, where extended family and community play central roles in addressing harm. These practices honor cultural values while addressing contemporary challenges.

In Europe, restorative justice is widely practiced, particularly in juvenile justice systems. Victim-offender mediation is available in most European countries, often as a diversion from prosecution or as a component of sentencing. The Council of Europe has issued recommendations encouraging member states to develop restorative justice programs. European approaches often emphasize professional facilitation, victim support, and integration with formal legal systems.

In North America, restorative justice has grown through both indigenous traditions and grassroots movements. Canadian indigenous communities have maintained healing circles and other restorative practices, which are increasingly recognized and supported by the justice system. In the United States, restorative justice programs have proliferated at every level—from school discipline to juvenile justice to adult criminal cases—often drawing on the work of community organizations and faith-based initiatives.

This diversity of cultural expressions reflects the universal appeal of restorative principles. Every human society must find ways to respond to harm, to hold offenders accountable, to support victims, to maintain community. Restorative justice offers a framework that can be adapted to diverse cultural contexts while maintaining core values. It is not a one-size-fits-all model but a set of principles that can be embodied in countless ways.

The biblical vision of a diverse humanity united in worship of God provides a theological foundation for this cultural diversity. The book of Revelation envisions a multitude from every nation, tribe, people, and language standing before the throne of God (Revelation 7:9). Diversity is not erased but celebrated. Each culture brings its unique gifts to the worship of God. So too with restorative justice: each culture brings its unique expressions to the practice of healing and reconciliation.

Legal Frameworks: Integration into Justice Systems

Some countries have integrated restorative justice into their legal systems, recognizing it as a formal option within the criminal justice process. This integration provides structure, legitimacy, and resources for restorative programs while ensuring that they operate within the framework of legal protections and accountability.

New Zealand's family group conferences are perhaps the most famous example of legislative integration. The Children, Young Persons and Their Families Act of 1989 formally incorporated Maori restorative practices into the youth justice system. When a young person offends, a family group conference brings together the offender, victim, their families, and other supporters to discuss the offense and develop a plan for accountability and restoration. This model has been widely adopted and adapted around the world.

European countries have integrated restorative justice through legislation, policy, and practice. Austria, Germany, France, and many other nations have victim-offender mediation programs operating within or alongside the criminal justice system. The Council of Europe has issued recommendations encouraging member states to develop restorative justice, and the European Union has funded research and training initiatives. European approaches often emphasize professional standards, victim rights, and integration with legal procedures.

In Canada, restorative justice is recognized in legislation and policy at both federal and provincial levels. The Youth Criminal Justice Act emphasizes restorative approaches for young offenders. The Correctional Service of Canada has restorative justice programs for federal offenders. Indigenous healing circles have been incorporated into sentencing and corrections. This legal recognition provides a framework for restorative practice while respecting indigenous traditions.

In the United States, restorative justice has been integrated at state and local levels through legislation, court rules, and prosecutor policies. Many states have statutes authorizing restorative justice programs, particularly for juvenile offenders. Some jurisdictions have established restorative justice courts or dockets. Federal legislation has supported restorative justice through grant programs and policy guidance from the Department of Justice.

This legal integration is essential for the sustainability and growth of restorative justice. It provides funding, standards, and accountability. It ensures that restorative programs operate within the framework of legal protections. It signals that restorative justice is not an alternative to the system but an integral part of it. It creates pathways for referral and collaboration between restorative programs and formal justice institutions.

The relationship between law and restorative justice in these contexts reflects the biblical tension between justice and mercy, between structure and grace. Law provides boundaries, accountability, and protection; restorative justice provides healing, restoration, and hope. Neither is sufficient alone; together, they point toward the fullness of God's justice.

Community-Based Initiatives: Justice From the Ground Up

In many parts of the world, restorative justice is implemented through community-based organizations and initiatives rather than as part of the formal legal system. These organizations address issues ranging from juvenile crime to domestic disputes, from neighborhood conflicts to school discipline. They represent justice from the ground up—initiatives rooted in local communities, responsive to local needs, sustained by local commitment.

Community-based restorative justice takes many forms. Neighborhood justice centers offer mediation and conflict resolution services to community members. Faith-based organizations provide restorative programming for offenders and support for victims. Schools implement restorative practices to address bullying and discipline. Community groups organize circles and conferences to address local conflicts. These initiatives are often more flexible, more accessible, and more culturally appropriate than formal system programs.

Community-based initiatives have several advantages. They are closer to those they serve, understanding local contexts and relationships. They are more accessible, with lower barriers to participation. They are more flexible, able to adapt to individual circumstances. They build local capacity and ownership, strengthening community resilience. They often operate at lower cost than formal system programs.

These initiatives also face challenges. They may lack stable funding, relying on grants and donations. They may struggle with quality assurance and accountability. They may be marginalized or ignored by formal systems. They may face resistance from those who prefer punitive approaches. Sustaining community-based restorative justice requires ongoing commitment, creative resource development, and strategic partnerships.

The early church provides a model for community-based restorative justice. The first believers did not rely on imperial institutions to address their conflicts or care for their members. They created their own structures—apostles, elders, deacons—to govern their community. They practiced mutual accountability, confessing sins to one another and praying for one another (James 5:16). They supported widows, orphans, and others in need (Acts 6:1-7). They resolved disputes through communal discernment (Acts 15). This was justice from the ground up, rooted in community and sustained by faith.

Community-based restorative justice continues this tradition. It recognizes that justice cannot be delegated entirely to professionals and institutions; it must be owned by communities. It builds on local knowledge, relationships, and resources. It strengthens communities even as it addresses harm. It is a vital expression of restorative justice in the global context.

Indigenous Practices: Ancient Wisdom for Contemporary Justice

Restorative justice aligns with many indigenous justice practices around the world. In some countries, these practices have been recognized and incorporated into the formal justice system. This recognition honors the wisdom of indigenous peoples and enriches contemporary restorative practice.

In Canada, indigenous communities have long practiced healing circles, sentencing circles, and other restorative approaches. These practices draw on traditional values of balance, harmony, and relationship. When harm occurs, the community gathers in a circle to address what happened, to support those affected, and to restore balance. The circle includes elders, family members, victims, offenders, and other community members. Everyone has a voice; everyone participates in finding a way forward.

The Canadian justice system has increasingly recognized and incorporated these indigenous practices. The Youth Criminal Justice Act requires consideration of restorative approaches for indigenous young offenders. Sentencing circles have been used in some jurisdictions as a form of restorative justice. Indigenous healing programs operate within corrections and community. This integration honors indigenous traditions while addressing contemporary justice needs.

In New Zealand, Maori restorative practices provided the foundation for family group conferencing. Traditional Maori approaches to justice emphasized community involvement, victim-offender reconciliation, and restoration of balance. The family group conference draws on these principles, bringing together victims, offenders, and their families to address harm and develop plans for restoration. This model has been so successful that it has been adopted around the world.

In Africa, indigenous justice systems have long practiced restorative approaches. Among the Kinga people of Tanzania, conflicts were addressed through community gatherings around a communal fire, where all parties spoke and the community worked toward reconciliation. In Nigeria, reconciliation was sealed through shared meals and symbolic acts. These practices embodied restorative principles centuries before the term was coined.

In the United States, Native American communities have maintained restorative traditions. The Navajo peacemaking courts, for example, bring together parties in conflict with community leaders to address harm and restore harmony. These courts operate alongside the formal justice system, offering an alternative rooted in Navajo values and traditions.

The recognition of indigenous restorative practices is not merely about incorporating ancient techniques into modern systems. It is about honoring the wisdom of peoples who have maintained restorative approaches despite centuries of colonization and oppression. It is about learning from traditions that have kept alive the understanding that justice is about healing, not punishment; about community, not isolation; about balance, not vengeance.

The biblical narrative includes its own indigenous wisdom—the practices of ancient Israel that embodied restorative values. The cities of refuge, the provisions for restitution, the Jubilee year of release and restoration—these were indigenous practices rooted in Israel's covenant relationship with God. They offer wisdom for restorative justice today.

Conflict Resolution and Peacebuilding: Addressing Deep Divisions

Restorative justice principles are applied in conflict resolution, peacebuilding, and transitional justice processes around the world. This approach has been used in post-conflict societies to address historical injustices and promote reconciliation. The principles of acknowledgment, accountability, and restoration that guide restorative justice in individual cases can also guide societies in addressing collective harm.

In South Africa, the Truth and Reconciliation Commission applied restorative principles to address the legacy of apartheid. The Commission provided a platform for victims to tell their stories, for perpetrators to acknowledge their actions, and for the nation to confront its history. While the Commission could not undo the harms of apartheid, it contributed to healing and reconciliation in ways that purely punitive approaches could not have achieved.

In Rwanda, the Gacaca courts addressed the aftermath of the genocide. These community-based courts encouraged perpetrators to confess their crimes, seek reconciliation with victims' families, and contribute to community restoration. The Gacaca process was imperfect—it faced enormous challenges and legitimate criticisms—but it demonstrated the potential of restorative approaches even in the most extreme circumstances.

In the Balkans, restorative initiatives have sought to promote reconciliation among ethnic groups divided by violent conflict. Organizations have brought together people from different backgrounds to share stories, build relationships, and work toward understanding. These efforts cannot undo the harms of war, but they can plant seeds of reconciliation that may grow over time.

In Colombia, restorative justice has been incorporated into peace negotiations and transitional justice processes. The 2016 peace agreement between the government and FARC guerrillas included restorative elements—acknowledgment of harm, victim participation, and measures for reconciliation. Restorative principles offer a path beyond the cycles of violence that have plagued the country for decades.

These applications of restorative justice to large-scale conflict and collective harm raise complex questions. How can restorative principles address harms that involve thousands of victims and perpetrators? How can acknowledgment and accountability be achieved when full truth may never be known? How can restoration occur when material resources are scarce? How can reconciliation be pursued when deep divisions persist?

These questions have no easy answers. But restorative principles offer guidance even in these challenging contexts. They emphasize that acknowledgment of harm is essential, even when full truth is impossible. They insist that victims' voices must be heard, even when their needs cannot be fully met. They recognize that accountability can take many forms—confession, apology, reparation, changed behavior—even when punishment is not possible. They hold out hope that healing and reconciliation are possible, even after the most terrible harms.

The biblical vision of reconciliation includes the hope that even the deepest divisions can be overcome. The prophet Isaiah envisioned a day when swords would be beaten into plowshares and nations would not learn war anymore (Isaiah 2:4). The apostle Paul proclaimed that in Christ, the dividing wall of hostility between Jews and Gentiles had been broken down (Ephesians 2:14). These visions inspire restorative approaches to conflict resolution and peacebuilding, reminding us that reconciliation is not naive optimism but faithful hope.

International Organizations: Supporting Restorative Justice

Restorative justice is promoted by international organizations like the United Nations as a means to promote reconciliation, transitional justice, and the reintegration of former combatants.

These organizations provide frameworks, standards, and support for restorative initiatives around the world.

The United Nations has adopted basic principles on the use of restorative justice programs in criminal matters. These principles, developed through consultation with experts and member states, provide guidance for developing restorative justice programs that respect human rights, ensure procedural safeguards, and promote effective practice. They encourage member states to develop restorative approaches and to integrate them into their justice systems.

The UN has also supported restorative justice in specific contexts. In post-conflict settings, UN peacekeeping missions have included restorative elements—truth commissions, community reconciliation processes, support for victims. In criminal justice reform, UN agencies have provided technical assistance for restorative program development. In human rights work, restorative principles have informed efforts to address violations and promote accountability.

Regional organizations have also promoted restorative justice. The Council of Europe has issued recommendations and sponsored research. The European Union has funded restorative justice initiatives and supported networking among practitioners. The African Union has recognized traditional restorative practices and encouraged their integration with formal systems. The Organization of American States has supported restorative justice development in Latin America.

International non-governmental organizations have played crucial roles. Organizations like Prison Fellowship International, the International Institute for Restorative Practices, and the European Forum for Restorative Justice have promoted restorative justice through research, training, advocacy, and networking. They have connected practitioners across borders, shared best practices, and built a global community of restorative justice advocates.

This international support is essential for the growth of restorative justice. It provides legitimacy, resources, and connections. It encourages governments to develop restorative programs. It facilitates learning across cultures and contexts. It builds momentum for restorative approaches at the global level.

The vision of a global community committed to justice and peace is deeply biblical. The prophets envisioned a day when all nations would stream to the mountain of the Lord to learn God's ways and walk in God's paths (Isaiah 2:2-3). The apostle Paul proclaimed that in Christ, there is neither Jew nor Greek, slave nor free, male nor female, for all are one (Galatians 3:28). The book of Revelation envisions a new heaven and a new earth, where God dwells with humanity and wipes away every tear (Revelation 21:1-4). International support for restorative justice participates in this vision, working toward a world in which justice and peace embrace.

Human Rights Focus: Restorative Justice and Human Dignity

Restorative justice intersects with human rights concerns, addressing issues such as the rights of victims, offenders, and marginalized populations. It has been used to promote accountability for human rights abuses and mass atrocities. This intersection reflects the deep connection between restorative justice and respect for human dignity.

Victims' rights are central to restorative justice. Victims have the right to acknowledgment of their suffering, to participation in processes that affect them, to information about their cases, to protection from further harm, to restitution and reparation, to support in healing. Restorative justice embodies these rights, giving them practical expression in processes that honor victims' dignity and address their needs.

Offenders' rights are also respected in restorative justice. Offenders have the right to due process, to legal counsel, to protection from coercion, to voluntary participation, to fair treatment. Restorative justice operates within the framework of these rights, ensuring that accountability does not become oppression.

Marginalized populations are often the focus of restorative justice. Indigenous peoples, racial and ethnic minorities, the poor, women, children, and others who have been systematically disadvantaged by conventional justice systems may find restorative approaches more accessible, more respectful, more effective. Restorative justice can address the harms that marginalized communities have suffered and can empower them to participate in shaping their own futures.

Accountability for human rights abuses is a critical application of restorative justice. Truth commissions, reparation programs, and community reconciliation processes have drawn on restorative principles to address massive human rights violations. These approaches cannot replace criminal prosecution for the worst offenders, but they can complement it, addressing the needs of victims and communities that prosecution alone cannot meet.

The Universal Declaration of Human Rights proclaims that "all human beings are born free and equal in dignity and rights." This affirmation of inherent human dignity is the foundation of both human rights and restorative justice. Every person, regardless of what they have done or suffered, possesses dignity that must be respected. Restorative justice embodies this respect, treating victims, offenders, and community members as persons, not cases.

The biblical doctrine of the imago Dei—that every human being is created in God's image—provides the theological foundation for this commitment to human dignity. Because we bear God's image, our worth is inherent, not earned. It cannot be erased by any action, no matter how heinous. The offender, no less than the victim, remains an image-bearer, deserving of dignity and capable of restoration. This truth undergirds the human rights focus of restorative justice.

Cross-Border Applications: Justice Without Borders

Restorative justice can cross borders in cases involving international crimes or disputes. It can facilitate reconciliation between nations and address transnational issues. In an increasingly interconnected world, the need for cross-border restorative approaches is growing.

International crimes—genocide, crimes against humanity, war crimes—often involve victims and perpetrators from different nations. Restorative principles can inform responses to these crimes, complementing international prosecutions with truth-telling, reparation, and reconciliation. The International Criminal Court has incorporated restorative elements, allowing victim participation and providing for reparations.

Transnational disputes—conflicts between nations, corporations, or groups that cross borders—can be addressed through restorative approaches. Diplomatic mediation, facilitated dialogue, and joint problem-solving can draw on restorative principles. The goal is not merely to resolve the immediate dispute but to restore relationships and build foundations for peaceful coexistence.

Cross-border restorative justice faces significant challenges. Different legal systems, cultural norms, languages, and power dynamics complicate restorative processes. Enforcement of agreements across borders may be difficult. Political considerations may override restorative goals. Yet the potential benefits—reduced conflict, improved relationships, sustainable peace—make these challenges worth addressing.

The international community has begun to develop structures for cross-border restorative justice. The United Nations and regional organizations have supported restorative initiatives in post-conflict settings. Transnational civil society networks have connected restorative practitioners across borders. International legal frameworks have incorporated restorative elements. These developments are still in early stages, but they point toward a future in which restorative justice operates across borders as well as within them.

The biblical vision of peace among nations inspires cross-border restorative justice. The prophet Micah envisioned a day when nations would "beat their swords into plowshares and their spears into pruning hooks" and "nation shall not lift up sword against nation, neither shall they learn war anymore" (Micah 4:3). This vision of international peace requires mechanisms for addressing conflicts when they arise—mechanisms that restore relationships rather than perpetuating cycles of violence. Cross-border restorative justice participates in this vision.

Victims' Rights: Global Recognition

Restorative justice supports the rights and needs of victims, which are increasingly recognized as a global concern. Initiatives like the Declaration of Basic Principles of Justice for Victims of Crime and Abuse of Power emphasize victim-centered approaches. This global recognition of victims' rights aligns with restorative justice principles.

The UN Declaration of Basic Principles of Justice for Victims, adopted by the General Assembly in 1985, articulates victims' rights to access justice, to fair treatment, to restitution, to compensation, to assistance. These rights reflect the understanding that victims are not merely witnesses to the state's case but persons deserving of respect, support, and redress. Restorative justice gives practical expression to these rights.

Victims' rights movements around the world have advocated for greater attention to victims' needs. They have pushed for victim impact statements, victim compensation programs, victim support services, and victim participation in justice processes. These advocacy efforts have created political will for restorative approaches that center victims.

Restorative justice responds to victims' rights by giving victims voice, choice, and agency. Victims can participate in processes that affect them. They can express their feelings and needs. They can shape outcomes that address their concerns. They can receive acknowledgment, apology, and restitution. They can find healing and closure. These experiences are not guaranteed in conventional justice systems; restorative justice makes them possible.

The biblical tradition consistently affirms the rights and needs of victims. God is described as one who "hears the cry of the oppressed" (Exodus 3:7), who "executes justice for the oppressed" (Psalm 146:7), who "defends the cause of the fatherless and the widow" (Deuteronomy 10:18). Jesus consistently reached out to those who were suffering—the leper, the paralytic, the bleeding woman, the grieving parent. The early church cared for widows and orphans, the most vulnerable victims of their society. This biblical witness undergirds restorative justice's commitment to victims.

Conflict Prevention: Stopping Harm Before It Occurs

Restorative justice is recognized as a tool for conflict prevention by addressing underlying issues, reducing recidivism, and fostering dialogue between groups with historical tensions. Prevention is ultimately more humane and less costly than response. Restorative justice contributes to prevention in multiple ways.

Addressing underlying issues prevents future harm. Restorative processes identify root causes of conflict—poverty, discrimination, trauma, addiction—and connect people with resources to address them. When these underlying issues are addressed, the conditions that produce harm are reduced. Prevention becomes possible.

Reducing recidivism prevents future victims. Offenders who participate in restorative justice are less likely to reoffend. Each prevented offense means one less victim, one less family traumatized, one less community disrupted. The cumulative effect of reduced recidivism is significant prevention.

Fostering dialogue between groups prevents escalation. When groups with historical tensions engage in restorative dialogue, they build understanding, reduce stereotypes, and develop relationships. These connections make it harder to dehumanize the other, easier to resolve conflicts peacefully. Prevention through dialogue is slow work, but it is essential for sustainable peace.

Building restorative cultures prevents harm at its source. When communities embrace restorative values—respect, empathy, accountability, reconciliation—they create environments in which harm is less likely to occur. Children raised in restorative families, schools, and communities internalize these values and carry them into adulthood. Prevention becomes woven into the fabric of daily life.

The biblical wisdom literature emphasizes prevention. Proverbs is filled with practical guidance for avoiding conflict, maintaining relationships, and living wisely. "A soft answer turns away wrath, but a harsh word stirs up anger" (Proverbs 15:1). "Starting a quarrel is like breaching a dam; so drop the matter before a dispute breaks out" (Proverbs 17:14). These proverbs are about prevention—avoiding harm before it occurs. Restorative justice, in its preventive dimension, embodies this wisdom.

Community Engagement: Shared Responsibility

In some regions, restorative justice is seen as a means to engage communities in addressing crime and conflicts, promoting a sense of shared responsibility for justice and healing. This community engagement is essential for sustainable justice and strong communities.

Community engagement in restorative justice takes many forms. Community members serve as volunteers in restorative programs—facilitating circles, mentoring offenders, supporting victims. Community organizations partner with restorative initiatives—providing resources, hosting meetings, connecting participants with services. Community leaders advocate for restorative approaches—speaking out for restorative justice, modeling restorative values, building political will.

Community engagement builds ownership. When communities are involved in restorative justice, they take responsibility for addressing harm and preventing its recurrence. They are not passive recipients of services provided by distant institutions but active participants in creating justice. This ownership strengthens communities and makes restorative justice sustainable.

Community engagement builds trust. When communities see restorative justice working—victims supported, offenders accountable, relationships restored—they gain confidence in the approach. This trust extends to the broader justice system, improving police-community relations, increasing cooperation with courts, and enhancing public safety.

Community engagement builds capacity. As community members gain experience with restorative processes, they develop skills they can use in other settings—families, workplaces, neighborhoods. Restorative values and practices spread through the community, creating a culture of dialogue, accountability, and reconciliation.

The early church modeled community engagement in justice. The Corinthian church was expected to resolve disputes among its members, not take them before secular courts (1 Corinthians 6:1-8). The Galatian churches were instructed to restore members caught in sin gently and humbly (Galatians 6:1). The community was responsible for justice within its fellowship. This model of community engagement continues to inspire restorative justice today.

Global Inspiration: Learning from Success

The adoption and application of restorative justice principles in various parts of the world to address local and global challenges provide inspiration for similar efforts everywhere. These examples demonstrate that restorative justice is not confined to one culture, region, or context but has universal relevance.

South Africa's Truth and Reconciliation Commission is one of the most iconic examples of restorative justice on a national scale. The TRC, chaired by Archbishop Desmond Tutu, provided a platform for victims and perpetrators of apartheid-era human rights abuses to share their stories and seek reconciliation. It did not achieve perfect justice—many perpetrators escaped accountability, many victims did not receive full reparations—but it contributed to national healing in ways that purely punitive approaches could not have achieved. The TRC has inspired truth commissions in other countries and demonstrated the potential of restorative approaches to address massive, systemic injustice.

Canada's Indigenous healing circles have gained recognition and inspired similar initiatives globally. These circles, rooted in Indigenous traditions, provide opportunities for dialogue, healing, and reconciliation, particularly in addressing historical injustices against Indigenous peoples. They have been incorporated into sentencing, corrections, and community programs, offering an alternative to conventional justice that respects Indigenous values and promotes healing.

Rwanda's Gacaca courts addressed the aftermath of the 1994 genocide through community-based justice. These courts encouraged perpetrators to confess their crimes, seek reconciliation with victims' families, and contribute to community restoration. While the Gacaca process faced enormous challenges—over a million cases, deep trauma, limited resources—it demonstrated the potential of restorative approaches even in the most extreme circumstances. It has inspired transitional justice initiatives in other post-conflict regions.

Scandinavian criminal justice systems have integrated restorative principles, focusing on rehabilitation, reconciliation, and reintegration rather than punitive measures. Norway's emphasis on humane treatment, education, and skills development in prisons has produced recidivism rates as low as twenty percent—far below those in the United States and many other countries. Sweden's restorative justice programs for young offenders have diverted many from the formal system and promoted accountability and healing. These successes have inspired criminal justice reforms around the world.

New Zealand's restorative justice practices, particularly within the youth justice system, have become a model for juvenile justice reform globally. Family group conferences bring together victims, offenders, and their families to address harm and develop plans for accountability and restoration. This approach has reduced recidivism, increased victim satisfaction, and strengthened families and communities. Other countries have looked to New Zealand's example in developing their own restorative programs.

Victims of crime support groups incorporating restorative principles have emerged in various countries. These groups offer victims opportunities to share their experiences, find support, and seek healing. They draw inspiration from the idea that victims' voices should be heard and their needs addressed. They demonstrate that restorative justice is not only about offenders but also about victims.

Community policing initiatives in some regions have adopted restorative approaches to address conflicts and build trust between law enforcement and the community. These models emphasize problem-solving, relationship-building, and community engagement rather than simply enforcement. They have inspired innovative law enforcement practices in different regions, improving police-community relations and public safety.

Interfaith peace and reconciliation initiatives in regions marked by religious or ethnic conflicts have embraced restorative justice principles. Organizations like the Sulha Peace Project in the Middle East facilitate encounters between people of different backgrounds, promoting dialogue, understanding, and reconciliation. These efforts demonstrate that restorative principles can bridge even the deepest divides.

The United Nations and international organizations have recognized the importance of restorative justice in various contexts, such as post-conflict peacebuilding and transitional justice. UN guidance on restorative justice, support for restorative initiatives, and integration of restorative principles into international frameworks have legitimized and promoted restorative approaches globally.

Numerous non-governmental organizations worldwide work to promote restorative justice principles in criminal justice, education, conflict resolution, and other areas. These organizations provide training, resources, advocacy, and networking for restorative practitioners. Their initiatives serve as global inspirations for grassroots restorative justice advocacy.

These global examples underscore the universal relevance of restorative principles in addressing a wide range of local and global challenges. They demonstrate the adaptability and effectiveness of restorative justice in various cultural, social, and political contexts. They serve as inspirations for similar efforts around the world, showing that restorative justice is not an impossible ideal but a practical reality.

The Vision for a Restorative Society

The vision for a restorative society is one where the principles of restorative justice are not merely an option but an integral way of life. It is a society that values healing over harm, understanding over judgment, and reconciliation over retribution. This vision is not utopian—it does not imagine a world without conflict or harm. But it does imagine a world in which conflict and harm are addressed in ways that heal rather than wound, restore rather than destroy, reconcile rather than divide.

In a restorative society, the default response to harm is healing. Instead of punitive measures that perpetuate cycles of violence and retribution, a restorative society prioritizes the recovery and well-being of all its members. Victims are supported, offenders are held accountable, and communities mend. Healing is not an afterthought but the primary goal.

In a restorative society, individuals are held accountable for their actions and encouraged to take responsibility for their wrongdoings. Accountability is not about punishment but about making amends and learning from one's mistakes. Offenders are given opportunities to understand the harm they have caused, to make things right, and to change. Accountability leads to transformation.

In a restorative society, empathy and understanding are the cornerstones of human interaction. People actively listen to one another, seeking to understand each other's perspectives, experiences, and needs. This understanding fosters compassion and promotes unity. Differences are not feared but engaged; conflicts are not avoided but addressed.

In a restorative society, reconciliation is the ultimate goal, even in the face of deep conflicts. Communities strive to rebuild trust through dialogue and acknowledgment of past wrongs. They understand that true reconciliation takes time but is worth the effort. Reconciliation is not about forgetting or pretending but about facing the past together and building a different future.

In a restorative society, strong emphasis is placed on preventing harm. Society invests in conflict resolution skills, education, and community-building initiatives to proactively address potential conflicts before they escalate. Prevention is recognized as more humane and less costly than response. Resources are devoted to creating conditions in which harm is less likely to occur.

In a restorative society, restorative justice is woven into the educational system, teaching the next generation the principles of healing, accountability, and reconciliation. Young minds grow up with an understanding of restorative values. They learn to resolve conflicts peacefully, to take responsibility for their actions, to empathize with others, to seek reconciliation. These values become second nature.

In a restorative society, communities play an active role in addressing conflicts and promoting healing. Neighborhoods, schools, workplaces, and faith communities are equipped with the tools and training to facilitate dialogue and reconciliation. Justice is not something done by distant institutions but something done by communities themselves.

In a restorative society, the criminal justice system undergoes a fundamental shift. Prisons are transformed into places of rehabilitation, where offenders are given opportunities for personal growth and transformation. Recidivism rates decrease significantly because offenders have been changed, not just punished. Victims are supported, and communities are strengthened.

In a restorative society, the principles of restorative justice from the Book of Romans serve as a source of inspiration not only within communities but also on a global scale. Nations come together to address international conflicts with the values of reconciliation, understanding, and healing. The same principles that guide interpersonal relationships guide international relations.

In a restorative society, diversity is embraced. Every individual is recognized as having inherent worth and dignity. Systemic inequalities are actively addressed, and oppressive structures are dismantled. The society works to ensure that all members can flourish, that no one is marginalized or excluded.

In a restorative society, restorative practices are employed in various sectors—family, schools, workplaces, international diplomacy. Conflicts are resolved with the goal of healing and preserving relationships. The same restorative principles apply whether the conflict is between two individuals or two nations.

In a restorative society, interfaith and interdisciplinary dialogues thrive. Shared values of justice, healing, and reconciliation are promoted. Collaboration across diverse faiths, disciplines, and cultures enriches the society's capacity to address complex issues. No single perspective is sufficient; many perspectives together create wisdom.

This vision for a restorative society is not a blueprint but a direction. It is not fully achievable in any finite time but is always worth pursuing. It acknowledges that transformation is a journey, requiring dedication and effort. But the potential for positive change in the lives of individuals, families, and communities is profound. It is a vision worth pursuing—one where reconciliation, understanding, and healing are at the heart of our shared human experience.

The biblical vision of shalom—peace, wholeness, flourishing—inspires this restorative society. The prophets envisioned a day when justice would roll down like waters and righteousness like an ever-flowing stream (Amos 5:24), when swords would be beaten into plowshares and nations would not learn war anymore (Isaiah 2:4), when every person would sit under their own vine and fig tree with no one to make them afraid (Micah 4:4). Jesus proclaimed the arrival of God's kingdom—a reign of justice, peace, and joy. The apostles envisioned a new heaven and a new earth, where God dwells with humanity and wipes away every tear (Revelation 21:1-4).

Restorative justice, in its global manifestations and in the vision of a restorative society, participates in this biblical vision. It is not the kingdom fully realized but a sign of the kingdom, a foretaste of what will be. It is work that matters, work that heals, work that points toward God's ultimate restoration of all things. As restorative justice continues to spread across the globe, adapted to diverse cultures and applied to diverse challenges, it bears witness to the universal relevance of restorative principles and the hope of a world made whole.

CHAPTER 15

RESTORATIVE JUSTICE IN EDUCATION

The school is a microcosm of society—a place where young people learn not only academic subjects but also how to relate to others, how to resolve conflicts, how to take responsibility for their actions, and how to become contributing members of their communities. For generations, schools have relied on punitive approaches to discipline—suspensions, expulsions, detentions—to maintain order and address misconduct. Yet these approaches have proven largely ineffective, disproportionately affecting students of color and those with disabilities, failing to teach lasting lessons, and pushing students out of school and into the criminal justice system in what has come to be known as the school-to-prison pipeline.

Restorative justice in education offers a fundamentally different approach. Rather than focusing on punishment, it focuses on repairing harm, restoring relationships, and building community. Rather than excluding students who misbehave, it seeks to reintegrate them after they have taken responsibility and made amends. Rather than treating discipline as something done to students, it treats it as something done with students, involving all affected parties in finding solutions. This approach aligns deeply with the teachings of Jesus, who consistently emphasized forgiveness, reconciliation, and the restoration of those who had gone astray.

This chapter explores the application of restorative justice in educational settings. We will examine how restorative practices address conflicts and misconduct, develop empathy and communication skills, empower students through peer mediation, build community, provide alternatives to punitive discipline, center the needs of victims, promote accountability and responsibility, reduce suspensions and expulsions, prevent bullying, create positive school climate, support reintegration, and teach life skills. Through this exploration, we will see that restorative justice in education is not merely an alternative discipline method but a comprehensive approach to forming young people in the values of respect, responsibility, and relationship that are essential for human flourishing.

The Crisis in School Discipline

To understand the significance of restorative justice in education, we must first understand the crisis in school discipline that it addresses. For decades, schools have relied on punitive, zero-tolerance approaches to discipline that have proven deeply problematic.

Zero-tolerance policies, adopted widely in the 1990s, mandated predetermined consequences—typically suspension or expulsion—for specific offenses, regardless of circumstances. These policies were intended to create safe, orderly schools by sending a clear message that misconduct would not be tolerated. Instead, they have created a host of unintended problems.

Research has consistently documented the failures of zero-tolerance discipline. Suspensions and expulsions do not make schools safer; they do not deter future misconduct; they do not teach students the skills they need to behave appropriately. Instead, they push students out of school, increasing their risk of academic failure, dropout, and involvement in the criminal justice system. Students who are suspended are more likely to repeat grades, drop out, and become involved with the juvenile justice system. The school-to-prison pipeline begins with school discipline.

Zero-tolerance discipline has also been applied disproportionately to students of color and students with disabilities. African American students are suspended at rates three to four times higher than white students, often for the same behaviors. Students with disabilities are also disproportionately disciplined. These disparities reflect and reinforce systemic racism and ableism, creating lasting harm for already marginalized students.

The punitive approach to discipline fails to address the underlying causes of misbehavior. When a student acts out, there is often a reason—trauma, family problems, mental health issues, learning difficulties, social conflict. Punishment does nothing to address these underlying issues. It simply removes the student from the learning environment, making it more likely that problems will persist or worsen.

The punitive approach also fails to teach students what they need to learn. When a student is suspended, they are removed from school, often with no alternative education provided. They miss instructional time, fall behind academically, and become further disengaged. They learn that the response to problems is exclusion, not engagement; punishment, not problem-solving. These lessons serve them poorly in future relationships and communities.

Perhaps most fundamentally, the punitive approach fails to address the harm caused by misconduct. When a student bullies another, steals from another, or damages property, the victim is left with no resolution, no acknowledgment, no repair. The focus is entirely on punishing the offender, not on addressing the needs of the one harmed. This leaves victims feeling ignored and invalidated, their wounds unaddressed.

The biblical tradition offers a different vision of discipline. The book of Proverbs speaks of the importance of training children in the way they should go (Proverbs 22:6). This training is not about punishment but about formation—shaping character, teaching wisdom, guiding toward right living. Discipline, in this sense, is about teaching, not punishing; about growth, not exclusion.

The apostle Paul writes about the purpose of discipline: "No discipline seems pleasant at the time, but painful. Later on, however, it produces a harvest of righteousness and peace for those who have been trained by it" (Hebrews 12:11). Discipline is not an end in itself but a means to an end—righteousness and peace. It looks toward the future, toward growth and transformation. This is the vision that restorative justice in education seeks to embody.

Conflict Resolution: Dialogue Instead of Punishment

Restorative justice practices are used to address conflicts, disputes, and disciplinary issues within schools. Rather than punitive measures, these processes promote dialogue and understanding. The goal is not to punish the offender but to address the harm, understand what happened, and find ways to move forward.

When a conflict arises in a restorative school, the first response is not "What punishment does this student deserve?" but "What happened, who has been harmed, and what needs to be done to make things right?" This shift in focus transforms how conflicts are addressed.

Restorative dialogue brings together those involved in the conflict. In a restorative conference, the offending student, the victim, and sometimes their supporters meet with a trained facilitator to discuss what happened. The offending student is asked to explain their actions, to listen to how they affected others, and to take responsibility. The victim is asked to describe the impact of the behavior, to express their feelings, and to say what they need to feel made whole. Together, they work out an agreement for how the harm will be repaired.

This process addresses the harm that punishment ignores. The victim receives acknowledgment and validation. The offending student gains understanding of the consequences of their actions. Both have a voice in determining the outcome. The relationship, if not fully restored, is at least addressed.

Restorative dialogue also addresses underlying issues. In the course of conversation, it often becomes clear why the offending student acted as they did—perhaps they were being bullied themselves, perhaps they were struggling with problems at home, perhaps they simply didn't understand the impact of their actions. These underlying issues can then be addressed, preventing future incidents.

The biblical tradition supports this approach to conflict resolution. Jesus taught His followers: "If your brother sins against you, go and tell him his fault between you and him alone. If he hears you, you have gained your brother" (Matthew 18:15). This is restorative dialogue—private, respectful conversation aimed at restoration. Only if this fails is the circle widened, involving others in the process.

The Apostle Paul instructed the Corinthians to address conflict within the community rather than taking disputes before secular courts (1 Corinthians 6:1-8). The community was to be the place where conflicts were resolved, where relationships were restored, where justice was done. This is restorative justice in practice.

Restorative dialogue in schools follows this biblical pattern. It addresses conflict at its source, involves those most affected, seeks understanding and repair, and aims at restoration. It is a more effective, more humane, and more educational approach to conflict than punitive discipline.

Empathy and Communication: Essential Skills for Life

Students are encouraged to develop empathy and communication skills through restorative justice practices. Restorative circles and discussions help students express themselves, listen to others, and build relationships. These skills are essential not only for school success but for life.

Empathy is the capacity to understand and share another's feelings. It is the foundation of moral development, enabling us to recognize the impact of our actions on others and to respond with compassion. Empathy is not innate but developed through experience and practice. Restorative practices provide opportunities for this development.

In restorative circles, students hear directly from those affected by their actions. A student who has bullied another hears from the victim about the fear, humiliation, and pain caused. This direct encounter is far more powerful than any abstract lesson about bullying. It develops empathy by making the other's experience real and personal.

Communication skills are also developed through restorative practices. Students learn to express themselves clearly, to articulate their feelings and needs, to listen actively to others, to ask questions for understanding, to respond respectfully even when they disagree. These skills are essential for healthy relationships, successful careers, and engaged citizenship.

Restorative circles provide structured opportunities for practicing these skills. The circle format—sitting in a circle, passing a talking piece, speaking and listening in turn—creates a safe space for expression and listening. Students learn to wait their turn, to attend to others, to speak from their own experience. These habits, practiced regularly, become second nature.

The biblical tradition places high value on empathy and communication. Jesus consistently demonstrated empathy, being "moved with compassion" by the suffering He encountered (Matthew 9:36; 14:14; 15:32). He listened deeply to those who came to Him, responding to their needs with understanding and care. He taught His followers to love their neighbors as themselves—a commandment that requires empathy, the ability to imagine oneself in another's place.

The Apostle Paul urged believers to "rejoice with those who rejoice, and weep with those who weep" (Romans 12:15)—a call to empathetic engagement with others. He encouraged speech that is "always with grace, seasoned with salt" (Colossians 4:6)—communication that builds up rather than tears down. These biblical values are embodied in restorative practices that develop empathy and communication skills.

Psychological research confirms the importance of these skills. Empathy is associated with prosocial behavior, reduced aggression, and better relationships. Communication skills are essential for academic success, career achievement, and personal fulfillment. Schools that develop these skills are preparing students not just for tests but for life.

Peer Mediation: Students as Peacemakers

Many schools implement peer mediation programs, where trained student mediators assist their peers in resolving conflicts. This approach empowers students to take an active role in addressing issues, developing leadership skills and ownership of the school community.

Peer mediation trains selected students in conflict resolution skills—active listening, neutral facilitation, problem-solving, agreement writing. These student mediators then work with their peers to address conflicts that arise—disputes between friends, disagreements in group projects, conflicts over relationships or resources. Mediation provides a structured process for resolving these conflicts constructively.

Peer mediation has multiple benefits. It resolves conflicts quickly and informally, before they escalate. It reduces the burden on teachers and administrators, freeing them for instructional tasks. It develops leadership skills in the mediators, who learn valuable abilities they will use throughout their lives. It empowers all students, who learn that they can resolve their own conflicts rather than relying on adults to solve problems for them.

Perhaps most importantly, peer mediation creates a culture of peacemaking in the school. When students see their peers successfully resolving conflicts, they learn that peaceful resolution is possible and expected. They internalize the message that conflict is not something to be avoided or escalated but something to be addressed constructively. The school becomes a community of peacemakers.

The biblical tradition supports this vision of students as peacemakers. Jesus pronounced a blessing on peacemakers, promising that they "shall be called sons of God" (Matthew 5:9). Peacemaking is not merely a skill but an identity, a way of being in the world that reflects God's own character. When students are trained as peer mediators, they are being formed as peacemakers—learning the skills and embodying the identity.

The Apostle Paul wrote to the Corinthians that God "has committed to us the word of reconciliation" (2 Corinthians 5:19). All believers are entrusted with the ministry of reconciliation, called to be agents of peace in a broken world. Peer mediation programs in schools are a practical expression of this calling, equipping young people for the work of reconciliation.

Research supports the effectiveness of peer mediation. Studies show that peer mediation programs reduce conflict, improve school climate, and develop valuable skills in student mediators. Students who participate in peer mediation, whether as mediators or as parties to conflicts, learn lessons that serve them throughout their lives.

Community Building: Circles of Trust and Respect

Restorative justice activities, such as circles, are used to build a sense of community within schools. These circles encourage trust, respect, and a feeling of belonging among students and staff. They create the relational foundation on which all learning depends.

Community building circles bring students together regularly to share experiences, express feelings, and build relationships. Unlike academic instruction, which focuses on content, circles focus on connection. Students sit in a circle, pass a talking piece, and respond to prompts that invite sharing—their hopes, their struggles, their successes, their concerns. Over time, this regular practice builds trust and understanding among students who might otherwise remain strangers.

Circles also build relationships between students and staff. When teachers participate in circles as equals—sitting in the circle, passing the talking piece, sharing from their own experience—they are seen in a different light. Students see them as human beings, not just authority figures. Trust deepens, communication improves, and the classroom becomes a community of learners.

Circles build a sense of belonging. In a large school, students can easily feel anonymous, unknown, unimportant. Circles ensure that every student is seen and heard regularly. Each student's voice matters; each student's presence is acknowledged. This sense of belonging is essential for engagement, motivation, and well-being.

Circles also build skills for community. Students learn to listen respectfully, to wait their turn, to speak honestly, to hold confidentiality. They learn that their voice matters and that others' voices matter too. These skills are essential for participation in any community—family, workplace, faith community, civic life.

The biblical tradition is rich with images of community. The early church gathered in circles—for teaching, fellowship, breaking bread, and prayer (Acts 2:42). They shared their lives with one another, bearing one another's burdens, rejoicing with one another, weeping with one another. This was not merely a collection of individuals but a community, a body, a family.

Jesus Himself gathered His disciples in a circle. At the Last Supper, they reclined around a table—a kind of circle—sharing a meal, sharing conversation, sharing themselves. He washed their feet, a act of humble service that symbolized the mutual care that should characterize community. He taught them that the greatest among them would be the servant of all (Mark 10:43-44). These are the values that restorative circles seek to embody.

Psychological research confirms the importance of belonging for student success. Students who feel connected to their school are more engaged, more motivated, and more likely to succeed academically. They have better mental health, fewer behavioral problems, and stronger relationships. Community building is not a distraction from education but an essential foundation for it.

Disciplinary Alternatives: Beyond Punishment

Restorative practices provide alternatives to traditional disciplinary actions. Students who engage in wrongdoing are encouraged to take responsibility, make amends, and learn from their actions rather than simply being punished. These alternatives address the harm caused by misconduct while keeping students engaged in learning.

Traditional discipline removes students from the learning environment through suspension or expulsion. This removal is itself harmful—students miss instruction, fall behind academically, and become disconnected from school. It does nothing to address the underlying causes of misbehavior or to repair the harm caused. It simply excludes.

Restorative alternatives keep students in school while holding them accountable. A student who has bullied another might participate in a restorative conference with the victim, hearing the impact of their actions and agreeing to make amends. A student who has vandalized property might meet with those affected and agree to repair the damage. A student who has disrupted class might work with the teacher and affected classmates to restore the learning environment.

These alternatives address the harm that punishment ignores. The victim receives acknowledgment and validation. The offending student learns from their mistakes and takes responsibility. The community is involved in finding solutions. The focus is on learning and growth, not on exclusion and punishment.

Restorative alternatives also address underlying issues. In the process of dialogue, it often becomes clear why the student acted as they did. Perhaps they are struggling with problems at home, with mental health issues, with learning difficulties. These underlying issues can then be addressed through counseling, support services, or other interventions. Prevention becomes possible.

The biblical tradition supports this approach to discipline. The prophet Ezekiel records God's words: "Do I have any pleasure at all that the wicked should die? says the Lord God, and not that he should turn from his ways and live?" (Ezekiel 18:23). God's desire is not punishment but transformation, not death but life. Restorative alternatives in schools reflect this divine desire, seeking not to punish but to restore.

Jesus' encounter with the woman caught in adultery illustrates this restorative approach. The religious leaders wanted to punish her according to the law—stoning. Jesus did not condemn her but called her to a changed life: "Go and sin no more" (John 8:11). He held her accountable while offering her a future. This is the model for restorative discipline.

Research supports the effectiveness of restorative alternatives. Schools that implement restorative practices report reductions in suspensions and expulsions, improvements in school climate, and better academic outcomes. Students who participate in restorative processes are less likely to reoffend and more likely to succeed in school. Restorative discipline works.

Victim-Centered: Honoring the Harmed

Restorative justice in education is victim-centered, focusing on the needs and perspectives of those harmed. Victims are allowed to share their experiences and influence the resolution process. This centering of victims is essential for healing and for justice.

In traditional discipline, victims are often ignored. The focus is on punishing the offender; the victim's needs are incidental. A student who has been bullied may never have the opportunity to tell their story, to express their pain, to receive acknowledgment. They are left to deal with the aftermath alone, their wounds unaddressed.

Restorative practices change this. Victims are central participants in the process. They are invited to share their experience—what happened, how it affected them, what they need to move forward. They are listened to with respect and compassion. Their needs shape the outcome—what the offender must do to make things right.

This victim-centered approach has multiple benefits. Victims feel heard and validated, which is essential for healing. They receive acknowledgment of their suffering, which counters the isolation that victimization often produces. They have a voice in determining what will happen, which restores a sense of agency and control. They are more likely to experience closure and to move forward.

The biblical tradition consistently affirms the importance of victims. God is described as one who "hears the cry of the oppressed" (Exodus 3:7), who "executes justice for the oppressed" (Psalm 146:7), who "defends the cause of the fatherless and the widow" (Deuteronomy 10:18). The prophets thunder against those who ignore the needs of the vulnerable. Jesus consistently reaches out to those who are suffering—the leper, the paralytic, the bleeding woman, the grieving parent.

The victim-centered approach of restorative justice in education embodies this biblical concern. It honors the dignity of those who have been harmed, addresses their needs, and supports their healing. It ensures that victims are not forgotten in the process of discipline.

Accountability and Responsibility: Learning from Mistakes

Offenders are held accountable for their actions and encouraged to take responsibility in restorative justice processes. This can involve actions like apologizing to the victim, performing community service, or making restitution. Accountability is not about punishment but about learning and growth.

Accountability in restorative justice means facing the consequences of one's actions—not in the sense of receiving punishment but in the sense of acknowledging harm, understanding impact, and making amends. The offending student must confront what they have done and its effects on others. This confrontation is essential for genuine change.

Responsibility means taking ownership of one's actions and their consequences. The offending student is not a passive recipient of punishment but an active participant in making things right. They must decide to apologize, to make amends, to change. This active engagement is far more likely to produce lasting change than passive acceptance of punishment.

Apology is often part of restorative accountability. A genuine apology acknowledges the specific harm caused, expresses remorse, accepts responsibility, and commits to change. Such an apology, offered freely and received genuinely, can be profoundly healing for both parties.

Restitution may also be required. A student who has stolen may need to return the property or compensate for its value. A student who has vandalized may need to repair the damage. A student who has harmed another may need to perform service that benefits the victim or the community. These actions make amends in tangible ways.

The biblical tradition emphasizes accountability and responsibility. The prophets called Israel to account for its sins, demanding acknowledgment and repentance. John the Baptist called people to "bear fruits worthy of repentance" (Luke 3:8)—actions that demonstrated genuine change. Zacchaeus, when he encountered Jesus, committed to restitution—restoring fourfold anything he had taken by fraud (Luke 19:8). Accountability and responsibility were essential to his transformation.

Psychological research confirms that accountability and responsibility are essential for change. Offenders who acknowledge their wrongdoing and make amends are less likely to reoffend. They have internalized the lessons of their experience and committed to a different path. Restorative justice in education creates conditions for this internalization.

Reduction in Suspensions and Expulsions: Keeping Students in School

Restorative justice can lead to a reduction in suspensions and expulsions by addressing the root causes of problematic behavior and promoting student understanding and growth.

Keeping students in school is essential for their academic success and future opportunities.

Suspensions and expulsions have well-documented negative effects. Students who are suspended are more likely to repeat grades, drop out, and become involved with the juvenile justice system. They fall behind academically, miss instruction, and become disengaged from school. The harms of exclusion often compound the harms that led to it.

Restorative practices reduce the need for exclusion by addressing problems at their source. When a student misbehaves, restorative processes seek to understand why—what underlying issues contributed to the behavior. These issues can then be addressed through counseling, support services, or other interventions. The student remains in school while receiving the help they need.

Restorative practices also reduce exclusion by providing alternatives. Instead of suspending a student, the school can use restorative conferences, circles, or mediation to address the harm and restore relationships. The student remains in school while being held accountable. The focus is on learning and growth, not on removal.

Research supports the effectiveness of restorative practices in reducing suspensions and expulsions. Schools that implement restorative approaches report significant reductions in exclusionary discipline. These reductions are often most pronounced for students of color and students with disabilities, groups disproportionately affected by punitive discipline. Restorative practices promote equity as well as effectiveness.

The biblical tradition values inclusion over exclusion. Jesus consistently reached out to those who were excluded—lepers, tax collectors, sinners, Samaritans, women, children. He welcomed them, ate with them, touched them, healed them. He taught that the shepherd leaves the ninety-nine to seek the one who is lost (Matthew 18:12-14). The goal is restoration, not rejection.

Restorative justice in education embodies this inclusive vision. It seeks to keep students in school, to address their needs, to support their growth. It refuses to give up on any student, believing that every student can learn and change. This commitment to inclusion reflects the heart of God.

Prevention of Bullying: Creating Safe Spaces

Restorative justice programs can be instrumental in preventing and addressing bullying. They create a safe space for victims and offenders to discuss their experiences and work toward resolution. They also address the underlying dynamics that enable bullying to occur.

Bullying is a pervasive problem in schools, with serious consequences for victims, offenders, and bystanders. Victims of bullying experience depression, anxiety, academic difficulties, and in extreme cases, suicide. Offenders are at increased risk for antisocial behavior and criminal involvement. Bystanders are affected by the climate of fear and intimidation. Traditional punitive responses to bullying—suspending or expelling the offender—often fail to address these complex dynamics.

Restorative approaches to bullying focus on understanding and repair rather than punishment. When bullying occurs, a restorative conference brings together the victim, the offender, and sometimes supporters and bystanders. The victim describes the impact of the bullying—the fear, the humiliation, the isolation. The offender is confronted with this impact and given the opportunity to take responsibility and make amends. Bystanders are asked about their role and what they might do differently in the future.

This process addresses the harm that punishment ignores. The victim receives acknowledgment and validation. The offender gains understanding of the consequences of their actions. Bystanders are challenged to become upstanders rather than passive observers. The entire community is engaged in addressing the problem.

Restorative approaches also address the underlying causes of bullying. In the course of dialogue, it often becomes clear why the offender acted as they did—perhaps they were being bullied themselves, perhaps they were struggling with problems at home, perhaps they simply didn't understand the impact of their actions. These underlying issues can then be addressed, preventing future incidents.

Restorative approaches create a school culture that discourages bullying. When students see that conflicts are addressed constructively, that victims are supported, that offenders are held accountable, that the community is engaged, they internalize these values. Bullying becomes less acceptable, less common, less tolerated.

The biblical tradition speaks strongly against bullying and for the protection of the vulnerable. The psalmist declares that God "executes justice for the oppressed" (Psalm 146:7). The prophets condemn those who "trample the head of the poor into the dust of the earth" (Amos 2:7). Jesus warns against causing "little ones" to stumble (Matthew 18:6). Restorative approaches to bullying embody this biblical concern for the vulnerable.

Research supports the effectiveness of restorative approaches in reducing bullying. Schools that implement restorative practices report decreases in bullying incidents and improvements in school climate. Students feel safer, more supported, more connected. Restorative justice works.

Positive School Climate: Foundations for Learning

Restorative justice practices contribute to a positive school climate where students, teachers, and staff feel respected, heard, and supported. This, in turn, can improve academic performance and overall well-being. School climate matters—it affects everything from attendance to achievement to mental health.

A positive school climate is characterized by respect, trust, and belonging. Students feel safe—physically, emotionally, and socially. They feel valued—their voices matter, their contributions are appreciated. They feel connected—to teachers, to peers, to the school community. These feelings are not incidental to learning; they are essential for it.

Restorative practices build positive climate by creating opportunities for connection. Regular circles help students and staff build relationships across differences. Restorative conferences address conflicts in ways that repair rather than damage relationships. Peer mediation empowers students to resolve their own disputes. These practices weave a fabric of connection that supports all members of the community.

Restorative practices also build positive climate by modeling respectful engagement. In circles, every voice is heard; every person is valued. In conferences, victims are centered; offenders are held accountable. In mediation, students learn to resolve conflicts peacefully. These practices teach by doing, embodying the values they seek to instill.

A positive school climate has documented benefits. Students in positive climates have better attendance, higher achievement, and fewer behavioral problems. They have better mental health and stronger relationships. Teachers in positive climates have higher job satisfaction and lower turnover. The entire community benefits.

The biblical vision of shalom includes the flourishing of all members of the community. Shalom is not merely the absence of conflict but the presence of right relationship—respect, trust, mutual care. It is the condition in which every person can flourish, can reach their full potential, can live in peace. A positive school climate is a small embodiment of shalom.

Jesus came that His followers might have life and have it abundantly (John 10:10). This abundant life includes the conditions for flourishing—safety, belonging, respect, support. Restorative justice in education, in building positive school climate, participates in Jesus' mission of abundant life.

Reintegration: Welcoming Back

Restorative justice helps reintegrate students who have been involved in wrongdoing back into the school community, promoting growth and learning from their mistakes. Reintegration is essential for preventing recidivism and for maintaining community.

When a student is suspended or expelled, they are removed from the school community. This removal severs relationships, disrupts learning, and creates distance between the student and the school. When the student returns, they often return to the same conditions that contributed to their misbehavior, with no support for change and no welcome from the community.

Restorative reintegration is different. Before the student returns, restorative processes address the harm that was caused. The student has taken responsibility, made amends, and committed to change. The victim has been heard and has had a voice in the outcome. The community has been involved in finding solutions. When the student returns, they return to a community that has been prepared to welcome them.

Reintegration may include a welcoming circle, where the returning student is welcomed back by teachers and peers. The circle may include expressions of support, commitments to help, and hopes for the future. The student is reminded that they are valued, that they belong, that the community believes in their ability to change.

Reintegration also includes ongoing support. The returning student may need mentoring, counseling, academic support, or other assistance to succeed. Restorative processes often include plans for this support, ensuring that the student has what they need to stay on track.

The biblical tradition emphasizes restoration and reintegration. The prodigal son, after his time away, was welcomed home with open arms (Luke 15:11-32). His father did not hold his mistakes against him but celebrated his return. He was restored to full membership in the family. This is the model for reintegration.

The Apostle Paul, writing to the Galatians, instructs: "Brethren, if a man is overtaken in any trespass, you who are spiritual restore such a one in a spirit of gentleness" (Galatians 6:1). Restoration, not exclusion, is the goal. And restoration is to be done gently, with care for the one being restored. This is the spirit of restorative reintegration.

Research supports the importance of reintegration for reducing recidivism. Students who are welcomed back and supported are less likely to reoffend. They have a stake in the community, relationships that matter, hope for the future. Reintegration works.

Life Skills: Preparing for the Future

Restorative practices teach life skills such as conflict resolution, effective communication, and empathy, which are valuable not only in school but also in students' future lives. These skills are essential for success in relationships, careers, and communities.

Conflict resolution skills are needed throughout life. In families, conflicts arise between spouses, between parents and children, between siblings. In workplaces, conflicts arise with colleagues, with supervisors, with customers. In communities, conflicts arise with neighbors, with service providers, with officials. Students who learn to resolve conflicts constructively are prepared for these challenges.

Communication skills are equally essential. The ability to express oneself clearly, to listen actively, to ask questions for understanding, to respond respectfully—these skills are needed in every sphere of life. Students who develop these skills through restorative practices carry them into their futures.

Empathy—the capacity to understand and share another's feelings—is perhaps the most fundamental life skill. Empathy enables us to form deep relationships, to respond compassionately to suffering, to navigate social situations with sensitivity. Students who develop empathy through restorative practices are prepared for lives of connection and care.

Restorative practices teach these skills through experience, not just instruction. Students do not just learn about conflict resolution; they practice it in real situations. They do not just hear about empathy; they experience it in circles and conferences. This experiential learning is deep and lasting.

The biblical tradition values wisdom—the practical knowledge of how to live well. The book of Proverbs is filled with instruction on how to navigate relationships, resolve conflicts, speak wisely, and act with integrity. This wisdom is for all of life, not just for religious contexts. Restorative practices in education impart this wisdom.

Jesus taught His followers to be "wise as serpents and innocent as doves" (Matthew 10:16)—combining practical wisdom with moral purity. Restorative practices develop this combination, teaching students to navigate conflicts wisely while maintaining integrity and compassion.

Research confirms that these skills are valuable for life success. Employers consistently rank communication, teamwork, and emotional intelligence among the most sought-after qualities in employees. Happy relationships depend on these skills. Engaged citizenship requires them. Restorative practices in education prepare students for lives of flourishing.

As we consider restorative justice in education, we see that it embodies the principles of the Jesus Paradigm. Its focus on conflict resolution reflects Jesus' teaching on peacemaking. Its emphasis on empathy and communication reflects Jesus' compassionate engagement with others. Its use of peer mediation empowers students to be peacemakers in their own communities. Its community-building circles create the kind of belonging that Jesus offered to all who came to Him. Its disciplinary alternatives reflect Jesus' call to repentance and transformation rather than condemnation. Its victim-centered approach honors the dignity of those who have been harmed, as Jesus always did. Its accountability and responsibility requirements embody Jesus' expectation that those who receive grace will bear fruit. Its reduction in suspensions and expulsions reflects Jesus' commitment to inclusion over exclusion. Its prevention of bullying protects the vulnerable, as Jesus always did. Its positive school climate creates conditions for flourishing, as Jesus promised abundant life. Its reintegration of offenders welcomes back the lost, as the father welcomed the prodigal. Its teaching of life skills prepares students for lives of wisdom, as Jesus taught His disciples.

Restorative justice in education is not merely an alternative discipline method but a comprehensive approach to forming young people in the values of the kingdom of God. It teaches them to be peacemakers, to love their neighbors, to forgive as they have been forgiven, to seek reconciliation, to build community. It prepares them not only for academic success but for lives of meaning, purpose, and relationship.

The Gospel of Restorative Justice in education is this: that every student matters, that every student can learn and change, that every student deserves to be part of a community where they are known, valued, and supported. It is a vision of schools as communities of shalom—places of peace, wholeness, and flourishing for all.

As restorative justice continues to spread in schools around the world, it bears witness to this gospel. It demonstrates that another way is possible—a way of healing rather than hurting, of restoration rather than exclusion, of love rather than punishment. It offers hope to students, teachers, and communities that the values of the kingdom can be embodied even in the challenging context of schools. And it prepares the next generation to carry these values into every sphere of life—families, workplaces, communities, and the world.

CHAPTER 16

RESTORATIVE JUSTICE IN FAMILY RELATIONSHIPS

The family is the first school of love, the primary context in which we learn to relate to others, to navigate conflict, to give and receive forgiveness, and to build the trust that sustains human community. It is within families that we first experience the joys of belonging and the pains of betrayal, the warmth of acceptance and the chill of rejection, the security of unconditional love and the vulnerability of being deeply known. When families function well, they provide the foundation for healthy individuals and thriving communities. When families are fractured by conflict, harm, and broken trust, the wounds can last a lifetime and ripple outward to affect every other relationship.

Restorative justice principles and practices offer powerful tools for addressing conflicts, healing emotional wounds, and rebuilding trust within families. These approaches, grounded in the teachings of Jesus and aligned with the deepest insights of psychology, philosophy, and theology, provide a path toward reconciliation and restoration that punitive or avoidant responses cannot achieve. This chapter explores the application of restorative justice in family and relationship contexts, examining how it can transform conflict into opportunity, harm into healing, and brokenness into renewed connection.

The Family as the Crucible of Relationship

The family is the fundamental unit of human society, the place where we first learn who we are and how to be with others. It is in families that we develop our capacity for attachment and trust, our understanding of boundaries and expectations, our patterns of communication and conflict resolution. The quality of family relationships shapes our mental health, our ability to form healthy relationships outside the family, and our sense of identity and worth.

Yet families are also places of profound vulnerability. Because we are deeply invested in these relationships, the harms that occur within them can be devastating. A parent's neglect, a sibling's betrayal, a spouse's infidelity, a child's rebellion—these wounds cut to the heart of who we are and what we most deeply need. The closer the relationship, the more painful the harm.

Traditional responses to family conflict often fail. Avoidance allows wounds to fester. Blame escalates conflict. Punitive responses deepen divisions. Legal intervention can be costly, adversarial, and damaging to relationships. Families need approaches that address harm while preserving relationship, that hold accountable while offering hope for restoration.

Restorative justice offers such approaches. Rooted in ancient wisdom and supported by contemporary research, restorative practices provide families with tools for addressing conflict constructively, healing emotional wounds, and rebuilding trust. These practices honor the complexity of family relationships while offering structured pathways toward resolution.

The biblical tradition is rich with stories of family conflict and restoration. The narrative of Joseph and his brothers (Genesis 37-50) depicts betrayal, loss, and ultimate reconciliation. Jacob's favoritism toward Joseph creates resentment among his brothers, leading them to sell Joseph into slavery. Years later, when Joseph has risen to power in Egypt and his brothers come seeking food during a famine, Joseph has the opportunity for revenge. Instead, he tests them, observes their growth, and ultimately reveals himself with tears and forgiveness. The family is restored, and Joseph declares that God used their evil for good (Genesis 50:20).

The parable of the prodigal son (Luke 15:11-32) portrays a family torn apart by a younger son's rebellion and an older son's resentment. The father's response to both sons—running to embrace the returning prodigal, going out to plead with the angry elder—models restorative love. He does not minimize the harm but welcomes repentance and extends grace. The family's restoration is possible because the father refuses to let brokenness have the final word.

These biblical narratives illuminate both the depths of family conflict and the possibilities of family restoration. They remind us that families are places where great harm can occur but also where great healing can happen. Restorative justice in families participates in this biblical vision, seeking to mend what is broken and restore what is lost.

Conflict Resolution: A Structured Approach to Family Disputes

Restorative justice offers a structured approach for resolving conflicts within families and relationships. This process encourages open communication, empathy, and understanding between parties. Unlike adversarial approaches that seek to determine who is right and who is wrong, restorative approaches seek to understand what happened, acknowledge the harm, and find ways to move forward.

Family conflicts can arise from many sources—differences in values or expectations, competition for resources or attention, misunderstandings or miscommunications, betrayals of trust or violations of boundaries. These conflicts, if unresolved, can poison relationships, create lasting resentments, and fracture family unity.

Restorative conflict resolution brings family members together in a structured setting to address the conflict constructively. A trained facilitator—perhaps a family therapist, a clergy member, or a trusted family friend—guides the conversation, ensuring that each person has the opportunity to speak and be heard. The focus is not on assigning blame but on understanding each person's experience, the impact of the conflict, and what is needed to move forward.

This structured approach has several benefits. It ensures that all voices are heard, including those that might otherwise be silenced. It creates safety for honest expression, reducing the risk that emotions will escalate into harmful words or actions. It keeps the focus on understanding and resolution rather than on winning and losing. It provides a framework for developing agreements that address the needs of all parties.

The process typically includes several stages. Preparation involves meeting with each party individually to explain the process, assess readiness, and identify concerns. The meeting itself includes opportunities for each person to share their perspective, to express feelings, to ask questions, and to hear others. Agreement development involves identifying what is needed to repair harm and restore relationship. Follow-up ensures that agreements are implemented and that ongoing support is available.

The biblical tradition offers examples of structured conflict resolution. When conflict arose between Paul and Barnabas over whether to take John Mark on their missionary journey, they "had such a sharp disagreement that they parted company" (Acts 15:39). While this particular conflict was not resolved restoratively, the early church elsewhere practiced structured approaches to conflict, as in the council at Jerusalem (Acts 15) where leaders gathered to discern together how to address a dispute threatening the unity of the church.

Jesus' teaching in Matthew 18 provides a framework for conflict resolution: "If your brother sins against you, go and tell him his fault between you and him alone. If he hears you, you have gained your brother. But if he will not hear, take with you one or two more, that by the mouth of two or three witnesses every word may be established. If he refuses to hear them, tell it to the church" (Matthew 18:15-17). This graduated approach—private conversation, small group involvement, community engagement—provides a structure for addressing conflict that keeps restoration as the goal at every step.

Psychological research confirms the importance of structured approaches to conflict resolution. Unstructured conflict conversations often escalate as emotions rise and communication breaks down. Structure provides containment, ensuring that the conversation remains productive rather than destructive. Facilitation provides guidance, helping parties navigate difficult emotions and communication challenges.

Dialogue and Communication: The Heart of Restorative Process

Restorative justice practices promote healthy dialogue and communication within families. Family members or partners have the opportunity to express their feelings, listen to each other, and find common ground. This dialogue is essential for understanding, for healing, and for rebuilding relationship.

Healthy communication is difficult, especially in the context of conflict. When emotions are high, we often speak without thinking, say things we regret, or shut down entirely. We may assume we know what the other person thinks or feels, without checking our assumptions. We may become defensive, blaming, or withdrawing. These patterns escalate conflict rather than resolving it.

Restorative dialogue creates conditions for healthy communication. The structured format ensures that each person has uninterrupted time to speak. The presence of a facilitator helps manage emotions and keep communication constructive. The focus on understanding rather than winning encourages genuine listening. The opportunity to ask questions and receive answers addresses the uncertainties that often fuel conflict.

In restorative dialogue, participants are encouraged to speak from their own experience using "I" statements—"I felt hurt when..." rather than "You always..." This ownership of one's own experience reduces blame and invites understanding. Participants are also encouraged to listen actively—to hear not only the words but the feelings and needs behind them, to reflect back what they have heard to ensure understanding.

This dialogue can be transformative. Family members who have been estranged for years may come to understand each other in new ways. Long-held resentments may begin to dissolve as each person's experience is acknowledged. Patterns of miscommunication may be identified and addressed. Common ground—shared values, mutual care, hopes for the future—may be rediscovered.

The biblical tradition places high value on honest, loving communication. The book of Proverbs is filled with wisdom about speech: "A soft answer turns away wrath, but a harsh word stirs up anger" (Proverbs 15:1). "The heart of the wise makes his speech prudent" (Proverbs 16:23). "Let another praise you, and not your own mouth" (Proverbs 27:2). These proverbs recognize the power of words to wound or to heal, to divide or to unite.

The Apostle Paul exhorts believers to speak the truth in love (Ephesians 4:15)—combining honesty with compassion, directness with care. He warns against unwholesome talk and encourages speech that builds up and gives grace to those who hear (Ephesians 4:29). These principles guide restorative dialogue, which seeks to combine truth-telling with love, honesty with care.

Psychological research confirms the importance of communication patterns for relationship health. Couples and families with healthy communication—who express feelings constructively, listen actively, and resolve conflicts collaboratively—report higher satisfaction and stronger relationships. Communication skills can be learned and practiced, and restorative dialogue provides a context for this learning.

Rebuilding Trust: The Slow Work of Restoration

In cases of betrayal or harm within a family or relationship, restorative justice can be a tool for rebuilding trust. Offenders can acknowledge their wrongdoing and work toward making amends. Trust, once broken, is not easily restored, but restorative processes provide a pathway.

Trust is the foundation of healthy relationships. It is the confidence that we can rely on others, that they will act in ways that respect and care for us, that they will keep their commitments and honor their promises. When trust is broken—through infidelity, deception, betrayal, abuse—the relationship is deeply wounded. The wounded party may feel unsafe, uncertain, and unable to rely on the one who harmed them.

Rebuilding trust requires several elements. The offending party must acknowledge the harm they have caused, without minimizing or excusing it. They must express genuine remorse, communicating that they understand the impact of their actions and are truly sorry. They must make amends, taking concrete steps to repair the damage. They must demonstrate changed behavior over time, showing through consistent actions that they can be trusted. And they must be patient, recognizing that trust is rebuilt slowly and that the wounded party needs time to heal.

Restorative processes provide a framework for this rebuilding. In a restorative meeting, the offending party can acknowledge the harm directly, hear from the wounded party about its impact, and commit to specific actions for making amends. Follow-up meetings can provide accountability and support for changed behavior. The process itself demonstrates commitment to restoration.

Rebuilding trust is not guaranteed. Some relationships may not survive the harm done. Some wounded parties may not be able to trust again. Some offending parties may not be willing to do the work required. But restorative processes create the best possible conditions for trust to be rebuilt, honoring the agency of all parties and supporting them in the difficult work of restoration.

The biblical tradition includes powerful stories of trust rebuilt. The relationship between God and Israel, repeatedly broken by Israel's unfaithfulness, is repeatedly restored through God's faithfulness. The prophet Hosea's marriage to Gomer, a woman who was unfaithful, becomes a metaphor for God's relationship with unfaithful Israel—a love that refuses to let go, that pursues even in the face of betrayal, that offers restoration again and again.

Peter's relationship with Jesus after his denial illustrates trust rebuilt. Peter, who had sworn he would never deny Jesus, did so three times on the night of Jesus' arrest. After the resurrection, Jesus sought Peter out and gave him three opportunities to affirm his love—one for each denial (John 21:15-19). Jesus entrusted Peter with the care of His sheep, demonstrating that trust could be restored. Peter went on to become the leader of the early church.

Psychological research on trust repair identifies several key factors. Acknowledgment of wrongdoing is essential; denial or minimization prevents repair. Remorse must be genuine; perfunctory apologies are ineffective. Amends must be proportionate to the harm; symbolic gestures are insufficient for serious wounds. Changed behavior must be sustained over time; trust is rebuilt through consistent actions, not momentary promises. Restorative processes address each of these factors.

Accountability and Responsibility: Owning Our Actions

Restorative justice encourages individuals to take responsibility for their actions. This can involve acknowledging the harm caused and taking steps to rectify it. Accountability is not about shame or punishment but about ownership and repair.

In families, accountability is often difficult. We may be tempted to minimize our actions, to make excuses, to blame others, to deny responsibility. These defenses protect our egos but prevent healing. They leave the harm unaddressed and the relationship damaged.

Restorative accountability requires us to face what we have done honestly. We must acknowledge the specific actions that caused harm, without minimizing or justifying. We must recognize the impact of those actions on others, listening to their experience without defensiveness. We must take ownership of our choices, accepting that we are responsible for what we did.

This accountability is not about wallowing in guilt or shame. It is about clearing the ground for repair. When we have acknowledged our wrongdoing, we can then take steps to make it right. We can apologize genuinely, expressing remorse for the harm we caused. We can make amends, taking concrete actions to repair the damage. We can commit to change, working to ensure that we do not cause similar harm in the future.

Restorative processes support this accountability. In a restorative meeting, we are invited to speak honestly about what we did, to listen to those we harmed, and to work with them to determine what will make things right. The process is structured to support accountability while also offering the possibility of forgiveness and restoration.

The biblical tradition emphasizes accountability. The prophets called Israel to account for its sins, demanding acknowledgment and repentance. John the Baptist called people to "bear fruits worthy of repentance" (Luke 3:8)—actions demonstrating genuine change. Zacchaeus, when he encountered Jesus, committed to restitution, restoring fourfold anything he had taken by fraud (Luke 19:8). Accountability was essential to his transformation.

David's response to Nathan's confrontation models accountability. When Nathan said, "You are the man!"—exposing David's sin with Bathsheba and against Uriah David did not deny or defend. He said simply, "I have sinned against the Lord" (2 Samuel 12:13). This acknowledgment opened the door to forgiveness and restoration. His subsequent psalm of repentance (Psalm 51) expresses the depth of his remorse and his commitment to change.

Psychological research confirms that accountability is essential for repair. When offenders take responsibility, victims are more likely to forgive and to experience closure. When offenders make amends, the tangible repair contributes to healing. When offenders change, relationships can be rebuilt. Accountability is not opposed to restoration but essential to it.

Apology and Forgiveness: The Healing Exchange

Apologies are a central part of restorative justice. Offenders may offer sincere apologies, and victims are given the opportunity to forgive. This exchange can be deeply healing, allowing both parties to let go of anger and resentment and to move forward.

A genuine apology is more than saying "I'm sorry." It involves several elements: acknowledgment of the specific harm caused, expression of genuine remorse, acceptance of responsibility, commitment to change, and offer of repair. A sincere apology names what was done, communicates understanding of its impact, expresses regret, and promises different behavior in the future.

Receiving an apology can be transformative for the wounded party. It validates their experience, confirming that the harm they suffered was real and recognized. It communicates that the offending party understands the impact of their actions and is genuinely sorry. It opens the door to forgiveness, making it possible to release resentment and begin healing.

Forgiveness is the wounded party's response to apology. Forgiveness is not forgetting, excusing, or condoning. It is not reconciliation, which requires the offending party's participation. Forgiveness is the decision to release the offending party from the debt of guilt, to let go of resentment, to relinquish the right to revenge. It is an act of grace that benefits the forgiver as much as the forgiven.

When victims forgive, they are not doing the offender a favor; they are freeing themselves. Research demonstrates that forgiveness reduces depression, anxiety, and anger; improves physical health; enhances relationships; and promotes overall well-being. Forgiveness breaks the cycle of rumination that keeps victims trapped in the past, allowing them to move forward.

The biblical tradition is rich with teaching on apology and forgiveness. Jesus taught His disciples to pray, "Forgive us our debts, as we forgive our debtors" (Matthew 6:12), linking divine and human forgiveness. He taught that forgiveness must be limitless—"seventy times seven" (Matthew 18:22). He illustrated this teaching with the parable of the unforgiving servant, who received forgiveness but refused to extend it, and was condemned for his hardheartedness.

On the cross, Jesus modeled ultimate forgiveness: "Father, forgive them, for they do not know what they do" (Luke 23:34). This forgiveness was extended to those who were actively crucifying Him—soldiers who nailed His hands, religious leaders who mocked Him, crowds who shouted for His death. It was forgiveness without condition, without waiting for repentance, without requiring acknowledgment. It was the purest expression of divine mercy.

Psychological research confirms the healing power of apology and forgiveness. Apologies reduce anger and promote reconciliation. Forgiveness reduces stress and improves mental health. The combination—genuine apology met with genuine forgiveness—can transform relationships and promote profound healing.

Restorative justice in families creates conditions in which apology and forgiveness can occur. It does not force them; they cannot be forced. But it brings family members together in settings where genuine encounter is possible. It provides support and facilitation that make these exchanges more likely. And it honors the choices that participants make, whether to apologize, to forgive, or not.

Family Meetings: Gathering for Healing

Restorative justice may involve family meetings or conferences where all members come together to discuss issues, reach resolutions, and work on healing relationships. These meetings provide a structured context for addressing family conflicts and promoting restoration.

Family meetings bring together all those affected by a conflict or harm—parents, children, siblings, extended family members, and sometimes others who are close to the family. A facilitator guides the meeting, ensuring that each person has the opportunity to speak and be heard. The focus is on understanding what happened, the impact on each person, and what is needed to move forward.

Family meetings can be used for a wide range of situations. They can address conflicts between parents and adolescents, disputes among siblings, issues related to separation or divorce, concerns about care for aging parents, or harm caused by one family member to another. They can also be used proactively, bringing families together to discuss values, expectations, and plans before conflicts arise.

The family meeting format has several advantages. It brings all voices to the table, ensuring that everyone's perspective is considered. It creates a safe space for honest communication, with the facilitator managing the process. It keeps the focus on understanding and resolution rather than on blame and punishment. It involves the whole family in developing solutions, increasing ownership and commitment.

Family meetings also honor the family's own wisdom and resources. The facilitator does not impose solutions but helps the family develop its own. The family knows its own dynamics, its own history, its own possibilities better than any outsider. The meeting taps into this knowledge, empowering the family to find its own way forward.

The biblical tradition includes examples of family gatherings for important purposes. The Passover meal brought families together to remember God's deliverance and to pass faith from one generation to the next (Exodus 12). The early church met in homes, gathering for teaching, fellowship, and prayer (Acts 2:46). These gatherings created space for relationship, for sharing, for mutual support.

Psychological research supports the effectiveness of family meetings. Structured family conversations can improve communication, resolve conflicts, and strengthen relationships. Involving all family members in decision-making increases commitment to outcomes. Regular family meetings can prevent conflicts by addressing issues before they escalate.

Victim-Centered: Honoring the Wounded

Restorative justice places the needs and experiences of victims at the forefront. It allows victims to have a voice, express their emotions, and actively participate in the resolution process. This victim-centered approach is essential for healing and for justice.

In family conflicts, victims are often overlooked. The focus may be on the conflict itself, on the behavior of the offending party, on maintaining family harmony, or on getting through a difficult situation. The victim's pain may be minimized, ignored, or even blamed. This neglect compounds the original harm, leaving victims feeling unseen, unheard, and uncared for.

A victim-centered approach changes this. The victim is invited to share their experience—what happened, how it affected them, what they have suffered. They are listened to with respect and compassion. Their feelings are validated, their pain acknowledged. They are asked what they need to heal, what would make things right. Their needs shape the outcome.

This victim-centered approach has multiple benefits. Victims feel heard and validated, which is essential for healing. They receive acknowledgment of their suffering, which counters the isolation that victimization often produces. They have a voice in determining what will happen, which restores a sense of agency and control. They are more likely to experience closure and to move forward.

The biblical tradition consistently affirms the importance of victims. God is described as one who "hears the cry of the oppressed" (Exodus 3:7), who "executes justice for the oppressed" (Psalm 146:7), who "defends the cause of the fatherless and the widow" (Deuteronomy 10:18). The prophets thunder against those who ignore the needs of the vulnerable. Jesus consistently reaches out to those who are suffering—the leper, the paralytic, the bleeding woman, the grieving parent.

The victim-centered approach of restorative justice in families embodies this biblical concern. It honors the dignity of those who have been harmed, addresses their needs, and supports their healing. It ensures that victims are not forgotten in the process of family restoration.

Long-Term Healing: Beyond Immediate Resolution

The focus of restorative justice in families is not merely on addressing immediate conflicts but on promoting long-term healing and understanding within families and relationships. Healing takes time; restoration is a journey, not an event.

Immediate resolution of a conflict is important, but it is not enough. The wounds that caused the conflict, and that the conflict created, may run deep. Patterns of communication and behavior that contributed to the conflict may be entrenched. Trust, once broken, takes time to rebuild. Long-term healing requires ongoing attention and care.

Restorative processes support long-term healing in several ways. They create agreements that address not only the immediate conflict but also underlying issues. They establish follow-up mechanisms to ensure that agreements are implemented and to provide ongoing support. They build skills—communication, conflict resolution, empathy—that families can use in future situations. They strengthen relationships, making families more resilient in the face of future challenges.

Long-term healing also requires patience. Families may experience setbacks, relapses into old patterns, new conflicts arising from unresolved issues. Healing is not linear; it involves two steps forward, one step back. Restorative approaches honor this reality, providing ongoing support rather than expecting quick fixes.

The biblical narrative is filled with stories of long-term healing. The people of Israel spent forty years in the wilderness, learning to trust God, before entering the promised land. Peter, despite his denial, was restored and went on to become a leader of the early church—but his restoration took time and involved multiple encounters with the risen Christ. The prodigal son's return was celebrated immediately, but the full restoration of family relationships, including the healing of the older brother's resentment, took longer.

Psychological research confirms that healing takes time. Trauma recovery is a process that unfolds over months and years. Relationship repair requires sustained effort and ongoing attention. Quick fixes are rarely lasting; deep healing requires deep work. Restorative justice in families honors this reality, committing to the long-term journey of restoration.

Prevention: Addressing Root Causes

Restorative justice practices can help prevent further harm by addressing the root causes of conflicts, reducing tension, and improving communication. Prevention is ultimately more humane and less costly than response. Restorative approaches contribute to prevention in multiple ways.

Addressing root causes prevents future conflicts. When families understand why conflicts arise—underlying needs, patterns of communication, unresolved issues from the past—they can address these causes rather than just managing symptoms. A family that learns to communicate more effectively will have fewer misunderstandings. A family that addresses the needs of all members will have less competition and resentment. A family that heals old wounds will be less likely to repeat old patterns.

Reducing tension prevents escalation. Families that practice restorative approaches learn to address conflicts early, before they escalate into major crises. They develop skills for managing emotions, for communicating concerns, for finding solutions. These skills prevent small disagreements from becoming large conflicts.

Improving communication prevents misunderstandings. Many family conflicts arise from miscommunication—words misinterpreted, intentions misunderstood, feelings unexpressed. Restorative practices teach families to communicate more clearly, to listen more deeply, to check understanding. Better communication prevents conflicts that arise from misunderstanding.

Building strong relationships prevents harm. Families with strong bonds of trust, respect, and care are less likely to harm each other. When relationships are healthy, members are more considerate, more forgiving, more committed to each other's well-being. Restorative practices strengthen these bonds, creating relationships that are resilient in the face of challenge.

The wisdom literature of the Bible emphasizes prevention. Proverbs is filled with practical guidance for avoiding conflict, maintaining relationships, and living wisely. "A prudent man foresees evil and hides himself, but the simple pass on and are punished" (Proverbs 22:3). Foresight—anticipating problems and taking preventive action—is a mark of wisdom. Restorative justice, in its preventive dimension, embodies this wisdom.

Empathy and Understanding: Transformative Connection

Participants in restorative processes are encouraged to develop empathy and understanding for each other's perspectives, which can be transformative in rebuilding relationships. Empathy—the capacity to understand and share another's feelings—is essential for healing and for connection.

Empathy allows us to see beyond our own experience to the experience of others. In the context of family conflict, empathy enables us to understand why the other person acted as they did, to feel the impact of our actions on them, to appreciate their needs and concerns. This understanding softens judgment, reduces anger, and opens the door to reconciliation.

Restorative processes cultivate empathy through direct encounter. When a family member hears another describe the pain they have caused, they cannot remain untouched. The abstract awareness that they have hurt someone becomes concrete, personal, real. This encounter can be transformative, breaking through defenses and awakening genuine remorse and compassion.

Empathy also benefits the wounded party. When an offending family member demonstrates understanding of the harm they caused, the victim feels validated and seen. The isolation of suffering is broken; someone else now shares the burden. This empathy can be profoundly healing, reducing feelings of anger and opening space for forgiveness.

The biblical tradition emphasizes empathy as a divine attribute and human calling. God is described as compassionate, merciful, and empathetic—entering into human suffering, sharing human grief, responding to human need. Jesus consistently demonstrated empathy, being "moved with compassion" by the suffering He encountered (Matthew 9:36; 14:14; 15:32). He calls

His followers to love their neighbors as themselves—a commandment that requires empathy, the ability to imagine oneself in another's place.

The Apostle Paul urges believers to "rejoice with those who rejoice, and weep with those who weep" (Romans 12:15)—a call to empathetic engagement with others. This empathy is not merely emotional but active, leading to mutual care and support. It is the foundation of Christian community and the heart of restorative relationship.

Psychological research confirms the power of empathy. Empathy reduces aggression, promotes prosocial behavior, and strengthens relationships. Empathy can be cultivated through practice, and restorative processes provide opportunities for this cultivation. Families that practice empathy are stronger, more resilient, more connected.

Resolution of Family Disputes: Wide Applications

In family settings, restorative justice can be used to address a wide range of disputes, including conflicts between parents and children, sibling rivalry, and issues related to inheritance or family property. The principles and practices of restorative justice are adaptable to diverse family situations.

Conflicts between parents and children are among the most common and challenging family disputes. Adolescents seeking autonomy clash with parents seeking to protect. Adult children making life choices conflict with parents holding different values. Aging parents needing care create tensions among siblings about responsibility. Restorative approaches bring all parties together to understand each other's perspectives and find mutually acceptable solutions.

Sibling rivalry is another fertile ground for restorative practice. Competition for parental attention, jealousy over perceived favoritism, conflicts over shared resources, and long-standing resentments can poison sibling relationships for decades. Restorative processes provide a structured context for addressing these issues, allowing siblings to express feelings, understand each other, and work toward reconciliation.

Inheritance and family property disputes can tear families apart. When parents die without clear plans, or when their plans are contested, siblings may find themselves in bitter legal battles that destroy relationships. Restorative approaches offer an alternative—a way for families to address these issues collaboratively, honoring the wishes of the deceased and the needs of the living, preserving rather than destroying family relationships.

Family businesses present unique challenges. Conflicts over leadership, strategy, compensation, and succession can threaten both the business and the family. Restorative practices bring family members together to address these conflicts constructively, finding solutions that honor both family relationships and business needs.

Blended families face complex dynamics as step-parents, step-siblings, and half-siblings navigate new relationships. Restorative approaches can help these families address conflicts, build trust, and develop healthy patterns of interaction.

The biblical tradition addresses many of these family situations. The stories of Jacob and Esau, Joseph and his brothers, David and his children, and the prodigal son and his brother all depict family conflicts and their resolution. These narratives offer wisdom for families navigating similar challenges today.

Couples Therapy: Restorative Principles in Practice

Restorative justice principles are integrated into couples therapy and relationship counseling to facilitate healthy conflict resolution and relationship repair. These approaches draw on restorative values—dialogue, accountability, empathy, forgiveness, restoration—to help couples heal and strengthen their relationships.

Couples face many challenges—communication difficulties, conflicts over values or priorities, betrayals of trust, growing apart over time, external stressors affecting the relationship. Traditional couples therapy addresses these challenges through various therapeutic approaches. Restorative principles enhance these approaches by providing a framework for addressing harm, accountability, and repair.

In restorative couples work, each partner is given the opportunity to express their experience—their feelings, their needs, their concerns. The therapist facilitates this dialogue, ensuring that each person is heard and that communication remains constructive. Partners are encouraged to take responsibility for their part in the relationship's difficulties, to acknowledge the harm they may have caused, and to commit to change.

Apology and forgiveness are central to restorative couples work. When one partner has harmed the other—through infidelity, deception, neglect, or abuse—a genuine apology is essential for healing. The therapist helps the offending partner craft an apology that acknowledges the specific harm, expresses genuine remorse, and commits to changed behavior. The wounded partner is supported in deciding whether and when to forgive.

Restorative agreements may be developed to address specific issues. These agreements might include commitments to changed behavior, plans for rebuilding trust, arrangements for addressing conflicts constructively in the future. Follow-up sessions provide accountability and support.

The biblical vision of marriage as a covenant relationship—faithful, committed, life-giving—provides a theological foundation for restorative couples work. The prophet Hosea's marriage to Gomer, despite her unfaithfulness, becomes a metaphor for God's faithful love for unfaithful Israel—a love that refuses to let go, that pursues even in the face of betrayal, that offers restoration again and again. This vision inspires couples to persevere in the hard work of relationship repair.

Psychological research supports the effectiveness of approaches that incorporate restorative elements. Couples therapy that addresses accountability, facilitates genuine apology, and supports forgiveness shows strong outcomes. Relationships can be healed, trust can be rebuilt, and couples can emerge stronger from the challenges they have faced.

Child Welfare: Protecting the Vulnerable

Restorative justice practices can be used in child welfare cases to address issues related to neglect, abuse, or parental disputes, with a focus on ensuring the child's well-being. These approaches prioritize the safety and welfare of children while seeking to address the underlying issues that have led to harm.

Child welfare cases are among the most sensitive and complex applications of restorative justice. The vulnerability of children, the seriousness of harm, and the need for protection require careful attention to safety and accountability. Restorative approaches in this context must be trauma-informed, child-centered, and focused on the well-being of the child.

In appropriate cases, restorative processes can bring together family members, child welfare professionals, and community supports to address the situation. The focus is on understanding what has happened, ensuring the child's safety, addressing the needs of all family members, and developing a plan for healing and restoration. The child's voice is central; age-appropriate opportunities for expression are provided.

Restorative approaches in child welfare emphasize accountability. Parents or caregivers who have harmed children must acknowledge their actions, understand their impact, and commit to change. They must engage with services—counseling, parenting education, substance abuse treatment—that address underlying issues. They must demonstrate over time that they can provide safe, nurturing care.

Restorative approaches also emphasize support. Families in crisis need resources—practical assistance, therapeutic services, community connections—to address the challenges they face. Restorative processes connect families with these resources and provide ongoing support for change.

The safety of the child is paramount. Restorative approaches do not replace child protection systems but complement them. They operate within the framework of legal requirements and professional standards, ensuring that children are protected while families are supported.

The biblical tradition emphasizes the protection of children. Jesus welcomed children, blessed them, and declared that the kingdom of heaven belongs to such as these (Matthew 19:14).

He warned against causing "little ones" to stumble, saying it would be better to have a millstone hung around one's neck and be drowned in the sea (Matthew 18:6). These strong words underscore the importance of protecting the vulnerable.

The Jesus Paradigm in Families

As we consider restorative justice in family relationships, we see that it embodies the principles of the Jesus Paradigm. Its focus on conflict resolution reflects Jesus' teaching on peacemaking within the household of faith. Its emphasis on dialogue and communication reflects Jesus' own practice of engaging with others in ways that honored their dignity and invited transformation. Its commitment to rebuilding trust reflects Jesus' willingness to entrust himself to flawed followers like Peter and the other disciples. Its insistence on accountability reflects Jesus' call to repentance and fruit-bearing. Its centrality of apology and forgiveness reflects the heart of Jesus' teaching and the core of His atoning work. Its use of family meetings reflects the communal nature of Jesus' ministry and the early church's practice of gathering in homes. Its victim-centered approach reflects Jesus' consistent care for those who were suffering and marginalized. Its focus on long-term healing reflects Jesus' patience with His slow-learning disciples and His commitment to their formation over time. Its preventive dimension reflects Jesus' wisdom in teaching His followers how to live in ways that avoid harm. Its cultivation of empathy reflects Jesus' own compassion and His call to love others as ourselves. Its application to diverse family situations reflects the universality of Jesus' message and its relevance to all of life. Its integration into couples therapy reflects Jesus' teaching on marriage as a covenant relationship. Its careful application in child welfare reflects Jesus' special concern for children and the vulnerable.

Restorative justice in families is not merely a set of techniques for resolving disputes but a comprehensive approach to living together in love, accountability, and grace. It embodies the values of the kingdom of God—forgiveness, reconciliation, restoration—in the most intimate sphere of human relationship. It offers hope to families fractured by conflict and harm, pointing the way toward healing and renewed connection.

The Gospel of Restorative Justice in families is this: that no family is beyond hope, that no relationship is irredeemable, that no harm is beyond the reach of God's healing grace. It is a vision of families as schools of love, places where we learn to forgive as we have been forgiven, to reconcile as we have been reconciled, to love as we have been loved. It is a vision worth pursuing, for the sake of families, for the sake of children, for the sake of the world.

CHAPTER 17

CASE STUDIES IN RESTORATIVE JUSTICE

The principles of restorative justice, for all their theoretical coherence and biblical grounding, find their fullest meaning in practice. It is in the lived experience of victims, offenders, and communities that restorative justice proves its worth—or reveals its limitations. Case studies provide windows into this lived experience, offering concrete examples of how restorative principles are applied in diverse contexts and with varying outcomes. They illustrate both the possibilities and the challenges of restorative practice, the successes and the struggles, the transformations and the limitations.

This chapter presents case studies from around the world, demonstrating the versatility and effectiveness of restorative justice in addressing a wide range of conflicts and offenses. We will examine victim-offender mediation in Germany, Maori restorative justice in New Zealand, restorative circles in schools, restorative justice in the Belgian criminal justice system, and the

Truth and Reconciliation Commission in South Africa. We will also consider additional cases that illustrate the application of restorative principles in other contexts. Through these case studies, we will see how restorative justice processes promote healing, reconciliation, and accountability while reducing recidivism and harm. We will also reflect on what these cases teach us about the Jesus Paradigm—the vision of justice rooted in love, compassion, forgiveness, and restoration that we have explored throughout this book.

Case Study 1: Victim-Offender Mediation in Germany

Germany has one of the most well-established systems of victim-offender mediation in the world, known as *Täter-Opfer-Ausgleich* (TOA). This system, which began developing in the 1980s, provides opportunities for victims and offenders to meet in a structured setting to address the harm caused by crime and to work toward resolution. The German approach to victim-offender mediation is notable for its integration into the formal justice system, its professional standards, and its strong research base.

Consider the case of a teenage offender, whom we will call Markus, who committed a property crime—breaking into a neighbor's home and stealing electronics and cash. Markus was sixteen years old, from a troubled family background, and had previous minor offenses. The victims, an elderly couple, were deeply affected by the burglary. Beyond the material loss, they felt violated, unsafe in their own home, and anxious about being alone.

Under Germany's juvenile justice system, Markus was offered the opportunity to participate in victim-offender mediation as an alternative to formal prosecution. A trained mediator met separately with Markus and the victims to prepare them for the process. Markus was initially defensive, minimizing his actions and blaming his circumstances. The victims were hesitant, unsure whether facing the offender would help or harm.

The mediation session brought together Markus, the victims, and the mediator. The mediator established ground rules for respectful communication and gave each party the opportunity to speak. The victims went first, describing their experience of the burglary—the fear of coming home to find their door broken, the sense of violation at a stranger having been in their private space, the ongoing anxiety that has made it difficult to feel safe. They spoke not with anger but with pain, and their words carried the weight of genuine suffering.

As Markus listened, something shifted. For the first time, he was confronted not with an abstract crime but with real people who had been hurt by his actions. He saw the tears in the elderly woman's eyes, heard the tremor in her husband's voice. When it was his turn to speak, he did not make excuses. He acknowledged what he had done, expressed genuine remorse, and asked what he could do to make things right.

The victims, after some discussion, said they wanted their property returned and some compensation for the damage to their door. They also wanted Markus to understand the impact of his actions—which, through the mediation, he already had. Markus agreed to return the stolen items that remained, to work to pay for the damage, and to write a letter of apology. The mediator helped them formalize these agreements.

Follow-up meetings ensured that Markus fulfilled his commitments. He returned the items, completed his work, and wrote a sincere apology. The victims reported feeling heard and validated; the mediation had given them a sense of closure that a court proceeding could not have provided. Markus, for his part, gained understanding and motivation to change. He did not reoffend.

This case illustrates several key principles of restorative justice. The process was victim-centered, giving the elderly couple voice and agency in addressing the harm they had suffered. Markus was held accountable not through passive punishment but through active responsibility—acknowledging his actions, understanding their impact, and making amends. The community, represented by the mediator and the broader system, supported the process without controlling it. The outcome focused on repair—returning property, compensating for damage, restoring relationship to the extent possible.

Research on victim-offender mediation in Germany supports its effectiveness. Studies have shown significant reductions in recidivism for offenders who participate in mediation compared to those processed through conventional means. Victims report higher satisfaction with mediation than with court proceedings, citing the opportunity to be heard, to receive answers, and to have a voice in outcomes. The German experience demonstrates that restorative justice can be successfully integrated into a formal legal system, operating alongside conventional processes and offering alternatives when appropriate.

From the perspective of the Jesus Paradigm, this case embodies several key themes. The victims' pain was acknowledged and validated, reflecting Jesus' consistent care for those who suffer. The offender was held accountable but also offered a path to restoration, mirroring Jesus' approach to sinners like Zacchaeus and the woman caught in adultery. The process created conditions for genuine apology and forgiveness, echoing Jesus' teaching on both. The outcome focused on repair and restoration, participating in the divine work of making things whole.

Case Study 2: Maori Restorative Justice in New Zealand

New Zealand has integrated Maori restorative justice practices into its legal system, particularly in the youth justice area. These practices, known as Family Group Conferences (FGCs), draw on traditional Maori approaches to justice that emphasize community involvement, victim-offender reconciliation, and restoration of balance. The FGC model has been so successful that it has been adopted and adapted around the world.

Consider the case of a Maori youth, whom we will call Tama, who was involved in a burglary of a family's home. Tama, along with two older youths, had broken into the home while the family was away, stealing electronics, jewelry, and cash. The family, when they discovered the burglary, felt violated and angry. Tama was apprehended and, under New Zealand's youth justice system, his case was referred for a family group conference.

The FGC brought together Tama, his extended family (including his parents, grandparents, and an uncle), the victims and their family, a youth justice coordinator, a police representative, and a cultural advisor familiar with Maori protocols. The conference was held in a community meeting house, with participants sitting in a circle—a format that reflects Maori values of equality and collective responsibility.

The conference began with a prayer and an acknowledgment of the cultural protocols. The youth justice coordinator explained the purpose of the meeting: to address the harm caused by the burglary, to hold Tama accountable, and to develop a plan for making things right. Each person was given the opportunity to speak.

The victims described the impact of the burglary—the sense of violation, the loss of treasured items, the fear that has made it difficult to feel safe in their own home. They spoke directly to Tama, expressing their anger and hurt but also their hope that he would learn from this experience and make better choices.

Tama's family spoke of their shame and disappointment, but also their love and commitment to helping Tama change. His grandmother, in particular, spoke of the importance of whakama—a Maori concept similar to shame but with connotations of honor and respect—and urged Tama to take responsibility and restore his place in the family and community.

When it was Tama's turn to speak, he was visibly moved. He acknowledged what he had done, expressed remorse, and apologized to the victims and his family. He said he had not understood the full impact of his actions until hearing their words. He asked what he could do to make things right.

The group then worked together to develop a plan. Tama would return any items that could be recovered. He would work to earn money to compensate the victims for their losses. He would participate in a cultural program to learn about Maori traditions and values, including the concept of kaitiakitanga—guardianship and respect for others' property. He would be mentored by his uncle, who agreed to spend regular time with him and provide guidance. The family would support Tama in fulfilling these commitments.

The conference concluded with a shared meal, a common Maori practice that symbolizes restoration of relationship and community. Follow-up meetings ensured that Tama was following through on his commitments. He completed the cultural program, developed a stronger connection to his heritage, and did not reoffend.

This case illustrates the power of restorative justice when it is culturally grounded. The FGC drew on Maori values of whanau (family), mana (dignity and authority), and whakapapa (connectedness) to create a process that was meaningful and effective for all involved. The involvement of extended family provided support and accountability that formal systems alone could not offer. The cultural elements—the circle format, the prayer, the shared meal—created a context of respect and relationship that facilitated honest communication and genuine resolution.

The New Zealand experience demonstrates that restorative justice is not a one-size-fits-all model but a framework that can be adapted to diverse cultural contexts. The success of FGCs in New Zealand has inspired similar approaches in other countries, including Australia, Canada, the United Kingdom, and the United States. These adaptations honor indigenous wisdom while addressing contemporary justice needs.

From the perspective of the Jesus Paradigm, this case embodies the communal nature of restorative justice. The involvement of extended family reflects the biblical understanding that we are members one of another, that healing requires community. The emphasis on cultural values echoes the incarnation—God's

Word becoming flesh in a particular culture, at a particular time, speaking in particular languages and through particular traditions. The shared meal at the conclusion points toward the Eucharist, the feast of reconciliation in which we anticipate the ultimate restoration of all things.

Case Study 3: Restorative Circles in Schools

Restorative circles are widely used in schools to address conflicts and behavioral issues. These circles draw on indigenous practices, particularly from North American First Nations, and have been adapted for educational settings around the world. They provide a structured process for addressing harm, building community, and teaching restorative values.

Consider the case of a high school that implemented restorative circles to address bullying and conflicts among students. The school, located in an urban area with diverse student population, had struggled with persistent bullying, racial tensions, and disciplinary incidents that seemed to escalate rather than resolve. Traditional punitive responses—suspensions, expulsions, zero-tolerance policies—had not improved the situation and had disproportionately affected students of color.

The school decided to implement restorative practices, beginning with training for staff and students. A restorative justice coordinator was hired to oversee the program. Teachers were trained in facilitating circles and restorative conversations. A group of students was trained as peer mediators. The school committed to using restorative approaches for all but the most serious disciplinary matters.

One incident involved a conflict between two groups of students that had escalated into a physical altercation in the cafeteria. Several students were involved, and tensions were running high. Rather than simply suspending those involved, the school convened a restorative circle.

The circle included the students directly involved, their parents, teachers who had witnessed the incident, and the school principal. The circle was facilitated by the restorative justice coordinator, who established ground rules for respectful communication and ensured that each person had the opportunity to speak.

The students involved in the altercation spoke first, describing what had happened from their perspectives. They expressed anger, frustration, and fear. They also listened as others described the impact of the incident—the fear of other students who witnessed it, the disruption to the school community, the concern of parents and teachers.

As the circle continued, deeper issues emerged. Some students spoke of feeling marginalized or disrespected. Others mentioned ongoing conflicts that had not been addressed. The racial dimension of the conflict was acknowledged, with students of color describing experiences of discrimination that had fueled resentment. Teachers acknowledged their own limitations in addressing these underlying issues.

The circle did not produce immediate solutions, but it created understanding. Students who had been opponents heard each other's experiences and began to see each other as human beings rather than enemies. Teachers gained insight into the dynamics that had led to the incident. Parents expressed appreciation for the opportunity to be heard.

Follow-up circles were held to continue the dialogue and develop action plans. Students worked together to organize activities that would build community across groups. Teachers committed to addressing issues of bias and inclusion in their classrooms. The school developed a peer mediation program to address future conflicts before they escalated.

Over time, the school climate improved. Bullying incidents decreased. Students reported feeling safer and more connected. Disciplinary referrals dropped. The restorative approach had not eliminated conflict—no approach can—but it had transformed how conflict was addressed, from punitive to restorative, from adversarial to collaborative, from reactive to proactive.

This case illustrates the power of restorative circles in educational settings. The circle provided a safe space for honest communication, allowing participants to express feelings and experiences that might otherwise remain hidden. The process addressed not only the immediate incident but the underlying issues that had contributed to it. The involvement of multiple stakeholders—students, parents, teachers, administrators—created shared ownership of both the problem and the solution. The focus on understanding and repair, rather than punishment and blame, promoted genuine learning and change.

Research on restorative practices in schools supports their effectiveness. Studies have shown reductions in suspensions and expulsions, improvements in school climate, decreases in bullying, and increases in academic achievement. Schools that implement restorative practices report stronger relationships, greater trust, and more positive learning environments.

From the perspective of the Jesus Paradigm, this case embodies several key themes. The circle's commitment to hearing every voice reflects Jesus' practice of attending to those who were often silenced—women, children, lepers, outcasts. The focus on addressing underlying issues echoes Jesus' concern for the root causes of human behavior, not merely its external manifestations. The involvement of the whole school community reflects the biblical vision of the body of Christ, in which each member contributes to the health of the whole. The transformation of school climate over time participates in the gradual growth of God's kingdom, like the mustard seed that becomes a great tree.

Case Study 4: Restorative Justice in the Belgian Criminal Justice System

Belgium has incorporated restorative justice into its legal system, particularly for juvenile cases. The Belgian approach emphasizes dialogue, reparation, and reintegration, offering alternatives to traditional punitive measures. Research on Belgian restorative programs has demonstrated positive outcomes for both victims and offenders.

Consider the case of a young offender, whom we will call Jean, who committed a theft. Jean was seventeen years old and had no prior record. He had stolen a laptop from a fellow student at his school, apparently to sell it for money to buy drugs. The victim, another student, was angry and felt violated. The school referred the case to the juvenile justice system.

Under Belgium's restorative justice provisions, Jean was offered the opportunity to participate in a restorative process as an alternative to formal prosecution. A mediator from a restorative justice service met separately with Jean and the victim to prepare them for a joint meeting.

The victim was initially reluctant. He was angry and wanted Jean to be punished. The mediator listened to his feelings, validated his anger, and explained the restorative process—how it would give him the opportunity to express his experience directly to Jean, to ask questions, and to have a voice in determining what Jean should do to make things right. After consideration, the victim agreed to participate.

Jean, for his part, was defensive at first. He minimized the theft, blaming his need for money and the pressures of his situation. The mediator helped him understand that the restorative process was not about making excuses but about taking responsibility and making amends. Jean agreed to participate.

The mediation session brought together Jean, the victim, and the mediator. The victim spoke first, describing the impact of the theft. The laptop contained schoolwork, personal photos, and other irreplaceable items. He had lost not only material value but also time and effort. He felt violated that someone he knew would steal from him. He wanted to understand why Jean had done it.

Jean listened, and as he listened, his defensiveness faded. He heard the genuine pain in the victim's voice. When it was his turn to speak, he acknowledged what he had done, expressed remorse, and answered the victim's questions honestly. He explained his struggles with drug use and the desperation that had led him to steal.

The victim, having heard Jean's explanation, was able to see him as a person rather than just an offender. He did not excuse the theft, but he understood it better. He agreed to a plan in which Jean would replace the laptop, participate in a drug treatment program, and perform community service at the school. Jean accepted these conditions.

Jean fulfilled his commitments. He replaced the laptop, completed the treatment program, and performed the community service. He did not reoffend. The victim reported feeling satisfied with the process and the outcome. He had been heard, his questions had been answered, and he had received restitution.

This case illustrates several key features of restorative justice in the Belgian system. The process was voluntary; both parties chose to participate. The mediator was trained and neutral, facilitating without imposing. The victim was central, his needs and voice shaping the outcome. The offender was held accountable through responsibility and amends, not merely punishment. The outcome focused on repair—replacing the stolen item, addressing the underlying drug issue, giving back to the community.

Research on Belgian restorative programs supports their effectiveness. Studies have shown high levels of victim satisfaction, reduced recidivism among participating offenders, and cost savings compared to traditional processing. The Belgian experience demonstrates that restorative justice can be successfully integrated into a civil law system, operating alongside conventional processes and offering meaningful alternatives.

From the perspective of the Jesus Paradigm, this case embodies the balance of accountability and grace that characterizes Jesus' approach to offenders. Jean was held accountable—he had to make amends, address his drug problem, and give back to the community. But he was also offered a path to restoration—an opportunity to change, to be reintegrated, to move forward. This combination of accountability and grace reflects the heart of the gospel.

Case Study 5: Truth and Reconciliation Commission in South Africa

The Truth and Reconciliation Commission (TRC) in South Africa represents one of the most ambitious applications of restorative principles on a national scale. Established in 1995 after the end of apartheid, the TRC was charged with uncovering the truth about human rights abuses committed during the apartheid era, providing a platform for victims and perpetrators to share their experiences, and promoting national reconciliation.

The TRC was not a purely restorative process—it operated alongside a criminal justice system that could prosecute those who did not participate or who committed particularly egregious offenses. But its core principles were restorative: acknowledgment of harm, accountability through truth-telling, victim-centered process, and the goal of reconciliation.

The TRC operated through three committees. The Human Rights Violations Committee heard testimony from victims, documenting the abuses they had suffered and providing a public platform for their stories to be heard. The Reparation and Rehabilitation Committee developed recommendations for how victims should be compensated and supported. The Amnesty Committee considered applications from perpetrators who sought amnesty in exchange for full disclosure of their crimes.

The amnesty provision was controversial. Critics argued that it allowed perpetrators to escape justice. Supporters argued that it was necessary to uncover the truth and to avoid the endless cycles of prosecution and counter-prosecution that could have destabilized the transition to democracy. Perpetrators who came forward, disclosed their crimes fully, and demonstrated that their actions were politically motivated could receive amnesty—not forgiveness, but legal immunity from prosecution.

The TRC hearings were deeply moving and often traumatic. Victims told stories of torture, murder, disappearance, and loss. Perpetrators described the atrocities they had committed. The nation watched and listened. For many South Africans, the TRC provided the first opportunity to confront the full reality of apartheid's horrors.

Archbishop Desmond Tutu, who chaired the TRC, articulated its restorative vision. He spoke of the African concept of ubuntu—the idea that a person is a person through other persons, that our humanity is bound up with one another. Ubuntu meant that the harms of apartheid had damaged not only victims but perpetrators and the whole society. Healing, therefore, required not punishment alone but acknowledgment, accountability, and reconciliation.

The TRC did not achieve perfect justice. Many perpetrators did not come forward. Many victims did not receive adequate reparation. The underlying economic and social structures of apartheid remained largely intact. But the TRC did achieve something remarkable: it allowed a nation to confront its past honestly, to acknowledge the suffering of victims, to hold perpetrators accountable through truth-telling, and to begin the long work of reconciliation.

The TRC has inspired similar processes in other countries—Rwanda, Sierra Leone, Peru, Canada, and elsewhere. It has demonstrated that restorative principles can be applied not only to individual crimes but to massive, systemic injustice. It has shown that truth-telling, acknowledgment, and reconciliation, while not sufficient, are necessary components of any comprehensive response to historical wrongs.

From the perspective of the Jesus Paradigm, the TRC embodies several key themes. Its commitment to truth reflects Jesus' declaration, "You will know the truth, and the truth will make you free" (John 8:32). Its victim-centered approach reflects Jesus' consistent care for those who suffer. Its emphasis on reconciliation reflects the heart of the gospel—God in Christ reconciling the world to Himself. Its understanding of ubuntu echoes the biblical vision of humanity as created for relationship, bound together in mutual responsibility and care. And its limitations—the incomplete justice, the ongoing struggles—remind us that full restoration awaits the coming of God's kingdom in its fullness.

Additional Case Studies

While the cases above illustrate the application of restorative justice in various contexts, many other examples could be cited. Each demonstrates the versatility and effectiveness of restorative principles.

Restorative Justice in Canada's Indigenous Communities: Indigenous communities in Canada have long practiced restorative justice through healing circles, sentencing circles, and other traditional processes. These practices have been increasingly recognized and incorporated into the formal justice system. In one case, a young Indigenous offender who had committed a serious assault was referred to a sentencing circle. The circle included the offender, his family, the victim, elders, and community members. Through the circle, the offender heard directly from the victim about the impact of the assault, accepted responsibility, and agreed to a plan that included counseling, community service, and cultural education. The process honored Indigenous traditions while addressing the harm and promoting healing.

Restorative Justice in Scandinavian Prisons: Scandinavian countries like Norway and Sweden have integrated restorative principles into their prison systems. In Norway's Bastøy Prison, for example, the focus is on rehabilitation, community, and preparation for reintegration. Prisoners live in a community setting, take responsibility for daily tasks, participate in education and work programs, and engage in restorative processes to address the harm they have caused. Recidivism rates are significantly lower than in more punitive systems. This approach reflects the restorative principle that offenders are more likely to change when they are treated with respect, given responsibility, and supported in their growth.

Restorative Justice in Post-Genocide Rwanda: After the 1994 genocide, Rwanda faced the impossible task of addressing crimes committed by hundreds of thousands of perpetrators against nearly a million victims. The formal justice system could not handle the caseload. In response, the government revived the traditional Gacaca courts—community-based tribunals that brought together victims, perpetrators, and community members to address the crimes. Perpetrators were encouraged to confess, seek reconciliation, and contribute to community restoration. While the Gacaca process was imperfect and faced significant challenges, it demonstrated the potential of restorative approaches even in the most extreme circumstances.

Restorative Justice in Northern Ireland: In the context of the Northern Ireland conflict, restorative justice has been used to address paramilitary violence and community tensions. Community-based restorative justice programs have brought together victims and perpetrators, addressed the harm caused by paramilitary "punishment" attacks, and contributed to the peace process. These programs demonstrate that restorative principles can be applied even in situations of deep political division and ongoing conflict.

Restorative Justice in Schools in Australia: Many Australian schools have implemented restorative practices to address bullying, conflict, and behavioral issues. In one case, a primary school used restorative circles to address a persistent bullying problem. Students who had been bullying others were brought together with their victims in circles facilitated by trained teachers. Through the circles, bullies heard directly about the impact of their actions, victims received acknowledgment and apology, and the school community developed strategies for preventing future incidents. The school reported significant reductions in bullying and improvements in school climate.

Restorative Justice in Faith Communities: Many faith communities have adopted restorative practices to address conflicts within their congregations. In one case, a church faced a serious conflict between the pastor and some members over worship style and leadership. Rather than allowing the conflict to divide the congregation, church leaders convened a restorative circle that included the pastor, the dissenting members, and other congregants. Through facilitated dialogue, the parties expressed their concerns, heard each other's perspectives, and developed a plan for moving forward that honored both tradition and innovation. The process strengthened rather than divided the congregation.

Restorative Justice in Workplace Conflicts: Restorative practices are increasingly used in workplace settings to address conflicts, harassment, and other issues. In one case, a company faced a complaint of harassment from an employee against a supervisor. Rather than simply terminating the supervisor, which would have left the underlying issues unaddressed, the company offered a restorative process. The supervisor acknowledged the behavior, apologized, and agreed to sensitivity training and ongoing monitoring. The employee felt heard and validated, and the workplace culture began to shift toward greater respect and accountability.

Restorative Justice in Family Disputes: Restorative practices are used in family disputes of all kinds. In one case, a family was torn apart by a dispute over the care of aging parents. Siblings who had not spoken in years came together in a family group conference facilitated by a social worker. Through the conference, they expressed their concerns, heard each other's perspectives, and developed a care plan that addressed everyone's needs. The process did not resolve all the underlying issues, but it reopened communication and created a foundation for ongoing collaboration.

Restorative Justice in Environmental Harm: Restorative principles are increasingly applied to environmental harm. In one case, a company that had polluted a river was brought into a restorative process with community members affected by the pollution. The company acknowledged responsibility, funded cleanup efforts, and supported community environmental projects. The process addressed not only the material harm but also the relational harm—the loss of trust, the sense of violation, the community's grief over damage to a beloved natural resource.

Restorative Justice in Historical Injustice: Restorative principles are applied to address historical injustices, such as the treatment of indigenous peoples, the legacy of slavery, and other systemic wrongs. In Canada, the Truth and Reconciliation Commission addressed the legacy of Indian Residential Schools, providing a platform for survivors to share their stories and for the nation to confront this history. In the United States, restorative processes have been used to address the legacy of racial injustice in specific communities, bringing together descendants of enslaved people and descendants of slaveholders to acknowledge the past and work toward reconciliation.

Lessons from the Case Studies

These case studies, diverse as they are, offer several important lessons about restorative justice.

First, restorative justice is adaptable. The principles of acknowledgment, accountability, and restoration can be applied in widely different contexts—criminal justice, schools, families, workplaces, communities, nations. The specific practices may vary—mediation, circles, conferences, truth commissions—but the underlying values remain consistent. This adaptability is one of restorative justice's greatest strengths.

Second, restorative justice is effective. Research across multiple contexts demonstrates positive outcomes: reduced recidivism, increased victim satisfaction, improved relationships, stronger communities. These outcomes are not guaranteed—restorative processes can fail—but when implemented well, they produce results that punitive approaches cannot match.

Third, restorative justice requires commitment. Successful restorative programs require trained facilitators, adequate resources, institutional support, and ongoing evaluation. They require patience—healing takes time, and outcomes may not be immediately apparent. They require courage—from victims who must face those who harmed them, from offenders who must take responsibility, from communities that must engage with conflict.

Fourth, restorative justice is rooted in relationship. The case studies consistently show that healing occurs through encounter—victims and offenders meeting, speaking, listening, understanding. Abstract processes cannot produce this healing; it requires real people, real dialogue, real relationship. Restorative justice creates conditions for this encounter.

Fifth, restorative justice reflects ancient wisdom. Many of the practices described in these case studies—circles, conferences, truth-telling—draw on indigenous traditions that long predate modern legal systems. Restorative justice is not an invention but a recovery, a return to ways of addressing harm that have sustained human communities for millennia.

Sixth, restorative justice aligns with biblical values. The case studies echo themes we have explored throughout this book: acknowledgment of harm, accountability of offenders, centrality of victims, involvement of community, apology and forgiveness, restitution and repair, healing and reconciliation. These are not merely secular values but deeply biblical ones, rooted in the character of God and the teaching of Jesus.

The Jesus Paradigm in the Case Studies

As we reflect on these case studies through the lens of the Jesus Paradigm, several observations emerge.

The German case reminds us that Jesus consistently reached out to those who had caused harm, offering them opportunities for repentance and restoration while also caring for those they had harmed. His encounters with Zacchaeus, with the woman caught in adultery, with Peter after his denial—all demonstrate this dual commitment to accountability and grace.

The New Zealand case reflects the communal nature of Jesus' ministry. He did not work alone but gathered a community of disciples, sent them out in pairs, and taught them to live as a new family. The involvement of extended family in the FGC echoes this communal vision.

The school case embodies Jesus' teaching about children. He welcomed them, blessed them, and declared that the kingdom of heaven belongs to such as these. Restorative circles in schools, by creating safe spaces for children to express themselves and resolve conflicts, honor this teaching.

The Belgian case illustrates Jesus' emphasis on both accountability and restoration. He did not let offenders off the hook—He called them to repentance and change. But He also offered them a path to restoration, a way back to community and wholeness. The restorative process in Belgium embodied this balance.

The South African case reflects the prophetic dimension of Jesus' ministry. He came to proclaim good news to the poor, freedom to the prisoners, recovery of sight to the blind—to announce God's concern for justice and liberation. The TRC, in confronting the evils of apartheid and seeking truth and reconciliation, participated in this prophetic work.

The additional cases further illuminate the Jesus Paradigm. The Canadian indigenous healing circles reflect Jesus' healing ministry. The Scandinavian prisons reflect Jesus' teaching about the last being first and the greatest being servant of all. The Rwandan Gacaca courts reflect the impossibility of justice without grace in the face of massive wrong. The Northern Ireland programs reflect Jesus' beatitude on peacemakers. The Australian schools reflect Jesus' welcome of children. The faith community case reflects Jesus' prayer that His followers might be one. The workplace case reflects Jesus' teaching about reconciliation before worship. The family case reflects Jesus' blessing on households. The environmental case reflects Jesus' concern for all creation. The historical injustice case reflects Jesus' proclamation of Jubilee—the year of the Lord's favor, when debts are forgiven and captives are freed.

The Gospel of Restorative Justice in Practice

These case studies demonstrate that restorative justice is not merely a theory but a practice—a way of responding to harm that can be implemented in diverse contexts with positive results. They show that victims can find healing, offenders can be transformed, and communities can be strengthened through restorative processes. They provide evidence that restorative justice works.

But these case studies also demonstrate something more: they show that restorative justice, at its best, embodies the values of the gospel. It reflects God's concern for victims, God's call to accountability, God's offer of forgiveness, God's work of reconciliation, God's hope for restoration. It participates in the divine mission of making all things new.

The Gospel of Restorative Justice is not a different gospel from the one proclaimed by Jesus and the apostles. It is that same gospel, applied to the specific challenge of responding to harm and wrongdoing. It is the good news that in Christ, God was reconciling the world to Himself, not counting our trespasses against us, and entrusting to us the ministry of reconciliation (2 Corinthians 5:18-19). It is the good news that healing is possible, that relationships can be restored, that even the deepest wounds can be transformed.

These case studies are signs of this gospel—glimpses of the kingdom breaking into a broken world. They are not the kingdom fully realized; they are partial, imperfect, incomplete. But they point toward the kingdom, toward the day when justice will roll down like waters and righteousness like an ever-flowing stream, when swords will be beaten into plowshares and nations will not learn war anymore, when God will wipe away every tear and death shall be no more.

As we continue to study, practice, and advocate for restorative justice, we do so in the light of these case studies. They remind us of what is possible. They encourage us in the face of challenges. They call us to persevere in the work of healing, reconciliation, and restoration. And they point us toward the one who is the ultimate model and source of restorative justice—Jesus Christ, in whom God was reconciling the world to Himself.

CHAPTER 18

RESTORATIVE JUSTICE AND THEOLOGY

The relationship between restorative justice and theology is not merely incidental but essential. Restorative justice, at its deepest level, is not simply a set of practices or a policy framework but a vision of reality—a vision that is profoundly theological. It makes claims about the nature of human beings, the meaning of harm, the possibility of healing, and the purpose of community that resonate with the deepest truths of Christian faith. To understand restorative justice fully is to understand its theological dimensions; to practice restorative justice faithfully is to participate in God's own work of reconciliation and restoration.

This chapter explores the intersections between restorative justice and theology, particularly Christian theology. We will examine how restorative justice embodies theological principles such as redemption and forgiveness, reconciliation, community and restoration, accountability, healing and transformation, non-retaliation, justice as love, empathy and compassion, liberation, and sacrificial love. We will also consider the ways in which restorative justice aligns with biblical teachings and the person and work of Jesus Christ. Through this exploration, we will see that restorative justice is not merely compatible with Christian faith but is, in many ways, a practical expression of it—a way of living out the gospel in response to harm and wrongdoing.

The Theological Foundations of Restorative Justice

Theology, at its simplest, is talk about God—about who God is, what God does, and what God requires of us. Restorative justice, while often discussed in secular terms, is deeply rooted in theological soil. Its core principles—that every person has inherent dignity, that harm damages relationships, that accountability requires repair, that healing is possible, that community matters—reflect theological convictions about creation, fall, redemption, and consummation.

The doctrine of creation affirms that every human being is made in the image of God (Genesis 1:26-27). This imago Dei is the foundation of human dignity and the source of our obligation to treat one another with respect. Restorative justice, in its commitment to honoring the dignity of victims, offenders, and community members, embodies this creation theology. It refuses to reduce any person to their worst act, insisting that even those who have caused great harm remain image-bearers, worthy of respect and capable of restoration.

The doctrine of the fall acknowledges that sin has disrupted God's good creation, fracturing relationships between God and humanity, between humans and each other, within the human heart, and between humanity and creation. Harm is real; wrongdoing has consequences. Restorative justice, in its honest acknowledgment of harm and its commitment to accountability, takes the fall seriously. It does not minimize wrongdoing or pretend that harm doesn't matter. It faces the brokenness of the world squarely.

The doctrine of redemption proclaims that God has acted in Jesus Christ to heal what sin has broken, to reconcile what has been estranged, to restore what has been lost. The cross and resurrection are the ultimate acts of restorative justice—the innocent one bearing the consequences of the guilty, opening the way to forgiveness and new life. Restorative justice, in its focus on repair, healing, and restoration, participates in this redemptive work. It is not the full realization of redemption—that awaits the consummation of all things—but it is a sign and foretaste of it.

The doctrine of the church affirms that God is creating a new community—a people reconciled to God and to one another, called to embody God's restorative purposes in the world. This community is to be a place of forgiveness, accountability, healing, and reconciliation. Restorative justice, in its emphasis on community involvement in the justice process, reflects this ecclesial vision. It recognizes that justice cannot be done by professionals alone but requires the participation of the whole community.

The doctrine of eschatology points toward the ultimate consummation of God's purposes—a new heaven and a new earth, where righteousness dwells, where God wipes away every tear, where death and pain are no more. Restorative justice, in its hope for healing and restoration, participates in this eschatological vision. It is not the kingdom fully realized, but it is a sign of the kingdom, a foretaste of what will be.

These theological foundations undergird everything that restorative justice seeks to do. They provide the ultimate justification for restorative practices and the ultimate hope that sustains restorative practitioners. They remind us that restorative justice is not merely a human invention but a participation in God's own work.

Redemption and Forgiveness: The Heart of the Gospel

Many theological traditions, including Christianity, emphasize the concepts of redemption and forgiveness. Restorative justice embodies these principles by providing opportunities for offenders to make amends, seek forgiveness, and ultimately redeem themselves in the eyes of both human society and the divine.

Redemption is the act of buying back, of freeing from bondage, of restoring to wholeness. In Christian theology, redemption is what God has done in Christ—paying the price for sin, freeing us from bondage, restoring us to relationship with God. This redemption is not earned but given, not achieved but received. It is an act of grace.

Restorative justice participates in this redemptive work. It creates conditions in which offenders can be redeemed—not in the ultimate sense, which is God's alone, but in the social sense of being restored to community, of having their relationships repaired, of being given a new start. When offenders acknowledge their wrongdoing, make amends, and change their behavior, they are redeemed in the eyes of those they have harmed and the community they have damaged.

Forgiveness is closely related to redemption. Forgiveness is the release of the offender from the debt of guilt, the decision to no longer hold the wrong against them. In Christian theology, forgiveness is what God offers to all who repent and believe—the free pardon of sins, the removal of guilt, the restoration of relationship. This forgiveness is costly—it required the death of Christ—but it is freely offered.

Restorative justice creates conditions in which forgiveness can occur. It brings victims and offenders together in settings where victims can hear offenders acknowledge their wrongdoing and express remorse, and where offenders can receive the gift of forgiveness if victims are able to offer it. Forgiveness cannot be forced; it must be freely given. But restorative processes make it possible.

The case of Zacchaeus illustrates the connection between redemption, forgiveness, and restorative justice. Zacchaeus, a tax collector who had defrauded many, encountered Jesus and was transformed. He declared, "Look, Lord, I give half of my goods to the poor; and if I have taken anything from anyone by false accusation, I restore fourfold" (Luke 19:8). Jesus responded, "Today salvation has come to this house" (Luke 19:9). Zacchaeus's restitution was evidence of his repentance and the fruit of his redemption. He was forgiven and restored.

The parable of the prodigal son also illustrates these themes. The younger son, who had squandered his inheritance in reckless living, returned home in humility, confessing his sin. The father, representing God, ran to meet him, embraced him, and restored him to full sonship. The son was redeemed and forgiven, not because he deserved it but because the father's love was greater than his sin.

Theological reflection on redemption and forgiveness deepens our understanding of restorative justice. It reminds us that offenders are not defined by their worst acts but remain image-bearers capable of change. It reminds us that forgiveness is not weakness but strength, not capitulation but liberation. It reminds us that redemption is possible, that no one is beyond the reach of God's grace.

Reconciliation: Restoring Relationship

Theological teachings often highlight reconciliation as a fundamental aspect of faith. Restorative justice actively promotes reconciliation, both between individuals and with the divine, in the context of conflicts and wrongdoing.

Reconciliation is the restoration of relationship after estrangement. It is what happens when those who have been divided are brought back together, when trust is rebuilt, when harmony is restored. In Christian theology, reconciliation is central to the gospel. The Apostle Paul writes that "God was in Christ reconciling the world to Himself, not imputing their trespasses to them, and has committed to us the word of reconciliation" (2 Corinthians 5:19). Reconciliation is God's work and the church's mission.

Restorative justice promotes reconciliation by bringing together those who have been separated by harm. Victims and offenders meet in settings where they can address the wrong that has been done, understand each other's perspectives, and work toward restoration. This process does not guarantee reconciliation—some relationships cannot be restored, and some parties may not be willing—but it creates the conditions in which reconciliation is possible.

Reconciliation is not the same as forgiveness, though they are related. Forgiveness can be offered unilaterally; the victim can forgive even if the offender remains unrepentant. Reconciliation requires the participation of both parties; it involves the rebuilding of trust and the restoration of relationship. Restorative justice seeks both—forgiveness where it can be offered, reconciliation where it can be achieved.

The biblical vision of reconciliation extends beyond individual relationships to encompass the whole creation. Paul writes that in Christ, God was pleased "to reconcile to Himself all things, whether things on earth or things in heaven, by making peace through His blood, shed on the cross" (Colossians 1:20). This cosmic reconciliation is the ultimate hope of the gospel—the restoration of all things to right relationship with God and with each other.

Restorative justice participates in this cosmic reconciliation. Every restorative process that heals a relationship, every victim who finds closure, every offender who is restored to community is a sign of the ultimate reconciliation that God intends for all creation. These small acts of restoration point toward the great act of restoration that is to come.

Community and Restoration: The Body of Christ

Restorative justice emphasizes the importance of community involvement and support in the justice process. This aligns with the theological concept of community and the role it plays in providing moral guidance, forgiveness, and healing.

In Christian theology, community is not merely a collection of individuals but a body—the body of Christ. Paul develops this image in 1 Corinthians 12, describing the church as a body with many members, each with its own function, all essential to the health of the whole. "If one member suffers, all suffer together; if one member is honored, all rejoice together" (1 Corinthians 12:26). This organic unity means that harm to any member harms the whole, and restoration of any member blesses the whole.

Restorative justice embodies this communal vision. It recognizes that crime wounds not only individual victims but the whole community. It involves the community in the process of healing, drawing on its resources, wisdom, and support. It seeks to restore not only individuals but relationships, not only victims and offenders but the social fabric that binds them together.

The community's role in restorative justice is multifaceted. Community members provide support to victims, surrounding them with care and assistance. They hold offenders accountable, offering guidance and encouragement for change. They participate in restorative processes, sharing their perspectives and contributing to agreements. They welcome returning offenders, helping them reintegrate and find their place. They address underlying conditions that contribute to crime, working to prevent future harm.

This communal approach reflects the biblical understanding of justice. In ancient Israel, justice was administered at the city gate, with elders and community members participating (Ruth 4; Deuteronomy 21:18-21). The community was present, witnessing proceedings, holding parties accountable, ensuring that justice was done. In the early church, conflicts were addressed within the community, with members supporting one another and working toward restoration (Matthew 18:15-20; 1 Corinthians 6:1-8).

Theological reflection on community deepens our understanding of restorative justice. It reminds us that we are not isolated individuals but members one of another, bound together in mutual responsibility and care. It reminds us that healing requires community, that we cannot recover alone. It reminds us that justice is not something done to communities but something done with them and by them.

Accountability: Responsibility Before God and Neighbor

The idea of moral accountability is central to many theological systems. Restorative justice holds offenders accountable for their actions while offering them a path to redemption, reflecting the theological belief in individual responsibility and accountability.

Accountability in Christian theology has both vertical and horizontal dimensions. We are accountable to God for our actions, for how we have lived, for what we have done with the gifts and opportunities we have been given. Paul writes that "each of us shall give account of himself to God" (Romans 14:12). This ultimate accountability shapes our accountability to one another.

We are also accountable to our neighbors. When we harm others, we owe them acknowledgment, remorse, and repair. The prophet Nathan held David accountable for his sin against Uriah and Bathsheba (2 Samuel 12). John the Baptist called people to "bear fruits worthy of repentance" (Luke 3:8)—actions demonstrating genuine change. Zacchaeus's restitution to those he had defrauded was evidence of his repentance (Luke 19:8).

Restorative justice embodies this dual accountability. Offenders are held accountable to victims—they must acknowledge the harm, express remorse, and make amends. They are also held accountable to community—they must demonstrate changed behavior, contribute positively, and rebuild trust. And they are invited to consider their accountability to God—to reflect on their actions in light of divine judgment and grace, to seek forgiveness and transformation.

This accountability is not about shame or punishment but about responsibility and repair. It is not about making offenders suffer but about making things right. It is not backward-looking only but forward-looking as well—concerned with preventing future harm and promoting future good.

Theological reflection on accountability deepens our understanding of restorative justice. It reminds us that accountability is not opposed to grace but is one of its expressions. Grace does not mean ignoring wrongdoing or letting offenders off the hook; it means holding them accountable in ways that lead to transformation rather than despair. It reminds us that accountability is not merely a human requirement but a divine expectation, rooted in the character of God who is just and righteous.

Healing and Transformation: New Creation

Both restorative justice and theology share a focus on healing and personal transformation. These approaches recognize that offenders can change, grow, and seek a more righteous path. They also recognize that victims need healing and that communities need restoration.

Healing in Christian theology is holistic—addressing body, mind, spirit, and relationship. Jesus' healing ministry was not merely physical; it restored people to community, to dignity, to purpose. The leper was cleansed and could rejoin society. The paralytic was forgiven and healed. The demoniac was liberated and sent home to testify. Healing was always more than the absence of disease; it was the presence of wholeness.

Transformation is also central to Christian faith. Paul writes, "Do not be conformed to this world, but be transformed by the renewing of your mind" (Romans 12:2). Transformation is the work of the Spirit, reshaping us into the likeness of Christ. It is a process, not an event—a journey of growth and change that continues throughout life.

Restorative justice seeks this kind of holistic healing and transformation. It addresses the wounds of victims—emotional, psychological, relational, spiritual. It supports offenders in changing—addressing underlying issues, developing new skills, building new relationships. It helps communities heal—rebuilding trust, strengthening bonds, addressing root causes. The goal is not merely to resolve the immediate conflict but to promote lasting healing and transformation.

The biblical narrative is filled with stories of healing and transformation. Saul of Tarsus, a persecutor of the church, was transformed into Paul the apostle, the greatest missionary in Christian history. Peter, who denied Jesus three times, was restored and became the leader of the early church. The woman at the well, with her complicated history, became an evangelist to her community. These transformations were not instantaneous or easy; they involved struggle, growth, and ongoing grace. But they demonstrate that change is possible, that no one is beyond the reach of God's transforming love.

Restorative justice participates in this transformative work. Every time a victim finds healing, every time an offender changes, every time a community is strengthened, it is a sign of the new creation that God is bringing about. These small transformations point toward the ultimate transformation when all things will be made new.

Non-Retaliation: The Way of Peace

Some theological teachings, such as the "turn the other cheek" principle in Christianity, emphasize non-retaliation and the pursuit of peace. Restorative justice aligns with these values by seeking non-punitive resolutions that focus on repair rather than revenge.

Jesus' teaching on non-retaliation is among His most challenging. "You have heard that it was said, 'An eye for an eye and a tooth for a tooth.' But I tell you not to resist an evil person. But whoever slaps you on your right cheek, turn the other to him also" (Matthew 5:38-39). This teaching does not mean passive acquiescence to evil but creative non-violent resistance—refusing to be drawn into the cycle of retaliation, choosing a different way.

The principle of lex talionis—"eye for eye, tooth for tooth"—had been given to limit vengeance, to ensure that punishment did not exceed the offense. Jesus calls His followers beyond even this limited retribution. He calls them to break the cycle of violence altogether, to respond to harm not with counter-harm but with creative, transformative action.

Restorative justice embodies this non-retaliatory approach. It refuses to respond to harm with more harm, to meet violence with violence, to perpetuate cycles of pain. Instead, it seeks to address the harm, to understand what happened, to hold offenders accountable through responsibility rather than punishment, to repair relationships, to restore community. This is not soft on crime; it is a different way of being tough—tough on the causes of crime, tough on the conditions that produce it, tough on the patterns that perpetuate it.

The Apostle Paul echoes this teaching: "Repay no one evil for evil. Have regard for good things in the sight of all men. If it is possible, as much as depends on you, live peaceably with all men. Beloved, do not avenge yourselves, but rather give place to wrath; for it is written, 'Vengeance is Mine, I will repay,' says the Lord" (Romans 12:17-19). Vengeance belongs to God; our role is to seek peace, to do good, to overcome evil with good.

Restorative justice, in its commitment to non-retaliation, participates in this biblical vision. It trusts that God's justice will ultimately prevail, that we do not need to take vengeance into our own hands, that we can focus on the work of healing and restoration. It embodies the way of peace that Jesus taught and lived.

Justice as Love: The Fulfillment of the Law

In some theological perspectives, justice is seen as an expression of divine love. Restorative justice embodies this concept by emphasizing love, empathy, and care in the process of addressing harm.

The connection between justice and love is rooted in the character of God. God is both just and loving; these are not competing attributes but complementary expressions of God's nature. God's justice is not cold and mechanical but warm and relational; it is justice that seeks to restore, to heal, to make whole. God's love is not soft and sentimental but strong and demanding; it is love that holds accountable, that calls to repentance, that refuses to let us stay as we are.

Jesus summarized the law in terms of love: "You shall love the Lord your God with all your heart, with all your soul, and with all your mind. This is the first and great commandment. And the second is like it: You shall love your neighbor as yourself. On these two commandments hang all the Law and the Prophets" (Matthew 22:37-40). Love is the fulfillment of the law, the principle from which all specific commands flow.

The Apostle Paul makes the same point: "Love does no harm to a neighbor; therefore love is the fulfillment of the law" (Romans 13:10). Whatever harms a neighbor is forbidden; whatever helps a neighbor is required. Love is not one commandment among many but the sum of all commandments, the measure of all actions.

Restorative justice embodies this understanding of justice as love in action. It seeks the good of victims by addressing their needs, giving them voice, supporting their healing. It seeks the good of offenders by holding them accountable, calling them to repentance, offering them restoration. It seeks the good of communities by involving them in healing, rebuilding trust, strengthening relationships. Restorative justice is love distributed to all affected by harm.

This understanding transforms how we think about justice. Justice is not about giving people what they deserve in some abstract sense but about loving them as neighbors. It is not about balancing scales through punishment but about restoring relationships through care. It is not about satisfying abstract principles but about meeting concrete needs.

Theological reflection on justice as love deepens our understanding of restorative justice. It reminds us that justice is not cold and mechanical but warm and relational. It reminds us that love is not soft and sentimental but strong and demanding. It reminds us that the goal of justice is not punishment but shalom—the peace, wholeness, and flourishing that God intends for all creation.

Empathy and Compassion: The Heart of God

Theological principles often stress the importance of empathy and compassion for others. Restorative justice encourages participants to empathize with one another and to approach conflicts with a compassionate mindset.

Empathy is the capacity to understand and share another's feelings. It is the ability to enter into another's experience, to see the world from their perspective, to feel something of what they feel. Empathy is essential for moral development, for healthy relationships, for compassionate action.

Compassion is empathy in action—the response of the heart to the suffering of another, the movement to alleviate that suffering, the commitment to stand with those who suffer. Compassion is not merely feeling sorry for someone but being moved to help.

In Christian theology, empathy and compassion are rooted in the character of God. God is described as "merciful and gracious, longsuffering, and abounding in goodness and truth" (Exodus

34:6). God hears the cry of the oppressed, sees the affliction of His people, knows their sufferings (Exodus 3:7). God's compassion is not passive but active, moving Him to deliver, to heal, to restore.

Jesus embodied this divine compassion. Again and again, the Gospels tell us that He was "moved with compassion" by the suffering He encountered (Matthew 9:36; 14:14; 15:32; Mark 1:41; 6:34). This compassion moved Him to act—to heal the sick, to feed the hungry, to teach the crowds, to welcome the outcast. His compassion was not merely a feeling but a motivation for action.

Restorative justice cultivates empathy and compassion. Victims are given the opportunity to share their experience, to express their pain, to be heard. Offenders are invited to listen, to understand, to feel something of what their victims have suffered. This encounter can be transformative, breaking through defenses and awakening genuine remorse. Community members are invited to care, to support, to stand with those who suffer. The process itself is an exercise in compassion.

Theological reflection on empathy and compassion deepens our understanding of restorative justice. It reminds us that these qualities are not merely nice additions to justice but essential to it. Justice without empathy becomes cold and mechanical; justice without compassion becomes harsh and punitive. Restorative justice, by cultivating empathy and compassion, embodies the heart of God.

Liberation Theology: Justice for the Oppressed

Liberation theology, which focuses on social justice and the marginalized, has strong connections with restorative justice.

Both approaches seek to address social inequalities and injustices, promoting healing and liberation for those who have been oppressed.

Liberation theology emerged in Latin America in the 1960s and 1970s, articulated by theologians like Gustavo Gutiérrez, Leonardo Boff, and Jon Sobrino. It reads Scripture from the perspective of the poor and oppressed, emphasizing God's preferential option for the poor and the call to work for justice and liberation. It challenges structural sin—the social, economic, and political systems that perpetuate poverty and oppression.

Restorative justice shares this concern for the marginalized. It recognizes that crime often arises from conditions of poverty, inequality, discrimination, and exclusion. It seeks to address these underlying causes, not merely to respond to individual offenses. It involves communities in the justice process, empowering them to address the conditions that produce harm. It prioritizes the needs of victims, many of whom come from marginalized communities.

Both liberation theology and restorative justice emphasize the importance of voice. The poor and oppressed must be able to speak for themselves, to name their own experience, to participate in decisions that affect their lives. Liberation theology calls this "the voice of the voiceless." Restorative justice calls it "victim participation." Both recognize that those who have been silenced must be heard.

Both also emphasize the importance of structural change. Liberation theology calls for transformation of the systems that produce and perpetuate poverty. Restorative justice calls for addressing the root causes of crime—the social, economic, and political conditions that contribute to offending behavior. Both recognize that individual change, while important, is not enough; systemic change is also necessary.

The biblical basis for liberation theology is found throughout Scripture. The Exodus story is the foundational narrative of liberation—God hearing the cry of His oppressed people and delivering them from bondage. The prophets consistently call for justice for the poor and oppressed. Jesus' inaugural sermon in Nazareth proclaims "good news to the poor," "liberty to the captives," and "recovery of sight to the blind" (Luke 4:18). The early church shared possessions so that there were no needy among them (Acts 4:32-35).

Restorative justice, in its concern for the marginalized and its commitment to addressing root causes, participates in this liberative vision. It is not merely about resolving individual cases but about transforming the conditions that produce harm. It is not merely about healing individual wounds but about creating a more just and equitable society. It is not merely about restoring relationships but about building a world where all can flourish.

Sacrificial Love: The Cost of Restoration

The concept of sacrificial love is present in many theological traditions. Restorative justice allows individuals to make amends for their wrongdoing, which can be seen as a form of sacrificial love in action.

Sacrificial love is love that costs something—that gives up something valuable for the sake of another. The ultimate example is the love of Christ, who "gave Himself for us" (Titus 2:14), who "humbled Himself and became obedient to the point of death, even the death of the cross" (Philippians 2:8). This sacrificial love is the heart of the gospel, the demonstration of God's love for sinful humanity.

In restorative justice, sacrificial love takes multiple forms. Victims practice sacrificial love when they extend forgiveness to those who have harmed them—releasing the offender from the debt of guilt, letting go of resentment, opening the door to reconciliation. This forgiveness costs something; it requires vulnerability, courage, and grace.

Offenders practice sacrificial love when they make amends for their actions—acknowledging wrongdoing, expressing remorse, paying restitution, changing behavior. This amends costs something; it requires humility, honesty, and effort. It may require giving up time, money, pride, or cherished patterns of behavior.

Communities practice sacrificial love when they welcome returning offenders, when they invest resources in restorative programs, when they commit to addressing root causes of crime. This welcome costs something; it requires trust, patience, and ongoing support.

The biblical concept of sacrificial love illuminates restorative justice. It reminds us that love is not cheap; it costs something. It reminds us that restoration is not easy; it requires sacrifice. It reminds us that the way of the cross—the way of sacrificial love—is the way of true justice.

The prophet Isaiah describes the suffering servant who "was wounded for our transgressions, He was bruised for our iniquities; the chastisement for our peace was upon Him, and by His stripes we are healed" (Isaiah 53:5). This is sacrificial love—the innocent one bearing the consequences of the guilty, opening the way to peace and healing. Restorative justice, in its own small way, participates in this sacrificial pattern.

The Unity of Theology and Restorative Justice

As we have seen, restorative justice and theology are deeply intertwined. The principles of restorative justice—acknowledgment of harm, accountability, forgiveness, reconciliation, community involvement, healing, transformation, non-retaliation, love, empathy, compassion, liberation, sacrificial love—are not merely secular values but deeply theological ones, rooted in the character of God and the teachings of Scripture.

This does not mean that restorative justice is only for Christians or that it requires religious faith to practice. Restorative justice stands on its own merits as a humane and effective approach to addressing harm. Its principles can be embraced by people of any faith or none. But for those who share the Christian faith, restorative justice is more than a useful technique; it is a way of embodying the gospel, of participating in God's work of reconciliation, of bearing witness to the kingdom.

The Jesus Paradigm, which we have explored throughout this book, is the integration of restorative justice with Christian faith. It sees in Jesus the model and source of restorative practice—His compassion for victims, His call to accountability, His offer of forgiveness, His ministry of reconciliation, His healing and transformation, His non-retaliatory love, His identification with the marginalized, His sacrificial death and victorious resurrection. It seeks to follow Jesus in responding to harm with grace and truth, in seeking restoration rather than retribution, in embodying love rather than revenge.

The Gospel of Restorative Justice is the good news that in Christ, God was reconciling the world to Himself, not counting our trespasses against us, and entrusting to us the ministry of reconciliation (2 Corinthians 5:18-19). It is the good news that healing is possible, that relationships can be restored, that even the deepest wounds can be transformed. It is the good news that we are called to be agents of this reconciliation in our families, our communities, our institutions, and our world.

As we continue to reflect on the relationship between restorative justice and theology, we are invited deeper into this vision. We are invited to see our own lives, our own relationships, our own responses to harm through the lens of God's restorative purposes. We are invited to practice restorative justice not merely as a technique but as a spirituality—a way of living in the world that reflects the heart of God. And we are invited to hope—to hope that God's restorative work will ultimately prevail, that all things will be made new, that justice and peace will embrace.

CHAPTER 19

FUTURE DIRECTIONS AND CHALLENGES

The journey of restorative justice is far from complete. What began as small experiments in victim-offender reconciliation, as the recovery of indigenous practices, as the vision of a few pioneering practitioners and scholars, has grown into a global movement with influence in criminal justice, education, family services, workplace relations, and international diplomacy. Yet for all this growth, restorative justice remains on the margins of most justice systems, an alternative rather than the norm, a complement rather than the foundation. The future of restorative justice holds both promise and challenge—opportunities for expansion and deepening, obstacles that must be overcome, questions that demand answers.

This chapter explores the future directions and challenges for restorative justice. We will examine the continued integration of restorative justice into mainstream justice systems, its global expansion, the need for robust research and evaluation, its potential for prevention and early intervention, the growth of restorative practices in education, the emergence of community-led initiatives, and the integration of technology. We will also consider the challenges that must be addressed—resistance from traditional systems, quality assurance, victim and offender safety, equity and access, funding and resources, cultural sensitivity, public perception, and complex cases. Through this exploration, we will see that the future of restorative justice is not predetermined but will be shaped by the choices we make, the commitments we keep, and the vision we pursue.

The Promise of Integration

One of the most significant future directions for restorative justice is its continued integration into mainstream justice systems. This integration is already underway in many countries, with restorative programs operating alongside conventional processes in criminal justice, family law, juvenile justice, and other areas. The future will likely see this integration deepen and expand.

Integration means that restorative justice is not merely an alternative for a few cases but an option available for many. It means that judges, prosecutors, defense attorneys, and other justice professionals are trained in restorative principles and practices, can identify appropriate cases for referral, and can support restorative processes. It means that restorative outcomes—restitution agreements, apology letters, community service plans—are recognized and enforced by the legal system. It means that restorative programs have stable funding, professional standards, and clear protocols.

The benefits of integration are significant. Victims have more opportunities to participate in justice processes that address their needs. Offenders have more opportunities to take responsibility and make amends. Communities have more opportunities to be involved in healing. Justice systems become more responsive, more effective, more humane.

Yet integration also poses risks. Restorative justice could be co-opted by systems that remain fundamentally punitive—used as a tool for system efficiency rather than a genuine alternative. It could be applied in ways that prioritize offender accountability over victim needs, or that pressure victims to participate against their will. It could lose its distinctive character, becoming just another program within a system that remains unchanged.

The challenge is to integrate without assimilating—to bring restorative principles and practices into mainstream systems while maintaining their integrity. This requires clear standards, strong advocacy, ongoing evaluation, and a commitment to restorative values that goes beyond mere compliance.

The biblical vision of leaven in the loaf (Matthew 13:33) offers a metaphor for integration. Leaven works from within, transforming the whole loaf by its presence. Restorative justice, integrated into mainstream systems, can work as leaven—transforming those systems from within, making them more responsive to victims, more accountable to communities, more focused on healing. This is the promise of integration.

Global Expansion: A Movement Without Borders

Restorative justice is likely to continue its global expansion, adapting to different cultural contexts and legal systems. International organizations and governments are increasingly recognizing its value in promoting reconciliation and addressing harm. The future will see restorative principles applied in new settings and adapted to new challenges.

The global expansion of restorative justice is already evident. The United Nations has adopted basic principles on restorative justice and encouraged member states to develop restorative programs. The European Union has funded restorative justice initiatives and supported networking among practitioners. The African Union has recognized traditional restorative practices and encouraged their integration with formal systems. In every region of the world, restorative justice is taking root.

This global expansion brings both opportunities and challenges. Opportunities include learning from diverse cultural expressions of restorative principles, adapting practices to new contexts, building a global community of restorative practitioners, and addressing transnational issues through restorative approaches. Challenges include ensuring that restorative justice is not imposed by dominant cultures on marginalized ones, that local traditions are honored, that practices are adapted appropriately, that quality is maintained across diverse settings.

The future of restorative justice will require ongoing attention to these challenges. It will require humility—recognizing that no single culture has a monopoly on restorative wisdom, that we have much to learn from others. It will require respect—honoring the integrity of local traditions, allowing communities to adapt restorative principles in ways that make sense for them. It will require connection—building networks that link practitioners across borders, facilitating learning and mutual support.

The biblical vision of a diverse humanity united in worship of God (Revelation 7:9) provides a framework for global expansion. The multitude from every nation, tribe, people, and language does not lose its distinctiveness but brings its unique gifts to the worship of God. So too, restorative justice in its global expression does not require uniformity but celebrates diversity—different practices expressing the same principles, different cultures embodying the same values, different contexts applying the same wisdom.

Research and Evaluation: Building the Evidence Base

Future directions for restorative justice include more robust research and evaluation of restorative justice programs. Gathering evidence of their effectiveness can help inform policy decisions and improve practices. The future will see continued growth in the research base for restorative justice.

Research on restorative justice has already produced impressive results. Studies have shown that restorative programs reduce recidivism, increase victim satisfaction, and cost less than conventional processing. Meta-analyses have confirmed these findings across multiple contexts and countries. Yet there is much we still do not know.

Future research should address several key questions. What types of restorative processes work best for what types of cases? What factors predict successful outcomes? How can restorative programs be implemented with fidelity while adapting to local contexts? What are the long-term effects of restorative justice on victims, offenders, and communities? How can restorative principles be applied to new areas—environmental harm, corporate wrongdoing, historical injustice?

Research should also address questions of equity. Do restorative programs serve all communities equally? Are there disparities in access, participation, or outcomes based on race, class, gender, or other factors? How can restorative justice be designed and implemented to promote equity rather than perpetuate inequality?

Evaluation is essential for continuous improvement. Programs need feedback on what is working and what is not, where they are succeeding and where they need to change. Rigorous evaluation, using both quantitative and qualitative methods, can provide this feedback. It can also build the case for restorative justice with policymakers, funders, and the public.

The biblical wisdom literature emphasizes the importance of knowledge and understanding. "Wisdom is the principal thing; therefore get wisdom. And in all your getting, get understanding" (Proverbs 4:7). Research and evaluation are forms of getting understanding—seeking to know what works, what doesn't, and why. They are expressions of the wisdom that seeks to do justice wisely and well.

Prevention and Early Intervention: Stopping Harm Before It Starts

Restorative justice can be applied as a preventive tool. Future efforts may focus on early intervention and the use of restorative practices to address conflicts and wrongdoing before they escalate. Prevention is ultimately more humane and less costly than response, and restorative approaches have much to offer.

Restorative prevention takes many forms. In schools, restorative practices teach students conflict resolution skills, build positive relationships, and create a climate of respect that prevents bullying and violence. In families, restorative approaches help members communicate effectively, address issues early, and strengthen bonds that prevent escalation. In communities, restorative initiatives build social cohesion, address underlying tensions, and create networks of support that prevent crime.

Restorative prevention addresses root causes. Rather than waiting for harm to occur and then responding, restorative prevention seeks to understand and address the conditions that produce harm. It asks why conflicts arise, why people offend, why communities fracture—and works to change those conditions.

Restorative prevention also builds capacity. By teaching restorative skills—communication, empathy, conflict resolution—to children and adults, it equips people to handle conflicts constructively throughout their lives. These skills, once learned, become resources for preventing harm in countless situations.

The biblical wisdom literature emphasizes prevention. Proverbs is filled with practical guidance for avoiding conflict, maintaining relationships, and living wisely. "A prudent man foresees evil and hides himself, but the simple pass on and are punished" (Proverbs 22:3). Foresight—anticipating problems and taking preventive action—is a mark of wisdom. Restorative prevention embodies this wisdom.

Restorative Practices in Education: Transforming Schools

The use of restorative practices in education is expected to grow. Schools are recognizing the benefits of creating a more inclusive, empathetic, and accountable learning environment. The future will see restorative practices become standard in educational settings, from early childhood through higher education.

Restorative practices in schools have already demonstrated significant benefits. They reduce suspensions and expulsions, improve school climate, decrease bullying, and increase academic achievement. They teach students essential life skills—communication, empathy, conflict resolution, accountability. They build stronger relationships among students, teachers, and families.

The future will likely see restorative practices integrated into every aspect of school life. Classrooms will use circles for community building and conflict resolution. Schools will have trained restorative practitioners on staff. Discipline policies will be rewritten to prioritize restorative approaches. Teacher preparation programs will include training in restorative practices. Parent engagement will include restorative principles.

Restorative practices in education also have the potential to transform communities. Students who learn restorative skills carry them into their families, their workplaces, their neighborhoods. Schools that model restorative values become resources for the wider community. The impact of restorative education ripples outward, affecting not only individual students but the whole society.

Jesus' welcome of children and His teaching about their importance in the kingdom (Matthew 19:13-15; 18:1-5) provide a theological foundation for restorative education. Children are not merely future adults but present members of the community, deserving of respect, worthy of care, capable of learning and growing. Restorative practices in schools honor this vision, treating students as full participants in the community of learning.

Community-Led Initiatives: Justice From the Ground Up

The future may see an expansion of community-led restorative justice initiatives that empower communities to address conflicts and harm on their terms. These initiatives reflect the principle that justice is not something done to communities but something done with them and by them.

Community-led restorative justice takes many forms. Neighborhood justice centers offer mediation and conflict resolution services. Faith-based organizations provide restorative programming for offenders and support for victims. Community groups organize circles and conferences to address local conflicts. Indigenous communities practice traditional restorative approaches. These initiatives are rooted in local knowledge, responsive to local needs, sustained by local commitment.

Community-led initiatives have several advantages. They are more accessible than formal system programs, with lower barriers to participation. They are more flexible, able to adapt to individual circumstances. They build local capacity and ownership, strengthening community resilience. They are often more culturally appropriate, reflecting community values and traditions.

Community-led initiatives also face challenges. They may lack stable funding, relying on grants and donations. They may struggle with quality assurance and accountability. They may be marginalized or ignored by formal systems. They may face resistance from those who prefer punitive approaches.

The future will require supporting community-led initiatives while addressing these challenges. This means providing resources without imposing control, offering training without demanding conformity, connecting initiatives without eroding local autonomy. It means recognizing that communities are the primary agents of justice, not merely recipients of services provided by others.

The early church provides a model for community-led initiatives. The first believers did not rely on imperial institutions to address their conflicts or care for their members. They created their own structures—apostles, elders, deacons—to govern their community. They practiced mutual accountability, confessing sins to one another and praying for one another (James 5:16). They supported widows, orphans, and others in need (Acts 6:1-7). This was justice from the ground up, rooted in community and sustained by faith.

Technology Integration: Expanding Reach

The use of technology, such as virtual conferencing and digital tools, may expand the reach of restorative justice processes, making them more accessible and efficient. Technology offers both opportunities and challenges for restorative practice.

Technology can increase access to restorative justice. Virtual meetings can connect participants who are geographically distant, who have mobility limitations, or who cannot meet in person for safety reasons. Online platforms can provide information about restorative justice, connect people with programs, and offer training for practitioners. Digital tools can support case management, documentation, and evaluation.

Technology can also enhance restorative processes. Video conferencing can allow participants to see each other's faces and hear each other's voices, preserving some of the benefits of in-person encounter. Online circles can bring together people from diverse locations, creating opportunities for dialogue that would otherwise be impossible. Digital agreements can be easily shared and tracked.

Yet technology also poses challenges. Virtual encounters lack the full richness of in-person interaction—the subtle cues, the shared physical presence, the embodied experience of encounter. Technology may create barriers for those without access or skills. Privacy and security concerns must be addressed. The relational core of restorative justice—genuine human encounter—must not be lost in technological mediation.

The future will require thoughtful integration of technology, using it to expand access and enhance practice while preserving the relational heart of restorative justice. This means developing best practices for virtual restorative processes, ensuring equitable access to technology, and remaining attentive to what is lost as well as what is gained when encounter is mediated.

The biblical vision of the body of Christ, with its many members connected across distance and difference (1 Corinthians 12), offers a framework for thinking about technology and restorative justice. Technology can connect members of the body who would otherwise be separated, enabling them to support one another, to share their experiences, to work together for healing. But technology must serve connection, not replace it; it must facilitate encounter, not substitute for it.

Resistance from Traditional Systems

Despite the growth of restorative justice, resistance from traditional justice systems remains a significant challenge. Many within those systems view restorative justice as a threat to established punitive practices, as soft on crime, as an unwelcome innovation. Overcoming this resistance requires sustained effort.

Resistance takes many forms. Some justice professionals simply do not know about restorative justice or misunderstand what it is. Others are skeptical of its effectiveness, doubting that it can really hold offenders accountable or protect public safety. Others are threatened by it—concerned that it might reduce their role, challenge their authority, or require them to learn new skills. Still others are ideologically committed to punitive approaches, believing that punishment is the only appropriate response to crime.

Addressing resistance requires multiple strategies. Education is essential—helping justice professionals understand what restorative justice is, how it works, and what evidence supports its effectiveness. Demonstration projects can show restorative justice in action, providing concrete examples of success. Relationship-building can create trust between restorative practitioners and system professionals, turning potential opponents into partners. Policy change can create incentives for restorative approaches, making them easier to use and more widely available.

The biblical story of Joseph (Genesis 37-50) offers wisdom for navigating resistance. Joseph faced resistance from his brothers, who sold him into slavery. He faced resistance from Potiphar's wife, who falsely accused him. He faced years of imprisonment and obscurity. Yet he remained faithful, used his gifts, and ultimately was elevated to a position of influence from which he could save many lives. His story teaches patience, perseverance, and trust that God can work even through resistance.

Quality Assurance: Maintaining Standards

Ensuring the quality and consistency of restorative justice programs and processes is a significant challenge. Proper training and adherence to best practices are essential. The future must include robust quality assurance mechanisms.

Quality assurance begins with training. Restorative practitioners need comprehensive training in restorative principles, communication skills, conflict resolution, trauma awareness, cultural sensitivity, and ethical practice. They need opportunities for supervised practice, ongoing professional development, and peer support. Training programs must be rigorous, accessible, and regularly updated.

Quality assurance also requires standards. Clear standards for restorative processes—preparation of participants, facilitation, confidentiality, agreement development, follow-up—can ensure consistency and protect participants. Standards for programs—staffing, policies, evaluation—can ensure accountability and effectiveness. Standards should be developed through inclusive processes involving practitioners, researchers, and community representatives.

Quality assurance involves oversight. Mechanisms for monitoring and evaluating restorative programs can identify problems, ensure compliance, and promote improvement. Complaint procedures can give participants recourse if things go wrong. Accreditation can recognize programs that meet high standards.

The biblical concept of "testing" applies to quality assurance. Paul urges believers to "test all things; hold fast what is good" (1 Thessalonians 5:21). Testing involves examining, evaluating, discerning—not accepting everything uncritically but distinguishing what is good from what is not. Quality assurance in restorative justice is a form of testing, ensuring that programs are worthy of the trust placed in them.

Victim and Offender Safety: Balancing Needs

Balancing the needs for victim and offender safety while conducting face-to-face meetings in restorative processes can be a challenge. Ensuring that all participants are safe—physically, emotionally, and psychologically—is essential.

Safety concerns are legitimate. Victims may fear facing those who harmed them, worrying about re-traumatization, intimidation, or further harm. Offenders may fear retaliation, humiliation, or unfair treatment. These fears must be taken seriously and addressed through careful preparation and appropriate safeguards.

Safety requires thorough preparation. Facilitators must meet separately with each participant before any joint meeting, explaining the process, assessing readiness, identifying concerns, and developing strategies for managing difficult situations. Participants need to understand what will happen, what their rights are, and what support is available.

Safety requires appropriate settings. Meetings should be held in neutral, accessible locations with adequate security if needed.

Participants should have support persons present if desired. Facilitators should be trained to manage difficult emotions and intervene if necessary.

Safety requires ongoing attention. Even after a successful meeting, participants may need follow-up support. Agreements should include provisions for ongoing safety. Programs should have protocols for responding to concerns that arise after the process concludes.

The biblical emphasis on保护 the vulnerable applies to safety in restorative justice. God is described as a refuge and strength, a very present help in trouble (Psalm 46:1). Jesus consistently protected those who were vulnerable—the woman caught in adultery from her accusers, the children from dismissive disciples, the outcasts from societal condemnation. Restorative justice must similarly protect the vulnerable, ensuring that participation does not expose them to further harm.

Equity and Access: Justice for All

Ensuring equitable access to restorative justice processes and addressing disparities in participation is a challenge that requires ongoing attention. Restorative justice must be available to all who need it, not only to those with privilege, resources, or connections.

Disparities in access are well-documented. Restorative programs are often concentrated in urban areas, leaving rural communities underserved. They may require participants to have transportation, childcare, or flexible schedules that not everyone can manage. They may be available only for certain types of offenses or certain categories of offenders. They may be culturally inaccessible to some communities.

Disparities in participation also exist. Research suggests that restorative programs may serve fewer people of color, fewer low-income individuals, fewer non-English speakers than their proportions in the justice system would predict. These disparities reflect broader inequalities and must be addressed.

Addressing equity requires intentional effort. Programs should be located in underserved communities, with outreach to ensure that all who could benefit know about them. Services should be provided in multiple languages, with cultural competence built into every aspect of practice. Barriers to participation—transportation, childcare, lost wages—should be addressed through support services. Data should be collected and analyzed to identify disparities and guide improvement.

The biblical vision of justice includes a special concern for the marginalized. The prophets consistently call for justice for the poor, the widow, the orphan, the stranger—those most vulnerable to exclusion and exploitation. Jesus' ministry was characterized by reaching out to those on the margins—lepers, tax collectors, sinners, Samaritans, women, children. Restorative justice, in its commitment to equity and access, participates in this biblical vision.

Funding and Resources: Sustaining the Work

Restorative justice programs often struggle with limited funding and resources, hindering their ability to reach their full potential. Sustainable funding is essential for the growth and effectiveness of restorative justice.

Funding challenges are multiple. Restorative programs often rely on soft money—grants, donations, short-term contracts—that makes long-term planning difficult. They compete for resources with established justice systems that have stable, ongoing funding. They may be seen as optional extras rather than essential services, making them vulnerable to budget cuts.

Adequate funding is needed for multiple purposes: trained staff, appropriate facilities, support services for participants, training and professional development, evaluation and research, outreach and education. Without adequate resources, programs cannot maintain quality or serve all who need them.

Addressing funding challenges requires advocacy. Restorative justice advocates must make the case to policymakers, funders, and the public that restorative programs are worth investing in. They must demonstrate, through research and testimony, that restorative justice produces better outcomes at lower cost than conventional approaches. They must build coalitions that amplify their voices and increase their influence.

Sustainable funding requires diverse sources. Government appropriations can provide stable base funding. Foundation grants can support innovation and expansion. Private donations can demonstrate community support. Fee-for-service arrangements can generate revenue. A diverse funding base reduces dependence on any single source and increases resilience.

The early church's practice of sharing resources (Acts 2:44-45; 4:32-35) offers a model for funding restorative justice. Believers pooled their resources, ensuring that no one was in need. This sharing was not compelled but voluntary, flowing from shared commitment. Funding restorative justice similarly requires shared commitment from diverse sources, each contributing according to its capacity.

Cultural Sensitivity: Honoring Diversity

Adapting restorative justice to diverse cultural contexts and ensuring cultural sensitivity is a challenge, as approaches may need to be customized to fit local norms and values. Restorative justice must be culturally appropriate, not culturally imposed.

Cultural sensitivity begins with recognition. Every culture has its own ways of addressing harm, resolving conflict, and restoring relationships. These traditional practices embody wisdom accumulated over generations. Restorative justice advocates must recognize and respect this wisdom, seeing themselves as learners as well as teachers.

Cultural sensitivity requires adaptation. Restorative practices cannot simply be transplanted from one context to another. They must be adapted to fit local values, norms, and traditions. This adaptation should be led by community members, not imposed by outsiders. It should honor what is already present while introducing new possibilities.

Cultural sensitivity involves humility. Outsiders cannot fully understand another culture; they will inevitably make mistakes, misunderstand, cause offense. Humility means acknowledging this, learning from mistakes, and relying on community members to guide the way. It means recognizing that we are guests in another's cultural home, not masters.

Cultural sensitivity also requires critical reflection. Not all traditional practices are good; some may be harmful, oppressive, or unjust. Cultural sensitivity does not mean uncritical acceptance of everything in a culture. It means engaging respectfully with community members to discern what is life-giving and what is not, what should be preserved and what should be changed.

The diversity of the early church offers a model for cultural sensitivity. The Jerusalem council (Acts 15) wrestled with how to include Gentiles without requiring them to become Jews. The decision—to require only essential things and respect differences—established a principle of cultural accommodation. Paul's practice of becoming "all things to all people" (1 Corinthians 9:22) reflects this same sensitivity. Restorative justice, in adapting to diverse cultures, follows this apostolic example.

Public Perception: Building Understanding

Overcoming public skepticism or misconceptions about restorative justice can be challenging, especially when it is seen as too lenient or as an alternative to traditional punishment. Public perception matters; without public support, restorative justice cannot thrive.

Misconceptions about restorative justice are common. Many people think it means letting offenders off without consequences. Others think it is only for minor offenses or first-time offenders. Others think it ignores victims' needs or fails to hold offenders accountable. These misconceptions create resistance and limit support.

Addressing misconceptions requires education. Public awareness campaigns can introduce restorative justice principles and practices to broad audiences. Media engagement can share stories of restorative justice in action, humanizing the approach and demonstrating its benefits. Community forums can provide opportunities for dialogue and questions. Schools can teach restorative values to the next generation.

Addressing misconceptions also requires demonstration. When people see restorative justice working—victims satisfied, offenders accountable, communities strengthened—they are more likely to support it. Successful programs, well-documented and well-publicized, build confidence in the approach.

Addressing misconceptions requires honesty. Restorative justice is not a panacea; it does not work in every case, for every person. Acknowledging limitations builds credibility. Being transparent about challenges and failures demonstrates integrity. The goal is not to persuade people that restorative justice is perfect but that it is valuable, that it deserves a place alongside other approaches.

The prophetic tradition's public proclamation offers a model for shaping public perception. Isaiah did not whisper his message; he cried aloud, sparing not his voice (Isaiah 58:1). Jeremiah did not hide his prophecy; he stood in the temple courts and proclaimed it to all who would hear (Jeremiah 7:2). John the Baptist preached in the wilderness, and crowds came out to hear him. Shaping public perception for restorative justice requires similar courage, similar visibility, similar persistence.

Complex Cases: Addressing Severe Harm

Certain complex cases, such as those involving severe violence or mass atrocities, pose challenges for restorative justice processes. These cases require special care, specialized expertise, and appropriate limits on what restorative justice can accomplish.

Severe violence—murder, rape, torture—creates wounds that may never fully heal. Victims may be deeply traumatized, unable or unwilling to face those who harmed them. Offenders may be dangerous, unrepentant, or incapable of genuine change. Communities may be divided, fearful, and angry. Restorative justice in these cases must proceed with extreme caution.

Mass atrocities—genocide, crimes against humanity, war crimes—involve harms on a scale that individual restorative processes cannot fully address. Thousands of victims, thousands of perpetrators, decades of trauma—no single process can do justice to such complexity. Restorative principles must be adapted, combined with other approaches, and pursued with humility about what can be achieved.

In these complex cases, restorative justice is not an alternative to accountability but a complement to it. Criminal prosecution may be necessary to hold perpetrators accountable and to affirm the seriousness of the harm. Truth commissions may be needed to document what happened and to give victims a voice. Reparations may be required to address material losses. Restorative processes can contribute to these efforts—by providing opportunities for victim-offender dialogue where appropriate, by supporting community healing, by promoting reconciliation.

The limits of restorative justice must be acknowledged. Not every harm can be repaired; not every relationship can be restored; not every offender can be changed. Restorative justice does not promise to fix everything; it promises to do what can be done, to seek healing where healing is possible, to pursue restoration as far as it can go.

The cross of Christ is the ultimate example of facing severe harm with restorative love. Jesus did not minimize the evil done to Him; He named it, bore it, and absorbed it. He did not retaliate; He forgave. He did not despair; He trusted in God's ultimate victory. The cross does not explain suffering or make it go away, but it transforms it—making it a source of hope rather than despair, of life rather than death. Restorative justice, in facing severe harm with courage and hope, participates in this mystery.

The Future and the Jesus Paradigm

As we consider the future directions and challenges for restorative justice, we do so through the lens of the Jesus Paradigm. This paradigm—rooted in the life and teachings of Jesus, grounded in the biblical vision of shalom, oriented toward reconciliation and restoration—shapes how we understand and pursue the future of restorative justice.

The Jesus Paradigm calls us to integration—not merely adding restorative programs to existing systems but transforming those systems from within, making them more responsive to victims, more accountable to communities, more focused on healing. It calls us to global expansion—not imposing one culture's practices on others but learning from diverse expressions of restorative wisdom, honoring local traditions while sharing common principles.

The Jesus Paradigm calls us to research and evaluation—not as an end in itself but as a means to better serve those who suffer, to understand what works and what doesn't, to be good stewards of the resources entrusted to us. It calls us to prevention and early intervention—addressing root causes, building capacity, creating conditions in which harm is less likely to occur.

The Jesus Paradigm calls us to restorative education—forming the next generation in the values of empathy, accountability, and reconciliation, creating schools that are communities of shalom. It calls us to community-led initiatives—empowering communities to be agents of their own healing, trusting local wisdom and local leadership.

The Jesus Paradigm calls us to thoughtful technology integration—using tools to expand access and enhance practice while preserving the relational heart of restorative justice, ensuring that technology serves connection rather than replacing it.

The Jesus Paradigm also equips us to face the challenges ahead. When we encounter resistance from traditional systems, we remember Jesus' patience with those who opposed Him, His willingness to engage rather than withdraw, His trust that God's purposes would ultimately prevail. When we struggle with quality assurance, we remember Jesus' attention to detail, His careful teaching, His investment in formation.

When we wrestle with safety concerns, we remember Jesus' protection of the vulnerable—His defense of the woman caught in adultery, His welcome of children, His healing of the outcast. When we confront inequity and access barriers, we remember Jesus' special concern for the marginalized—His reaching out to lepers, tax collectors, Samaritans, women, sinners.

When we face funding challenges, we remember Jesus' reliance on the generosity of others—the women who supported His ministry out of their means (Luke 8:1-3), the crowds who shared loaves and fishes, the early church's practice of holding everything in common. When we struggle with cultural sensitivity, we remember Jesus' own cultural embeddedness—His Jewish identity, His engagement with Samaritans and Gentiles, His ability to transcend cultural boundaries while honoring cultural particularity.

When we confront public skepticism, we remember Jesus' patience with misunderstanding, His willingness to explain, His trust that the truth would ultimately be known. When we face complex cases of severe harm, we remember the cross—God's own entry into the darkest places of human suffering, God's refusal to abandon us even there, God's promise that death does not have the final word.

The Ongoing Journey

The future of restorative justice is not yet written. It will be shaped by the choices we make, the commitments we keep, the vision we pursue. It will be shaped by practitioners who show up day after day to facilitate difficult conversations, by victims who find courage to face those who harmed them, by offenders who take responsibility and make amends, by communities that embrace the work of healing. It will be shaped by researchers who ask hard questions and seek honest answers, by advocates who make the case to policymakers and the public, by educators who teach restorative values to the next generation.

The challenges are real. Resistance, quality concerns, safety issues, equity gaps, funding shortages, cultural complexities, public skepticism, the difficulty of severe cases—these are not imagined problems but genuine obstacles. They will not disappear on their own; they must be addressed with wisdom, persistence, and creativity.

But the promise is also real. Integration into mainstream systems, global expansion, robust research, prevention and early intervention, restorative education, community-led initiatives, thoughtful technology use—these are not fantasies but possibilities, already being realized in many places, capable of being extended much further.

The Gospel of Restorative Justice is that God is in the business of making all things new. This is not a promise that everything will be easy or that all obstacles will be overcome. It is a promise that God's restorative purposes will ultimately prevail, that the future belongs to shalom, that the work we do now participates in something eternal.

As we look to the future, we do so with hope—not naive optimism that ignores challenges but faithful hope that trusts in God's promises. We do so with commitment—not casual interest that fades when difficulties arise but deep dedication that perseveres through trials. We do so with joy—not grim determination that drains life but joyful participation in the work of healing that gives life.

The journey continues. The future awaits. And the one who is the pioneer and perfecter of our faith, who for the joy set before Him endured the cross, goes before us. We follow in His steps, walking the way of restorative justice, embodying the Jesus Paradigm, bearing witness to the Gospel of Restorative Justice, until the day when all things are made new.

CHAPTER 20

EMBRACING RESTORATIVE JUSTICE THROUGH THE LENS OF JESUS

We have journeyed far together through these pages. From the ancient codes of Mesopotamia to the teachings of the Hebrew prophets, from the parables of Jesus to the writings of the Apostle Paul, from the indigenous healing circles of Africa and North America to the restorative programs of modern Europe and New Zealand, from the challenges of institutional resistance to the promise of global expansion—we have traced the contours of a vision of justice that is as old as humanity and as new as the latest innovation in restorative practice. Throughout this journey, one figure has stood at the center, illuminating the path and embodying the principles we have explored: Jesus of Nazareth, the one in whom the justice and mercy of God are perfectly revealed.

As we come to the conclusion of this exploration, we are invited to embrace restorative justice through the lens of Jesus. This is not merely an intellectual exercise or a policy preference; it is a calling, a way of life, a participation in the very work of God. The lens of Jesus transforms how we see everything—how we understand justice, how we respond to harm, how we relate to victims and offenders, how we build community, how we hope for healing. Through this lens, we discover that restorative justice is not simply a set of techniques or programs but a profound expression of the gospel itself.

The Journey Summarized: A Vision Unfolding

We began this book by exploring the nature of restorative justice, contrasting it with punitive approaches and grounding it in the biblical vision of shalom. We saw that restorative justice is not a novel invention but a recovery of ancient wisdom—wisdom embedded in the Law of Moses, proclaimed by the prophets, embodied by Jesus, and practiced by the early church. We learned that restorative justice focuses on harm rather than rule-breaking, on victims rather than the state, on accountability through responsibility rather than punishment, on healing rather than retribution, on community involvement rather than professional control.

We then examined the teachings of Jesus on justice, discovering that His message consistently prioritizes love, compassion, forgiveness, and reconciliation over legalism, retribution, and exclusion. The Sermon on the Mount, the parables of the Good Samaritan and the Prodigal Son, the encounters with Zacchaeus and the woman caught in adultery, the command to forgive seventy times seven—these and countless other passages reveal a vision of justice that is fundamentally restorative.

We explored the parables of Jesus as narratives of restoration, finding in them profound illustrations of restorative principles. The Good Samaritan showed us what love in action looks like.

The Prodigal Son revealed the heart of a God who runs to meet returning sinners. The Unforgiving Servant warned us of the consequences of refusing to extend the mercy we have received. The Lost Sheep and Lost Coin reminded us of the value of every person and the joy of restoration. The Workers in the Vineyard challenged our merit-based calculations and invited us into God's generous grace.

We delved into forgiveness and reconciliation, discovering that these are not optional extras for the especially virtuous but essential practices for all who would follow Jesus. We learned that forgiveness is not forgetting or excusing but releasing the offender from the debt of guilt. We learned that reconciliation is not always possible but always worth pursuing. We saw that both forgiveness and reconciliation are rooted in the character of God and made possible through the work of Christ.

We examined restorative justice in biblical context and in the church, discovering that the Christian community is called to be a restorative community—a place where confession and repentance are practiced, where forgiveness and reconciliation are extended, where mediation and accountability are offered, where victims are supported and offenders are restored, where the values of the kingdom are embodied in daily life.

We traced the historical development of justice, from ancient codes to modern systems, from retributive philosophies to restorative alternatives. We saw that the seeds of restorative justice were present from the beginning—in the restitution provisions of the Law of Moses, in the communal practices of indigenous peoples, in the teachings of Jesus and the apostles. We also saw how punitive approaches came to dominate Western legal systems, and how restorative justice has reemerged in recent decades as a critique of and alternative to those approaches.

We explored modern restorative justice, examining its principles, practices, and evidence base. We saw that restorative justice is victim-centered, offender-accountable, community-involved, healing-oriented, and evidence-supported. We learned that it is being applied in criminal justice, education, family services, workplaces, and international diplomacy. We discovered that it has been recognized by the United Nations, supported by governments, and embraced by communities around the world.

We considered Jesus as the model for restorative justice, examining how His compassion, forgiveness, reconciliation, accountability, community involvement, restoration of dignity, healing, and love provide a comprehensive paradigm for restorative practice. We saw that Jesus did not merely teach about restorative justice; He embodied it in His life, His ministry, His death, and His resurrection. We learned that those who follow Jesus are called to the same ministry of reconciliation.

We examined restorative justice in Christian communities, exploring how churches can become centers of restorative practice. We saw that this requires education and training, victim support, offender accountability, community engagement, and a commitment to holistic ministry. We learned that the church, as the body of Christ, is uniquely positioned to model restorative values and to extend restorative practices to the wider community.

We considered the challenges and critiques that restorative justice faces—theological differences, institutional resistance, resource limitations, participant unwillingness, societal skepticism, equity concerns, measurement difficulties, legal gaps—and we explored strategies for overcoming these obstacles. We learned that these challenges are real but not insurmountable, and that addressing them requires patience, wisdom, and persistence.

We examined restorative justice and healing, discovering that restorative processes are designed to facilitate healing for victims, offenders, and communities. We learned that healing requires acknowledgment of harm, empowerment of victims, accountability of offenders, apology and forgiveness, restitution and repair, community support, prevention of recidivism, resolution of trauma, humanization of all parties, personal growth, healing circles, and catharsis and closure. We saw that healing is holistic, relational, communal, and possible.

We compared restorative justice and criminal justice, seeing the contrasts between punitive and restorative approaches, between government-led and community-led processes, between adversarial and collaborative methods, between victim as witness and victim as central, between limited and extensive victim participation, between sentencing and restitution. We learned that these approaches can coexist and that restorative justice offers a way to humanize the justice system.

We explored restorative justice in the global context, discovering its adaptability to diverse cultures and its application to a wide range of challenges. We learned from South Africa's Truth and Reconciliation Commission, New Zealand's family group conferences, Canada's indigenous healing circles, Rwanda's Gacaca courts, Scandinavia's rehabilitative prisons, and many other examples. We saw that restorative justice is not confined to one culture or context but has universal relevance.

We examined restorative justice in education, discovering its power to transform schools, reduce bullying, improve climate, teach life skills, and keep students in school. We learned that restorative practices in education are not merely disciplinary alternatives but comprehensive approaches to forming young people in the values of respect, responsibility, and relationship.

We explored restorative justice in family relationships, discovering its application to conflicts between parents and children, among siblings, in couples therapy, in child welfare, and in other family contexts. We learned that restorative practices can heal emotional wounds, rebuild trust, and strengthen the bonds that hold families together.

We considered case studies in restorative justice, learning from real examples in Germany, New Zealand, schools, Belgium, South Africa, and other contexts. We saw that restorative justice works—that victims find healing, offenders change, communities are strengthened, and recidivism is reduced. We learned that restorative justice is not merely theoretical but practical, not merely idealistic but effective.

We reflected on restorative justice and theology, discovering the deep connections between restorative principles and theological themes—redemption and forgiveness, reconciliation, community and restoration, accountability, healing and transformation, non-retaliation, justice as love, empathy and compassion, liberation, sacrificial love. We learned that restorative justice is not merely compatible with Christian faith but is, in many ways, a practical expression of it.

And finally, we looked to the future, considering the directions restorative justice may take and the challenges it must overcome. We saw promise in integration with mainstream systems, global expansion, research and evaluation, prevention and early intervention, restorative education, community-led initiatives, and technology integration. We acknowledged challenges in resistance from traditional systems, quality assurance, victim and offender safety, equity and access, funding and resources, cultural sensitivity, public perception, and complex cases. We learned that the future of restorative justice is not predetermined but will be shaped by the choices we make and the commitments we keep.

The Lens of Jesus: A Transformative Vision

Throughout this journey, we have looked at restorative justice through the lens of Jesus. This lens is not merely one perspective among many; it is the perspective that gives coherence and meaning to all the others. Through this lens, we see that restorative justice is not a human invention but a divine revelation—a glimpse into the heart of God, who is Himself the great Restorer.

Through the lens of Jesus, we see that every person has intrinsic worth and dignity because every person is created in the image of God. This imago Dei is the foundation of restorative justice, the reason we cannot give up on anyone, the source of hope that even the worst offenders can change. Jesus demonstrated this dignity in every encounter—touching lepers, speaking with Samaritans, eating with tax collectors, welcoming children. He saw beyond labels and sins to the human being created in God's likeness.

Through the lens of Jesus, we see that harm is real and must be acknowledged. Jesus did not minimize sin or pretend that wrongdoing doesn't matter. He confronted the Pharisees with their hypocrisy, called sinners to repentance, wept over Jerusalem's unbelief, and bore the weight of the world's sin on the cross. Restorative justice, following His example, insists on honest acknowledgment of harm as the first step toward healing.

Through the lens of Jesus, we see that accountability is essential. Jesus held people responsible for their actions—the rich young ruler for his idolatry, Peter for his denial, the Pharisees for their hypocrisy, Judas for his betrayal. But His accountability was always aimed at restoration, not destruction. He called people to account not to condemn them but to save them, not to destroy them but to restore them.

Through the lens of Jesus, we see that forgiveness is possible and powerful. Jesus taught His disciples to pray, "Forgive us our debts, as we forgive our debtors." He told parables about forgiveness, commanded limitless forgiveness, and modeled ultimate forgiveness on the cross: "Father, forgive them, for they do not know what they do." Restorative justice, following His example, creates conditions in which forgiveness can occur—not forced, not cheap, but genuine and healing.

Through the lens of Jesus, we see that reconciliation is the goal. Jesus came to reconcile us to God and to one another. He broke down dividing walls, created one new humanity from hostile factions, and entrusted to us the ministry of reconciliation. Restorative justice, following His example, seeks to restore relationships, rebuild trust, and reunite communities.

Through the lens of Jesus, we see that love is the way. Jesus summarized the law in two commands: love God and love neighbor. He taught that love for enemies is the mark of His followers. He demonstrated that love is not merely a feeling but an action—laying down one's life for others. Restorative justice, following His example, seeks to address harm with love, to respond to wrongdoing with care, to overcome evil with good.

Through the lens of Jesus, we see that healing is possible. Jesus healed the sick, gave sight to the blind, made the lame walk, cleansed lepers, cast out demons, raised the dead. His healing was never merely physical but always holistic—restoring people to community, to dignity, to purpose. Restorative justice, following His example, seeks healing for victims, offenders, and communities—healing that is physical, emotional, psychological, relational, and spiritual.

Through the lens of Jesus, we see that transformation is real. Jesus transformed fishermen into fishers of men, tax collectors into disciples, persecutors into apostles, deniers into leaders. His encounters changed people—Zacchaeus gave away his wealth, the woman at the well became an evangelist, the demoniac became a witness. Restorative justice, following His example, believes that people can change, that offenders can become restorers, that victims can become survivors, that communities can become stronger.

Through the lens of Jesus, we see that community matters. Jesus gathered a community of disciples, sent them out together, taught them to love one another, prayed for their unity. The early church understood itself as a body, each member connected to every other, each contributing to the health of the whole. Restorative justice, following this example, involves the community in the work of healing, recognizing that justice cannot be done by professionals alone.

Through the lens of Jesus, we see that the cross is the ultimate act of restorative justice. On the cross, Jesus absorbed the worst that humanity could do and responded with forgiveness. He bore the consequences of sin, satisfied the demands of justice, and opened the way to reconciliation. The cross is not a model of retribution but of restoration—the innocent one suffering for the guilty, not to inflict pain but to heal, not to condemn but to save.

Through the lens of Jesus, we see that the resurrection is the ultimate hope of restorative justice. The resurrection proclaims that death does not have the final word, that evil cannot ultimately triumph, that God's restorative purposes will prevail. It assures us that even the deepest wounds can be healed, even the most broken relationships can be restored, even the worst tragedies can be redeemed. The resurrection is the promise that restorative justice is not wishful thinking but divine reality.

Integrating the Disciplines: A Holistic Understanding

The lens of Jesus also brings into focus the contributions of other disciplines to restorative justice. Law, psychology, philosophy, and theology each offer insights that enrich our understanding and practice.

Law provides the framework within which restorative justice operates. It establishes the rights of victims and offenders, the procedures that must be followed, the limits of what can be done. It ensures accountability, protects against abuse, and provides recourse when things go wrong. Restorative justice, seen through the lens of Jesus, honors law while also recognizing its limitations. Jesus came not to abolish the law but to fulfill it—to bring it to its intended completion in love. Restorative justice seeks to fulfill law in the same way, not by discarding legal protections but by infusing them with the spirit of love and reconciliation.

Psychology provides insight into the human dynamics of harm and healing. It helps us understand trauma and its effects, the conditions that promote healing, the factors that contribute to change. It confirms what Jesus taught and demonstrated—that acknowledgment, empathy, apology, and forgiveness are essential for healing. Psychology also reminds us of the complexity of human beings, the depth of our wounds, the difficulty of change. Restorative justice, informed by psychology, approaches each person with humility, recognizing that healing is a process, not an event.

Philosophy provides the conceptual framework for thinking about justice. It asks the fundamental questions: What is justice? What do we owe to one another? What is the purpose of punishment? What is the meaning of forgiveness? The answers to these questions shape how we design and implement restorative programs. The lens of Jesus brings a distinctive philosophical perspective—one that prioritizes love over retribution, relationship over rules, restoration over punishment. This perspective challenges purely retributive philosophies and offers an alternative vision of what justice can be.

Theology provides the ultimate grounding for restorative justice. It reminds us that justice is not merely a human construct but a divine requirement—rooted in the character of God, revealed in Scripture, embodied in Christ, and promised in the new creation. It gives us the language of sin and redemption, of grace and forgiveness, of reconciliation and restoration. It provides the hope that sustains us when the work is hard and the outcomes uncertain. The lens of Jesus, informed by theology, sees restorative justice not as a secular program but as participation in God's own work.

These disciplines are not in competition but in cooperation. Law provides structure; psychology provides insight; philosophy provides conceptual clarity; theology provides ultimate meaning. Together, they enrich restorative justice, making it more robust, more nuanced, more effective. The lens of Jesus integrates them all, bringing them into harmony with the vision of justice that He embodied and taught.

The Gospel of Restorative Justice

At the heart of this book is a message we have called the Gospel of Restorative Justice. This is not a different gospel from the one proclaimed by Jesus and the apostles; it is that same gospel, applied to the specific challenge of responding to harm and wrongdoing. The Gospel of Restorative Justice is the good news that in Christ, God was reconciling the world to Himself, not counting our trespasses against us, and entrusting to us the ministry of reconciliation (2 Corinthians 5:18-19).

The Gospel of Restorative Justice proclaims that God is a God of justice—not retributive justice that demands payment but restorative justice that seeks healing. God's justice is not satisfied by the punishment of sinners but by their restoration. This is the message of the cross: that God in Christ bore the consequences of our sin, not to inflict pain but to open the way to forgiveness and new life.

The Gospel of Restorative Justice proclaims that every person is created in God's image and possesses inherent dignity and worth. This dignity is not erased by any action, no matter how heinous. The offender, no less than the victim, remains an image-bearer, deserving of respect and capable of restoration. This conviction undergirds restorative justice's commitment to treating all persons with dignity.

The Gospel of Restorative Justice proclaims that forgiveness is possible and that it is the path to freedom. When we forgive, we are not doing the offender a favor; we are freeing ourselves from the prison of resentment. Forgiveness does not mean forgetting or excusing; it means releasing the offender from the debt of guilt and opening the door to reconciliation. This is the forgiveness that Jesus taught and modeled.

The Gospel of Restorative Justice proclaims that reconciliation is the goal. God in Christ was reconciling the world to Himself, and He has entrusted to us the ministry of reconciliation. This means that our relationships matter, that brokenness can be healed, that estrangement can be overcome. It means that the work of bringing people together, of rebuilding trust, of restoring community is not merely a human project but a divine calling.

The Gospel of Restorative Justice proclaims that healing is possible. The same God who raised Jesus from the dead can heal our deepest wounds, restore our most broken relationships, and transform our most damaged communities. This healing is not always complete in this life, but it is always possible, always worth pursuing, always a sign of the kingdom that is coming.

The Gospel of Restorative Justice proclaims that love is the way. Jesus summarized the law in two commands: love God and love neighbor. He demonstrated that love is not merely a feeling but an action—laying down one's life for others. He taught that love for enemies is the mark of His followers. This love is the foundation and goal of restorative justice.

The Gospel of Restorative Justice proclaims that hope is justified. The resurrection assures us that death does not have the final word, that evil cannot ultimately triumph, that God's restorative purposes will prevail. This hope sustains us in the difficult work of restorative justice, reminding us that our labor is not in vain.

Embracing the Call

As we come to the end of this book, we are faced with a choice. We can close these pages and return to business as usual, continuing to think about justice in the same old ways, responding to harm with the same old punitive instincts. Or we can embrace the vision we have explored—the vision of restorative justice through the lens of Jesus—and commit ourselves to living it out.

Embracing restorative justice through the lens of Jesus is not merely about adopting a set of practices or supporting certain programs. It is about a fundamental reorientation of how we see the world, how we understand justice, how we respond to harm, how we relate to others. It is about seeing every person as an image-bearer, every conflict as an opportunity for healing, every harm as a call to restoration. It is about embodying the values of the kingdom—love, compassion, forgiveness, reconciliation—in every relationship and every situation.

For those who work in the criminal justice system—judges, lawyers, police officers, corrections officials, probation officers—embracing restorative justice means seeing your work in a new light. It means asking not only "What law was broken and what punishment does it deserve?" but "Who has been harmed and what do they need?" It means looking for opportunities to refer cases to restorative processes, to support victims and offenders in healing, to collaborate with community programs. It means being agents of restoration within a system that has often been content with punishment alone.

For those who work in education—teachers, administrators, counselors, staff—embracing restorative justice means transforming how you handle discipline, how you build community, how you teach students to relate to one another. It means using circles and conferences, not just suspensions and expulsions. It means teaching empathy and communication skills, not just enforcing rules. It means creating schools where every student feels known, valued, and supported.

For those who work in ministry—pastors, priests, lay leaders, volunteers—embracing restorative justice means making your faith community a place of healing and reconciliation. It means preaching and teaching on forgiveness, not just judgment. It means offering mediation and support for those in conflict, not just advice from a distance. It means reaching out to victims and offenders, prisoners and their families, the marginalized and the broken. It means embodying the gospel in your community life.

For those who work in families—parents, children, siblings, extended family—embracing restorative justice means learning to address conflicts constructively, to apologize and forgive, to rebuild trust when it is broken. It means holding family meetings, not just avoiding difficult conversations. It means teaching children by example, not just by precept. It means creating homes where love, accountability, and reconciliation are practiced daily.

For those who work in communities—neighborhood leaders, community organizers, volunteers—embracing restorative justice means building the social fabric that prevents harm and supports healing. It means organizing circles and dialogues, not just waiting for problems to escalate. It means supporting restorative programs, not just complaining about crime. It means creating communities where people know each other, care for each other, and hold each other accountable in love.

For all of us, embracing restorative justice through the lens of Jesus means letting His vision shape our lives. It means practicing forgiveness in our daily relationships, not just in dramatic moments. It means seeking reconciliation when we have been wronged, not just nursing grievances. It means extending compassion to those who have harmed us, not just to those we like. It means working for justice that heals, not justice that hurts.

The Challenges Ahead

Embracing restorative justice through the lens of Jesus does not mean ignoring the challenges. The obstacles we have explored throughout this book are real—theological differences, institutional resistance, resource limitations, participant unwillingness, societal skepticism, equity concerns, measurement difficulties, legal gaps. These challenges will not disappear simply because we have embraced a new vision.

The path ahead requires patience. Change does not happen overnight; systems and mindsets shift slowly. We must be willing to work for the long haul, to celebrate small victories, to learn from failures, to persist when progress seems slow. The parable of the growing seed reminds us that growth happens mysteriously, gradually, in ways we cannot control. Our job is to plant and water; God gives the increase.

The path ahead requires wisdom. There are no simple formulas, no one-size-fits-all solutions. Each situation is unique, each community different, each person complex. We must be willing to listen, to learn, to adapt. We must draw on the insights of multiple disciplines—law, psychology, philosophy, theology—and integrate them with practical experience. We must be humble enough to know that we do not have all the answers.

The path ahead requires courage. Restorative justice challenges powerful interests and deeply ingrained habits. It will be resisted by those who benefit from the status quo, by those who fear change, by those who are simply comfortable with what they know. Speaking truth to power, advocating for change, standing with the marginalized—these require courage. But courage is not the absence of fear; it is acting in spite of fear, trusting that God goes with us.

The path ahead requires hope. There will be setbacks, disappointments, failures. Cases will go badly; programs will struggle; progress will be slow. Without hope, we will give up. But hope is not naive optimism; it is trust in God's promises, confidence that God's restorative purposes will ultimately prevail. The resurrection is the ground of this hope—the assurance that death does not have the final word, that God can bring life out of death, that restoration is possible even when all seems lost.

A Vision for the Future

What would it look like if restorative justice, seen through the lens of Jesus, became not an exception but the norm? What would our world be like if healing, accountability, and reconciliation were the default responses to harm?

Imagine a criminal justice system where victims are central, where their needs are addressed, where they have voice and agency. Imagine a system where offenders are held accountable not through passive punishment but through active responsibility—acknowledging harm, making amends, changing behavior. Imagine a system where communities are involved in healing, where the social fabric is strengthened, where recidivism is reduced because offenders have been transformed.

Imagine schools where discipline is not about exclusion but about learning, where conflicts are resolved through dialogue rather than punishment, where students learn empathy and communication skills alongside academic subjects. Imagine schools where every student feels known, valued, and supported, where bullying is rare because the culture does not tolerate it, where teachers and students work together to build community.

Imagine families where conflicts are addressed constructively, where apologies are offered and received, where trust is rebuilt when it is broken. Imagine families where members know how to communicate, how to listen, how to forgive. Imagine families that are schools of love, preparing children for lives of healthy relationship.

Imagine communities where neighbors know each other, where disputes are resolved locally, where those who have caused harm are supported in changing. Imagine communities that take responsibility for addressing the conditions that produce crime—poverty, inequality, discrimination, trauma. Imagine communities that are resilient, cohesive, and just.

Imagine a world where nations address their conflicts through dialogue rather than violence, where historical injustices are acknowledged and reparations made, where reconciliation is pursued even after the most terrible harms. Imagine a world where the principles of restorative justice inform international law, diplomacy, and peacebuilding. Imagine a world moving toward the peace that the prophets envisioned—swords beaten into plowshares, nations not learning war anymore.

This vision is not utopian. It is not a fantasy of a perfect world that can never exist. It is a vision of what is possible, grounded in what is already happening in thousands of restorative programs around the world. It is a vision of what can be, if we have the courage and commitment to pursue it. And it is a vision that reflects the heart of God, who is even now reconciling the world to Himself.

The Final Word

As we close this book, we return to where we began: the person of Jesus Christ. He is the lens through which we have seen restorative justice. He is the model we have sought to follow. He is the source of the hope that sustains us. He is the goal toward which all our efforts point.

In Jesus, we see the perfect embodiment of restorative justice. His compassion for the suffering, His forgiveness of sinners, His reconciliation of the estranged, His healing of the broken, His transformation of the lost, His love for all—these are the principles and practices of restorative justice incarnate. In His death, we see the ultimate act of restorative love—the innocent one bearing the consequences of the guilty, opening the way to forgiveness and new life. In His resurrection, we see the ultimate hope of restorative justice—the assurance that death does not have the final word, that God's restorative purposes will prevail.

Those who follow Jesus are called to continue His work. We are called to be agents of reconciliation in a world torn by conflict. We are called to be healers in a world wounded by harm. We are called to be restorers in a world broken by sin. We are called to embody the values of the kingdom—love, compassion, forgiveness, reconciliation—in every relationship and every situation.

This calling is not easy. It will cost us. It will require us to forgive when we would rather hold grudges, to seek reconciliation when we would rather walk away, to love when we would rather hate, to hope when we would rather despair. It will require us to stand with victims and to reach out to offenders, to challenge systems of injustice and to build communities of healing. It will require us to take up our crosses and follow Jesus.

But this calling is also joyful. It is participation in the most important work in the world—the work of restoration. It is alignment with God's own purposes, cooperation with the Spirit's action, anticipation of the kingdom's coming. It is the privilege of being ambassadors of Christ, agents of reconciliation, ministers of the gospel of restorative justice.

As we go from these pages into the world, may we carry this vision with us. May we see every person through the lens of Jesus—as an image-bearer, worthy of dignity and capable of restoration. May we respond to every harm with the values of restorative justice—acknowledgment, accountability, amends, forgiveness, reconciliation. May we build communities that embody shalom—peace, wholeness, flourishing for all. And may we never lose hope, trusting that the God who raised Jesus from the dead will also bring to completion the good work He has begun in us.

The journey continues. The work goes on. The future awaits. And the one who is the pioneer and perfecter of our faith, who for the joy set before Him endured the cross, goes before us. We follow in His steps, walking the way of restorative justice, embodying the Jesus Paradigm, bearing witness to the Gospel of Restorative Justice, until the day when all things are made new.

Amen. Come, Lord Jesus.

www.ingramcontent.com/pod-product-compliance
Lightning Source LLC
LaVergne TN
LVHW052208200926
848481LV00001B/55